Worship and Culture

Worship and Culture

Foreign Country or Homeland?

Edited by

Gláucia Vasconcelos Wilkey

WILLIAM B. EERDMANS PUBLISHING COMPANY

GRAND RAPIDS, MICHIGAN / CAMBRIDGE, U.K.

Published 2014 by
Wm. B. Eerdmans Publishing Co.
2140 Oak Industrial Drive N.E., Grand Rapids, Michigan 49505 /
P.O. Box 163, Cambridge CB3 9PU U.K.
www.eerdmans.com

Printed in the United States of America

20 19 18 17 16 15 14   7 6 5 4 3 2 1

Library of Congress Cataloging-in-Publication Data

Worship and culture: foreign country or homeland? / edited by Gláucia Vasconcelos Wilkey.
    pages   cm
Includes bibliographical references.
ISBN 978-0-8028-7158-9 (pbk.: alk. paper)
1. Worship.   2. Christianity and culture.   3. Lutheran World Federation.
I. Wilkey, Gláucia Vasconcelos, 1941-, editor.

BV15.W653   2014
264 — dc23
                                                            2014031257

Cover Art

This six-foot banner, now hanging on a wall in the narthex leading to the chapel at the denominational offices of the Presbyterian Church (USA) in Louisville, was created for the Peacemaking Offering for 1997. Leaders in that PCUSA office had asked this volume's editor, who was then serving as Associate for Theology and Worship at the PCUSA headquarters, to suggest an art piece that would serve for posters and covers of Worship Aids, which were to be used nationally in PCUSA churches. Maureen O'Connor, who was responsible for arts in denominational publications, and I settled on verses from Ezekiel 47:1-12, Isaiah 49:10-12, Revelation 22:1-5, and Luke 13:29 as biblical foundations for the art that was to be prepared. Looking closely at this picture, one can see peoples of all nations, colors, and races in the multitude. Note the flowing water, the table laden with food, animals and trees, and the sliver of moon — all symbolizing the created order gathering under the Light, who is Christ, the Sun of Righteousness.

This design was originally rendered in oil on canvas by the artist Dorothea B. Kennedy, and it was transferred to fabric for the banner by Gloiela Yau Dolak. The four women involved in this project — Vasconcelos Wilkey, O'Connor, Kennedy, and Dolak — formed their own quartet of cultural diversity. In the same way as the mountains and hills rejoice, the thirsty of all nations are invited to come to the water, and the hungry are invited to come to the table. Everyone is welcome. No one is a stranger or foreigner. All belong.

In memory of

S. Anita Stauffer and Anscar J. Chupungco, OSB
and

In honor of participants
who today yet seek the meaning of these things

Contents

PART II: CHRISTIAN WORSHIP: UNITY IN CULTURAL DIVERSITY

PART III: BAPTISM, RITES OF PASSAGE, AND CULTURE

Preface and Acknowledgments

Gláucia Vasconcelos Wilkey

The LWF Worship and Culture Study Series Then and Now

In March 2010, the journal *Worship,* known and respected for its engagement of discourse on liturgical renewal, published an essay entitled "Liturgy, Culture, and the Challenge of Catholicity" by Margaret Mary Kelleher, OSU, professor of theology at the School of Theology and Religious Studies at The Catholic University of America.[1] A particular sentence in that essay caught my attention: "The efforts of the Lutheran World Federation to engage in an ecumenical and interdisciplinary study of the relationship between Christian worship and cultures offer a model for future attempts at such collaboration." Kelleher was speaking about a seven-year-long study that resulted in the publication of three volumes: *Worship and Culture in Dialogue* (1994); *Christian Worship: Unity in Cultural Diversity* (1996); and *Baptism, Rites of Passage, and Culture* (1998). All three were edited by the late S. Anita Stauffer and published by the Geneva offices of the Lutheran World Federation (LWF). Stauffer, of dear memory, facilitated the long process of research, case studies, and reflections on the reports by participants. Alas, these volumes were out of print years before Professor Kelleher's appraisal.

The central reason for my interest in what Kelleher suggests is that during the 2009 meeting of Societas Liturgica in Australia, which focused precisely on the issue of worship and culture, an informal conversation took place during a lunch. At the table, my husband and I were joined by Fr.

1. Kelvin Seasoltz, OSB, ed., *Worship* 84, no. 2 (March 2010): 119-20.

Anscar A. Chupungco, OSB (now also, sadly, deceased), and Gordon W. Lathrop, a Lutheran pastor and professor. As we discussed the various lectures we were enjoying at that gathering, I ventured to suggest to those two scholars, the primary theological "pillars" of the LWF work, that perhaps it was time for them to consider ways to revisit, renew, enrich, and thus expand the LWF findings. The idea seemed to take root in that conversation. Two weeks after we returned home from that gathering in Australia, Lathrop suggested that I take on that effort. As a dear friend and teacher, he knew of my commitment to the vision set forth in the LWF project and the questions it sought to address.

The desire to revisit the history and the life of that large body of study engaged me to such a degree that now here I am, writing this preface for a volume that is precisely what we envisioned in that Societas lunch meeting. Indeed, the essays in this volume — both those reprinted from the original sources and those recently composed — seek to revisit, offer models, critique, expand, and thus enrich the conversation on worship and culture. They also seek to encourage questions and engage the life of pastors, liturgists, teachers, students, and churches in reflection on the connections between local and global cultures vis-à-vis the gospel of Jesus Christ.

Original Project Texts

To fully grasp the contents of this book, one needs to keep in mind the history and vision of the LWF project. Norman Hjelm's gracious and historically well-informed introduction at the beginning of this volume accomplishes precisely that. Speaking from his own experience with the project, Hjelm helps us understand the historical contexts of both the original and the current project. The earliest texts were written between 1992 and 1999, and they can be seen in the very structure of this present collection of essays. For example, note that each of the full texts of the "Statements" — coming out of the meetings of the original LWF project participants in Cartigny, Nairobi, and Chicago — make up the first chapters of each of the three parts of this book. Named for the cities in which they were drafted by the participants in each conference, these statements provide the titles, and thus the focus, of each of the three parts.

Stauffer, Chupungco, and Lathrop

LWF's entire "Study Series on Worship and Culture" was facilitated and ably guided by Anita Stauffer, who died in 2007 after a long illness. But among her many contributions were essays that she wrote for the original projects. In this collection we include two of those essays: "Christian Worship: Toward Localization and Globalization" (Part I, pages 35-42) and "Ecumenical Core and Cultural Context" (Part II, pages 200-213).

Both Anscar Chupungco and Gordon Lathrop agreed in the initial phase of this collection to critique their original contributions and offer new insights on those texts. Thus we reprint Chupungco's original essays, "Reenvisioning 'Liturgy and the Components of Culture'" (Part I, pages 68-83) and "Methods of Liturgical Inculturation" (Part II, pages 262-75). A most amazing gift for this volume is a new essay by Anscar Chupungco, which he sent me just a few weeks before his sudden death in January 2013. This essay was originally prepared as a lecture entitled "Inculturation of Worship: Forty Years of Progress and Tradition" (Part II, pages 276-86); it appears here, followed by a warm and thoughtful "In Memoriam" to Chupungco by Gordon Lathrop.

I must note the significance of the role that Gordon Lathrop has played in the preparation of this volume. His work in the past trajectory of the LWF study series has been of great importance, and the reader will see his name quoted in many of the chapters that make up this book. And his own contributions are central to the purpose and vision of this volume. For example, were the cast of writers in this collection presenting their contributions as lectures at a conference, Lathrop's theological introduction, "Every Foreign Country a Homeland, Every Homeland a Foreign Country: On Worship and Culture," would be the keynote address, because in it he sets the whole collection of essays in a theological context and worldview, showing the way for all the other contributors. Also, in some concluding thoughts at the end of this volume (pages 379-86), Lathrop reenvisions his original essay "The Shape of the Liturgy: A Framework for Contextualization," viewing it from a current perspective.

Mark Bangert

Church musician Mark Bangert provides a thoughtful text on music in worship that was first printed as "Dynamics of World Musics: A Methodology for Evaluation" in the LWF consultation volume of 1994. Bangert here revisits that original text (Part I, pages 124-33) and substantially updates it in the second half of that chapter under the subheading "Last Words." In Bangert's chapter we also encounter what for this ethnomusicologist is a model hymn, one from Africa that is in many of today's hymnals.

New Riches in New Texts

All original LWF-project-related essays are clearly named as such, with the original places and dates of publication identified in the first footnote of each chapter. Also significant are the contributions of original participants in the LWF study series, identified in Appendix A. Here we find the names of witnesses to the inclusiveness of the gospel, and we encounter the questions they, too, raised in the study process. We gratefully recognize and honor the gifts of all those involved: participants, churches that sponsored them, and entities that facilitated case-study projects all over the world; "culture study teams," including various consultants, ecumenical partners, and resource persons; also local pastors and leaders and LWF staff members at the time the study projects took place — far too many to name, yet whose gifts continue to aid in the fulfillment of the project's vision.

In this volume, contributions from recent contemporary scholarship seek to encourage questions and engage the life of liturgical scholars, pastors, liturgists, teachers, church musicians, students — all in reflection on the connections between local and global cultures and their impact on Sunday assemblies everywhere, this day and time, each in his or her own language. Gospel lenses provide the sine qua non frame for discourse on worship in the postcolonial, postmodern, migrating, hybrid, intermingling, multilayered, and massively digital culture systems of today. The following are the new contributors who wrote fresh essays for this collection, thus supplying new riches for the worship and culture project.

Benjamin M. Stewart

Stewart adds to his theological lenses a deep knowledge of anthropology and ecology. Revealing to us the fact that some experts consider the idea of taking into account the world's cultures as "ultimately more misleading than helpful," Stewart wonders about the distance between liturgical theologians and the "noisy way" the cultures of the world are often expressed. Stewart invites his readers to a humble listening perspective on the matter, and yet he asks, "How do we listen?" in his chapter, entitled "What, Then, Do Theologians Mean When They Say 'Culture'?" (pages 43-51).

Margaret Mary Kelleher, OSU

Kelleher is deeply committed to exploring the connections between liturgy, culture, and the catholicity of the church. She names the number of convergences between the texts on liturgy in the Vatican II documents and those in the volumes from the LWF study series. A delightfully ecumenical worldview, with fidelity to her own theological and ecclesiological stances, has led her, in "Vatican II and the LWF Project: Points of Convergence," to find the LWF case studies and published texts to be models "for responding to the challenge of catholicity" (Part I, pages 52-67).

Scott Anderson

In this chapter we hear the voices of the people of the U.S. Pacific Northwest via the narrative of one congregation's life, patterns of worship, and vision. The congregation and its pastor, Scott Anderson, live in the midst of what is now widely known as the "None Zone," the region of North America where the highest percentage of residents declare "none" as their choice of religious affiliation. In its liturgical life and sense of mission, St. Andrew Presbyterian Church in Renton, Washington, seeks to see Christ as just as marginalized as are many people in the Seattle/Renton area. This marginalization is most acutely sensed by those oppressed by racism, sexism, ableism, classism, imperialism, and all the many "isms" of the world today (Part I, pages 84-106).

Stephen Burns

An Australian Anglican liturgical theologian, Burns brings to this conversation table the current discourse and debate on the nature of the *ordo,* or shape, of Christian liturgy. Inviting participants in the conversation to at least an "adequate study" of the Nairobi text, Burns cites postcolonial questions as the heart of the issue (in "A Fragile Future for the *Ordo*?" Part II, pages 143-61), and he invites readers to a conversation that includes what theorists call "contrapunctuality": point and counterpoint of open, respect-ful, and humble listening and speaking woven to form a rich tapestry of inclusiveness.

Dirk Lange

In a profound way, Stewart's and Burns's questions need to be read in tandem with another set of questions, those proposed by Lange's provocative chap-ter, entitled "Worship: Translating the Untranslatable" (Part II, pages 162-81). For Lange, the paradigms in the Nairobi texts could "betray a metaphys-ical prejudice." In his point of view, worship is a form of "translation," but in the end it is impossible to translate because of its intrinsically "traumatic" nature — for the Christ event is itself traumatic. Lange's essay takes issue with the Nairobi paradigms, for instance, saying that "word and sacrament are not transcultural." Yet he also tells us that what the Nairobi Statement proposes for the interaction between worship and culture can "invite faith communities toward countercultural reflection."

Joseph A. Donnella II

A worship service in the Crucian community in the Danish West Indies (now the U.S. Virgin Islands) is the focus of the chapter by Joseph Donella. He describes what he identifies an "Afri-Caribbean/West Indian" celebration of New Year's Eve, known locally as "Old Year's Night." The Nairobi paradigms serve as a framework for much of this text. The Crucian narrative gives par-ticular emphases to the reconciliation within the community, which is ex-pressed in public ways. The narrative goes on to tell of the journey of a group of college students to Taizé, drawing the reader into the parallel between Taizé and the Crucian islanders' gatherings. For both groups, the community of the baptized is reconciled, the old is gone, and a new life has begun (Part II, pages 182-99).

Thomas F. Best

The theologian-ecumenist Best contributes two essays to this collection. The first is a touching and eye-opening piece that details Best's denomination's journey into fuller life in Christ, entitled "Christian Unity and Christian Diversity, Lessons from the Liturgical Renewal: The Case of the Christian Church (Disciples of Christ)" (Part II, pages 214-38). This chapter gives an account of what could well be models for engaging questions on the nature of the church (ecclesiology), worship (liturgy), and how that worship life in word and table might serve to manifest the de facto unity of the body of Christ (theology).

Best's second essay, written explicitly for this book, is entitled "A Faith and Order Saga: Towards *One Baptism, Toward Mutual Recognition*" (Part III, pages 302-19). This chapter sheds light on the relationship between the LWF Study Series on Worship and Culture and the WCC's Faith and Order work on baptism and its place in the ecumenical movement and vision (see also this editor's essay at the end of this collection). The journey of WCC/Faith and Order reached a high point with the birth of the study text "One Baptism: Towards Mutual Recognition." Best explores the implications of that document, which is vital to the story of the ecumenical movement. In so doing he also leads us to reflect on the best-known volume on ecumenism, "Baptism, Eucharist, and Ministry" (BEM). My own passion and commitment to the vision of a visible expression of the body of Christ's unity leads me to offer Thomas Best my deepest gratitude for his leadership in the world of churches and the life of unity in the growing diversity in which we live as peoples and churches.

Julio Cézar Adam

This Brazilian theologian's chapter questions life in worship in Brazil. He questions, as do Monro and Burns, the metaphors for worship that come out of the Northern Hemisphere and are "translated" into the Southern Hemisphere ("Worship with a Brazilian Face," Part II, pages 239-61). Such liturgical language may be disjointed when lived in his part of the world. Adam sees in his country a worship life moored still in its history as a "mission field," where churches until recently have given scant honor to the cultural ethos of the geographical, cultural, and historical place of Brazil. As a Brazilian myself, I urge readers to hear the multiple insights of theologians from that nation, and to marvel with me at the wisdom of fresh voices from liturgical theologians in the Southern Hemisphere.

Anita Monro

Monro, already well known for her writings, offers an astounding set of metaphors from Australia, her place of life and ministry. She brings together mythic creatures from her part of the world (e.g., a frog who swallows up the world's waters!) and Christian traditions, questioning the nature of baptism in its "ambiguity/alterity" between faith and culture. Monro invites readers to uphold Christic baptismal identity as constituting the church and sealing it in solidarity with the whole creation, both by the gracious gift of God and through the "limited, grasping, searching human response to that undeserved gift" ("Of Frogs, Eels, Women, and Pelicans," Part III, pages 320-34).

Gail Ramshaw

Continuing as one of the most prolific and gracious liturgical theologians and linguists of our time, Gail Ramshaw proposes foundational guides for local yet global liturgical language. Her gifts in the area of liturgical language are universally recognized and lauded. Here Ramshaw offers two models, one a prayer of thanksgiving at the font, and then a prayer of thanksgiving at the table (Part III, pages 335-41). In these prayers, and the texts that accompany them, she invites us to name, for example, local pools, rivers, streams, local bread and wine in our all-too-important prayers at the font and the table. These two prayers reflect liturgical language at its most inclusive — and enticing.

Melinda Ann Quivik

In this essay Quivik examines the findings of the case studies named in the "Chicago Statement on Worship and Culture," as well as in the rites of passage found in various church orders, all in the light of the themes proposed by the four categories in the "Nairobi Statement on Worship and Culture." Many churches refer to the rites here as "Occasional Services." For Quivik, the most significant issues of these services is the question of purpose, particularly as marriage, healing, and funeral rites are so deeply embedded in secular cultural practices in all parts of the world. Intriguing expressions of localized, contextual practices from various countries elicit wonder in Quivik's chapter, and we are pulled into the questions she asks here. Yet the challenges remaining for the theologians, pastors, and churches that engage them is vast. What gifts can we share across cultural, national, or ecclesial borders? In the end, Quivik guides us to see all these occasions and their rites in a baptismal light. For her, Christian baptism reveals that "belonging to Christ is the most profound source of comfort at the times of greatest sorrow" (Part II, pages 342-66).

Martha Moore-Keish and Joyce Ann Zimmerman, CPPS

One of the greatest — yet largely ignored — events in the history of the discourse on baptism in churches everywhere is the dialogue that Roman Catholic and Reformed theologians embraced in the United States between 2003 and 2010. The dialogue's reports are nothing short of astonishing. The title of the first one is: "Common Agreement on Mutual Recognition of Baptism: Roman Catholic-Reformed Dialogue (U.S.) Contained in *These Living Waters.*" The document was adopted by the Roman Catholic Church and by each of the five Reformed communions in the dialogue. This significant document is included here (Part III, pages 367-68), followed by reflections on the processes, visions, and results of the discourse by two participants in it: Moore-Keish, from the Presbyterian Church (USA), and Zimmerman, from the Roman Catholic Church. Centuries of misunderstandings and divergent cultural misgivings led participants in the dialogue to lay those misgivings and misunderstandings "down by the riverside," as the African American gospel hymn has it.

All of the essays in this book will lead readers to see that, given the instant nature of global communication media, borders and territorial lines are fast disappearing in many places of the world, and the sense that we live in a global village as a growing reality. These things beg our commitment for life in and out of the Christian liturgy. For while Christ, in the power of the Holy Spirit, calls the church into being from baptism in the waters of local fonts, pools, streams, and rivers, and in texts and actions peculiar to local cultural contexts, it is the same Spirit who speaks, leading us to the Pentecost question: "How is it that we hear each in our own language" — in all our diverse languages and cultures? Readers, welcome!

"To Whom Honor, Honor"

Two Guides

Many people have made this effort and book possible. Gordon W. Lathrop trusted and supported me, and he was an ever-present friend indeed when questions arose during these five years since that 2009 lunch in Australia. Words are insufficient to express the depth of my gratitude and respect for this beloved teacher and fellow participant in liturgy. Yet I try again in the language of my heart, Portuguese: *Muito obrigada* (literally "much obliged," but in normal speech, simply "Thank you").

Professor Lathrop introduces us to the theological context for this work, suggested in the title of this volume. Lathrop's support was enriched by Dr. Norman A. Hjelm, who served as liaison between me and the Geneva officers in the LWF, leading eventually to the publisher for this book, William B. Eerdmans. In his essay, Hjelm introduces us to the historical contexts of the original work and this current volume. For his guidance and consistent grace, *Muito obrigada!*

Publisher

Bill Eerdmans, the chairman of the publishing company and his very knowledgeable managing editor, Linda Bieze, along with her staff, particularly editor Reinder Van Til, have been as patient as they have been gracious from the outset of the conversations with this general editor, going beyond the expected to unexpected help. Thus, to Mr. Eerdmans, Ms. Bieze, and helpers — *Muito obrigada!*

LWF Officers

From my first contacts with the current staff at the Lutheran World Federation in Geneva, I was amazed by the good will and enthusiasm for this project and the helpful information set forth by those leaders. I pray that God will continue to inspire such work as we see in the three volumes published in the 1990s and in this current edition. Dr. Stephen Larson (no longer in that office), my first contact in Geneva, was helpful and supportive from the beginning. Larson shared my work with the general secretary of the

LWF, Rev. Martin Junge (from the Evangelical Lutheran Church in Chile) and with Dr. Hintikka Kaisamari, current director of the Department of Theology and Studies. Subsequently, Norman Hjelm and I also contacted Iris Benesch, who was responsible for publication concerns and was particularly helpful in dealing with matters related to copyright permissions. To these faithful servants of Christ, working on behalf of the church in every culture and place, *Muito obrigada!*

Unexpected Gifts

One of the problems I faced in putting together this book was that the original manuscripts were sometimes impossible to locate, and I needed the texts of the originals so that we could reprint them *ipsissima verba*. A surprising solution appeared in the person and work of Dr. Melanie Hoag Bliss, of Southwestern University in Georgetown, Texas, where my husband and I live. As a professor of instructional technologies at her institution, she had the answer and access to the solution, and she offered to "convert" texts from the books directly to my computer's files. As you will see, the list of texts includes the "Statements" named above, various original essays, a listing of participants in the original process, and the international bibliography relating to that work in the back of this book. However, Dr. Hoag Bliss had to work from original and "clean" books, and my volumes would not do. Fortunately, Dr. Donald Keeny, director of the library at the Seminary of the Southwest in Austin, loaned us the three clean volumes we needed — again, free of cost. These two colleagues, one from a Methodist academic context, the other from an Episcopal one, went beyond the expected to unexpected acts of grace. So to them I say, *Muito obrigada!*

Family

Then to my family: our daughters were always supportive and endured my rumblings and need of time and space as I worked on one essay or another. To them and to their children, delights of our life — *Todo meu amor, e muito obrigada.* My husband, Jay, has been anchor, solace, help, teacher, friend, counselor, and inspiration. He endured this editorial process with patience and gave me answers, for example, to questions related to the usage of English, not my first language. So, to him, church musician par excellence,

companion in the life of liturgical assemblies and in the life of our home —
Todo meu amor, e muito obrigada!

The Writers

Then to you, writers for this volume, I also say, *Muito obrigada.* But I must
say more, because I recognize the depth of your insights individually and
collectively. I must praise your fidelity in asking daring questions and engaging concepts from multiple sociological and theological disciplines. Your
texts are truly eye-opening. As you were asked to do, you have taken us back
to the LWF project, but you have also set our eyes and minds to the future
beyond that work, critiquing insights and asking questions not previously
expressed. The newness of it all is surprisng and refreshing. That you are able
to do this through the lenses of theology is a gift. You have given us, the
readers, new metaphors for liturgical language and life from various parts of
the world. You have also enticed us into seeking to make visible the unity of
the body of Christ in the middle of the rich tapestry of diversity of cultures
and churches in the world. You have indeed proposed theological, ecclesiological, and anthropological questions and visions that will serve liturgical
thinkers and participants in worship alike for years to come.

During the Seattle Summer Institute for Liturgy and Worship, which is
referred to elsewhere in this volume, we expressed our gratitude to presenters when we sang, "Gloria in Excelsis Deo." I sing now the same text as I
think of you, the contributors to this volume. And as we sang in Seattle when
we sent presenters to the wide world beyond the institute, this I also sing,
even as I pray: "May you cling to Wisdom, for she will protect you, and if
you follow her, she will keep you safe."[2]

I write this preface on October 15, 2013, when the church collectively gives
thanks to God for the life of Teresa of Avila, sometimes called the "Renewer
of the Church," who said, "Pray for the Lutherans." Today I will say, "Yes,
but also for all others of us in churches anywhere."

---

2. Text from Proverbs 4; adaptation and music, Steven C. Warner, Octavo, Portland,
OR. Copyright 1993 © World Library Publications.

Contributors

JULIO CÉZAR ADAM is a pastor in the Igreja Evangélica de Confissão Luterana no Brasil (Evangelical Church of the Lutheran Confession in Brazil) and a professor in the *Escola Superior de Teologia* (EST), a seminary in São Leopoldo, Rio Grande do Sul, Brazil. He is also the editor of the journal for his denomination's liturgical life, *T.E.A.R.,* and he serves as coordinator for a research group on Christian worship in Latin America.

SCOTT ANDERSON is a Presbyterian (PCUSA) pastor currently serving St. Andrew Presbyterian Church in Renton, Washington. He was a member of the board for the School of Theology and Ministry of Seattle University's Summer Institute of Liturgy and Worship.

MARK P. BANGERT is a pastor in the Evangelical Lutheran Church in America and the John H. Tietjen Professor Emeritus of theology, worship, and music at the Lutheran School of Theology at Chicago. Pursuing an interest in multicultural church music, he has studied in Japan, Tanzania, Zimbabwe, Taiwan, and the Philippines. He was also a U.S.A. representative to the five-year LWF study team on worship and culture addressed in this volume.

THOMAS F. BEST is a pastor in the Christian Church (Disciples of Christ); he retired in late 2007 as director of the Faith and Order Commission of the World Council of Churches. He was closely involved in the development of the text *One Baptism: Towards Mutual Recognition,* and he has written and spoken extensively on issues of worship and ecclesiology with regard to the unity of the church and the ecumenical movement, including publishing articles in *Studia Liturgica.*

STEPHEN BURNS is a Church of England priest and Carter Distinguished Lecturer on Liturgical and Practical Theology, Associate Dean and Director of Ministerial Formation at Trinity College, University of Melbourne, Australia. His recent publications include *Pilgrim People: An Invitation to Worship in the Uniting Church* (2012); *Christian Worship: Postcolonial Perspectives* (coauthor with Michael N. Jagessar, 2011), and *Christian Worship in Australia: Inculturating the Liturgical Tradition* (coeditor with Anita Monro, 2009).

ANSCAR CHUPUNGCO, OSB, was a Roman Catholic priest and Benedictine monk who served as one of the "theological pillars" of the work of the Lutheran World Federation's project and study series on worship and culture, where he brought to bear his love for the ecumenical vision. Readers will note Chupungco's comments on this work in his chapter on inculturation; they will also note the "In Memoriam" to Chupungco (at the end of chapter 16) provided by his colleague and close friend, Gordon W. Lathrop. A member of the Abbey of Our Lady of Montserrat in the Philippines, Chupungco was president of the Pontifical Liturgical Institute in Rome and director of the Paul VI Institute of Liturgy in the Philippines. He was scheduled to receive the *Pro Ecclesia et Pontifice* award from Pope Benedict XVI when he died suddenly in January 2013. Chupungco published many books, including *What, Then, Is Liturgy? Musings and Memoir* (Collegeville, MN: Liturgical Press, 2010). This volume is dedicated to his memory, along with that of Anita Stauffer.

JOSEPH A. DONNELLA II is an African American pastor in the Evangelical Lutheran Church in America and the chaplain at Gettysburg College, in Gettysburg, Pennsylvania, where he also teaches liturgical theology. He lived and served on the island of St. Croix in the Caribbean, where he observed, studied, and participated in the liturgical life and issues of inculturation of liturgy in the particular community of Crucians, and their story is at the center of his essay in this volume.

NORMAN A. HJELM is a pastor in the Evangelical Lutheran Church in America. A respected ecumenical theologian, Hjelm played a vital role in the process of the publication of this volume, serving as a liaison between the editor, the publisher, and the leadership of the Lutheran World Federation in Geneva, which he served as director from 1985 to 1991. Hjelm is the retired director of the Commission on Faith and Order of the National Council of Churches of Christ in the U.S.A.

MARGARET MARY KELLEHER, OSU, is a professor in the School of Theology and Religious Studies of The Catholic University of America, in Washington, D.C. She has published many essays on liturgical theology and practice, and has served on the bishops' advisory committee of the International Commission on English in the Liturgy (ICEL). Her essay on the catholicity of the church, written for the journal *Worship* 84, no. 2 (March 2010), calls attention to the work of the LWF and thus is vital to this volume.

DIRK G. LANGE is a pastor in the Evangelical Lutheran Church in America, Associate Professor of Worship, and Chair of the History and Theology Division at Luther Seminary. During the 1980s, he was a brother in the Taizé community, and worked with peoples in the Eastern European underground. He is a member of the North American Academy of Liturgy where he founded and convenes the seminar on Liturgy and Postmodern Questions. He is well known as the author of *Trauma Recalled: Liturgy, Disruption, and Theology.*

GORDON W. LATHROP is a pastor in the Evangelical Lutheran Church in America and a retired professor of liturgical studies. He has taught recently at the Pontifical University of St. Thomas Aquinas in Rome, the University of Copenhagen, and Yale Divinity School. After teaching for twenty years at the Lutheran Theological Seminary at Philadelphia, he was named an emeritus professor there in 2004. Most recently he published *The Four Gospels on Sunday: The New Testament and the Reform of Christian Worship* (Minneapolis: Fortress, 2012). This present volume is dedicated to his honor as a "participant in the liturgy" and to his work on making clear "the meaning of these things."

ANITA MONRO is a pastor in the Uniting Church in Australia. She is currently the principal of Grace College, a residential college in the University of Queensland, under the auspices of the Uniting Church and the Presbyterian Church of Queensland. She is the author of *Resurrecting Erotic Transgression: Subjecting Ambiguity in Theology* in the Gender, Theology, and Spirituality Series (London: Equinox, 2006), and has edited, with Stephen Burns, *Christian Worship in Australia: Inculturating the Liturgical Tradition* (Strathfield, NSW: St Paul's, 2009).

MARTHA MOORE-KEISH is a Presbyterian Church (USA) pastor and a professor of theology at Columbia Theological Seminary in Decatur, Georgia. She was part of the group of theologians who met for seven years in the Dialogue on Baptism and Eucharist between the Roman Catholic Church and the Reformed churches. The final document of agreement between those bodies, and Moore-Keish's reflection on that event, are part of this volume, side by side with a testimonial from one of her Roman Catholic counterparts, Sr. Joyce Ann Zimmerman, CPPS.

MELINDA A. QUIVIK is a pastor in the Evangelical Lutheran Church in America. She has taught worship and preaching at the Lutheran Theological Seminary at Philadelphia. Today she serves the wider church as a liturgical and homiletical scholar by presenting workshops and lectures on worship and preaching, along with a number of writing projects. Her latest contribution to the church's liturgical discourse is *Leading Worship Matters: A Sourcebook for Preparing Worship Leaders* (Minneapolis: Augsburg, 2013).

GAIL RAMSHAW, retired from the religion department of La Salle University, where she taught for twenty-two years, now studies and crafts liturgical language from her home. Among her many publications are *Treasures Old and New: Images in the Lectionary* (Minneapolis: Augsburg Fortress, 2002) and *Christian Worship: 100,000 Sundays of Symbols and Rituals* (Minneapolis: Fortress, 2009).

BENJAMIN M. STEWART is the Gordon A. Braatz Assistant Professor of Worship and Dean of Augustana Chapel at the Lutheran School of Theology at Chicago. Stewart's contributions to the discourse on the convergences between liturgy and ecology single him out as a forward-thinking theologian. Indeed, he is convener of the Ecology and Liturgy seminar at the North American Academy of Liturgy and is author of *A Watered Garden: Christian Worship and Earth's Ecology* (Minneapolis: Augsburg Fortress, 2011).

JOYCE ANN ZIMMERMAN, CPPS, is the founder and director of the Institute for Liturgical Ministry in Dayton, Ohio, and the editor of that institution's journal, *Liturgical Ministry*. With her Presbyterian counterpart in this volume, Martha Moore-Keish, Zimmerman was one of the Roman Catholic theologians in the Roman Catholic and Reformed churches' dialogue on baptism and Eucharist.

EDITORS

LWF Study Series: S. Anita Stauffer, Editor (1947-2007)
Worship and Culture in Dialogue (1994)
Christian Worship: Unity in Cultural Diversity (1996)
Baptism, Rites of Passage, and Culture (1998)

S. ANITA STAUFFER, a Lutheran theologian, served on the worship staffs of the Lutheran World Federation, the Evangelical Lutheran Church in America, and the Lutheran Church in America. She wrote several books, including *Altar Guild Handbook* (1985). Most significantly, Dr. Stauffer facilitated and contributed to the LWF Study Series on Worship and Culture, serving the wider church from the LWF home offices in Geneva. She is the author of two of the essays in the original study series, which are reprinted in full in this volume. This new collection of essays and texts is dedicated to her memory in thanksgiving for her life and contributions.

Current Volume
Worship and Culture: Foreign Country or Homeland?
Gláucia Vasconcelos Wilkey, Editor

GLÁUCIA VASCONCELOS WILKEY is a native of Brazil and a Presbyterian Church (USA) pastor. Her first academic appointment was as a professor in Rio de Janeiro's Seminário Batista do Sul do Brasil for ten and a half years. After a six-year ministry in Canada with a multicultural and multilingual congregation, she served in two PCUSA congregations and in the Presbyterian (USA) General Assembly's Office of Theology and Worship. In 2008 she retired from Seattle University's School of Theology and Ministry, where she taught liturgical theology for more than nine years, served as coordinator for that institution's ecumenical liturgical life, and founded — and for seven years directed — the Summer Institute for Liturgy and Worship.

INTRODUCTION

From the Past to the Future: The LWF Study Series on Worship and Culture as Vision and Mission

Norman A. Hjelm

At a meeting of the Council of the Lutheran World Federation (LWF) in the early 1990s, a proposal was brought by the LWF's Division for Theology and Studies that a global study of worship and culture be undertaken. Leadership of this study was to be provided by the Rev. S. Anita Stauffer (1947-2007) of the Evangelical Lutheran Church in America (ELCA), who was then the division's study secretary for Worship and Congregational Life. The proposal was adopted, even though a few members of the council, the LWF's deliberative body, opposed it, largely on the grounds that its subject was at best peripheral, if not irrelevant, to the pressing needs of churches in the world. In sharp contrast to that opposition, Viggo Mortensen, the director of Theology and Studies, wrote in 1994: "I do not think that there is a single other issue which is discussed more keenly among both clergy and laity than the question of how Gospel and culture relate to one another, especially with regard to worship."[1]

Thus it was that for several years major attention was given to the transcultural, contextual, and countercultural aspects of Christian worship within expressions of the Lutheran tradition in all parts of the world. This enterprise produced three stimulating volumes of essays (in 1994, 1996, and 1999) and three "statements" that are now seen as having enduring value. To be sure, it is a truism that, within churches and interchurch organizations, "of the making of studies there is no end" and that most such studies are both expensive

---

1. Viggo Mortensen, preface in S. Anita Stauffer, ed., *Worship and Culture in Dialogue: Reports of International Consultations — Cartigny, Switzerland 1993, Hong Kong 1994* (Geneva: Department for Theology and Studies, Lutheran World Federation, 1994), p. 6.

and short-lived. And that is certainly true of communions of churches such as the LWF as well. However, it is quite generally acknowledged that the Worship and Culture study, as published in those three volumes, has assumed a life of its own, making a striking and enduring contribution to the global and ecumenical church. Much of the credit for that should be attributed to the insight, perseverance, and dedication of the late Anita Stauffer, one of the persons to whom this book is gratefully dedicated.

The Worship and Culture study can be seen, from one angle, as a natural outgrowth of earlier studies conducted within the LWF, especially the major project of the 1970s on "The Identity of the Church and Its Service to the Whole Human Being."[2] Of that project it has been said:

> Hardly any other theological project in the history of the Federation was ever undertaken with comparable creativity and enthusiasm. Hardly any other initiative taken by the staff in Geneva was ever marked by the same degree of happy interaction between the secretariat, which assumed careful and dynamic leadership, and representatives of member churches, who exhibited extraordinarily high degrees of cooperation. And, to maintain balanced and honest historical judgment, hardly any other theological work of the Federation aroused more controversy and debate on practically all levels than this "ecclesiology study."[3]

While the long-term endurance of this ecclesiology study within the Lutheran family can perhaps be doubted, it surely set a tone at two points: the LWF has remained occupied, quite correctly, with questions of *ecclesiology;* and the many issues that surround the problem of *contextuality* have continued to claim prominence. Like the work of the 1970s and 1980s — including "Confessing Christ in Cultural Contexts" (1976-83), which involved Lutheran churches in Indonesia, Germany, Tanzania, Sweden, Japan, and the United States — many subsequent LWF study enterprises have come and gone. But the fundamental problematic of the life and nature of the church in myriad situations — ecclesiology and contextuality — has continued to be of great importance. Witness: Worship and Culture.

Worship and Culture is also notable for its attention to ecumenical and

2. LWF, Department of Studies, *The Identity of the Church and Its Service to the Whole Human Being* (Geneva: LWF; Final Volume I, 1976; Final Volume II, 1977).

3. Jens Holger Schjørring, Prasanna Kumari, and Norman A. Hjelm, eds., *From Federation to Communion: The History of the Lutheran World Federation* (Minneapolis: Fortress, 1997), p. 194.

global concerns. Lutherans can no longer, as in past generations, confine themselves to their particular confessional tradition alone; nor can their focus be on the classical Lutheran areas of Europe and North America. Reflection on the nature and practice of worship has of necessity become thoroughly ecumenical. Thus participation in the project, as in this book, has included persons from a variety of communions, perhaps most notably one of its key leaders, Anscar J. Chupungco, OSB (1939-2013), the second person to whom this volume is dedicated. Churches from all parts of the globe — and their contexts — were represented both among its participants and as the source of concrete case studies.

It is, moreover, of considerable significance that even as the LWF developed its concern for worship and culture, the World Council of Churches (WCC) was pursuing the theme of "Gospel and Culture." As early as 1973, at the WCC International Missionary Conference in Bangkok, a section on "Culture and Identity" had declared, under the rubric "On Conversion and Cultural Change":

> Christian conversion gathers people into the worshiping community, the teaching community and the community of service to all men. Even if Christians are not called out of their culture and separated from the society in which they were born, they still will form cells of worship, of reflection and of service within their original cultures.[4]

The question of culture received considerable attention at the 1991 WCC Assembly in Canberra, leading to the formation of some sixty study groups around the world and the publication of a series of eighteen small books under the title *Gospel and Culture.*

In this framework the time was right in the 1990s for the LWF to embark on its global study of worship and culture. The first of three parts to the study reached its culmination in the publication in 1994 of *Worship and Culture in Dialogue.* In his preface to that book, Viggo Mortensen says:

> How are we to proclaim Christ in different cultures? The message must first embrace us, and speak not only to our brains and senses but also to

4. Michael Kinnamon and Brian E. Cope, eds., *The Ecumenical Movement: An Anthology of Key Texts and Voices* (Grand Rapids: Eerdmans; Geneva: WCC Publications, 1997), p. 354. See also Birgitta Larson and Emilio Castro, "From Missions to Mission," in John Briggs, Mercy Amba Oduyoye, and Georges Tsetsis, eds., *A History of the Ecumenical Movement,* vol. 3, 1968-2000 (Geneva: WCC Publications, 2004), pp. 139-41.

our hearts. In order for this to happen it must be incarnated in the life of the people and their culture, just as it took root in one specific culture for the first time. Thus the issue of how Gospel and culture relate always has been and always will be with us as we reflect on how to be God's Church. Being a perennial issue, it is one which calls for continued reflection. This is what we are trying to do in our study on worship and culture.[5]

This first part of the study was undertaken by about twenty-five representatives from Lutheran churches, and with participants from the Roman Catholic Church, the Anglican Communion, and the WCC. Their work resulted in the "Cartigny Statement on Worship and Culture: Biblical and Historical Foundations" (1993). The second phase of the study resulted in the publication of *Christian Worship: Unity in Cultural Diversity* (1996).[6] It involved regional research that faced questions such as the following:

1. What is the cultural situation in a given region/subregion of (a) the population as a whole, and (b) the Lutheran church(es)? To what extent is the situation homogeneous and monocultural, heterogeneous, indigenous, immigrant, and so forth? What are the cultural values and patterns?
2. What cultural patterns might be brought into Christian worship? Why?
3. In what respects should Christian worship in this region/subregion be countercultural? Why? In what sense should worship (a) contradict the culture, or (b) reinterpret the culture?
4. What resistance is there to (a) contextualization, and (b) the countercultural? Why?[7]

These questions and others were applied in various regions of the world — Africa, Asia, Europe, Latin America, North America — to elements of liturgical worship: eucharistic prayers, church year calendar and liturgical colors, hymn texts and music, church architecture, art, and furnishings, vessels and vestments, lectionary, baptism, healing rites, and so forth. The product of this phase of the study was "The Nairobi Statement on Worship

---

5. S. Anita Stauffer, ed., *Worship and Culture in Dialogue,* pp. 5-6, 129-135. This latter statement is also to be found in the present volume, p. 390.
6. S. Anita Stauffer, ed., *Christian Worship: Unity in Cultural Diversity* (Geneva: LWF, Department for Theology and Studies, 1996).
7. Stauffer, ed., *Christian Worship,* p. 9.

and Culture: Contemporary Challenges and Opportunities" (1996).[8] The third and final part of the study resulted in *Baptism, Rites of Passage, and Culture* (1999).[9]

In 1998, the fourth and final consultation of the Worship and Culture study took place in Chicago. In this consultation, case studies provided a basis for considerations of how local cultures are related to several rites that are at least relatively universal: baptism (a sacrament, to be sure, and not just a "rite of passage"), healing rites, funeral rites, and marriage rites. In addition, the consultation also considered the relationship of culture to church architecture and to the preaching ministry. A fourfold dynamic, identified earlier in the 1996 Nairobi Statement, was applied to the study.

> Worship is and should be:
> - *Transcultural:* the same substance everywhere, transcending cultures.
> - *Contextual:* the transcultural substance expressed locally, adapted from the natural and cultural contexts through the methods of dynamic equivalence or creative assimilation.[10]
> - *Countercultural:* challenging and transforming cultural patterns that are inconsistent with the gospel of Jesus Christ.
> - *Cross-cultural:* sharing across and between local cultures.[11]

The Chicago consultation again prepared a statement that built "upon the prior Cartigny and Nairobi Statements, applying their insights to the topics considered at the Chicago consultation."[12]

Earlier in this introduction, I made the commonplace point that in church bodies, in global communions, and in ecumenical frameworks, "of the making of studies there is no end." To put it cynically, such studies come and go even if the issues with which they wrestle are truly consequential. There are exceptions — certain papal encyclicals, statements from some ec-

---

8. Stauffer, ed., *Christian Worship*, pp. 23-28. This statement is also to be found in the present volume, pp. 137-42. It has been widely quoted and used, e.g., in Charles E. Farhadian, ed., *Christian Worship Worldwide: Expanding Horizons, Deepening Practices* (Grand Rapids: Eerdmans, 2007), pp. 285-90.

9. S. Anita Stauffer, ed., *Baptism, Rites of Passage, and Culture* (Geneva: LWF, Department for Theology and Studies, 1999).

10. See below, Anscar Chupungco, OSB, "Methods of Liturgical Interpretation."

11. S. Anita Stauffer, preface to *Baptism, Rites of Passage, and Culture*, p. 10.

12. Stauffer, *Baptism, Rites of Passage, and Culture*, pp. 13-24. The statement is found in the present volume, pp. 290-301.

umenical dialogues, a few assembly documents; but it still seems that most studies and statements come and go.

The present volume, carefully and lovingly conceived and edited by Gláucia Vasconcelos Wilkey, who builds on the work of her dear friends Anita Stauffer, Anscar Chupungco, and Gordon W. Lathrop, is based on the confidence that the LWF Worship and Culture study, with its three statements and its three published books, is a study of enduring importance. In this book, the three statements — Cartigny, Nairobi, Chicago — are to be found, along with two original essays by Anita Stauffer, original essays by Gordon Lathrop and Anscar Chupungco (with authors' revisions), and a host of new essays developing the Worship and Culture studies from historical and recent ecumenical and international perspectives.

But more. This book demonstrates that the worship of the triune God — at all times and in every culture — is the heart of the church's life. And it demonstrates that worship and culture is not to be regarded as an ossified item in ecclesiastical archives. Rather, it is to be seen as a step in a never-ending journey. To relate the worship of God to the realities of culture and of particular cultures is a perennial task, and this book moves us ahead — from the past to the future. The Chicago Statement from the Worship and Culture study concludes with a challenge that is broadly global and broadly ecumenical:

> We continue to call on all . . . to undertake further intentional study and efforts related to the transcultural, contextual, and counter-cultural natures of Christian worship, and its cross-cultural sharing. We call on all . . . to recover the centrality of Baptism for their life and worship, and as the foundation of rites of human passage, and to do so whenever possible in ecumenical partnerships with wide participation. The challenge is to develop and use forms of worship which are both authentic to the Gospel and relevant to local cultural contexts.[13]

Worship takes form in tradition. Culture provides contexts for all things human. Together they shape and reshape each other, offering resources of faith, consolation, and mission. One author, Gordon Lathrop, who contributed deeply to the Worship and Culture study and who is honored in the present book, has used the expression "conserve and critique" as a key to opening the treasure of the tradition, of worship itself. That key is what this

---

13. Stauffer, *Baptism, Rites of Passage, and Culture*, p. 124.

book is all about: to conserve the Worship and Culture study and to offer critique. For what has been learned is that worship is "both conservative and critical, centered and open, catholic and evangelical, free and bound, local and more-than-local, God's action and our action."[14] Perhaps what was done in the original study from the 1990s and what is done now in this book is well understood in the oft-cited charge of Johann Wolfgang von Goethe:

What you have as heritage,
Take now as task:
For thus you will make it your own!

14. Gordon W. Lathrop, "The Problems Facing Churches in the Light of the LWF Project."

Every Foreign Country a Homeland, Every Homeland a Foreign Country: On Worship and Culture

Gordon W. Lathrop

Among the many early expressions of Christian thought that have come down to us, one interesting, incisive voice might be especially important to hear at the outset of a book devoted to cultural diversity and cultural relevance in Christian liturgical practice. The voice is that of the Epistle to Diognetus, a second- or third-century writing that was preserved for us in only one thirteenth- or fourteenth-century manuscript. We know very little about the provenance of the writing or of the writer; nonetheless, we can recognize in the work a particular voice expressing clearly the faith and practice that was becoming orthodox, faithful Christianity in the early centuries. The following passage, from the fifth chapter of the Epistle to Diognetus, may be relevant to us here and now:

> Christians are not distinguished from the rest of humanity either in locality or in speech or in customs. For they do not dwell off somewhere in cities of their own, neither do they use some different language, nor do they practice an extraordinary style of life. . . . But while they dwell in the cities of Greeks and barbarians as the lot of each is cast, and follow the local customs, both in clothing and food and the rest of life, the constitution of their citizenship is nevertheless quite amazing and admittedly paradoxical. They dwell in their own countries, but only as sojourners; they share all things as citizens and suffer all things as strangers. Every

---

This essay was first given as a lecture at the Summer Institute for Liturgy and Worship of the School of Theology and Ministry of Seattle University in 2006.

foreign country is a homeland to them, and every homeland is a foreign country.[1]

The writer then continues with several examples of the cultural correspondences and the cultural differences of Christians:

They marry as do all people and have offspring, but they do not expose their children. They set out an hospitable, open table but not an open bed.[2]

"Every foreign country a homeland and every homeland a foreign country." Notice that it does not say "heaven is my home," but "every foreign country." Note also that that it does not simply say "resident aliens," but "aliens who are at home here." It is a remarkable vision, one that can be especially helpful to us now, as we affirm both human cultural rootedness and something larger than such rootedness, and as we invite Christians to find themselves in sympathy with — even "at home" in — every culture, at the same time that they also need to exercise a certain criticism of every culture.

Indeed, perhaps we can be drawn to this ancient voice precisely because of our own worldwide cultural moment, the conversation and argument not only among Christians but among everyone in our own cities of today: How do we treasure difference and yet find common values? How does specific cultural identity not simply become the source of violence and exclusion? How do the universal patterns of global consumerism not rob us of the ancient wisdom of local cultures? How do we avoid both cultural imperialism and ethical relativism? And how do we avoid simply giving up in despair, regarding the only defensible value to be found in the private choices of the individual consuming self? And why do these questions matter so much?

"Every foreign country a homeland and every homeland a foreign country." Especially in that first phrase, this is an idea not unlike the ancient proposal of the Greek Cynics — and then of the Roman Stoics — that they called themselves "cosmopolitans," a proposal that was itself a metaphor straining into a paradox.[3] In ancient Greek thought and practice, "politans"

---

1. Epistle to Diognetus 5:1-5 (my translation). The Greek text can be found in Kirsopp Lake, ed., *The Apostolic Fathers II* (Cambridge, MA: Harvard University Press, 1959), pp. 358, 360.

2. Epistle to Diognetus 5:6-7.

3. See Kwame Anthony Appiah, *Cosmopolitanism: Ethics in a World of Strangers* (New York: Norton, 2006), p. xiv.

(to make up an English word from the Greek *polites*) are citizens, city-dwellers, this-city people: the free and responsible participants in the "political" life of a city, a polis, one city against the others. The cosmos — the whole universe seen as an ordered whole — is not a city. But the astonishing proposal of these "cosmopolitans," a philosophical proposal sometimes seen as useful by later Christians, was that the wise human should be such a citizen, such a locally invested and responsibility-bearing participant, of the universe.

Of course, caring about the universe can easily lead to caring about no particular local place at all, dismissing and undermining differences. So it is that more recent cosmopolitan thinkers, such as the remarkable Kwame Anthony Appiah, have called themselves "partial cosmopolitans," seeking both to support some basic universal values and to celebrate local differences.[4] One of the most interesting ancient assertions of this view, struggling toward both local particularity and more-than-local value, was that of the second-century B.C.E. Roman playwright Terence in his famous dictum *homo sum: humani nil a me alienum puto* ("I am a human being: nothing that is human is alien to me").[5]

Christians can and should rejoice in this line from Terence. Indeed, I think that Christians can and should find themselves allied with the partial cosmopolitans, over against all imperialists (on the one hand) and all identity purists (on the other). Just so, I think that Christians today should treasure, for example, the history of the remarkably mixed, tolerant, and learned cultures of the Muslim caliphate of Cordoba and its successor states in early-medieval Andalusia, called Al-Andalus (original home to both Averroes and Maimonides), as they should also lament the fierce end of that rich history of tolerance in the name of an appallingly narrow and self-serving so-called Christian orthodoxy.[6]

And Christians should delight in and learn from any stories of people who become "amphibians," capable of swimming and walking in more than one culture, even when that ability was gained from decidedly mixed motives.[7] Such amphibians, by the way, are not just the educated elite or the traders and merchants or the world tourists; they are, more particularly, the

4. Appiah, *Cosmopolitanism*, p. xvii.
5. Quoted in Appiah, *Cosmopolitanism*, pp. 111-12.
6. See Maria Rosa Menocal, *Ornament of the World* (Boston: Little, Brown and Company, 2002).
7. E.g., the famous William Johnson, Anglo-Irish, adopted Iroquois agent of late British America. See Finian O'Toole, *White Savage* (New York: Farrar, Straus and Giroux, 2005).

immigrants and refugees found everywhere today, or the country folk who have come to the city for economic reasons, or the city folk who have sought refuge in the countryside, or the First Nation folk (as Native Americans are called in Canada) who, simply by being alive in present-day Canada or the United States, are living mixed cultural lives, balancing values, learning new ways. The amphibians are often us. And the "cultures" that are so mixed are not simply ethnicities — though they are also that! — but they represent all the ways people specifically teach their children to order and navigate the world, all the locally specific languages and symbols and habits we use to organize human life. For Christians to intentionally and willingly join these amphibians, to find "every foreign country a homeland," to treasure other cultures in whatever way is possible, bit by particular bit, and to learn more and more from them, indeed, to seek to hold more than one idea about how to live at one time — none of this is easy. But it is the invitation held out by the writer of the Diognetus. Even more, I think, Christians should join in the growing postcolonialist acknowledgment that cultures themselves are always mixed, even "mongrel," ever-changing internal arguments, "hybrid, impure, intermingled things," to quote Salman Rushdie.[8] We are all are living in, and even enjoying, the fruits of many cultures. You and I, dear reader, are inevitably living such lives right now.

But in Terence's play *The Self-Tormentor,* that phrase occurs in a comedy, as a comic justification for gossip — that wonderful, painful, busybody investigator of all things human! Accused of being a gossip, Terence's protagonist says, "I am a human being! Nothing that is human is alien to me!" We laugh with Terence, see the truth in the humor, but we also know that in Christian use, the same idea is anchored in theology itself. And that theology is anchored in the biblical stories. God has made all things, all people. All people, from all nations and all times, are invited to gather before God with their gifts. "People will bring into that city the glory and honor of the nations," says the vision at the end of the Bible (Rev. 21:26). "Praise the LORD, all you nations; extol God, all you peoples," says Psalm 117:1.[9] I am part of that all. Still, for Christians, there is more: all things are in need of God, all human beings are in utter need of grace. And I am also part of that all. "But nothing unclean will enter it . . ." says the same Revelation text (21:27). "In Adam's fall, we sinned all," says the old Christian sampler phrase that was sewn into many a

8. Quoted in Appiah, *Cosmopolitanism,* p. 112.

9. See the Psalter in *Evangelical Lutheran Worship* (Minneapolis: Augsburg Fortress, 2006).

nineteenth-century Anglo-American girl's handwork, girls who as yet knew very little of the global cultures embraced by that "all" (except, perhaps, what they knew of the tea they were learning to drink in china teacups, brought to their shores by sailing ships). Nothing that is human — the great gifts and the great need, the beauty and the sin — is alien to me.

That assertion of universal giftedness and universal need is one reason why the Gnostic idea, popular once again in such writings as the Gospel of Judas, is such a bad idea: according to that idea, God did not really make the world. Not to mention the idea that humanity is divided up between the really large group of fleshly people who do not get it and the tiny group of spiritual people who do. For those espousing such an idea, most of what is human is alien to me — if I am one of the enlightened — and I am destined to get out of here, away from all these fleshly diversities, escaping into the pure, unmixed Idea of the utterly spiritual One.

But orthodox Christians have not needed Gnosticism to fuel their rejection of the other. Think of those "Catholic monarchs" in Spain and think of their Inquisition in its relationship to Muslims and to Jews. Or, closer to us, think of the Puritan colonizers of New England in their relationship to the peoples of the land, peoples of the forest, a relationship that became an oft-repeated and murderous pattern in North America.

The melancholy stories go on. Indeed, unless we use the biblical idea of an "elect people" — a people "on the hill" giving light to the world — very, very carefully, it can carry within itself the uncriticized idea that we are the elect and that our current culture is God's own approved, superior culture. You have heard — perhaps you have even used — the language that calls the United States the "best country in the world." This is not innocent language.

No. Every foreign country a homeland and every homeland a foreign country. It is a paradox and it is surely nearly impossible to actually live out, but it is a better, more biblical idea than either the Gnostic proposal or the uncriticized use of an idea of "the elect." It is an idea more in accord with the deep story of Israel — of Israel as a separate priestly people only to exercise that priesthood for the sake of the life of all peoples (Exod. 19:5-6) — and more in accord with the account of Jesus in the four Gospels, the four diverse, flesh-honoring, "sarcophilic" Gospels, as John Dominic Crossan says.[10] In those Gospels, for example, is found both the Lukan use of

10. John Dominic Crossan, *The Birth of Christianity* (San Francisco: Harper, 1998), pp. 36-38. See also Gordon W. Lathrop, *The Four Gospels on Sunday: The New Testament and the Reform of Christian Worship* (Minneapolis: Fortress, 2012), pp. 8-9.

the originally Hellenistic cultural idea of "benefaction," reworking that cultural idea as a mark of Christianity, and the Johannine prayer that says, "I am not asking you to take them out of the world, but I ask you to protect them from the evil one. They do not belong to the world, just as I do not belong to the world. Sanctify them in your truth . . ." (John 17:15-17).[11] Indeed, many Christians down through the ages have tried to live by this idea, finding diverse ways to bring to expression both their "being at home" and their being sojourners, suffering and criticizing the institutions of local culture.

Of course, the appropriate balance between being at home and being strangers has been one source of Christian disagreement, one side or the other of the balance sometimes being lost. Early Egyptian monasticism, for example, sought to be entirely strange, entirely at odds with any homeland, whereas Byzantine state religion at more or less the same time could seem to be utterly at home in one imperial place. But the reformed monasticism of Benedict sought to be clearly at odds with some of the values of its surrounding cultures, while it also sought to be at home in the actual local world, the very local land, deeply treasuring the virtue of stability and harboring some of the best of local human cultural (and agricultural) expressions. And it was Roger Schutz, the prior of the ecumenical monastic community of Taizé — thus, a monk, by definition a kind of sojourner, and in this case one with his own history of resisting the French version of the purist identity ideology of National Socialism and its concomitant persecution of the Jews — who gave us a modern Christian version of Terence's dictum or a modern exhortation formed from the wisdom of the Diognetus letter: "Open yourself to all that is human," says his Rule of Taizé, "and you will find that every vain desire to escape from the world disappears."[12]

How might we do that?

In what follows, this book will argue that the ecumenical liturgical renewal movement has within itself, if we pay attention, the seeds of a lively and helpful, biblically rooted balance between being at home in every culture and being a stranger. The renewed liturgy can be one source of wisdom for us among the current urgent questions of cultural identity and multicultural encounter. But how is that so? Every foreign country a homeland and every homeland a foreign country. How will we find this proposal in the

---

11. See Lathrop, *The Four Gospels on Sunday*, p. 117.

12. Roger Schutz, "The Rule of Taizé," in *Parable of Community* (London: Mowbray, 1990), p. 13.

liturgy? In fact, this idea is profoundly helpful as a hermeneutical key in approaching the history of Christian worship.

For one thing, Christians, from the beginning, have struggled with a balance between the local and the universal in their worship. That balance of the local and universal, the cultural and the transcultural, is a particularly liturgical way of enacting the saying of Diognetus. The local assembly is church. So is the worldwide assembly, the hoped-for communion of all the assemblies. When they are healthy, the celebrations of Christians always make use of local languages, local people, local food and water, local architecture, local patterns of gathering with others, local cultural matters; but they are also always in touch with others away from here, strange to this culture. Indeed, Christian assemblies receive their ministers as sent by the others, read their Scripture, and confess their faith together with the others who are not here, in more-than-local patterns. When gestures toward the universal came to dominate, as in the late-medieval imposition of an idealized Roman practice everywhere in Western Europe, the liturgy could quickly become impenetrable, unhelpful to local assemblies, and much in need of reform. Such imposition can and does continue to occur.

But, similarly, when the liturgy becomes too local, uncorrected by the more-than-local communion, it could finally wander away from the Christian faith itself, as in the communities that became Gnostic or Manichaean. Such local distortions also still occur. In any case, liturgy in the vernacular and as responsible and participating in local assembly is a continuing monument to the assertion "every foreign country a homeland." And the Bible itself, that collection of books from other cultural times read with authority in our midst — not to mention the creeds or the patterns of ministry or the very *ordo* of the liturgy or the more-than-local patterns of observance called "rites" — these are monuments to the assertion "every homeland a foreign country." Read the Bible, dear friends! Really. It is strange to us, not easily domesticated, at odds with our values, inviting us to be strangers here.

Furthermore, it was a liturgical judgment that Tertullian made when he said that "whatever belongs to those that are of us, belongs to us."[13] Being at home in other cultures may be hard, but liturgical customs spread nonetheless, inviting us into at least a fragment of multiculturalism. Local practice becomes a cultural mix. The assembly practices of the Christians assimilate and are assimilated to local cultural patterns, and the resulting mix — often

13. Tertullian, *De virginibus velandis* 2:2. See also Gordon W. Lathrop, *Holy People: A Liturgical Ecclesiology* (Minneapolis: Fortress, 1999), pp. 119ff.

because of its very brilliance — can then be adopted much more widely, with growing meanings.

So today, in the renewed liturgy, we keep a revised version of the ancient Asian Christian reworking of the Jewish Passover to become our Pascha, or Easter, the ancient Roman (and then northern European) Christian reworking of the pagan winter solstice has now become our Christmas, as well as the eastern Mediterranean (and perhaps ancient Spanish) creation of Epiphany and the ancient Egyptian and African creation of Lent.

Nothing is more traditional among faithful Christians, says Anscar Chupungco, than the constant inculturation of the liturgy, including the resultant spread of the creative assimilations.[14] Somebody started to anoint the newly baptized or clothe them with a clean white garment. Somebody began to light candles at evening prayer or light a fire at Pascha. Somebody started to use an Advent wreath or a Christmas tree. The original stories are complex, partly hidden, but they involved cultural practices. And they have spread nearly everywhere.

Indeed, the Sunday liturgy itself is a kind of palimpsest of cultures, a manuscript reused and rewritten again and again, one image and one hand over another, like the paintings heaped on top of each other in the paleolithic caves of Lascaux and Altamira. It is very possible that in your own assembly, this past Sunday, you sang a European entrance hymn, a Greek *kyrie*, a Syrian *gloria*, an African *alleluia*, an Asian and then a Latin American song during communion, while you read old Hebrew and Greek writings and celebrated a meal with Hellenistic-Jewish roots. Your leaders may have been dressed in ancient Mediterranean clothing. And yet you did it all in an elegant form of current American English, perhaps mixed with some current American Spanish (or Korean or Navajo!), and with patterns of participation that echo current American democratic values as well as ancient Christian baptismal ones. Dear friends, hurrah for the mixture! Hurrah for the gifts of the nations! Hurrah also for the many particular local cultural ways, ethnic ways, and ways beyond ethnicity that have flowed into the wider mixture that is our liturgy. Nothing that is human should be alien to us. It is as if, in liturgical history, the churches have meant to act out that image of the city in Revelation, the city of God of which we are to be citizens: "Its gates will

14. See Anscar Chupungco, *The Cultural Adaptation of the Liturgy* (New York: Paulist, 1982). On "creative assimilation," see also Chupungco, "Two Methods of Liturgical Inculturation," in S. Anita Stauffer, ed., *Christian Worship: Unity in Cultural Diversity* (Geneva: LWF, 1996), pp. 78-81; see also the Nairobi Statement on Worship and Culture, 3.4 (reprinted below, pp. 137-42).

never be shut by day — and there will be no night there. People will bring into it the glory and honor of the nations" (Rev. 21:25-26).

The very most central matters of Christian liturgy — Scripture being read and preached, the meal being celebrated, the bath with which the community is constituted, and the very idea of assembly itself — are themselves old cultural artifacts, most of them from specific Hellenistic-Jewish (mixed!) cultural moments not our own.[15] And even though these central matters are stylized, made to connect with the basically human transcultural realities of assembling, bathing, storytelling and meal-keeping, and so to connect profoundly with us as well as with other peoples in other places and times, this bath, word, table, and assembly trail something of that foreign country with themselves, training us to be at home in every foreign place.

There is more. These very material, central things of Christian worship, wherever they are celebrated — if the celebration allows these things to stand forth in clarity and strength — are always straining to make use of local water, local agriculture, local speech, and thus they are inviting us all to treasure every foreign ecosystem, every foreign local culture, relearning the ways in which culture itself is at its best when it is solidly connected to the land and to communities passing on to their children the most helpful ways they have found to live in the land.

Indeed, for Christians, the deepest ground for this "being at home" in every foreign land comes not from cosmopolitan insight but from the gift of that central Christian bath. At least according to current attempts at understanding this gift, the baptismal bath itself washes us into identification not just with our own local group, but with Jesus Christ, who in his death and resurrection identifies with all people, especially in their great need.[16] To be baptized, then, is not to be distinguished from humanity but, paradoxically, to be identified with the one who identifies with all.

For Christians, it is Jesus Christ who is the "elect one," and in him an "elect community" must be with him and like him. For Christians, paradoxically, "election" — being a chosen one of the insiders — has an utterly new meaning: in Christ, we are to be at home in every foreign land. Such being

15. On baptism and Eucharist as Christian reworkings of cultural artifacts, see the articles in S. Anita Stauffer, ed., *Worship and Culture in Dialogue* (Geneva: LWF, 1994), pp. 17-102. Some of those articles were themselves reworked, with additional attention to assembly and the observance of time, in chaps. 7-9 of Lathrop, *Holy People*.

16. See the Chicago Statement on Worship and Culture, 2.3 (reprinted below, pp. 293-301). See also "Baptismal Ordo and Rites of Passage in the Church," in S. Anita Stauffer, ed., *Baptism, Rites of Passage and Culture* (Geneva: LWF, 1998), pp. 34-35.

at home does not come easily, but it is our vocation. In this sense, "you are a chosen race, a holy nation, God's own people, in order that you may proclaim the mighty deeds" of this God (1 Pet. 2:9).[17]

All very well, you may say. At least when it was renewed, Christian liturgy classically welcomed and affirmed diverse cultures, symbolizing the open gates of the city of God and inviting Christians who are in communion with each other to find every foreign country to be a homeland. But what about the other side of the saying? What about "every homeland a foreign country"? What about the critique of cultures?

A certain critique of cultures also belongs to the ecumenical liturgical renewal, but it is more difficult to articulate, perhaps most difficult about one's own cultural patterns. The very fact the Christian liturgy is made up of a variety of diverse cultural materials is already some help. Fierce, uncriticized local identity, resisting and rejecting all others, is harder when some of the most important things in our lives — hymns in which we sing our faith, for example, not to mention the patterns and central matters of the holy communion itself — come at least partly in forms that we did not make up and that do not come from here.

Even more, the very Scripture passages read at the heart of our meetings are themselves not a uniform, cultural whole. They are a kind of canonical argument: for example, Job with Deuteronomy, or Ruth with Ezra and Nehemiah, or Mark with Matthew, or Paul with James, a way to let two or more conflicting ideas about "identity" be held at once in the very center of our assemblies. Where such mutually critical sacred Scripture texts are read — and where they are heard — it will be harder to establish only one cultural way.

Again, the most central matters of our liturgy — bath and word, prayers and table, to use one summary list — can demonstrate ways that culture is not only welcomed and celebrated, but criticized. These central matters are made up of local, ordinary cultural materials from daily life: storytelling and meals, of course, but also appeals to the divine and baths to mark a new beginning. But these matters are now used in critical and reorienting association with Jesus, with his reversals of religious meaning and his attack on religious boundaries, with his death and the communal practice of his resurrection.

---

17. The Epistle goes on to urge its readers to live as "aliens and exiles" (2:11-12) and as a free people (2:16), and yet to accept the "authority of every human institution" (2:13), among which we may include cultural institutions.

In many cultures, local words ordinarily tell local stories with conventional endings in which people get what they deserve. But in the four Gospels and in liturgy that is faithfully in continuity with them, traditional stories are given surprising, mercy-filled endings. The disfigured child is not thrown away. The curse becomes a place of blessing. Communal meals are a universally local cultural phenomenon, in which our small group assures itself of its own survival and passes on its own culture — but only for our group. But in the four Gospels and the letters of Paul, and in the liturgies that keep the Lord's Supper in company with them, commensality with Jesus is combined with an open door to the outsider and the sending of food to the poor. This cultural criticism belongs to the heart of Christianity, to the very continued proclamation and discernment of the crucified and risen body of Christ. Furthermore, when humans are in need, prayers arise from practically every set of local lips, to anything that might be regarded as being able to help — for us and for ours. There are richly diverse cultural forms for such prayer throughout the world. But in the four Gospels, and in the reformed liturgy, the community is invited to pray for others beyond this ordered circle, others besides itself, to pray for the earth itself, and thus to pray in Jesus' name. And as we have seen, even water and its local cultural uses gets reoriented in healthy Christian practice to mark not so much purity and distance from the unclean as participation in the need of all the world. This is the bath, as I have tried to say, that makes us dirtier. The word and the sacraments at the heart of Christian worship are ordinary human, cultural matters, criticized and reused to bear the gospel of Jesus Christ, thereby giving us an image of God criticizing and saving our cultures. Every homeland a foreign country.[18]

As we have seen, when the last book of the Bible made that promise about the gifts of the nations streaming into the city of God, it also added the warning: "But nothing unclean will enter it, nor anyone who practices abomination or falsehood, but only those who are written in the Lamb's book of life" (Rev. 21:27). Christians have certainly sometimes adopted ideas of purity, as if ritual uncleanness were the "unclean thing" that cannot enter the city, and as if Christian versions of cultural taboos were the way to protect the gates. Consider the idea that women are unclean, especially during their periods, and thus should not come near the holy things, an idea found

18. See Gordon W. Lathrop, "Bath, Word, Prayer, Table: Reflections on Doing the Liturgical Ordo in a Postmodern Time," in Dirk G. Lange and Dwight W. Vogel, eds., *Ordo: Bath, Word, Prayer, Table* (Akron, OH: OSL, 2005), pp. 216-28.

in some cultural contexts. It is also an idea found in various places throughout the history of Christian practice.

Or consider the idea that lower castes are unclean and should approach Holy Communion only after the higher castes have received the elements. These cultural ideas, or diversities, have indeed always been present in parts of Christianity. But they are wrong. A better, deeper, more biblical insight, I say, is that the very idea of purity — as it raises its head in every culture and as a locally constructed establishment of identity — is the unclean thing, the lie, the abomination. Even among the purity rules of Leviticus, argues our semicosmopolitan Kwame Appiah, there are "appeals to values that are universal and that discipline the demands made by the taboos."[19]

But for Jesus and his company, the exclusions created by purity rules can no longer determine identity (e.g., Mark 7:1-30) and should not be welcome in the liturgy. For the letter to Diognetus, being a stranger at home, a citizen with distance, a foreigner in every homeland, means hospitality without free sex, marriage without infanticide. For those of us in Christian liturgy, it means an intentional community, welcoming many cultures, but with permeable boundaries and without the identity dynamics of purity. "As many of you as were baptized into Christ have clothed yourselves with Christ," writes Paul. "There is no longer Jew or Greek, there is no longer slave or free, there is no longer male and female; for you are all one in Christ Jesus" (Gal. 3:27-28). And for us, in the Christian liturgy, it must mean celebrations that accentuate God's free grace, not our achievements and distinctions and self-made identities. There are our larger principles to discipline every cultural taboo. "Every homeland a foreign country."

The open city criticizes our identity purities; the leaves of the tree of God's grace heal our broken cultures. "Who am I?" There is the identity question. Reoriented by the gospel, by biblical lament, by the cross and resurrection of Jesus Christ held out in word and sacrament, the answer can be, I am a woman, I am a man, who stands before God's mercy with all the other beggars. Now. Here. "Every homeland a foreign country."

The very word used in the letter to Diognetus ("homeland") is actually *patris* in the Greek — literally, "fatherland." That word still has, in our own times, enough of the resonance of *Vaterland* about it, the stench of Nazi purity and exclusion and nationalist group identity wherever it occurs, that we can immediately see the importance of being a stranger in such a highly identified, purely boundaried country. It may be more difficult for us to see

---

19. Appiah, *Cosmopolitanism*, p. 57.

it in our own country or our own ethnic group or our own congregation. But it is a very important point to emphasize among people who care about liturgy: in every homeland, fatherland, motherland, and foreign country, we need to know that ritual practice inevitably marks off the ritualizing group from other groups. Ritual is one of the tools of social differentiation.

But then what about Christian ritual? Of course, Christians, too, will do ritual that so differentiates. If our ritual is important, if we keep working to learn it well and become adept in its practice, it will exclude. That is also human, and nothing that is human is alien to us, including such structural sin. But the Christian ritual, when it is renewed and reformed, includes within its practice a criticism of itself, a pattern of broken symbols and holes in our walls. This rite is not nearly enough, we say. "We have only done our duty," we quote. Or, better, "the sacrifices of God are a broken spirit," which is all we have to bring. Or simply: "God be merciful to me, a sinner." If we are impure publicans gathered here, then open wide the door. This assembly of beggars must be about telling other beggars where there is bread.

These proposals from reformed Christian liturgy are not themselves the full answer to the current worldwide cultural quandary. But they are a pattern, a symbol, an important model, a gift to our need, a balance to our frequent imbalance. And they are also easy to forget.

So what shall we do with this — that is, in our own liturgical communities? How shall every foreign country be for us a homeland and every homeland still be for us a foreign country as we go to church?

Here are a series of concluding proposals and examples. I hope that they will function as a beginning to the book that follows and an opening to further conversation.

1. Learn the excellent Nairobi Statement on Worship and Culture, reprinted below, or at least learn its major point: Christian worship is marked by a transcultural, contextual, cross-cultural, and countercultural relationship to every culture. All four. Gathered around a few transcultural central things — important to us because of their association with Jesus as well as their long centrality in Christian practice — Christian liturgy seeks to arrive in every cultural place, welcoming local and distant, contextual and cross-cultural gifts into its hybrid practice, while it also seeks to resist the dangerous, sometimes murderous, practices of local cultures, including especially their practices of identity purity. This brief statement, while formed in a Lutheran conversation, can be a tool for us all.

2. Continue to work on the clarity and largeness of the central matters — bath, word, prayer, table, and the participating assembly — as truly the

center of your gathering, and learn from them about Christianity and culture. Basic human cultural materials — meals and storytelling, for example — are the very heart of Christian worship, teaching us to love these same things in every foreign country. Yet these very things are broken to the purposes of Jesus and his Spirit, welcoming outsiders and the unclean, teaching us to be strangers in every homeland that is too delimited. Set out the central things as now, in your real context, the very city where the gifts of the nations — your own cultural gifts — are brought, welcomed, pruned, reoriented, and healed.

3. Continue to welcome many new gifts to come to this assembly. Continue to write on the palimpsest of cultures that is our Sunday assembly. Let change and a centered mixture characterize us: word and sacrament with hybrid music and mixed genres, the familiar holy Eucharist done in a new way.

4. Welcome cross-cultural gifts — songs and gestures, for example — that are born in another Christian context. Be careful and respectful of their origin, especially of the suffering that marked their origin. Learn as much as you can of their original context and meaning. Do not use such gifts without also praying for the people from whom they come and for their situations of injustice and sorrow, frequently the very situations from which these gifts arose. Do not steal from someone who rightly should be rewarded for his or her labor for the community. (For example, I profoundly believe in a living and just wage for musicians and writers.) But, at the same time, do not give in to the idea that cultural goods cannot travel to new contexts, cannot be claimed and reused with growing new meanings. That idea can be another form of a dangerous identity purity that is contradictory to our baptismal identity. Be very careful not to give the impression, for example, that only black musicians can lead authentic African-American Christian music, only Hispanic musicians can lead Hispanic songs, and so forth. "Whatever belongs to those who are of us, belongs to us," as Tertullian says. And vice versa. Do not forbid people from using "your stuff."

5. Avoid capturing people in culture-preservationist and culture-romantic stereotypes. Not all people of Latin or African or Asian or European or Native American origin like or do the same things. These days, all of us are hybrids. In your community, talk with the people themselves about the many gifts that may be practiced in your place.

6. If your assembly has a particular cultural cast, as it may very well have if it is a strong community, focus on at least some holes in that fabric — some people who are not part of the great majority of your congregation and yet

have leadership roles, for example, some music that is not "ours" — and focus on continuous and strong prayers for people and things beyond the usual boundaries.

7. Resist the use of symbols that stand for identity purity in the Christian assembly, or at least insist that they not be the central symbols, such as national or denominational flags, national garb, national festivals, and so on. Perhaps North American life is a place where our local dominant culture needs to be criticized and resisted. One exercise in thinking about Diognetus's dictum might be to consider the hymn "This is My Song," written by Lloyd Stone and Georgia Harkness and found in the national song section of many current hymnals.[20] Here is a model, in song, of being at home — yet not.

8. Continue thus to work on the ecumenical liturgical renewal movement. Engaged as an ongoing movement and an ongoing conversation, the renewed liturgy has resources for us to see anew that every foreign country is our homeland just as every homeland continues to be a foreign country.

9. And, as a beginning, read the book that follows. The authors here are revisiting the "Worship and Culture Study" of the LWF. Their essays are gathered around the three "statements" made by that study, statements that have had a wide, ecumenical discussion but have become increasingly difficult to find. Those statements are reprinted here. At the same time, in a time at least a decade beyond that study and with a community that is even more intentionally ecumenical than was the study itself, the authors here are also rethinking the issues of worship and culture.[21] One of the most important characteristics of that rethinking involves attention to a matter that did not yet come to expression in the LWF study: the widespread existence of "hybridity" in cultures, in postmodern and postcolonialist societies, but also everywhere as "amphibious" behavior has increasingly come to mark us all in this time of global exchange. We need this rethinking. Do join it.

This Christian proposal of the Epistle to Diognetus is not the usual contemporary attitude — liberal or conservative — to cultural identity. But I think it is the deep Christian attitude and, while difficult, I think it can invite us into patterns of living, amid the manifold gifts of human life, that are humbly respectful of cultures, yet aware of our sin and also the need in our cultures; curious to learn more of the others around us, yet critical of all that

20. E.g., see *Evangelical Lutheran Worship*, p. 887.
21. But it is important to remember that the LWF study team included Anscar Chupungco, a Roman Catholic scholar, as one of its principal resource persons, and the team always had Methodist or Anglican or Disciples of Christ participants.

lies and hurts and kills; and standing before the merciful triune God, trusting that our identity finally comes through the grace of that God, not through our cultural differences.

So, again, with our anonymous writer and with the wisdom of the liturgy, with the new cosmopolitans of our world, but, most of all, with and because of our Lord Jesus Christ, let Christians know that "they dwell in their own countries, but only as sojourners; they share all things as citizens and suffer all things as strangers. Every foreign country is a homeland to them, and every homeland is a foreign country."

PART I

WORSHIP AND CULTURE IN DIALOGUE

The Cartigny Statement on Worship and Culture: Biblical and Historical Foundations

Lutheran World Federation, 1993

Preface

This statement was prepared at the first consultation of the Lutheran World Federation's study on "Worship and Culture" held in Cartigny, Switzerland, in October 1993. Those invited to participate make up the LWF's ongoing international study team for the project; the participants represent all continents of the world. At this initial consultation, the study team focused on the biblical and historical (early church and Lutheran Reformation) foundations of the relationship between worship and culture. The study team met again in March 1994, in Hong Kong, to explore contemporary issues and questions of the relationship between culture and liturgy, church music, and church architecture. Following the Hong Kong consultation, it is envisioned that the study will move into a regional phase, in which regional study teams will encourage and assist in the identification and exploration of particular issues related to worship and culture as they exist in the LWF's regions, subregions, and member churches; this exploration is to be at the pastoral as well as the theological level. Phase III of the study is to synthesize and reflect globally on the regional findings. Phase IV is to conclude the study with a wide variety of seminars and workshops to implement the explorations of the study, as each region and LWF member church decides is helpful.

Ipissimis verbis S. Anita Stauffer, ed., *Worship and Culture in Dialogue,* LWF Department for Theology and Studies: Reports of International Consultations in Cartigny, Switzerland, 1993; Hong Kong, 1994 (Geneva: The Lutheran World Federation, 1994).

Therefore, the contents of this Cartigny Statement are conclusions only of the study team's initial consultation, with its specific focus on biblical and historical foundations; it is not a final statement on the topic as a whole.

1. Introduction

1.1. With gratitude to God, the LWF study team on Worship and Culture acknowledges the efforts of the church throughout the ages to adapt to current and local situations. We ourselves are also particularly grateful that the LWF and its member churches have given us a mandate to begin a new study of this central aspect of our Christian life.

1.2. We began our work with the conviction that, even during our own times, the Word of God must be interpreted within the context of a changing world. Through the Holy Spirit, Jesus Christ is present in our own diverse cultural contexts today, just as his presence was incarnated in the life situation of the first century.

1.3. We acknowledge the need in our time to make worship both authentic to the Word of God and relevant to given cultures. The church is called upon to continue the ongoing task of reformation so that the gospel might faithfully be proclaimed among the various cultures of today's world. In the final analysis, the church is an assembly of believers in a given place and time where the Word of God is preached according to Scripture and the sacraments administered following the letter and spirit of the gospel (cf. Augsburg Confession 7). It has been our Lutheran tradition — indeed, it belongs to the Christian tradition as a whole — that the Word of God should be rendered understandable to all and that the sacraments should be accessible to all believers. This is understood in the context of God's grace and what Christ does for us.

1.4. In the incarnate Christ the witness and service of congregations become meaningful to our societies. The church — in its worship, which is the central expression of celebrating our life in Christ — should be seen as an ongoing incarnation of the gospel.

2. First Questions

2.1. As member churches of the LWF from across the world begin to explore how the gospel can be rooted in cultural patterns, it is clear that such an exploration is not a luxury, but an imperative. Further, it is clear that the process of localizing worship is not something new, but rather is an age-old ecclesial inclination attested by well-known examples from the past.

2.2. But the rich and complex record of the faith compels us to take more than a cursory look at the past. It seemed right, then, to engage ourselves in a more comprehensive search for the roots and methods that could provide directions and energy for present opportunities and challenges.

2.3. The process for the first consultation grew from a profound recognition that Jesus Christ himself is God incarnate in human culture. This pre-eminent inculturation led us first to the New Testament, where we could discover how the liberating Word for the world met culture. Then we were propelled into a study of the early church, where the Word continued to be incarnated in several different cultures. And, finally, the consultation focused on the Lutheran Reformation as a particular time when that creating Word was experienced anew, challenging and transforming culture. The ecumenical importance of this process led to several non-Lutheran participants being involved in our deliberations.

2.4. A sense of the dynamic life-giving relationship between worship and culture derives from more than an examination of theological development. Therefore, this study by definition searches for illumination from the histories of liturgy (text and action), church architecture, and church music as well, giving the study the kind of breadth required by current cultural contexts.

2.5. The deliberate intent to discover how the church in the past has sorted out the issues and processes amending the worship/culture dynamic has yielded considerable insight and prospects for future fruitful interaction. Examples: (A) The church, as a continuing incarnation of Christ in the world, is always taking root in culture as that place where Christ can be experienced anew. To recognize the cultural component of the church's worship, however, is to reckon with the rich presence of God's diverse creation in the references and materials of Christian worship. A focus on the cultural leads the church toward a more responsible relationship with creation itself. (B) Asking inculturation questions of the church's history has made it clear that there are identifiable core elements of baptism and Eucharist that perdure through nearly every time and place. (C) The church's liturgy is most authentic when it resists crystallization by permitting the gospel to interpret and direct the contextualization process.

2.6. The focus on history, therefore, quite naturally draws attention to contemporary issues, as Christian communities live the gospel in worship in their various cultures. At the Hong Kong consultation in 1994, the study team turned toward specific contemporary concerns, seeking to find common methods and mutual encouragement as the churches carefully attended to the issues.

3. Models and Methods

3.1. An examination of the history of the church, from its inception in the Hellenistic-Jewish milieu to the current modern contexts, reveals that it has struggled continually with how to relate Christian worship to the cultures in which it is located. The process of understanding and answering this question has been alternately called contextualization, indigenization, localization, and inculturation. Each of these terms has been used in different ways, in different places in the world; it should be noted that no one single term adequately expresses the process.

3.2. Nonetheless, it remains the case that the Christian assembly for worship, with its music and its spatial environment, stands at the intersection of Christian faith and cultural patterns. Out of this complex interplay of Christianity and culture, three areas for consideration readily become apparent — the cultural, the countercultural, and the transcultural. The task of relating worship and culture, then, involves asking the following three questions:

3.3. First, what are the cultural elements in Christian worship (including liturgical texts, gestures, vestments, furnishings, art, music, and architecture) that give expression to the particularity of the gathered people? Cultural elements have been used in worship throughout the history of the church (e.g., the adaptation of basilican architecture in the Constantinian church) to help engage Christian worship with a particular context, while yet remaining faithful to the gospel. In the same way, the churches in every generation and in every context must ask what cultural elements can/should be used in their worship in order to help locate the worshiping community in its particular cultural context.

3.4. Second, what are the countercultural elements in Christian worship that challenge the culture in which it is located? Throughout its history the church, by its faithful proclamation of the gospel, has challenged the status quo and the social injustices of its day (e.g., Christ and his disciples sharing meals with the socially unaccepted people of their day). In the same way, the churches in every generation and in every context must ask what in their worship can/should be countercultural, challenging the culture in which it exists and ultimately facilitating its transformation.

3.5. Third, what are the transcultural elements in worship that place it clearly within the universality of the Christian liturgical tradition? Throughout its history the church has consistently observed certain core elements within its worship as a way to identify itself with the universal tradition of the church, which transcends time and place (e.g., the use of water in baptism). In the same way, churches in every generation and in every context must ask in what ways their worship practice can/should transcend their particular culture, placing them within the universal Christian tradition.

3.6. Therefore, the task of relating worship and culture is ultimately concerned with finding the balance between relevance and authenticity, between particularity and universality, while avoiding eclecticism and/or syncretism. While it is clear that each church, within its cultural context, will need to ask these questions for itself and find answers appropriate to its own situation, it is also clear that this inquiry will require each church to attend to the experiences of the other churches and to the treasures of other cultures.

3.7. An examination of the tradition, from the biblical witness, the early church, and the Lutheran Reformation, reveals the core of Christian worship to be Word, baptism, and Eucharist. The pattern, or *ordo,* of entry into the community is teaching and baptismal bath. The pattern of the weekly gathering of the community on the Lord's Day is the celebration centered in the Word and eucharistic meal. These core elements are clearly evident in the historical witnesses of the Christian worship tradition. Further, it is evident that the purpose of this pattern of worship is faithfully to receive and faithfully to proclaim the gospel of Jesus Christ.

3.8. One helpful model, then, that is evident throughout the history of the church is found where the worshiping community is able to receive and use the important elements of the culture (and thus be localized in a particular context), while at the same time critically shaping these elements so that they may bear witness to the gospel of Christ, who transcends and transforms all cultures (and thus may be rooted in the universal Christian tradition): "See, I am making all things new" (Rev. 21:5; NRSV).

4. Prospects

4.1. The consultation studied processes of interaction between worship and cultural settings in the New Testament, the early church, and the Lutheran Reformation. It identified the use of different models and methods and recognized in these patterns an ongoing process.

4.2. The study team wishes to invite the churches to join in this study of the common roots of Christian worship, believing that the study offers important tools for the analysis of their worship (liturgy, music, architecture, art, etc.) within their various cultural settings.

4.3. The study team will continue its work by examining contemporary relationships between worship and cultures. In specific topics for further consideration, the study will seek to clarify the interrelationship between form and content in liturgy; the use of language, gestures, symbols, and music in varying cultural contexts; and the shaping of worship space, with the goal of the inclusive participation of all people, exploring what is cultural, countercultural, and transcultural in these elements.

4.4. The sacramental practices of baptism and the Eucharist need to be examined and adapted to recover their full meanings within the churches' current diverse cultural contexts, in order that the gift of God's grace may be offered to all.

4.5. The churches are challenged to be creative as they develop forms of worship that are both authentic and relevant, responding both to their cultures and to the gospel. Through the power of the Holy Spirit, the churches can find for themselves — and offer to the many societies of the world — an alternative model of life.

Christian Worship: Toward Localization and Globalization

S. Anita Stauffer

From the four corners of the earth, about twenty-five people from the Lutheran Communion, with observers from the Anglican Communion, the Roman Catholic Church, and the World Council of Churches (WCC), gathered in a quiet little Swiss town in October 1993 for a common purpose: to examine the roots of Christian worship, the common roots of what Christians do on Sunday morning as the baptized people of God. The group examined the Jewish matrix and the Hellenistic-Jewish heritage out of which Christian worship developed, and how the early church contextualized its worship in Greco-Roman cultures.

The purpose was not to dig for these roots as an end in itself, but to aid in the richer growth of the branches in the cultures of each of the world's continents. The meeting was to begin a major study of Christian worship as that consequential activity that stands between Christ and culture, to help enable churches around the world to work toward both contextualization and transformation, both localization and globalization, in order that congregational worship might be both authentically Christian and more culturally relevant. Therefore, the group gathered a second time, in March 1994, in Hong Kong, to consider contemporary issues related to the relationship between worship and culture.

This volume contains the major papers from these two international

Ipsissimis verbis S. Anita Stauffer, ed., *Worship and Culture in Dialogue,* LWF Department for Theology and Studies: Reports of International Consultations, Cartigny, Switzerland, 1993; Hong Kong, 1994 (Geneva: LWF, 1994), pp. 7-15.

consultations. The topic is not new for the Lutheran World Federation. From 1976 through 1983 the LWF conducted a study on "Confessing Christ in Cultural Contexts," involving Lutheran churches in Indonesia and Germany, Tanzania and Sweden, Japan and the United States.[1] In 1981 the LWF held a seminar in Tantur, Israel, for Third-World pastors on the "Significance of the Jewish Heritage for the Task of Contextualization."[2] From 1978 through 1983, a series of LWF conferences was held, which culminated in the Northfield Consultation.[3] Finally, the LWF sponsored the Latin American Lutheran Consultation on Liturgy in Caracas, Venezuela, in 1986.[4]

Nor is the topic new for the wider church. Roman Catholics, especially, have been addressing the issues for decades, and both the Anglican Communion and the WCC have also had the matter on their agendas. The relationship between culture and Christian worship is of ecumenical interest; the questions, the issues, the dynamics are shared across confessional lines. All Christians share "the same baptismal water of the same Spirit," who creates the church everywhere.[5] Though there are a variety of cultures on the continents of this earth, there is one baptism, one gospel, one faith, one Lord. The core of Christian worship — its Jewish roots and its development in the early church — is shared across our confessional and cultural lines. That core, those roots, constitute a common ecumenical foundation.

But there are different presuppositions, different perspectives, in examining these roots and addressing the matter of worship and culture. Personal histories and cultural backgrounds shape these perspectives. It is useful to set the specific topic of worship and culture within its larger framework, which is the relationship between Christ and culture. One helpful model for considering this larger theological context is a typology developed by

1. Yoshiro Ishida, "Introduction," in Maren Mattiesen, ed., *Confessing Christ in Cultural Contacts* (Geneva: LWF Department of Studies, 1981), pp. 1-12.

2. See the resulting "Tantur Report on Worship, 1981," in Eugene L. Brand, ed., *Worship Among Lutherans* (Geneva: LWF Department of Studies, 1983), pp. 15-23.

3. See the "Northfield Statement on Worship," in Brand, *Worship Among Lutherans,* pp. 5-14 (esp. sections C and E).

4. See the resulting *Declaración de Caracas sobre Liturgia* (Buenos Aires, 1986: English translation by Gerhard M. Canfold, *Caracas Statement on Liturgy* (Buenos Aires: Committee of Presidents of the Lutheran Churches in Latin America; LWF Department of Studies, 1987).

5. J. M. R. Tillard, *L'Église d'Églises* (Paris: Cerf, 1987), p. 30; English translation in Joseph A. Komonchak, "The Local Church and the Church Catholic: The Contemporary Theological Problematic," *The Jurist* 52, no. 1 (1992): 443.

H. Richard Niebuhr in his book *Christ and Culture,* where he laid out five possible relationships:[6]

Christ against culture
Christ of culture
Christ above culture
Christ and culture in paradox
Christ, the transformer of culture

The *Christ against culture* scenario sees culture negatively — something hostile to Christianity. In much of the early church, and especially during the persecutions, it was natural that Christ and Christianity would be completely contrary to the culture. In much of the twentieth century the communist world once again set culture and Christ in mutual hostility. And in other societies of the world, where another religion (such as Hinduism) totally pervades the culture, perhaps the paradigm of Christ against culture is still operative to varying degrees.

The *Christ of culture* scenario sees culture positively — something consonant with Christianity. Christ is absorbed into the culture, and Christianity is seen as a "prop" for the culture. The problem is that this approach "risks reducing Christ to a culture-hero."[7] The culture and the Christian faith are identified with each other, and it is very difficult to critique the culture. These first two paradigms are the two extremes; in between them Niebuhr sets three types of relationships.

Christ above culture is a synthesis: Christ is neither opposed to the culture nor absorbed into it. Rather, Christ is seen as coming to perfect the culture. Culture is seen as essentially good: it is preparation for the ultimate communion with God.[8] The danger here is that the culture becomes absolutized, and its provisional character is forgotten.[9]

Christ and culture in paradox is the dualist approach: Christ is the good, and human culture is sinful and corrupt.

The final position is the most central one. *Christ the transformer of culture* is more hopeful about culture: culture is not inherently evil, though it

---

6. See Niebuhr's book *Christ and Culture* (New York: Harper and Row, 1951), as well as Geoffrey Wainwright's application of it to worship in his book *Doxology* (London and New York: Oxford University Press, 1980), chap. 11.

7. Wainwright, *Doxology,* p. 390.

8. Niebuhr, *Christ and Culture,* p. 195.

9. Wainwright, *Doxology,* p. 392.

is the locus of disorder and sin. What is needed is conversion or transformation of the culture, à la the death/resurrection model of baptism in Romans 6. If these five positions were put onto a map, people from various cultures could place themselves in one of the positions — or in some mixture or variation of them. It is important to be conscious of one's own perspectives, based on one's own background within one's own cultural context.

Interlocking Content

To consider the relationship between worship and culture is to be concerned with three interlocking areas of content. Worship itself is multifaceted: it includes not only texts but also actions, not only music but also the space or place in which worship happens. The topic is interdisciplinary. It involves not only liturgy — its texts and actions, and church music in its many forms — but also church architecture, furnishings, and art. Christian worship is profoundly shaped in one way or another by the space in which it happens. The design and iconography and symbol systems of church buildings (particularly the worship space) are expressions of theology just as much as the liturgical texts that are spoken. The consideration of the topic thus includes such things as what is beauty in various cultures.[10]

Overlaid on the three disciplines of liturgy, music, and architecture are three questions that are crucial to worship: How, in a given culture, can worship be hospitable to those who come? How can the community or communal dimension be expressed? And how, in a given culture, can reverence be expressed in response to encountering the God who is holy and transcendent?

Tensions

The dynamics between worship and culture can be considered in the context of several tensions; these are not tensions in a negative sense, but in the sense of several sets of values at opposite ends of a continuum, or axis:

---

10. See the chapter entitled "Contemporary Questions on Architecture and Culture" below.

authentic — relevant
Lutheran — catholic
local — global
Christocentric — anthropocentric

The first tension is between the *authentic* and the *relevant*. This is the need for balance between worship being faithful to our common Judeo-Christian roots and being meaningful in each given culture. Our taproot is Jesus, and his death and resurrection, which itself is Jesus' new interpretation of the whole Passover event. This is the central core of the Christian faith, and it provides a pattern for everything we do, including our worship, the pattern for baptism, and the pattern for Eucharist. The test of authenticity is the gospel and the apostolic tradition, which are themselves patterned on Jesus the Christ.

For Christian worship there is no such thing as a tabula rasa, no blank slate. In matters of faith and liturgy we do not start from scratch. The starting point is already given in the death and resurrection of Christ, and in the Upper Room, where the meaning of it all was made clear and the pattern for our own celebration of it was established. As Eugene Brand has said:

> Because of the historical and incarnational aspects of Christian faith, the Church's worship has remained anchored to the historical person of Jesus and the culture in which he lived. Since Jesus was a Jew, Christian worship has retained a Jewish character. . . . Adherence to liturgical forms rooted in the Judaism of Jesus' day is what marks Christian worship as authentic. The sharing of the loaf and the cup in the context of thanksgiving is the chief example.[11]

The balance to authenticity — the other end of the axis — is relevance. Again, we might think in terms of roots and branches: the roots as authenticity, the branches as cultural relevance. How can worship be meaningful to people in a given culture? How can the common core of worship be "clothed" in such a way that it relates to people in a given culture? How can worship be "at home" in a given culture? How can the worship life of congregations be meaningful and inviting to people in the diverse cultures of the world? How can the taproot of the Christian faith — the death and resurrection of Jesus — itself take

11. Eugene L. Brand, "A Lutheran Agenda for Worship after Dar-es-Salaam," in *A Lutheran Agenda for Worship* (Geneva: LWF Department of Studies, 1979), p. 25.

root in the world's cultures? How can liturgy and church music and church architecture and art be both truly Christian and truly Chinese, or truly Christian and truly East African, or truly Christian and truly Brazilian, and so on?

There are dangers at both extreme ends of this authenticity-relevance continuum. The danger on the authenticity end is that worship can become culturally irrelevant, out of touch, meaningless; on the other end of the spectrum, the relevance end, the danger is that worship can become captive to a given culture, isolated from the whole church of Christ, and, at the worst, syncretistic through becoming detached from Christian roots.

The second and third tensions could both be considered under a more general heading of the tension between universality and particularity, but it is worth looking at them separately. The second tension is that between *Lutheran and catholic,* between the confessional and the ecumenical. Christian roots in faith and worship are shared with the whole Christian church, the church catholic. Each one of us is baptized into the Christian church. There is no such thing as being "baptized Lutheran" or "baptized Roman Catholic," or anything other than "baptized Christian." There is one baptism because there is one Lord. Likewise, there is no such thing as "Lutheran worship" or "Lutheran liturgy." There is worship as Lutherans do it, liturgy as Lutherans do it; but the liturgy does not belong to Lutherans any more than it belongs to any other confessional communion. What is done in word and sacrament is shared at its core, at its roots, with the whole church of every time and every place. To be sure, the manifestation of liturgical convergence is more apparent in some places in the world than in others. But the ecumenical reality exists — thanks be to God! It is only a matter of recognizing and manifesting it more and more.

The Lutheran Confessions express liturgical continuity with the wider church. Article 24 of the Augsburg Confession says it clearly: "Our churches are falsely accused of abolishing the Mass. Actually, the Mass is retained among us and is celebrated with the greatest reverence." The Apology of the Augsburg Confession repeats and goes on: "We do not abolish the Mass but religiously keep and defend it. In our churches Mass is celebrated every Sunday and on other festivals. . . . We keep traditional liturgical forms, such as the order of the lessons, prayers, vestments, etc." For Lutherans there is no starting from scratch in matters of worship. We are not a sect; our worship is not idiosyncratic. The liturgical heritage we share with the wider Christian church is an inherent part of our identity as Lutherans. We are part of the whole *communio,* the whole communion of saints. As we strive toward the contextualization or inculturation of worship, we do it not only in the context of various world cultures but also "within the context of the catholic and ecumenical Church."[12] That is why ecumenical cooperation in contextualization is vital, internationally and regionally.

The third tension is between the *local and the global,* between the contextual and the transcultural. Like the second tension, this is also a variation on the theme of the particular and the universal. On the one side is the local, the particular cultural context of a given people, a given group of congregations. How can cultural richness be reflected in worship? What are the thought patterns and linguistic styles that should shape how prayers and sermons and liturgical texts are written? What aspects of indigenous music should find their way into hymns and other music in the church? What aspects of the aesthetics, the artistic styles, the symbol systems, the architectural prototypes in a given culture should be reflected in the rooms in which worship takes place? What gestures and postures from the culture can be meaningfully incorporated into Christian worship? What are the cultural manifestations of gathering into a community, of offering hospitality, of expressing reverence? All of this can be termed localization, or contextualization, or inculturation.

These efforts all need to be kept in balance with the other end of the spectrum, what could be called globalization. Worship needs not only to reflect the local, but also the wider Christian community. The God whom Christians worship is transcendent and transcultural, and there is no point in substituting one form of cultural captivity for another. No one cultural form can do justice to the God of the whole cosmos. One fruit of contextualization efforts is that worship resources from one cultural setting can be shared around the world. Not only, for example, might churches in Ethiopia and Papua New Guinea and in the Sami areas of the Nordic countries find ways to enable their worship to be more truly at home in their cultures, but also some of the riches of those cultures can be shared with the wider church. Would such global sharing not enrich the life of the whole church and strengthen the sense of *communio*? Such cross-cultural and ecumenical sharing, such global enrichment, is the opposite of tribalization, apartheid, segregation, and ethnic cleansing. Worship should be both contextual and transcultural, as a testament to the unity of the church and to the God who is "far beyond our mind's grasp."[13]

---

12. Eugene L. Brand, "Lutheran Worship in Cultural Context," *Lutheran Forum* (Reformation 1982): 17.

13. This is the first line of the eucharistic hymn text by Filipino composer and writer

A further facet of the localization-globalization balance is that the church is called not only to inculturate but also to be countercultural. Not everything in any given culture is worthy or appropriate of Christian worship. Everything human always needs to be critiqued by the light of the gospel. Ultimately, Christ came to transform all things human, including our selves and our cultures. We are called not to conform to the world, in the final analysis, but to be transformed ourselves (Rom. 12:2) and, in turn, to transform the world.

The final tension is that between *Christocentricity and anthropocentricity,* the balance between Christ-centeredness and human-centeredness. It is, on the one hand, vitally urgent that we strive to make worship at home in our variety of cultures. That requires considerable attention to our cultures — to our selves, in a sense. But we must not forget that we worship Christ, the crucified and risen one, the Lord of the whole church. We do not worship ourselves or our cultures.

Christian worship must be culturally relevant; it must be meaningful to those who worship in a given place. But at the same time, we must not lose Christ as the focus, or we will have cut off our root — and will have killed the branches.

Francisco F. Feliciano. See hymn 82 in *Sound the Bamboo,* a hymnal published in 1990 jointly by the Christian Conference of Asia and the Asian Institute for Liturgy and Music.

What, Then, Do Theologians Mean
When They Say "Culture"?

Benjamin M. Stewart

Introduction

There are experts who devote all of their scholarly attention to culture. Given the extensive conversation among such experts, why should liturgical theologians be anything other than attentive listeners in the conversation? In other words, why not leave questions of culture to anthropologists, ethnographers, sociologists, historians, cultural theorists and activists, and artists and theorists of art? Indeed, the diverse and considerable body of knowledge about the world's cultures (including questions about whether the concept of culture is ultimately more misleading than helpful) calls liturgical theologians to a posture of thoughtful listening, learning, and observation.[1] The appropriate epistemic disposition involves modesty and humility.

Given a noisy, wide, and diverse conversation about culture that stretches far outside the disciplines of theology, how then do liturgical theologians, as a first move, make decisions about how to listen and where to pay special attention within such a conversation? To ask it another way: What are the specifically *theological* interests that Christian liturgical theologians bring to questions of culture? In this chapter I identify a number of focal points to which liturgical theologians give special attention in questions of culture, and I identify some of the theological interests that motivate such

---

1. For a brief overview of recent debates concerning these questions, see Tomoko Masuzawa, "Culture," in Mark C. Taylor, ed. *Critical Terms for Religious Studies* (Chicago: University of Chicago Press, 1998), pp. 70-93.

attention. But there is the prior question: What do theologians mean by culture?

By and large, they mean the same thing indicated by many other contemporary theorists of culture. At a most basic level, culture represents the more or less shared patterns of life practiced by a group of people.[2] However, for theologians — liturgical and otherwise — what emerges most importantly is not a lexical definition of culture but rather a recognizable constellation of cultural loci brought into focus and relationship by specific theological commitments.

Common Cultural Places

Much recent thinking about culture has rightly emphasized cultural diversity and local distinctiveness.[3] Nevertheless, liturgical theologians approach culture with a sacramental lens that brings into focus a particular set of *universals* in human culture: communal gathering, storytelling, bathing, and meal-sharing are perhaps most central of those universals. It is worth emphasizing that universal cultural practices form the foundation of Christian worship.[4] These practices, shared among all cultures on earth, are identified by Christian tradition as sites suited for strong encounters with the divine, anchoring the central liturgical-sacramental acts of gathering for worship, sharing Scripture, baptism, and Eucharist.

The list of cultural universals of interest to liturgical theologians is longer still. Other universal cultural practices (e.g., singing, timekeeping, healing,

---

2. See the expanded definition of culture in Anscar J. Chupungco, "Liturgy and the Components of Culture," in S. Anita Stauffer, ed., *Worship and Culture in Dialogue,* LWF Studies 3 (1994), pp. 154-65. For a definition more focused on the symbolic dimension of life, see Gordon W. Lathrop, "Baptism in the New Testament and Its Cultural Settings," in Stauffer, *Worship and Culture in Dialogue,* LWF Studies 3 (1994), p. 17.

3. See "local distinction" below.

4. This claim relies on a wider definition of culture than some traditions allow. Some definitions of culture incorporate — problematically, many believe — a strict delineation between what is "biological" or "genetic" and what is "cultural," or "constructed" or "learned." This strict delineation increasingly appears to be philosophically and scientifically untenable, as the social and biological dimensions of human creatureliness overlap and complexly interact: biological and ecological factors influence patterns of human teaching and learning, and learned technical knowledge is altering "nature" and genetics in increasingly dramatic ways. In any case, such a strict delineation would nearly rule out the possibility of identifying *any* human cultural universals.

the marking of death, giving thanks and expressing need, the tending and critiquing of group boundaries, the practices of leadership) form further important layers in the composition of Christian worship. These layers of Christian worship — the central and the next-to-central — are made up of matters that are not culturally arcane or idiosyncratic but are rather shared among all cultures without exception.

In engaging questions of culture, liturgical theologians strongly emphasize that humanity shares some central, comprehensible patterns of life, and that this commonality is meaningful and worth noticing. That conviction alone is no small thing. But even more profound is a theological insistence that the living God of Israel is active and can be known and encountered in cultural practices and locations found among all people everywhere. God acts through means of grace that are not secret and elite but public and common. God's desire is salvation for every culture, for all within each culture, and by means that are known and comprehensible across cultures. The focus by liturgical theologians on a number of universal cultural practices is not only an anthropological observation. It arises from faith in the God, who "pours out the Holy Spirit on all flesh," giving birth to a life in the Spirit that is public, intelligible, and accessible to people of all cultures.[5]

Local Distinction

Theories of culture have long noted the ways in which patterns of human civilization are influenced by local land and history, the great diversity of which — including, for example, the American Gulf Coast bayou, the Andean mountains, and the Saharan sands, each with different human histories — contributes to a corresponding diversity of local and regional cultures.

---

5. When others interpret an occurrence of dramatic cross-cultural and cross-linguistic intelligibility as a foolish delusion, Peter interprets the phenomenon as the long-prophesied work of God's Spirit: "Peter, standing with the eleven, raised his voice and addressed them: 'Men of Judea and all who live in Jerusalem, let this be known to you, and listen to what I say. Indeed, these are not drunk, as you suppose, for it is only nine o'clock in the morning. No, this is what was spoken through the prophet Joel: 'In the last days it will be, God declares, that I will pour out my Spirit upon all flesh, and your sons and your daughters shall prophesy, and your young men shall see visions, and your old men shall dream dreams. Even upon my slaves, both men and women, in those days I will pour out my Spirit; and they shall prophesy. . . . Then everyone who calls on the name of the Lord shall be saved'" (Acts 2:14-18, 21, citing Joel 2:28-32).

Much of the work regarding worship and culture in recent decades has described itself as being concerned chiefly with the localization or contextualization of liturgical life, which is to say, the process by which the classic elements of Christian liturgy become expressed by means of local culture.[6] Anita Stauffer describes the localizing emphasis in the LWF project to be a corrective of earlier efforts that largely left the local dimension ignored.[7]

Undergirding the interest in local culture in its diversity are theological commitments. The incarnation of Christ includes Christ's honoring of local cultural patterns including dress, language, cuisine, time-keeping, gesture, and relationship with local ecology, and so on. As Anscar Chupungco has insisted, the church as the body of Christ rightly honors each local culture in which it is incarnated by similarly assuming the givenness of local patterns, grounded in the scriptural memory that, in Christ, God comes to the world "deep in the flesh" of local culture.

Scriptural imagery portrays diversity within the church as a characteristic of flourishing life in Christ: one Spirit grants a diversity of gifts, one body of Christ has diverse members, and many of the early reports of apostolic ministry reflect profoundly theological efforts — like ours, often stumbling or inadequate — to honor local diversity in cultural practice as the one gospel is shared in new places and cultures.

While cultural theorists have helped liturgical theologians understand that there are no completely pure local cultures to defend from contamination by other cultures (all culture is always hybrid, never unmixed), nonetheless liturgical theologians, especially in recent decades, have valued local dimensions of culture over against the culturally homogenizing force of global capitalism and consumerism, spread increasingly by symbolic discourse carried over electronic media and by the aggressive mechanized reconfiguration of the physical environment. The theological emphasis here is not simply on diversity but on solidarity with those threatened with exploitation or extinction.

6. See Gordon W. Lathrop's account of the "localizing" work of the Worship and Culture project in "Worship: Local yet Universal," in S. Anita Stauffer, ed., *Christian Worship: Unity in Cultural Diversity*, LWF Studies 1 (1996), pp. 47-66.

7. S. Anita Stauffer, "Worship: Ecumenical Core and Cultural Context," in Stauffer, *Christian Worship*, LWF Studies 1 (1996), p. 7.

Patterns

Liturgical theologians are trained to analyze the event of Christian worship with particular attention to its rich field of metaphor and symbol. Thus, such theologians are perhaps especially aware of the ways in which culture, too, is understood by way of pattern and symbol — an observation shared with many theorists of culture as well as scholars in cognitive sciences.

The universality of pattern in meaning-making results in the blending of symbolic patterns across boundaries of culture and liturgy. Thus, for example, biblical typology does not end at the cover of the Bible or the boundary of the liturgy, but extends into cultural patterns of meaning. Israel's liberation from slavery serves as a pattern for understanding the hope for the return from exile, the pattern of which informs the significance of Christian baptism, all of which contributes to a patterned interpretation of the experience of slavery and racial discrimination in North American culture. God, as the pattern of salvation history had shown, liberates slaves and guides them on an exodus to the Promised Land. The biblical patterns known in the Ancient Near East helped create and interpret cultural patterns in recent American history. Because Scripture and liturgy use typological and metaphorical patterns for meaning-making, liturgical theologians are especially attentive to the patterns by which culture is known and organized, assuming that scriptural-liturgical patterns will interact meaningfully — even salvifically — with cultural patterns. Thus, for liturgical theologians, the patterns that order cultural life are especially worthy of theological attention. This is one major entry point for Christian ethics: the theo-ethically significant patterns of Scripture and liturgy are placed in dialogue with cultural patterns of life, including economic and social dimensions.

Ecology

Gordon Lathrop has sometimes described culture as the conversation between generations about how best to live on the land.[8] This definition of culture brings into prominence a layer of meaning associated with culture that has sometimes remained subterranean. *Culture* is etymologically related to "cultivate," the nurturing of the growth of the living landscape. In addition

---

8. Plenary lecture, Seattle University Summer Institute for Liturgy and Worship, July 2006.

BENJAMIN M. STEWART

to the insights from fields of study such as human geography, which chart the patterns of interaction between humans and local ecology, liturgical theologians today are increasingly attentive to cultural patterns that give rise to, are impacted by, or seek to heal or prevent anthropogenic ecological disruption.[9]

Three of the most prominent theological insights orient this interest in ecological dimensions of culture. The opening chapter of the Bible, in something like a liturgical cadence, teaches that the whole creation is inherently "good," even "very good."[10] Liturgical theologians are interested in how cultures regard the earth reverently as "very good" — and, on the other hand, the extent to which they treat the earth only as inferior raw material until it is "developed" by humans. Second, liturgical theologians recognize that what is sometimes compartmentalized as "the environment" actually refers to all of creaturely existence, including all humans. Therefore, "environmental" health is a matter of theological ethics and justice concerning humans and all other creatures. Third, scientific discoveries have enabled humans to understand the earth more fully in its cosmic context: it is a relatively small and rare (unique, as far as we know thus far) crucible of life in a sprawling universe, almost all of which seems hostile to life. We have come to see the earth not as our ancestors did (as something like the ground floor of the universe, making up roughly half of the cosmos), but rather as a creature, like us — living, mortal, fragile, created good, in need of healing, beloved by God. Thus do liturgical theologians, out of theological concern, inquire into the ecological dimensions of culture: How do human cultures honor the inherent goodness of the earth, relate ethically to earth's bounty and dangers, and interact with the earth as a living creature in need of healing?

Arts and Aesthetics

With many other theorists of culture, liturgical theologians are interested in the cultural patterns of human creativity and adornment sometimes catego-

9. This emphasis, at its best — at least implicitly — also corrects some approaches to culture that identify the defining characteristic of "culture" as its distinction from "nature." This approach was both unrealistic (all human activity is thoroughly biological, or, in theological terms, "incarnational") and unhelpful (the idea of human distinction or alienation from nature can be part of a vicious self-reinforcing cycle).

10. The first creation narrative (Gen. 1) depicts God declaring the cosmos "good" six times, and then finally declaring it definitively "very good" (Gen. 1:4, 10, 12, 18, 21, 25, 31).

48

rized as aesthetics or the arts. These elements of culture include music; dance and gesture; material craft in the making of shelter, furniture, tools, and clothing; various forms of adornment (sometimes including paint, dyes, stones, plants, clay, and cloth); patterns of speech; representational and abstract images; and methods of heightening attention to interactions with the wider natural world, including its creatures and cycles. The creative power of the human spirit derives from the spirit of God and rightly seeks alignment with the will and mission of God.[11]

These cultural signs of creativity and adornment are especially important for liturgical theologians in their role in proclaiming the word of God in worship in ways that are comprehensible and beautiful to local cultures. While Christianity has at times drawn back from appreciation of the arts and aesthetics out of a desire to avoid idolatry or hedonism, Lutherans especially have valued both the incarnated nature of the arts and their role as servants of the word of God.[12] Liturgical theologians seek out artistic forms in culture for adorning the proclamation of the word of God, signifying the goodness of creation and incarnation and highlighting the primary actions of the assembly in their encounter with the means of grace. Accordingly, cultural art forms can resist hedonism and consumerism by being drawn into service of the word of God.

The Word about the Cross

Among some theorists, definitions of religion and culture have been essentially coextensive: culture is religion and vice versa. However, Christian liturgical theologians consistently seek out the *margins* of any culture in order to discover one crucial *center* of religious significance: the hungry and thirsty, the strangers, the naked, those who are sick or in prison — all those who may be characterized as "the least of these." One of Jesus' sayings in Matthew strikingly depicts this still-surprising cultural remapping:

11. For a musical theological reflection on this dynamic, see the recent hymn text by David Mowbray, "Come to Us, Creative Spirit," text © 1979 Stainer and Bell Ltd. and the Trustees for Methodist Church Purposes Administration (Hope Publishing Co.). For this chapter, see also *Evangelical Lutheran Worship,* © 2006 Evangelical Lutheran Church in America (Minneapolis: Augsburg Fortress, 2006), p. 687.

12. For a theological account of Christian approaches to aesthetics and beauty, see Edward Farley, *Faith and Beauty: A Theological Aesthetic* (Burlington, VT: Ashgate, 2001).

> [T]he righteous will answer, "Lord, when was it that we saw you hungry and gave you food, or thirsty and gave you something to drink? And when was it that we saw you a stranger and welcomed you, or naked and gave you clothing? And when was it that we saw you sick or in prison and visited you?" And the king will answer them, "Truly I tell you, just as you did it to one of the least of these who are members of my family, you did it to me." (Matt. 25:31-46)

The theological commitment at the heart of this remapping of the cultural landscape is "the word about the cross" (1 Cor. 1:18, 27-31) that seeks the holiness of God in the most vulnerable and apparently Godforsaken of cultural locations:

> [T]he message about the cross is foolishness to those who are perishing, but to us who are being saved it is the power of God. . . . God chose what is foolish in the world to shame the wise; God chose what is weak in the world to shame the strong; God chose what is low and despised in the world, things that are not, to reduce to nothing things that are, so that no one might boast in the presence of God. He is the source of your life in Christ Jesus, who became for us wisdom from God, and righteousness and sanctification and redemption, in order that, as it is written, "Let the one who boasts, boast in the Lord."

This cruciform reading of culture connects again to the motif of *cultivation*. The way of the cross — the encounter with God, who brings life where we expect to find death — is the central way in which Christian liturgy looks for the renewal of all cultures. Thus the often contentious and sometimes violently abused notion that a culture can be "improved" is here reoriented to a reverent and honest solidarity with the suffering and marginalized. The margins become the center. The cross of Christ becomes God's cultivation of the tree of life in every culture. It is through God's presence with the crucified of every culture that the world is being brought from death to life.

Concluding Observations

Liturgical theologians carry out their work as part of a much wider and lively conversation about culture. They listen attentively and learn from many sources. At the same time, the interests of Christian theology and liturgy direct special attention to a number of points within culture, drawing out patterns of significance in every culture that are in turn engaged by the patterns of Christian worship: the common cultural places of communal gathering, storytelling, bathing, and meal sharing, among others; the particularities of each local culture; the patterned nature of all cultural life; the ecological dimensions of human life; the artistic and aesthetic dimensions of culture; and the privileged place of those pushed to the margins of every culture who share in the sufferings of Christ and thus share profoundly in God's favor and in the promise of salvation. Christian liturgical theologians highlight a constellation of interests among the world's cultures, rooted in the faith that God in Jesus Christ is present in and renewing all the cultures of the world.

The question of the relationship between liturgy and culture has sometimes been reduced to a binary choice between two opposing dispositions toward culture: "traditional" and "contemporary." These categories not only present a false choice; they also distort and mask enormous complexity. The Nairobi Statement on Worship and Culture, among its many conceptual virtues, calls for vigorous, theologically driven attention to *both* tradition and reform in liturgy and culture. This virtue alone allows it to break through what has been a profoundly unhelpful (and variously named) binary dilemma. Similarly, the statement resists cultural imperialism/homogeneity, on the one hand, and resists approaches to diversity that move toward postmodern incomprehensibility and permanent cultural alienation, on the other. The statement sounds themes of deep honor and profound critique into every culture — including (though perhaps in a muted way) a word of critique concerning the "culture" of ritual itself. The brilliance of the statement lies not principally in its text but in the four modes of engagement between liturgy and culture that it describes: together they form a kind of conceptual ecology that resists a number of stubborn distortions of culture, gospel, and liturgy. The challenge in coming years may be to account for and engage unprecedented patterns of technologically empowered cultural aggressiveness in areas such as emerging patterns of digital communication, global capitalism, and consumerism, militarism, and ecological disruption.

Vatican II and the LWF Project: Points of Convergence

Margaret Mary Kelleher, OSU

I first encountered the work of the Lutheran World Federation (LWF) some years ago when I discovered *Worship and Culture in Dialogue* in the course of doing some research on the topic of liturgy and culture. It was exciting and enriching to read the Cartigny Statement and the essays by such scholars as Anita Stauffer, Gordon Lathrop, Anscar Chupungco, and others. In more recent years, when I was exploring the interrelationship of liturgy, culture, and catholicity, I returned to that volume and also read *Christian Worship: Unity in Cultural Diversity*. Once again, I learned much from the essays in both books.

In addition, I found the inclusion of international case studies on the topic of worship and culture to be a model for responding to the challenge of catholicity. It is an honor to be invited to contribute to this volume.

Since the celebration of the fiftieth anniversary of the Second Vatican Council has begun, I thought it would be interesting to explore points of convergence that appear in the three volumes of the LWF study and selected documents of Vatican II. In the essay that follows I will address the following points of convergence: the foundational nature of baptism for Christian worship; the relationship between worship and ecclesial identity; the significance of worship for a local church; the relationship between local churches and the universal church; the concern for catholicity with respect to worship; the centrality of word and Eucharist in Christian worship; the foundational nature of the incarnation for the relationship between liturgy and culture; and the church's relationship with culture as one of mutual enrichment and critique.

Baptism as Foundational for Christian Worship

The affirmation of baptism as the foundation for life in the church is one of the most important principles set out in the documents of Vatican II. *Sacrosanctum Concilium (SC)* 6 states that "by Baptism men and women are implanted in the paschal mystery of Christ; they die with him, are buried with him, and rise with him (see Rom. 6:4; Eph. 2:6; Col. 3:1; 2 Tim. 2:11)."[1] The constitution goes on to present baptism as the basis for the right and duty of participation in liturgical celebrations because baptism has made the Christian people "a chosen race, a royal priesthood, a holy nation, a redeemed people" (1 Pet. 2:9, 4-5; *SC* 14). *Lumen Gentium (LG)*, "The Dogmatic Constitution on the Church," confirms that "through Baptism we are formed in the likeness of Christ" and united with his death and resurrection (*LG* 7). It goes on to say that "incorporated into the church by Baptism, the faithful are appointed by their baptismal character to Christian religious worship" (*LG*11).

The foundational nature of baptism is also affirmed in the three statements associated with the LWF project. Baptism and word and Eucharist are identified as the "core of Christian worship" in the 1993 Cartigny Statement.[2] In discussing the cross-cultural nature of worship three years later, the Nairobi Statement notes that "by virtue of Baptism, there is one Church."[3] The Chicago Statement begins with an elaboration of why and how baptism is a foundational event for Christian communities everywhere. Among the reasons given in support of this position is the fact that baptism constitutes the church as a "royal priesthood" (1 Pet. 2:9). Baptism is also presented as the burial of Christians with Christ so that they can be raised with him to newness of life (Rom. 6:4)[4] It is striking to find the same New Testament sources appearing in documents of Vatican II and in statements from the

1. English translation in *Vatican Council II: Constitutions, Decrees, Declarations,* ed. Austin Flannery, O.P. (New York: Costello, 1996). All subsequent quotations from conciliar documents will be taken from this translation.

2. "Cartigny Statement on Worship and Culture: Biblical and Historical Foundations," 3.7, in S. Anita Stauffer, ed., *Worship and Culture in Dialogue* (Geneva: LWF, 1994), pp. 129-35.

3. "Nairobi Statement on Worship and Culture: Contemporary Challenges and Opportunities," 5.1, in S. Anita Stauffer, ed., *Christian Worship: Unity in Cultural Diversity* (Geneva: LWF, 1996), pp. 23-28.

4. "Chicago Statement on Worship and Culture: Baptism and Rites of Life Passage," 1.1, in S. Anita Stauffer, ed., *Baptism, Rites of Passage, and Culture* (Geneva: LWF, 1998), pp. 13-24.

LWF and to recognize the shared use of the New Testament as the main source for both in exploring the meaning of baptism.

Worship and Ecclesial Identity

If baptism is foundational for membership in the church and participation in liturgy, then the liturgical actions of any church, beginning with baptism, will disclose something of the church's identity. This principle appears in several places in *Sacrosanctum Concilium*. For example, *SC* 2 presents the liturgy, especially the Eucharist, as "supremely effective in enabling the faithful to express in their lives and portray to others the mystery of Christ and the real nature of the true Church." A later passage describes liturgical services as "celebrations of the Church" that "make it visible and have effects on it." (*SC* 26) The Cartigny Statement makes a similar point when it presents the church's worship as "the central expression of celebrating our life in Christ" (1.4). This theme will also appear in a number of the essays in the LWF study.

Gordon Lathrop identifies the "central identity-creating signs of Christians" as "the washing or bathing which gathers a person into the Christian community, the reading and preaching of the Scriptures, and the thanksgiving meal, which the community holds weekly as the memorial of Jesus."[5] Both Lathrop and Anita Stauffer quote the definition of the church given in the Augsburg Confession as "the assembly of all believers among whom the Gospel is preached in its purity and the holy sacraments are administered according to the Gospel."[6]

Of course, it is the realization that the church's identity is disclosed in worship that gives rise to questions about liturgical inculturation and contextualization. Anita Stauffer recognized this in her commentary on Cartigny's identification of the core of Christian worship as word, baptism, and Eucharist. After noting that such a core "assumes a body of Christians assembled around Jesus Christ who is manifest and present in that core of Word and sacrament," she explores a number of questions about church art and architecture that reveal her sensitivity to issues of cultural diversity and ecclesial identity.[7] For example, she wonders how the cultural heterogeneity

5. Gordon W. Lathrop, "Baptism in the New Testament and its Cultural Settings," in Stauffer, *Worship and Culture in Dialogue*, p. 20.

6. See Stauffer, *Christian Worship*, pp. 11, 68.

7. S. Anita Stauffer, "Contemporary Questions on Church Architecture and Culture," in Stauffer, *Worship and Culture in Dialogue*, p. 169.

of a multicultural congregation can be reflected in architecture and iconography. Although she is aware of the challenging nature of such a goal, she thinks that "it is important that no one feels excluded."[8]

Significance of Worship for Local Churches

Questions such as the one just mentioned imply that ecclesial identity is revealed and shaped in the worship of local churches. This principle is clearly stated in *Sacrosanctum Concilium,* which equates the principal manifestation of the church with the liturgical celebrations of God's holy people presided over by the bishop of a diocese (*SC* 41) Since it is impossible for bishops to preside over the liturgical celebrations of the whole local church or diocese in any regular manner, the constitution recognizes the significant role played by smaller groupings of the faithful, such as parishes, in mediating ecclesial identity (*SC* 42).

With the Augsburg Confession in mind, the Cartigny Statement presents the church as "an assembly of believers in a given place and time where the Word of God is preached according to the Scriptures and the Sacraments administered following the letter and spirit of the Gospel" (1.3). The Nairobi Statement elaborates on the significance of the worship of local churches when it states that "Christian worship is always celebrated in a given cultural setting" (1.2), and it calls on all the member churches of the LWF to explore the local elements of liturgy, language, and so on — "so that their worship may be more truly rooted in the local culture" (6.1). In agreement with such statements, Gordon Lathrop notes that the church "is always a local gathering of people with their leaders, around the Scriptures and the sacraments, knowing Christ risen and here." However, he also affirms the importance of conversation among local churches as a means "whereby worship that is localized also remains worship that is catholic or universal."[9]

8. Stauffer, "Contemporary Questions," p. 180.

9. Gordon W. Lathrop, "Worship: Local Yet Universal," in Stauffer, *Christian Worship,* pp. 48-49.

Local Churches in Relationship to the Universal Church

The relationship between local churches and the universal church makes an appearance in several ways in discussions of the contextualization of Christian worship. One question has to do with identifying the elements that are constitutive of ecclesial identity. What has to be present for a local congregation to be identified as a church? The clearest statement made by Vatican II about this appears in *Lumen Gentium* 26, and it bears repeating:

> This church of Christ is really present in all legitimately organized local groups of the faithful which, united with their pastors, are also called churches in the New Testament. For these are in fact, in their own localities, the new people called by God, in the Holy Spirit and with full conviction (see 1 Thess. 1:5). In them the faithful are gathered together by the preaching of the Gospel of Christ, and the mystery of the Lord's Supper is celebrated. . . . In any community of the altar, under the sacred ministry of the bishop, a manifest symbol is to be seen of that charity and "unity of the mystical body, without which there can be no salvation." In these communities, though they may often be small and poor, or dispersed, Christ is present through whose power and influence the one, holy, catholic and apostolic church is constituted.

It is not difficult to find the similarities between the elements listed above and those identified by Lathrop when he names the "instruments of communion" that allow local churches to be in communion with one another. They are the presence of the gospel of Jesus Christ, the use of Scripture, baptism and formation in faith, the holy Eucharist, and "a recognized ministry serving the assembly around these central things."[10]

Another way in which the relationship between the local and universal church appears is in the desire that the liturgical worship of local churches be linked with the broader tradition of worship in the church. In its section on the reform of the liturgy, *Sacrosanctum Concilium* sets out the twofold goal of retaining sound tradition and being open to legitimate progress. It notes that "any new forms adopted should in some way grow organically from forms already existing" (*SC* 23). The Nairobi Statement makes a similar point in its discussion of methods for contextualizing worship. It declares that an important criterion to be used "is that sound or accepted liturgical traditions

10. Lathrop, "Worship: Local Yet Universal," p. 49.

are preserved in order to keep unity with the universal Church's tradition of worship, while progress inspired by pastoral needs is encouraged" (3.6).

The Cartigny Statement's interest in identifying "the transcultural elements in worship, which place it clearly within the universality of the Christian liturgical tradition," leads into a discussion of core elements in Christian worship. (3.5) Is there a core of Christian worship that can be found in all cultural contexts? As I noted earlier, the Cartigny Statement identifies such a core as consisting in word, baptism, and Eucharist (3.7). It goes on to present the pattern, or *ordo*, of entry into the community as teaching and the baptismal bath and the pattern of the weekly gathering on the Lord's Day as "the celebration centered around the Word and Eucharistic meal" (3.7). Lathrop refers to these statements when he suggests that "the *ordo*, or shape of classic Christian worship, provides local Christian communities with a basic, trans-cultural link to other such communities" as well as "an immensely important tool for the ongoing work of localization."[11]

Concern for Catholicity with Respect to Worship

Discussions of the relationship between local churches and the universal church naturally lead into the topic of catholicity. What is meant by this term? Vatican II made a significant statement about catholicity in *Lumen Gentium* 13:

> The universality which adorns the people of God is a gift from the Lord himself whereby the catholic church ceaselessly and effectively strives to recapitulate the whole of humanity and its riches under Christ the Head in the unity of his Spirit. In virtue of this catholicity, each part contributes its own gifts to other parts and to the entire Church, so that the whole and each of the parts are strengthened by the common sharing of all things and by the common effort to achieve fullness in unity.

This vision of diversity in unity is grounded in the shared gift of the Holy Spirit, the source of communion among all those who make up the one people of God throughout the world.[12] While *Sacrosanctum Concilium* does

---

11. Gordon W. Lathrop, "Preaching in the Dialogue of Worship with Culture," in Stauffer, *Baptism, Rites of Passage, and Culture*, p. 245.

12. Joseph Komonchak has suggested that Vatican II redefined catholicity as diversity

not use the language of catholicity, the principle of diversity in unity is present in the statement that "in the liturgy the church does not wish to impose a rigid uniformity in matters which do not affect the faith or the well-being of the entire community" (*SC* 37). The principle also appears in *Gaudium et Spes (GS)*, the "Pastoral Constitution on the Church in the Modern World," which recognizes that the church has made use of the resources of diverse cultures "to spread and explain the message of Christ . . . and to express it more perfectly in the liturgy and in the life of the multiform community of the faithful" (*GS* 58).

Attention to the catholic nature of the church's worship appears in several of the essays contained in the three volumes of the LWF project. After discussing a number of questions related to the topic of church architecture and culture, Anita Stauffer identifies one principle as being related to all of them: "The architecture and art of a worship space should speak both the universality of the Gospel and the church catholic, as well as the particularity of a congregation's own cultural background(s) and identity."[13] In his exploration of the local yet universal nature of Christian worship, Lathrop calls attention to the value of the international conversation that was central to the LWF project. He saw it as "one modest means whereby worship that is *localized* also remains worship that is *catholic* or universal, one modest evidence that the call to localization is itself one of the deepest gifts of catholic worship."[14]

In his discussion of the inculturation of baptism, Anscar Chupungco says that "the framework for inculturation is diversity in unity." In identifying the core that provides baptismal unity among the churches, he says that "they acknowledge one Baptism for the forgiveness of sins, and they baptize in water invoking the name of the Blessed Trinity." Fidelity to this core is the foundational criterion for inculturating the baptismal rite. At the end of his discussion of criteria for faithful inculturation, he suggests that the method of dynamic equivalence has the potential to allow churches throughout the world to "remain united in a common understanding of the message of Baptism, but each according to one's particular expression."[15]

---

in unity (Komonchak, "The Theology of the Local Church: State of the Question," in William Cenkner, ed., *The Multicultural Church: A New Landscape in U.S. Theologies* [New York: Paulist, 1996], p. 37).

13. Stauffer, "Contemporary Questions," p. 180.

14. Lathrop, "Worship: Local Yet Universal," p. 48.

15. Anscar J. Chupungco, "Baptism, Marriage, Healing, and Funerals: Principles and Criteria for Inculturation," in Stauffer, *Baptism, Rites of Passage, and Culture*, pp. 54, 55, 59.

Centrality of Word and Eucharist in Christian Worship

While baptism is foundational for membership in the Christian community, the word and the Eucharist play a central role in the life of these communities. We have already seen that the Cartigny Statement identified word, baptism, and Eucharist as constituting the core of Christian worship (3.7). The Nairobi Statement called on the churches of the LWF "to recover the centrality of Baptism, Scripture with preaching, and the every Sunday celebration of the Lord's Supper — the principal transcultural elements of Christian worship and the signs of Christian unity" (6.1). Exploring the shape of Christian liturgy, Lathrop identifies word and meal as "what we do on Sunday because they are the means of our encounter with the very presence of the crucified, risen Christ."[16]

One of the exciting aspects of the documents of Vatican II is the evidence in them of a retrieval of the centrality of the word in the life of the church. *Sacrosanctum Concilium* 24 recognizes that "sacred scripture is of the greatest importance in the celebration of the liturgy." In accord with this statement, the constitution states that "the treasures of the bible are to be opened up more lavishly so that a richer fare may be provided for the faithful at the table of God's word" (*SC* 51). *Dei Verbum (DV)*, "The Dogmatic Constitution on Divine Revelation," uses the image of "the one table of the word of God and the Body of Christ" (*DV* 21). The constitution ends with a significant statement about the centrality of word and Eucharist in the life of the church. "Just as from constant attendance at the Eucharistic mystery the life of the church draws increase, so a new impulse of spiritual life may be expected from increased veneration of the word of God, which 'stands forever' (Isa. 40:8; 1 Pet. 1:23-25)" (*DV* 26). The centrality of word and Eucharist in the creation and nurturing of young churches is clearly stated in the following statement from *Ad Gentes Divinitus*, the "Decree on the Church's Missionary Activity":

> The principal instrument in this work of implanting the church is the preaching of the gospel of Jesus Christ. It was to announce this gospel that the Lord sent his disciples into the whole world, that men and women, having been reborn by the word of God (see 1 Pet. 1:23) might, through baptism, be joined to the church, which, as the Body of the Word incar-

---

16. Gordon W. Lathrop, "The Shape of the Liturgy: A Framework for Contextualization," in Stauffer, *Christian Worship*, p. 68.

nate, lives and is nourished by the word of God and the Eucharist (see Acts 4:23).

In his discussion of methods for carrying out liturgical inculturation, Anscar Chupungco reaffirms the one table "of God's Word and Christ's sacrament." In reflecting on the challenge of inculturating liturgical space and furnishings, he notes that "the lectern and the Eucharistic table should symbolize the unity between the Word and Christ's body."[17] The intimate unity between word and Eucharist is also manifest in Lathrop's discussion of the place of preaching within the liturgy. He makes the point that "the juxtaposition of this sermon to the celebration of the Lord's Supper makes it most clear that this is a Word which is to be eaten and drunk in faith, just as the Eucharist is a meal which preaches (1 Cor. 11:26)."[18]

The Incarnation as Foundational for the Relationship between Liturgy and Culture

At the beginning of its discussion of the church as the people of God, *Lumen Gentium* makes the significant statement that God "willed to make women and men holy and to save them, not as individuals without any bond between them, but rather to make them into a people who might acknowledge him and serve him in holiness" (*LG* 9). This statement is repeated in *Gaudium et Spes (GS)* 32, which goes on to say that "this communitarian character is perfected and fulfilled in the work of Jesus Christ, for the Word made flesh willed to take his place in human society." In doing so "he sanctified those human ties, above all family ties, which are the basis of social structures." *GS* 32 notes that, in his preaching, Christ called upon people to treat one another as sisters and brothers and that he prayed that his followers would be one. After his death and resurrection, he established "a new communion of sisters and brothers . . . the communion of his own body, the church, in which all as members one of the other would render mutual service in the measure of the different gifts bestowed on each." In discussing the missionary work of the church, *Ad Gentes (AG)* 10 recognizes that the church must implant itself

17. Anscar J. Chupungco, "Two Methods of Liturgical Inculturation," in Stauffer, *Christian Worship*, p. 87.

18. Gordon W. Lathrop, "Preaching in the Dialogue of Worship with Culture," in Stauffer, *Baptism, Rites of Passage, and Culture*, p. 250.

among groups of people "in the same way that Christ by his incarnation committed himself to the particular social and cultural circumstances of the women and men among whom he lived." The decree elaborates on this by saying that, "just as happened in the economy of the incarnation, the young churches, which are rooted in Christ . . . borrow from the customs, traditions, wisdom, teaching, arts and sciences of their people everything which could be used to praise the glory of the Creator, manifest the grace of the savior, or contribute to the right ordering of Christian life" (*AG* 22).

Within the context of a description of the process followed by member churches of the LWF in their exploration of how the gospel could be rooted in culture, the Cartigny Statement notes that the recognition "that Jesus Christ himself is God incarnate in human culture" led them "to the New Testament where we could discover how the liberating Word for the world met culture" (2.3). Cartigny presents the church in its worship as "an ongoing incarnation of the Gospel" (1.4). The Nairobi Statement reaffirms this principle when it identifies the mystery of Jesus' incarnation as "the model and the mandate for the contextualization of Christian worship" (3.1). In his reflections on baptism in the early church, Anscar Chupungco shows how the church practiced what we would call liturgical inculturation. It had to do this in order to make it possible for the liturgy to communicate the faith of the church to people in various cultural contexts. He notes that the faith "had to become recognizably incarnate, that is, as having taken flesh in the cultural milieu of the worshipers."[19]

Church and Culture: A Relationship of Mutual Enrichment and Critique

Sacrosanctum Concilium's affirmation of the possibility of liturgical diversity, cited above, was a very significant step in light of centuries of liturgical uniformity in the Roman Catholic Church. This openness to pluralism in the liturgy was one of the fruits of research on the history of liturgy in the church, which provided evidence of diversity in liturgical practice. It was also a manifestation of Vatican II's openness to the world and its recognition of cultural pluralism. After declaring that the church does not wish to impose a rigid uniformity in the liturgy, *SC* 37 goes on to say the following:

---

19. Anscar J. Chupungco, "Baptism in the Early Church and its Cultural Settings," in Stauffer, *Worship and Culture in Dialogue*, p. 40.

Rather does it cultivate and foster the qualities and talents of the various races and nations. Anything in people's way of life which is not indissolubly bound up with superstition and error the church studies with sympathy, and, if possible, preserves intact. It sometimes even admits such things into the liturgy itself, provided they harmonize with its true and authentic spirit.

SC 38 and 39 go on to set out possibilities for diversity in the revised liturgical books, allowing for legitimate variations and adaptations within the elusive criterion that "the substantial unity of the Roman rite is preserved." *SC* 40 allows for the possibility of "an even more radical adaptation of the liturgy." In such cases it would be up to local conferences of bishops to "carefully and prudently consider which elements from the traditions and cultures of individual peoples might appropriately be admitted into divine worship." In subsequent sections of the constitution these principles reappeared with regard to liturgical music and art. For example, *SC* 119 recognizes the importance of musical traditions in the religious and social life of some people and notes that, because of this, "their music should be held in due esteem and should be given a suitable role . . . in adapting worship to their native genius." *SC* 123 recognizes that "the church has not adopted any particular style of art as its own," and goes on to say that "the art of our own times from every race and country should also be given free scope in the church, provided it bring to the task the reverence and honor due to the sacred buildings and rites."

The openness to the cultural expressions of diverse peoples that appear in the first document issued by Vatican II reappeared in a number of subsequent documents about the church. Just before the definition of catholicity presented in *Lumen Gentium* 13, the document makes a point of declaring that the church "fosters and takes to itself, in so far as they are good, people's abilities, resources and customs. In so taking them to itself it purifies, strengthens and elevates them." *Gaudium et Spes* 58 is even more positive in its statement about the relationship between the church and culture. After recognizing that throughout its history the church has made use of the resources of different cultures to spread Christ's message and to express it in the liturgy and life of the faithful, the document makes the following statement about cultural diversity in the church:

> Nevertheless, the church has been sent to all ages and nations and, therefore, is not tied exclusively and indissolubly to any race or nation, to any

one particular way of life, or to any set of customs, ancient or modern. The church is faithful to its traditions and is at the same time conscious of its universal mission; it can, then, enter into communion with different forms of culture, thereby enriching both itself and the cultures themselves.

This idea of mutual enrichment appears also in the Council's discussion of young churches that are created as a result of the church's missionary activity. *Ad Gentes* 19 makes it clear that "the faith should be imparted by means of a well-adapted catechesis and celebrated in a liturgy that is in harmony with the character of the people." It goes on to reflect on the communion of the young churches with the whole church and says "they should graft elements of its tradition on to their own culture and thus, by a mutual outpouring of energy, increase the life of the mystical body."

The importance of incorporating elements of culture into Christian worship, as well as the need to bring a critique to any culture, appears in the Cartigny Statement, which says, "We acknowledge the need in our time to make worship both authentic to the Word of God and relevant to given cultures" (1.3). The task of relating worship and culture includes the identification of cultural elements in Christian worship that "give expression to the particularity of the gathered people" (3.3) and the identification of "the countercultural elements in Christian worship which challenge the culture in which it is located" (3.4). The Nairobi Statement gives a concrete example of Christian worship as countercultural when it says that the "contextualization of Christian faith and worship necessarily involves challenging of all types of oppression and social injustice wherever they exist in earthly cultures" (4.1). Nairobi also recognizes that the cross-cultural nature of worship in the one church involves the sharing of elements of worship across cultures. This "helps enrich the whole Church and strengthen the sense of the communion of the Church" (5.1). The authors of the document comment that the cross-cultural sharing of elements of worship is especially appropriate in multicultural congregations. While calling on the member churches of the LWF to recover the transcultural elements of Christian worship, Nairobi also challenges them to explore local elements such as language, music, art, and architecture "so that their worship may be more truly rooted in the local culture" (6.1). The Chicago Statement recognizes transcultural aspects of the *ordo* of baptism but also calls for the contextualization of this transcultural gift in each local place (2.1; 2.2). Since baptism calls Christians to solidarity with all people, there will be countercultural elements in its liturgical celebration. The examples given emphasize the dignity and equality of all human beings who "will stand here on equal footing, equally in need of God's mercy, equally gifted with the outpoured Spirit" (2.3).

The significance of incorporating elements of local culture into Christian worship, as well as the need to bring a critique to those cultural elements, appears in the essays of several of the scholars who contributed to the LWF project. In his study of baptism and culture in the New Testament, Lathrop indicates that, while the early Christian communities made use of washing symbolism that they received from their cultural contexts, this cultural symbolism was "broken" and "turned to the purpose of proclaiming God's grace in Christ."[20] He offers this dynamic of reception and critique as a "model for the ongoing cultural dialogue with Christian worship." Lathrop presents the same dynamic at work in the shaping of the Eucharist within early Christian communities. He notes that "in the Eucharist the New Testament communities both continued and critically re-formed Hellenistic-Jewish meal practice."[21] Lathrop develops this dynamic of reception and critique in his essay "A Contemporary Approach to Worship and Culture: Sorting out the Critical Principles." Here he presents a principle of Lutheran liturgical hermeneutics that is rooted in Martin Luther's ability to distinguish the central from the secondary in celebrations of the Eucharist. Lathrop suggests that Lutheran liturgical hermeneutics offers two guiding principles for decisions about the relationship between worship and culture. The first is that "in worship, the center must be clear: the assembly gathers around the gift of Christ in Word and sacrament." The second guiding principle is that the gifts of diverse cultures are to be welcomed and honored but "these cultural patterns must not become their own new law or usurp the place of the center. . . . [T]hey must be broken to the purpose of Christ." In the pages that follow, Lathrop gives some concrete examples of the kinds of cultural elements that might be welcomed in Lutheran worship and those that should be rejected. He suggests using a method of juxtaposition as the best way of critically associating cultural gifts with the purpose of the Christian assembly. "What is brought in must be capable . . . of serving the gathering of the people as they find the Word and the sacraments at the center." It is Lathrop's conviction that "cultural symbols will bring their own strongest gifts to voice when they can be set next

20. Lathrop, "Baptism in the New Testament," p. 38.
21. Gordon W. Lathrop, "Eucharist in the New Testament and its Cultural Setting," in Stauffer, *Worship and Culture in Dialogue,* p. 73.

to the biblical Word, full of the power of God's saving grace, and be used to illuminate the continuing strength of that Word."[22]

In her essay "Contemporary Questions on Church Architecture and Culture," Anita Stauffer offers a fascinating introduction to the complexity of this topic. Following the Cartigny Statement, she identifies the core of Christian worship as word, baptism, and Eucharist, but then goes on to explore what that core requires spatially. The simple answer is that "worship requires a place for the people to assemble (whether outdoors or indoors), a place from which to proclaim the Word, a pool in which to baptize, and a table on which to celebrate the sacramental meal." The complexity of the issue becomes evident once one tries to ascertain how these things should be influenced by the cultural context in which an assembly is gathering. In reflecting on the matter of the relationship between Christian faith and the cultural patterns of a given people, Stauffer wonders: "Are there certain inherited or current cultural forms or influences which are inappropriate for use in a Christian worship space?" She also asks, "What are the aesthetics of a given culture, and how does the aesthetic system relate to a sense of the Holy?" As she makes clear, any attempt to answer such a question means asking further questions about the understanding of beauty and holiness in a given cultural context. After reflecting on these and a number of other questions, Stauffer concludes that "the contextual, the countercultural, and the transcultural all have a place in architecture for Christian worship."[23]

In reflecting on baptism and culture in the early church, Chupungco makes the point that "the Church not only welcomes culture; it also critiques culture."[24] He notes that only those cultural elements or patterns were assimilated into Christian worship which could "be reinterpreted in the light of God's revelation." In his discussion of the Eucharist and culture in the early church, he introduces the subject of the language of worship. Noting the importance of language for expressing a people's cultural traits and identity, he says that "the option of the early Church in the West to use Greek and Latin, that is, the living languages of her converts, opened the door wide to inculturation." The language of the people was seen as capable of being able to express God's revelation. As a result, both Christian worship and the

---

22. Gordon W. Lathrop, "A Contemporary Lutheran Approach to Worship and Culture: Sorting Out the Critical Principles," in Stauffer, *Worship and Culture in Dialogue*, pp. 138-39, 147, 148.

23. S. Anita Stauffer, "Contemporary Questions on Church Architecture and Culture," in Stauffer, *Worship and Culture in Dialogue*, pp. 170, 173, 178, 181.

24. Chupungco, "Baptism in the Early Church," p. 41.

local cultures were enriched by the process. Chupungco emphasizes the centrality of the domestic character of the Eucharist for understanding the inculturation of it in the early church. This domestic character of the Eucharist was evident in the places where the communities gathered (houses), in the vessels used for the liturgy, as well as in the language of worship. Chupungco even suggests that "this domestic character of the Eucharist is the Church's countercultural message today to a world broken by individualism, anonymity, and absence or even denial of family values."[25]

The principles of mutual enrichment and critique are certainly present in Chupungco's presentation of creative assimilation and dynamic equivalence as methods for liturgical inculturation. The Christian liturgy was enriched by its incorporation of cultural ritual practices such as "anointing at Baptism, the giving of the cup of milk and honey, and the footwashing of neophytes." However, Chupungco sets out critical questions that should be asked before any cultural element is added to the liturgy. One of his questions asks: "Do the local elements enhance the theological understanding of the Christian rite?" His final question on efforts at inculturation asks: "Do people accept them as an authentic contribution of their culture to the enrichment of Christian worship?" At the end of his presentation of a series of steps that should be taken in the process of deciding what cultural patterns might be incorporated into a community's liturgical *ordo,* he notes that "the old adage *sacramenta sunt propter homines,* sacraments are for the good of the people, should be the ultimate aim of inculturation."[26] The faith of the people — the faith of the church — is to be enriched.

Concluding Thoughts

As I read through the three volumes of the LWF project and the documents of Vatican II in preparation for writing this essay, I was surprised by the many points of convergence that I found. In retrospect, I should not have been surprised. *Lumen Gentium* 13 presents the shared gift of the Holy Spirit as the source of communion among all those who make up the one people of God throughout the world. The examples of convergence between the work of Vatican II and that of the LWF research project are manifestations of this

25. Anscar J. Chupungco, "Eucharist in the Early Church and its Cultural Settings," in Stauffer, *Worship and Culture in Dialogue,* pp. 87-88, 100.
26. Chupungco, "Two Methods of Liturgical Inculturation," pp. 79, 80, 93.

shared gift. The vision of catholicity that is presented in *Lumen Gentium* 13 is one that is grounded in the gift of the Holy Spirit, but it is also one that calls diverse communities to share their gifts with one another in order to promote fullness in unity. In an article I published a couple of years ago in *Worship,* I suggested that the efforts of the LWF to engage in an ecumenical and interdisciplinary study of the relationship between Christian worship and cultures provides a model for this task of realizing catholicity.[27] After working on this project I have become even more convinced that the LWF research project is an example of catholicity at work. This appears especially in the efforts to bring representatives of various local churches together to reflect on what has been done with regard to the inculturation or contextualization of worship and to identify what questions have been raised. In his report on discussions of marriage rites, Marcus Felde includes an account of the conversation that took place among the participants in order to illustrate "the character of the stimulating interchange."[28] The language of "stimulating interchange" seems to be a good way of describing the dynamic of mutual enrichment and critique as it has appeared in the conversations of members of local Christian communities throughout the world on the topic of worship and culture.

27. Margaret Mary Kelleher, "Liturgy, Culture, and the Challenge of Catholicity," *Worship* 84, no. 2 (2010): 120.

28. Marcus Felde, "Summary on Marriage Rites," in Stauffer, *Baptism, Rites of Passage, and Culture,* p. 239.

Reenvisioning "Liturgy and the Components of Culture"

Anscar J. Chupungco, OSB

Introduction

Over the centuries the church, both in the East and the West, has been in constant dialogue with the culture of every race and nation. One remarkable result of such a dialogue is that the church often assimilated various components of culture into the liturgy. We may say that it became one of the church's ways of incarnating the gospel in the life and history of peoples. To state the matter more simply, by integrating new cultural components into the liturgy, the church allowed the liturgical shape to be influenced by culture. Thus, soon after Christianity had been transplanted into the Greek and Roman soil, it came about that the liturgy was rooted in a culture other than and in addition to the Jewish culture.[1]

We need only consider the shape of baptism and Eucharist to realize how in the course of time these Jewish-Christian rites became so Hellenistic, so Roman, so Franco-Germanic, that it is not always easy for us to define their original core. In fact, one of the difficulties people encounter when they

---

1. A. Chupungco, "Inculturation," *The New Westminster Dictionary of Liturgy and Worship* (New York: Westminster John Knox, 2002), pp. 244-51.

This essay is a revised version of Anscar Chupungco, OSB, "Liturgy and the Components of Culture," in S. Anita Stauffer, ed., *Worship and Culture in Dialogue* (Geneva: LWF, Department for Theology and Studies, 1994), pp. 153-65.

work on inculturating the liturgical *ordo* is how to distinguish between what is immutable in the liturgy and what is subject to change.

The Components of Culture

Culture may be defined according to its components. Cultural anthropologists name three: values, patterns, and institutions.[2]

Values

Values are principles that influence and give direction to the life and activities of a community and its members. They are formative of the community's attitude or behavior toward social, religious, political, and ethical realities. The value of hospitality, for example, shapes the active vocabulary of a community and creates pertinent rites to welcome, entertain, and send off guests. The value of family ties brings members back to parental homes for family meetings and annual celebrations. The value of leadership is extolled by titles of honor and pledges of loyalty on the part of the community and by the corresponding promise of active service by the leader.

The liturgy also has its set of values. These are parallel to human values, though they are obviously to be viewed from a Christian perspective. Hospitality, for example, acquires a distinctly Christian meaning in the baptismal celebration, when the community receives the newly baptized. It is expressed by the openness with which the community welcomes strangers to its eucharistic table. The Sunday ministers of hospitality are not mere ushers; they perform the task of Christian hospitality toward not only strangers but also the members of the household. Surely we claim the *domus ecclesiae* as our home, but we do not wish to get in and out of our home anonymously: we expect to be welcomed and seen off at the door.

Another important liturgical value is community spirit, which is a

2. See F. Keesing, *Cultural Anthropology: The Science of Custom* (New York: Rinehart, 1958); V. Turner, *The Ritual Process* (Chicago: University of Chicago Press, 1969); J. Shaughnessey, ed., *The Roots of Ritual* (Grand Rapids: Eerdmans, 1974); T. Tentori, *Antropologia culturale* (Rome, 1980); C. Di Sante, "Cultura e liturgia," in *Nuovo Dizionario di Liturgia* (Rome, 1984), pp. 341-51; A. Terrin, *Leitourgia: Dimensione fenomeonologica e aspetti semiotici* (Brescia, 1988); A. Triacca and A. Pistoia, eds., *Liturgie et anthropologie: Conférence Saint-Serge, XXXVI Semaine d'études liturgiques* (Rome, 1990).

broader version of family ties. The following remark is often heard from people who find the Sunday liturgy boring, if not quite meaningless: "Why go to church, if one can worship God at home, in the privacy of one's room?" Such an attitude is easily generated by a liturgy in which the horizontal or community aspect is dispensed with. But if the liturgy is viewed as a cultural reality possessing its own value of community spirit or family ties, coming together every Sunday in order to celebrate as a Christian community or family should not be too difficult to understand. Nor should it come as a surprise that people get deeply involved in church affairs and remain loyal to it because of the community spirit.

The value of leadership is a basic ingredient of the liturgical assembly. The liturgy is essentially the worship of an assembled community, a particular image of Christ's church that is organically structured — or, we might also say, structurally organized. We refer here to the relationship between the presider and the assembly. Whether we speak of an episcopal or presbyterial hierarchy or of the presidency of regional synods, we are dealing with no less than the office of church leadership and consequently with liturgical leadership. This is a value that is inherent in the very nature of community worship, as it is in every secular assembly and institution, not excluding democratic systems. In our mainstream tradition we cannot conceive of acephalous liturgical celebrations. Even in those liturgies where the hierarchical representative does not preside, there is always a lay leader, a *primus inter pares* — yet *primus*.

Cultural Patterns

The second component of culture is cultural patterns. These represent the typical way members of a society think or form concepts, express their thoughts through language, ritualize aspects of their lives, and create art forms. Thus the areas covered by cultural patterns are: thought, language, rites and symbols, literature, music, architecture, and all other expressions of fine arts. We call them cultural patterns because they are rather predictable, in the sense that they follow an established course. Things are thought out, verbalized, and done according to a certain pattern, in much the same way that we expect cherry trees to blossom in spring. Hence every cultural group has its typical way of thinking, articulating concepts, expressing values, and so on.

It might be useful to note in passing that the law of cultural patterns is verified not only in social groupings but in individuals as well. Each of us personally operates according to set individual patterns. Commonplace things like putting on shoes, first on the left foot and then on the right, are day-to-day examples. When we think we know a person sufficiently, we tend to comment after hearing or seeing something from him or her, "Typical, isn't it?"

Cultural patterns are so named also because they are the society's norms of life into which a person is born and reared. Through the process of what anthropologists call inculturation, a person is initiated and trained to behave according to such patterns that these become like second nature to every member of the community. That is why anything that happens outside the normal pattern is regarded as something exceptional or anomalous, and the person as demigod or semi-mad. Although cultural patterns do not eliminate individuality, they shape members of society within the established bounds of social acceptability. For this reason we should have no scruples distinguishing one society from another, or one racial group from another. The extent to which we accept the profound influence cultural patterns have on members of a society or race is shown when we say things like, "Don't be surprised when she does things that way — she's Asian, that's why." Comments like this are not necessarily judgmental; rather, they express a perception, namely, that cultural patterns have the power to shape the life of an individual, as they conform him or her to the image that society has of itself and its members.

Cultural patterns are at the root of social and racial identities. The typical way a group thinks, speaks, and ritualizes allows us to distinguish one cultural group from another. Each cultural group thus has its thought, language, and ritual patterns with which to express the values of hospitality, community spirit, and leadership.

Thought Pattern

At this point it is wise to engage in a process of introspection in order to identify one's own cultural patterns. What comes immediately to mind when a guest or a stranger is announced? In other words, we are dealing with thought patterns, with concepts and images that spontaneously arise in the mind. Typical of the biblical world is theophany: God visits his people in the person of strangers. The sixth-century Rule of Benedict directs the porter of the monastery to welcome guests as Christ himself, and to answer those who knock at the monastery door with the exclamation, "Thanks be to God!"

Language Pattern

From thought pattern we move on to language pattern. What words and phrases do we readily associate with the value of hospitality? What are the first words we address to a guest? A number of cultural groups, especially in Asia, waste no time with set formularies such as "welcome," "how are you?" "I hope you had an enjoyable trip," "have a seat," and so on, depending on the situation. Instead, the host's first words are: "Have you eaten yet?" Language patterns reveal what is uppermost in the mind of a welcoming host: concern for the well-being of guests. Throughout the duration of a visit, guests are given the reassurance of being welcome and cared for with words like "feel at home," "you are family," or "yell when you need something."

Ritual Pattern

From language pattern we turn to rites. The value of hospitality is ritualized according to established patterns. Handshakes, embraces, slight bows of the head, hands pointed toward the forehead, kissing the right hand of the elders or placing it on one's forehead are some of the ritualizations of welcoming and leave-taking. Guests who are familiar with these ritual patterns expect to receive them from their hosts. It is not surprising that no less a person than Jesus was offended when his host Simon failed to kiss him and offer water for his feet as he entered his house. In the ancient world, footwashing was a ritual of hospitality and certainly a source of physical comfort for those who traveled on foot. As late as the sixth century, the Rule of Benedict required the abbot and community to wash the feet of incoming guests.

Different cultural groups have different rituals for entertaining guests. Some of these are details of social refinement, the ignorance or omission of which constitutes a faux pas in hospitality. Examples are the ritual of introducing the guests, the assignment of places at table, the order of serving the food. Sometimes the children are tasked by their parents to perform for the guests by singing, playing musical instruments, reciting poems, or dancing. In a sense, the host will not spare anything to please the guest. It is not unusual in some cultures for a family to bring out the best it can afford in terms of food and lodging; alas, sometimes they get into unnecessary debt because of hospitality. Guests are sacred, and the ritual patterns of hospitality are often as extravagant as the furnishings used for sacred worship.

Ritual patterns of hospitality manifest themselves not only when guests are welcomed and entertained, but also when they are sent off. Leave-taking can be as elaborate as the rite of welcoming; indeed, in some cultures saying farewell can last forever, which happens because the host, out of a sense of hospitality, tries to hold back the guest, even if at times this might prove inconvenient for those who have a schedule to keep or a plane to catch. The rites used for welcoming are normally also those for leave-taking, but the formularies express various sentiments from the prayer-like "adieu" or "adios," to the hopeful "arrivederci" or "see you soon," and even to the apologetic "I wish I could have done more."

Cultural patterns of hospitality are the typical ways groups of people think or form concepts and images about guests, speak to them and about them, and perform rites to welcome, entertain, and send them off. How do these things affect the liturgy? If we regard the liturgy as a cultural reality, though with a divine component, and consider that one of its values is hospitality, it becomes evident that it, too, follows a system of cultural patterns. In other words, the liturgy has its particular and specific way of thinking and speaking about hospitality and of expressing it in ritual form. We find this in liturgical *ordo,* which — due to its consistency and predictability — is called typical, that is, an exemplar or model to be imitated. The *ordo* contains the typical way the liturgy handles the value of hospitality.

Although we can ultimately trace our liturgical origins to the Jewish tradition, we have to accept the fact that in the West the Christian liturgy has been influenced by the Roman cultural patterns. The Western liturgies, as they are known today among Roman Catholics, Lutherans, Anglicans, and others, are a conglomeration of cultural patterns from the Jewish to the Christian medieval times. Nonetheless, they all possess a distinct and typical style of formulary and rituality that we can identify as being typically Roman: sober, concise, direct, and practical. It is this kind of cultural pattern that has by and large shaped the patterns of hospitality in the Western liturgies.

A strikingly Roman pattern affecting hospitality in the liturgy is the abruptness with which the assembly is sent off. In concise and direct words the Roman assembly was told: *Ite, missa est.* The equivalent in modern English would simply be "Meeting adjourned" at the conclusion of a meeting. Under the influence of this Roman pattern, the liturgical assembly is quickly blessed and sent away in three words. Some even call this rite of leave-taking the rite of dismissal, which can be quite offensive and absolutely lacking in social refinement. I should add something apropos here: That people do not take offense at being dismissed is a sure sign that they do not take the words they hear seriously enough or that they have formed the habit of not regarding the liturgy as a cultural reality. The Roman genius for brevity, applied to the leave-taking in the liturgy, can cause uneasiness among societies where it takes considerable time and art to say good-bye. It is understandable that some liturgists try to elaborate this part of the liturgy in an effort to incorporate into it the local pattern of hospitality.

Perhaps the most significant expression of liturgical hospitality is in the greetings "The Lord be with you" and "Peace be with you." These greetings, which are said at various moments in the celebration, serve as words of welcome, as reassurance of Christ's presence, and as parting words. Some presiders replace them with more contemporary formulas, or else juxtapose them, thereby giving the wrong impression that these Christological greetings do not have the same value of hospitality that contemporary greetings such as "Good morning" or "Good evening" have.

Institutions

The third component of culture is institutions. These are society's traditional rites whereby it celebrates the different phases of human life from birth to death. Thus do we speak of initiation rites, rites of marriage and parenthood, rites of taking the office of leadership, and rites connected with sickness, death, and funerals. Other institutions are society's celebrations to mark the advent of the seasons of the year, especially spring and summer for shepherds and farmers respectively, and to commemorate memorable legends in its mythology or significant events in its history. These rites are celebrated as feasts. They engage the family, the neighborhood, or the entire community. They are celebrated with great regularity and fervor, and with a fidelity to traditional rites that exceed the demands of rubrical liturgists. In other religions the efficacy of the institution depends on the exact and minute observance of ritual details. Such is the power and influence that institutions have on the life of communities.

The liturgy also has its institutions. It possesses special rites to accompany the faithful in important events in life, from birth to maturity in the faith, to critical moments such as marriage, assumption of community leadership, and life's decline. Tradition has given the generic name "sacraments" to these institutions, though some churches distinguish between sacraments, on the one hand, and sacramentals and blessings, on the other. Foremost among them are the rites of Christian initiation and the Eucharist. Tradition points clearly to Christ as author of some of these sacraments and to the church as author of sacramentals and blessings. There is no uniform teaching among the churches regarding the kind and number of sacraments authored directly by Christ. But what interests us here is the fact that all of these institutions correspond to a particular situation in the life of the Christian community and its members. Likewise, as institutions they have been profoundly influenced by the values, cultural patterns, and institutions of various cultures, as I have pointed out on several occasions. They are, in other words, institutions.

Besides the sacraments, the liturgy has other institutions that are called feasts. These are celebrated at various times of the year according to a calendar system, an institution in itself, which is known as the "liturgical year." A couple of feasts originate in the Jewish world of Jesus and his disciples: Sabbath, Easter, and Pentecost. In the course of time a great number have been added: from religious and secular feasts — Epiphany, Nativity, John the Baptist; others have a political coloring because they were introduced in times of uneasy relationship between the church and politics — Christ the King and Joseph the Worker; and lastly, some feasts were occasioned by turbulence and calamities — Michael the Archangel, Rogations Days. The church instituted these feasts as any human society would. The difference is that we are dealing with Christian institutions here: they celebrate the mystery of Christ and the church, though they do so in the context of the culture and traditions of the celebrating assembly.[3]

Cultural Components and the Eucharistic *Ordo*

To illustrate the relationship between cultural components and the liturgy, let us focus on the eucharistic ordo. Let us consider those moments in the *ordo* where values, patterns, and institutions appear prominently.[4]

---

3. E. James, *Seasonal Feasts and Festivals* (New York: Barnes and Noble, 1965); A. Chupungco, "The Liturgical Year: The Gospel Encountering Culture," *Studia Liturgica* 40 (2010): 46-64.

4. M. Witczak made a detailed study of the Order of Mass of Pope Paul VI, with suggestions on how it can be refined, taking into account both liturgical tradition and contemporary needs ("The Sacramentary of Paul VI," in *Handbook for Liturgical Studies* [Collegeville, MN: Liturgical Press, 1999], pp. 133-75).

Entrance Rites

In the rite of gathering or entrance rites, for example, we are able to identify the values of hospitality and community spirit. We express hospitality by the openness with which community leaders welcome visitors and strangers to the eucharistic table. The Sunday ministers of hospitality welcome back members of the parish community and lead them to their seats. In the usage of the Roman Catholic Church, the purpose of the rite of gathering "is that the faithful who are assembling should become a community and dispose themselves to listen properly to God's word and to celebrate the Eucharist worthily."[5] The entrance song, which accompanies the procession of the ministers to the sanctuary, is also intended to enhance the community spirit. Singing together in assembly creates a bond of unity. Indeed, the entire celebration should be a musical liturgy.[6] Other traditional elements, such as the *Kyrie, Gloria,* and Collect, foster the spirit of worship as a community act.

The challenges of dynamic equivalence and creative assimilation are many. In some communities there might be a need to bring to greater consciousness some of the elements of the eucharistic gathering. Who welcomes whom to the celebration? How is hospitality made to interplay with leadership and ministerial functions? What role does the procession of ministers play at this point? Does the entrance song create community spirit? Is the seating arrangement indicative of equality and mutual respect among members of the assembly? As one ancient writer has impressively put it, "A special welcome is to be given to the poor, even if the bishop has to surrender his chair and sit on the floor."[7] Is the rite of gathering confined to words and songs, or are gestures and material things also used to signify the meaning of the eucharistic gathering? What impact does the traditional greeting "The

5. *General Instruction of the Roman Missal,* chap. 2, no. 46 (Washington, DC: USCCB, 2002), p. 15.

6. The Roman musical tradition for the Eucharist consisted of singing the liturgical texts; it meant singing the liturgy more than singing hymns, e.g., in the liturgy. Today the option exists of singing entrance, offertory, and communion hymns in place of the assigned liturgical text. See J. Gelineau, *Voices and Instruments in Christian Worship* (Collegeville, MN: Liturgical Press, 1964), pp. 59-65; E. Foley, "Liturgical Music," in *The New Dictionary of Sacramental Worship* (Collegeville, MN: Liturgical Press, 1990), p. 855; E. Schaefer, *Catholic Music through the Ages* (Chicago: University of Chicago Press, 2008).

7. Quoted in R. Cabié, "The Eucharist," in *The Church at Prayer,* vol. 2 (Collegeville, MN: Liturgical Press, 1986), p. 39.

Lord be with you" have on the assembly's perception of faith that Christ is present in the assembly?

The Liturgy of the Word

In the traditional eucharistic *ordo* the structure of the liturgy of the word consists of biblical readings, psalmody and alleluia, homily, and intercessions. As a unit they appear as a dialogue between God, who proclaims the word, and the community, which listens and replies to the word. The liturgy of the word can be described as the word of God proclaimed in the readings, explained by the homily, and responded to in the recitation of the Apostles' Creed and in the intercessory prayer. In this part of the *ordo* the community leader occupies the presider's chair and interprets the word of God through the ministry of preaching. The assembly listens as the word of God is proclaimed and explained, and thereafter utters or sings words of praise, thanksgiving, and supplication. The word of God is addressed to the assembly as a community, and the response, which the assembly makes through supplications, is the prayer of those who have gathered for the entirety of humankind.

Here again, the methods of dynamic equivalence and creative assimilation present challenges to local churches. Some liturgical assemblies will need a more solemn — perhaps even dramatic — presentation of the book of Scripture. It should be noted that the Roman tradition has no special introduction to the liturgy of the word; this begins quite abruptly with the first reading. There are cultural groups that feel uneasy about this system. Another challenge is the formation of readers who will combine the nature and qualities of liturgical reading with the cultural pattern of public proclamation, giving attention to voice pitch, rhythmic cadence, and public presence. The posture of the assembly during the readings also has a cultural significance that should not be ignored. Liturgical tradition tells the assembly to sit at the readings, except during the gospel reading when the assembly stands to listen in silent respect. However, in some cultures the posture of standing while someone of authority is speaking is considered disrespectful, an indication of boredom, or of an eagerness to take leave.

The presider is also challenged to preach on the basis of the word that has been proclaimed. To do otherwise can be as culturally shocking as ignoring an official message addressed to the assembly. In the Middle Ages, when the sermon had lost any relationship to the biblical reading, pulpits were built in the center of the church, thus aggravating the problem of relating the homily to the proclaimed word of God. The idea of having a homiletical book independent of the lectionary disrupts the flow of liturgical dialogue between God and the assembly.

The intercessions should likewise be inspired by the word proclaimed and explained. If we take the concept of dialogue seriously, the intercessions as the assembly's response cannot entirely ignore the proclaimed word. Unrelated intercessions bring to mind the image of two deaf people trying to engage in a conversation. The challenge also includes the formulation of intercessions, using the local community's language pattern. Lastly, it might be useful to note that the traditional Roman posture during the intercessions is standing, perhaps a reference to the priestly character of the assembly, to the *Ecclesia Orans*. In some cultural situations, however, kneeling might express more convincingly an aspect of the intercessory prayer, namely, humble petition.

The methods of dynamic equivalence and creative assimilation challenge us also in the area of liturgical space and furnishings.[8] For example, the ambo (lectern) and the eucharistic table should symbolize the unity between the word and Christ's body. This will be more clearly manifested if the material and decoration (which should be of local inspiration) of the ambo are identical with those of the eucharistic table. There is indeed one table — the table of God's word and Christ's sacrament. Furthermore, where should these furnishings, together with the chairs of the presider and ministers, be located with respect to the assembly? What cultural pattern does the community follow in the arrangement of the liturgical space? Does it correspond to the special feature of liturgical gathering, which denotes both community participation and leadership?

The Liturgy of the Eucharist

The meal of thanksgiving, also called the liturgy of the Eucharist, has a plan whose essential elements can be traced from a report of Justin Martyr in about A.D. 165.[9] Bread and wine (mixed with water) were presented to the presider,

8. C. Valenziano: *Architetti di chiese* (Palermo, 1995), pp. 167-266; A. Stauffer: "Inculturation and Church Architecture," *Studia Liturgica* 20, no. 1 (1990): 70-80.

9. Justin Martyr, *1 Apology,* c. 65 and 67, ed. L. Pautigny (Paris, 1904); partial English translation: W. Jurgens: *The Faith of the Early Fathers* (Collegeville, MN: Liturgical Press, 1970), p. 57.

who recited a lengthy prayer of thanksgiving over these elements. At the end the people shouted out "Amen" to express assent to the prayer made in their name. The eucharistic elements were then distributed to the assembly and to those who could not be present. Justin mentions that collection is made for widows and orphans and for the sustenance of the guests of the community. In the Roman liturgy revised by Vatican II, these various elements are represented by the preparation of the gifts, the eucharistic prayer, and communion. The various elements of the eucharistic liturgy project the values of community spirit, leadership, and hospitality. In the ancient *ordo,* observed in Rome and North Africa, the assembly offered bread and wine for the community's communion. What was superfluous — and we can presume that there was much — was distributed to the needy members of the church. The Eucharist became an occasion to be generous to the poor; that is, communion became like a token meal, in order to have enough to give to the hungry. We can, to some extent, understand the stern words addressed by Cyprian of Carthage to a wealthy person who came to church, Sunday after Sunday, bringing no gifts for the community, yet "dared to eat," he said, "the bread offered by the poor." The Eucharist urges the rich and the poor alike to share their possessions with the members of the community. It is through this generous sharing of goods that the community spirit is fostered.

The challenge here is to find appropriate rites for presenting the gifts to the community. What are the words exchanged at this moment between the person who offers and the person who receives? What gestures are involved? At what time of the celebration is the presentation of the gifts most appropriate — at the rite of gathering or at this part of the celebration? What kinds of gifts, other than the accepted tradition of bread and wine, can be brought to the community for its needs and the needs of the poor?

In the recitation of the eucharistic prayer, the role of the presider as leader has been evident from as far back as the second century C.E. Witnesses are Justin Martyr in the second half of the second century and Hippolytus, in *Traditio Apostolica,* in the third century.[10] It is worth noting that this long and solemn prayer was recited by "the one who presides," the *proestòs,* in the name of the assembly. That is why Justin remarks that the assembly shouted out its "Amen" to signify that it consented to what the presider had prayed in everyone's name. We can say that during the eucharistic prayer there was interplay between the values of leadership and com-

---

10. Justin Martyr, *1 Apology,* c. 65 and 67; see also Hippolytus, *Traditio Apostolica* 9, ed. B. Botte (Münster, 1989), p. 28.

munity. In the liturgical thinking of the third- and fourth-century Christian writers, the two fundamental roles of the presider at the Eucharist consisted of the homily and the eucharistic prayer. In the tradition of the Roman Church, the collect, the prayer over the gifts, and the prayer after communion are also called "presidential prayers."

The challenge of the eucharistic prayer is its composition, which is not only integral (dialogue, preface, narration of the institution, prayer of anamnesis and epiclesis, intercessions for the church and the world, and final doxology), but also localized in its language and use of images.[11] Language is not only a compendium of words and phrases; it is above all a mirror of the people's thoughts and values. That is why liturgical language, especially for the central prayer of the Eucharist, should assimilate the linguistic qualities of the assembly: noble and beautiful, but accessible; prayerful and uplifting, but rhetorical, using what is proper to the local language, such as idioms, proverbs, and maxims.[12] Failure to use the literary qualities of a language produces prosaic prayers, failing to impress on the hearers anything memorable and anything that can accompany them spiritually through life.

Another challenge is the way to pronounce the eucharistic prayer and the rites that should accompany it. How are solemn orations proclaimed by a leader in a given culture, and what are the traditional gestures or postures assumed by the assembly to express the attitude of reverence and communion with the leader — bowed heads, hands lifted up, standing, sitting, or kneeling? The rite of communion has much to say about community spirit. The common recitation of the Lord's Prayer and the sign of peace, if it is done at this moment, are some of the more significant expressions of community spirit. Originally, as we find in Justin Martyr, the sign of peace was placed after the intercessions, thus acquiring in the writings of Tertullian the name *sigillum orationis,* or "seal of prayer." Pope Gregory I transferred it at this point as a *sigillum communionis* ("seal of communion").

The central and eloquent symbol of the value of community is, of course, the New Testament "breaking of bread," the name for the Eucharist given in Acts 2:42. The one bread must be broken, like the body of Christ "broken" violently on the cross, in order to be shared. For there is no sharing unless

11. For the Roman tradition, see E. Mazza, *The Eucharistic Prayers of the Roman Rite* (New York: Pueblo, 1986).

12. P. De Clerck, "Le language liturgique: sa nécessité et ses traites spécifiques," *Questions liturgiques* 73, nos. 1-2 (1992): 15-34; see also A. Echiegu, *Translating the Collects of the "Sollemnitates Domini" of the "Missale Romanum" of Paul VI in the Language of the African* (Münster, 1984).

there is a breaking, and there is no Eucharist unless there is a sharing. Likewise, the communal cup mentioned in 1 Corinthians 10:16-17 suggests unity among the members of the assembly. The principle of a communal cup would make us believe that, before the age of the basilicas, the size of the cup was determined by the size of the community.[13] The later practice of prebroken bread might have come about as a practical solution to the large number of communicants or — what seems a more likely explanation — as a consequence of the use of thin wafers, called "hosts." In the seventh-century papal Mass recorded by Roman Ordo I, a "main cup" was used, thus implying that there were other cups, probably for the communion of the assembly.[14] These practical solutions should not make us forget the basic value of community spirit expressed by the one bread that is broken and the one cup that is shared.

The methods of dynamic equivalence and creative assimilation present cultural challenges in connection with communion. For example, the appropriate manner of giving the sign of peace is a question that torments both ecclesiastical authorities and liturgists alike, and probably it will take several more years before a suitable cultural sign can satisfy each member of a local community. There is also a need to study the ritual pattern of sharing food and drink in community. Who offers them? How are they presented to the people? What words are used by the one who offers and what reply is given by the one who receives?

At this point it is important to note that the eucharistic communion does not tolerate cultural patterns where a distinction is made between races, sexes, and social positions. To affirm the nature of Christian service, it might even be helpful for the leader to receive communion last. In some cultures, in fact, parents eat after feeding the children, and hosts eat after ministering to their guests.

Concluding Rites

The value of leadership and community spirit surfaces again at the concluding rites. The presider, in the capacity of community leader, invokes God's

---

13. See E. Foley: *From Age to Age: How Christians Celebrated the Eucharist* (Chicago: University of Chicago Press, 1991); D. Power, *Unsearchable Riches: The Symbolic Nature of the Liturgy* (New York: Pueblo, 1984); K. Richter, *The Meaning of the Sacramental Symbols* (Collegeville, MN: Liturgical Press, 1990).

14. *Les Ordines Romani du haut moyen âge*, vol. 2, ed. M. Andrieu (Louvain, 1971), p. 104.

blessing on the assembly before sending them off. Something of the parents' action of blessing their children as these leave the house seems to be evoked by this gesture. The practice of some presiders to take leave of the assembly and see them off at the door of the church heightens the sense of family or community spirit.

It has become fashionable nowadays to emphasize the aspect of mission on the basis of the words *Ite, missa est.* Although such a connection does not enjoy etymological and historical support, one cannot deny that the dynamism of the Eucharist is such that it compels the assembly to be preachers and doers of the word and sharers of Christ's gift of himself.

The challenge presented by dynamic equivalence and creative assimilation is to examine the local pattern for ending a gathering. Do people say — politely and in so many words — "go" at the end of a meeting or a visit, or do they normally say, "Come back soon"? But words at this point can be deceiving. In some cultures it is possible to say, "You go now, while I stay here," to mean "I am sad that you must go." What gestures are performed by people as they take leave of each other, even if for a short period of time?

Summary: Methodological Steps

To sum up, we review the methodological steps to be undertaken when we inculturate. The first step is to examine closely the official liturgical *ordo* of the church or communion: its history and theology, structure, fundamental elements, and cultural background. It is obvious that we should not institute modifications or alterations on any system unless we are thoroughly informed about its nature and component parts. Furthermore, we need to determine how the liturgical *ordo* expresses cultural values, patterns, and institutions. In other words, we need to analyze the cultural patterns of the *ordo.*

Although we can ultimately trace our liturgical origins to the Jewish tradition, we have to accept the fact that, in the West, the Christian liturgy has been influenced by Roman cultural patterns. Even after other European cultural patterns, such as the Franco-Germanic, had modified the Western liturgy, the style of its formulary and its ritual traits continued to retain Roman characteristics: sobriety, conciseness, and practicality. Therefore, the eucharistic *ordo* of most churches was, by and large, shaped by the Roman cultural patterns, even if medieval Europe added its own contributions and the Reformation amended some of them.

Having analyzed the *ordo,* we come to the second step. We should determine which of its elements may be — or should be — reexpressed in the culture of the people, without prejudice to its original meaning or intention. Like any structure, the liturgy possesses elements that are not subject to change: food and drink for the Eucharist (tradition speaks of the bread that is broken and the cup of wine that is shared), water for baptism (tradition speaks of natural water, while giving preference to flowing water), and so on. This goes hand in hand with the study of one's own culture. We, each in his or her own cultural ambit, need to enter into a process of research and introspection in order to define the cultural patterns at play in such values as hospitality, community spirit, and leadership. What images arise in our minds when we speak of these values? What are the words, phrases, idiomatic expressions, proverbs, and maxims with which we associate them? Are we able to identify the rites, symbols, and institutions by which our society signifies these values? In short, we need to study those components of culture that share similar traits with the liturgical *ordo* and are able to reexpress the *ordo* adequately.

The third step consists of comparing the patterns of the liturgical *ordo* with the cultural patterns of a local community. This step aims to establish the similarities and differences that exist between the two patterns. Does a particular linguistic expression, for example, convey the same sense as the liturgical anamnesis or epiclesis? Does a local ritual gesture correspond to the liturgical laying on of hands? Does orange color say the same thing as the liturgical white? Does the practice that the host or parent eats last express the same value as the traditional rite of communion? The questions can be as numerous as the elements of celebration. If we are able to establish such similarities and differences, we can begin to apply the method of dynamic equivalence by replacing parts of the liturgy with equivalent cultural components.

In the process we shall need to remember the cautions concerning doctrinal and moral critique that leads to purification. Certain cultural "values," might be diametrically opposed to Christian values and must in no way be incorporated in the liturgical *ordo*. On the other hand, we might in some instances have recourse to biblical types in order to ensure that the cultural equivalents are suitably integrated into the Christian *ordo,* or, in other words, that they are assumed into the history of salvation.

Lastly, we should not lose sight of the pastoral and spiritual benefits that our people should derive from the changes or modifications brought about by inculturation. The old adage *sacramenta sunt propter homines* ("sacraments are for the good of the people") should be the ultimate aim of inculturation.

Context, Margins, and Ministry:
A Church in the Pacific Northwest's "None Zone"

Scott Anderson

*If God was in Jesus-Christ,
the people of God must also be marginal people.*[1]

*Throughout American history periods of upheaval over
social and economic and political inequality have very often been periods of religious revival aimed at redressing
that inequality.*[2]

Advent

Baptism is not:
- A purity bath to identify insiders against outsiders. Baptism is a bath
  to identify us with Jesus Christ, who identifies with everyone. It
  makes us dirtier. It constitutes the identity of the church as a community drawn to the world.
- A thing we do to make God happy. God acts: God runs out with the
  robe and the ring. We are Lazarus, raised from the dead into the life
  of the triune God.

1. Jung Young Lee, *Marginality: The Key to Multicultural Theology* (Minneapolis: Fortress, 1995), p. 4.
2. Robert Putnam and David E. Campbell, *American Grace: How Religion Divides and
Unites Us* (New York: Simon and Schuster, 2010), p. 258.

- Done for you alone: Lazarus is surrounded by his sisters and by the community. Symbolically, he becomes a type not of when we die, but of when we live. Lazarus now walks in God's good earth. Baptism is for living.[3]

I remember the confusion I felt when I went looking for the baptismal font soon after my beginning as the pastor of St. Andrew Presbyterian Church. I asked around; in fact, I asked several people over a few days. I finally found someone who took me into the kitchen and brought out from one of the cupboards a small gold-colored chalice, made of some kind of acrylic. "I think this is what we've used," she said. Obviously, it had been a while since there had been a baptism there. The vessel was so insubstantial that when I lifted it, it almost flew out of my hand. That's not to say there wasn't a certain and significant vitality in the congregation that had drawn me as a pastor. They shared their joys and concerns with one another. They had birthed a regional mental-health ministry, and they spoke of mental illness along with other struggles in a way that was vulnerable, empathetic, knowledgeable, and true to their engagement with people on the margins of families and society. They had a long history of community engagement and local ecumenical leadership. Membership and church attendance had remained steady in recent years. They had built an addition and paid it off in a third of the time they had anticipated.

The font was not the first thing I thought of when I moved across Washington state to become their fourth installed pastor in forty years of existence. Honestly, it was a few months into my ministry there before I thought to look. I had attended a week-long ecumenical gathering hosted by the School of Theology and Ministry at Seattle University. At its Summer Institute for Liturgy and Worship I encountered a way of worship and thinking about worship that, much to my astonishment, made room for virtually every generative thing I had experienced in my life in the church. From the fundamentalism that had shaped my youth to becoming the pastor of this rather liberal PCUSA congregation in the "none zone" of the Pacific Northwest — it was all there.[4]

---

3. Gordon Lathrop, Reflections at the conference "Baptismal Living, Baptismal Ethics," St. Paul's Episcopal Church, Seattle, March 10, 2012 (from my notes of Lathrop's comments on baptismal living, drawn from John's Gospel, particularly the story of Lazarus).

4. Those who, in response to questions indicate no religious affiliation are referred to as *nones*. In the 2001 American Religious Identification Survey, 63 percent of Pacific Northwesterners indicated they were not affiliated with a religious group (compared to 41 percent

From my earliest years, the church had always been a place of belonging and strength, and perhaps most remarkably when I was seventeen and lost my father to cancer in only six months. The community held our whole family in ways that gave Jesus' question "Who are my mother and my brothers?" sudden and lasting resonance. I remember being gathered in his hospital room, counting his last breaths, and having a sudden epiphany: all the members of my family had beside us our dearest friends, holding us. And they were all from the church. It took my breath away.

But I was always something of a misfit. I was deeply uncomfortable with the pressure to evangelize strangers with a message that, even when I was a teenager, was frankly something of an embarrassment. Its literalism was incompatible with the critical thinking I was learning in school. It seemed to me that its commitment to proselytizing was uninterested in understanding or engaging — just converting. And yet I was profoundly nurtured there.

I found myself deeply disturbed by the assumption of superiority we brought to our evangelism, what Letty Russell has written about as the deformation of the church's witness and service fueled by the imperialistic assumption that those who share the gospel and bring Christ have an elevated role that makes them superior to others.[5] It was, in fact, precisely this perceived hypocrisy and judgmental attitude that was responsible for what Robert Putnam and David Campbell refer to as the "second aftershock" to the seismic upheaval of the 1960s in their book *American Grace: How Religion Divides and Unites Us*.[6] So many of those raised in my generation of the 1970s, and even more of those raised in the 1980s and 1990s, left the church in reaction to the religious right and its cocktail of religious literalism, elevated importance of certainty, traditional social positions, and conservative political activism (p. 98).[7] Yet, rather than leaving the church through the back door, as so many of my friends did, I found myself called to it for its

---

of Americans as a whole), while 25 percent claimed no religious identity (compared to 14 percent nationally), thus the "none zone." This summary is drawn from the *Christian Century* online: http://www.christiancentury.org/article/2008-12/none-zone.

5. Letty Russell, *Just Hospitality: God's Welcome in a World of Difference* (Louisville: Westminster John Knox, 2009), pp. 43ff. Russell notes that one of the elements of a feminist hermeneutic of hospitality is giving priority to the perspective of the outsider.

6. Putnam and Campbell, *American Grace,* pp. 8off. Hereafter, page references to this work appear in parentheses within the text.

7. Putnam and Campbell note that the defection actually began with the boomer generation, though it was largely masked. In 1971, for example, church attendance, while steady overall, was 28 percent among those ages 18-29, compared to 51 percent for the same age group in 1957.

power to share life and give meaning, even as I found my religious affiliation shift to a denomination where, for me, head and heart could dwell together in greater unity.

Putnam and Campbell's analysis fills out this metaphor of the broad demographic trends of religion in the last fifty years by noting that the first aftershock to the long sixties was the birth of the religious right in the 1970s and '80s. Some young and some older Americans, so appalled by what they saw as the moral and spiritual decay of the era, flocked toward evangelical and conservative churches. By 1980, conservative politics became the most visible aspect of religion in America.

Indeed, the polarization of red- and blue-state America that we know so well today is rooted, according to Putnam and Campbell, in these three seismic phases. The rise of evangelicals at the most conservative end of the religious spectrum was followed after 1990 by "nones" at the most liberal end of the spectrum, squeezing the moderate center to an ever-smaller contingent (p. 104). In 1973, evangelicals and "nones" made up 30 percent of the population; in 2008 they made up 41 percent. And while the evangelical boom of the 1970s was over by the early 1990s (p. 105), the trends toward secularization have every sign of continuing (p. 123).[8]

Come to the Waters

> For many Americans, religion pulls together people with a common ethnic background into particular denominations and, within denominations, into particular congregations. But this symbiosis also means that, across denominations and congregations, religion has pushed apart people of different ethnicities. (p. 288)

The personal significance of what I encountered at the Summer Institute for Liturgy and Worship is hard to describe. In less than a week I found room for all those experiences and hungers and hopes that had become a part of me over my lifetime in the church. An astonishing array of what I then saw as new worship practices was on display. But I came to see that there were no "worship wars" here, or "new worship practices." Rather, the question was made moot by an ecumenical commitment to an ancient structure, the

---

8. Putnam and Campbell note that cohorts who are 5 percent nonreligious are being replaced by cohorts of whom 25 percent claim no religious affiliation.

ordo of the meeting. The music was chosen not first for style, but for how it served the liturgy, which aimed to support the meeting at every point in its movement — logically, imaginatively, thoughtfully, prophetically — as did every other element and action. Performance gave way to doxology, a praise and a lamentation that included songs from all over the world. Thinking walked hand in hand with acting and dancing and washing and bowing. Beauty and awe, astonishment and lament, laughter and silence were all welcome companions. Systematic theologians and artists, thinkers and feelers, were given room around the word and the table. The sanctuary was filled with people from many parts of the world, from many denominations, from many ethnicities and cultural traditions. Christ was proclaimed in the pulpit and at the table and at the font. Love and justice were preached and enacted as we were gathered and then sent. The earth and all its people were our concern. The sacraments were celebrated in ways that all of life became holy; the holy was praised in ways that all life became sacramental.

Most simply, it was a conference at which we worshiped and then reflected on worship — primary and secondary liturgical theology, as I later learned.[9] As I have said to many over the five years that I participated in the institute, many of whom I brought along from my congregation, I found what I had been looking for all my life. Along with the Samaritan woman, I had found water as a spring of life; along with the Syrophoenician woman, I had found healing grace and grace's source; like the merchant, I thought I had found a pearl of great price that everyone would value right along with me.

So I went looking for the baptismal font, and I began to mess with worship.

Things Next to Each Other

Meaning occurs through structure, by one thing set next to another. The scheduling of the *ordo,* the setting of one liturgical thing next to another in the shape of the liturgy, evokes and replicates the deep structure of biblical language, the use of the old to say the new by means of juxtaposition.[10]

9. Gordon Lathrop, *Holy Things: A Liturgical Theology* (Minneapolis: Fortress, 1993, 1998), pp. 4ff.

10. Lathrop, *Holy Things,* p. 33.

Gordon Lathrop has observed that the *ordo* of worship — the ritual ordering and shape of the liturgy, the words and actions of the Christian assembly and its leaders from meeting to meeting, Sunday to Sunday — propose to us a realistic pattern for interpreting our world, for capturing our human experiences and enabling action and hope. Liturgy, the "work of the people," is made up of one thing against another, so that at least two things together is the way of speaking faithfully about God, for example: Gathering | Sending; Confession | Forgiveness; Water | Fire; Word | Table; Scripture | Preaching; Silence | Song; Assembly | Presider; Crucified | Risen.

> The Sunday meeting of Christians, no matter what the denominational tradition, has focused around certain things: primarily a book, a water pool, bread and wine on a table; and secondarily fire, oil, clothing, a chair, images, musical instruments. These things are not static, but take on meaning in action as they are used, especially as they are intentionally juxtaposed. Even the assembly itself, the place of those juxtapositions, may be regarded as a thing . . . that is, a gathering of people with a purpose, an assembly of the free and responsible ones.[11]

In this way of understanding worship — an ancient way, adapted by early Christianity and patterned in the Gospels themselves — I found a way toward the deeper mysteries of God that critiqued the certitude and literalism of my past while refusing to betray it. It was a way of bridging the gap between head and heart. It was a way of moving out from under the shadow of the Enlightenment and its imperialist implications without returning to primitive thinking — a move to a new-old way of understanding that presented endless possibilities for shaping Christian worship and discipleship.[12] It was a way of holding onto this ancient wisdom while recovering the heart of authentic religion as the place of meaning-making and generativity, inviting the kind of cultural critique that leads to justice.

Letty Russell looks to Kwok Pui-lan's postcolonial theological critique, which makes the connection between the Enlightenment project of the West and its practices of colonization. The Enlightenment led to a codification of knowledge that occurred hand in hand with developing scientific views of historical criticism and theological discourse that made normative the Western worldview: "It is not much of an exaggeration to say that every aspect

---

11. Lathrop, *Holy Things*, p. 10.
12. Russell, *Just Hospitality*, pp. 32ff.

of the lives of colonized peoples was written about by their colonizers, whose scientific study of the history of India, Indonesia, and other nations provided these colonizers with knowledge that helped them politically dominate the colonized people they were studying." Similarly, Russell refers to Musa Dube's understanding of imperialism as "a structural imposition of a few standards on a universal scale that assumes that the "other" is a blank slate to be (1) inscribed with a universal (Western) culture in disregard of their own particular culture, and (2) rendered dependent on those who maintain these standards.[13]

The *ordo* sets next to these imperial powers the unassuming power of the sacramental practices of the worshiping church. Rather than definitions, the ancients resorted to metaphors and images. God's action in baptism is a mystery of grace that defies explanation. God's action in the bread and the wine is better experienced than described. The mystery of God must be met by symbols not literalism and its reductionist, fearful quest for certainty. And yet, when the assembly is gathered, when the claim and welcome of baptism is enacted, when the words of forgiveness are spoken, when Scripture is read and the word rightly proclaimed and the bread is broken and the wine poured, the eschatological moment comes. Jesus is once again raised in the assembly; the risen crucified one is encountered for the life of the world. In bread, wine, word, and assembly next to each other, "[t]heir eyes [are] opened and they recognize him." None is "colonized" or a "colonizer," none a foreigner or a stranger, but they are equal citizens — even more, all members of the same body of life, all in the same "homeland," all in the same foreign country (see Lathrop's chapter on theological context in this volume).

Here was a way for me as a seeker to fully welcome the gifts of the church, my encounters with the risen Christ from my youth with the fullness of life in this new place. Here was a way for me to invite those for whom church was a good place for building relationships and organizing community service to see it in its particularity as a place for conversion, *metanoia,* the church away from here, for the world beyond it, where not only something authentic and reliable about God was said, but also something true and transformative about ourselves and our world.[14] Here was a way for the contradictions and tensions that always seem to be present in our lives and in the deepest truths to live together in creative unity — a Christian way.

So in our church we borrowed a table that matched the style of the

13. Russell, *Just Hospitality,* p. 27.
14. Cf. Lathrop, *Holy Things,* p. 3.

pulpit and the communion table, and we purchased a large ceramic bowl to use as a font. We began to speak our gathering words there, our words of forgiveness as the water was seen and heard. We began to intentionally lead the prayers of intercession from the table where the people were invited to share their gifts and offerings. We were blessed and sent out into the world, sometimes from the font, which reminds us that we are baptized in the waters that unite us with Christ and those with whom Christ united, and sometimes from the table, where we remember that we become Christ's body broken for the world.[15]

Those who teach leadership from a systems perspective caution us never to do adaptive leadership alone.[16] When challenges require innovation and new learning, they also require the management of loss and grief. Humans don't necessarily resist change, but we do resist loss.

Maggie was a church member, a thirty-something mother of three, and a sojourner from Scotland with a husband who had been raised in the same congregation. Maggie often says of her precarious upbringing in Scotland that, while the church of her youth wasn't especially good at caring for her, the liturgy held her. Maggie was among the small group of my church's members who began attending the annual institute in Seattle. As her interest deepened, her considerable gifts were also noticed. She was called by the congregation first to youth ministry; then she was taken under care as an inquirer in the PCUSA; and then she was a student at the ecumenical School of Theology and Ministry (STM) at Seattle University. Her trajectory toward a bivocational ministry that is rooted in the worship life of a particular congregation is the result of her discernment, in partnership with a discerning community, during a tumultuous five years that have seen her slowly accepted into the center of the church community's life as a dynamic, transformative, and trusted leader.

It didn't start that way. Maggie was among a core group of people who responded wholeheartedly to the conversations about worship and the potential for renewal in the church's life. They appreciated the shifts in worship, the attention to all of our senses, the invitation to movement, the careful and

15. The publication *Invitation to Christ: A Guide to Sacramental Practices* (Louisville: PCUSA, 2006) is an excellent resource for understanding and exploring these practices. It can be found online: http://www.pcusa.org/resource/invitation-christ/.

16. See, e.g., Ronald A. Heifetz and Marty Linsky, *Leadership on the Line: Staying Alive through the Dangers of Leading* (Boston: Harvard Business School Press, 2002); see also Edwin Friedman, *A Failure of Nerve: Leadership in the Age of the Quick Fix* (New York: Seabury, 2007).

intentional shaping of the liturgy. The effects of anchoring children and youth deeply in the life of the congregation through worship were especially striking. Her ministry was embodied, creative, and relational — a continuous dialogue among its basic elements involving a "participating assembly."

By the time she became a staff member of her congregation, Maggie had been identified with a particular group in the midst of a growing rift within the congregation — a rift that focused on worship. Yet she was also fully aware of the importance of her work and the power of the young to transform our life together in the kingdom of God.

When Maggie began as our youth director in 2007, she painted her office blue. I had painted my office when I had moved in three years earlier, and no one said a word — except of praise. But when Maggie painted her walls, it became a controversy that spread like a virus through all extremities of church life.

Prepare the Way

The Nairobi Statement on Worship and Culture sets four basic principles of Christian worship next to each other, which challenge every local assembly into a continuous and creative critique of its worship — and ultimately of its life together and in the world.[17]

- *Worship is transcultural.* The triune God transcends any and all cultural contexts, so there are elements in authentic Christian worship that always transcend what occurs in any particular time or place.
- *Worship is contextual.* The incarnational mystery of Christ in Jesus was located within a specific time, place, and culture. The challenge of Christian worship, then, is to re-present the values of the gospel within each particular time and place.
- *Worship is countercultural.* All people and all cultural patterns, in the perspective of the gospel, need critique and transformation. Christian liturgy ultimately challenges and transforms cultural components that are sinfully dehumanizing, thus contradictory to the values of the gospel.

17. "Nairobi Statement on Worship and Culture: Contemporary Challenges and Opportunities," prepared by the third international consultation of the Lutheran World Federation's Study Team on Worship and Culture, Nairobi, Kenya, January 1996.

- *Worship is cross-cultural.* Jesus Christ came to be the Savior of all people, so treasures shared across all cultural barriers contribute to the full expression of the gospel. The hybridity of the world's cultures and of Christians everywhere are to be faithfully reflected in Christian liturgy.

> *A multicultural community is not one where otherness is obliterated.*
> *It is a community of hospitality in which the richness of individual*
> *gifts and the mystery of the other are celebrated.*[18]

While the Nairobi paradigms are not necessarily embraced everywhere, or go unchallenged in today's discourse on worship and culture, they offer a deeply considered set of lenses through which to examine questions on the issue, as some authors in this volume propose. In fact, postcolonial interpretation, in its concept of "hybridity," understands that we live out our familial, cultural, political, and economic contexts as both colonizer and colonized. We live both outside and inside the institutional power structures. But this in no way means that all people experience — even remotely — a level playing field. The history of Western imperialism has ensured that cultural domination is much more familiar to and sustained for someone who looks like me (a white Euro-American male) than it does to almost anyone else in the world. Asian theologian Kwok Pui-lan has pointed to at least four keys for analyzing how the Christian theological tradition has been shaped by Europe and North America, that is, by "colonizing countries of the North."[19]

- *Codification of knowledge*: The systematization and methodization of all kinds of knowledge, including theology and biblical studies, developed hand in hand with colonialism. The modern academy emerged in Europe in the nineteenth century and with it the understanding of theological method, colonial expansion, and the study of native peoples. It continues to enjoy a privileged place to this day.
- *Decolonizing the mind*: Postcolonial theory recognizes that the historical process is so comprehensively embedded that we all carry with us layers upon layers of deep-seated assumptions that need examination. We inadvertently reinforce Western thinking as correct and better, and we

18. Brian K. Blount, and Leonora Tubbs Tisdale, ed. *Making Room at the Table: An Invitation to Multicultural Worship* (Louisville: Westminster John Knox, 2001), p. xi.
19. See Russell, *Just Hospitality*, pp. 31ff.

shape data collection and analysis so that the "other" is taught what he or she should be in order for domination to continue.

- *Framework of mutually constituted oppressions*: The many "isms" of cultural, political, and relational realities (e.g., racism, sexism, ableism, classism, imperialism) are woven together, and many people are doubly and triply oppressed — so that they do not have access to what they need to flourish or even survive. In other words, oppressions are mutually constituted — interrelated and reinforcing.
- *Focus on North American imperialism*: Salman Rushdie speaks of the "empire writing back to the center" — claiming a power to narrate, contest, and reconstruct meanings. Postcolonial theology is particularly concerned with the global, political, economic, and cultural domination that affects the way people of all cultures and nations live within the United States and other countries, and the global impact of American foreign policy. Postcolonialism calls us to intentionally interpret biblical and church traditions from perspectives other than our own, paying particular attention to how these traditions reinforce unjust social structures. Admittedly, this discussion is focused on a particular congregation within a particular region of the United States. The amount of diversity addressed here is miniscule compared to the global concerns represented by postcolonial theologians.[20]

There is danger in another act of imperial aggression, which yet again colonizes these ideas, repurposing and domesticating them by diminishing their breadth and sidestepping the broader implications of the postcolonial critique. These keys are also instructive in a culture that increasingly suffers from the fractionalizing that has resulted from its imperial practices — its wedge politics, its massive and still widening gaps between "haves" and "have-nots," and the pervasive rhetorical use of "us" and "them."[21] The pressure is great, particularly in anxious times, to divide into polarized groups even on a smaller scale, such as a local church, each subgroup assuming a

---

20. Russell, *Just Hospitality*, p. 36.

21. On social class, educational attainment, and wealth, see Putnam and Campbell, *American Grace*, pp. 246ff. "In short, over the last three to four decades Americans have been increasingly polarized into haves and have-nots — living increasingly segregated and unequal lives." Among other trends, Putnam and Campbell note that while the income distribution became more equal during the first two-thirds of the twentieth century, the latter third has seen sudden shifts. Greater social inequality exists now than at just about any time in American history (p. 231).

privileged place, each neglecting to examine deep-seated assumptions, ignoring layers of oppression that exist within our relatively privileged community and "writing back to the center" by claiming the power to construct the narrative according to our own preferences.

Indeed, polarization is the frequent experience of churches in conflict. It was certainly the experience of St. Andrew. Moreover, there is little doubt that Maggie's experience of marginalization was especially acute. Even as my experiences of being scapegoated took its toll, there were many more layers to her experience of vulnerability than for someone like me, who enjoyed much greater privilege. This continues to be true, though our life together, integrated by the liturgy and its transcultural, contextual, countercultural, and cross-cultural implications, has invited deeper awareness and changes in priorities among our leadership and within our community.

It was here that the *ordo* revealed yet another of its treasures. Within the ordering of worship is an ongoing conversation, an ongoing invitation to analyze our own traditions in juxtaposition with the gospel as we encounter it in the symbols of the liturgy, with a world that claims us when we gather at the font around our common baptism and give thanks at a table that is at once local, global, and cosmic, whose small amount of food and drink is sufficient to restore creation. Samuel Torvend beautifully notes the pull of the table toward the world:

> The ethical interpretation of the eucharist was clearer in the liturgical practice of the early church. Each communicant brought wine and bread to the Sunday liturgy. Deacons and deaconesses would collect this abundant offering, reserving a smaller portion for the eucharist and setting aside the rest. Immediately after the liturgy, the larger and remaining gifts were given to the poor, sent to orphans and widows, and carried to the sick. Without speaking a word, the church set forth the worldly implications of its holy eating and drinking.[22]

Some in the St. Andrew congregation were beginning to gain "eyes to see" the implications of our renewed worship and the logic of centering the church by way of its worship life, even as the frustration, distress, and resistance of others increased to the breaking point.

---

22. Samuel Torvend, "How Does the Liturgy Serve the Life of the World?" in Gordon Lathrop, ed., *Open Questions in Worship,* vol. 6: *What Are the Ethical Implications of Worship?* (Minneapolis: Augsburg, 1996), p. 32.

Fire and Water

> Since, then, there is a cleansing virtue in fire and
> water, they who by the mystic water have washed
> away the defilement of their sin have no further
> need of the other form of purification, while they
> who have not been admitted to that form of purga-
> tion must needs be purified by fire.[23]

The catechumenate is the ancient way of baptism. It is a pregnancy — the
way the church makes space in its own body for the new life that the Holy
Spirit is birthing. The catechumenate process is a ministry of the whole
church that is expecting the coming of God in the guise of the stranger, born
at the margins rather than the center. It is an immersion into the verities and
complexities of humanity by way of intense liturgical participation and intentional reflection.

The way it has evolved over six years at St. Andrew, the catechumenate
also shares a similarity in form with the small-group (accountability) movement I was acquainted with from my evangelical past, though with a deeper
connection to the church's particular and ecumenical worship life. Inquirers
and sponsors are brought together for a season of meetings around the
weekly liturgy, the lectionary texts, the theologies and patterns of the
church, the texts of our own lives, and a meal. The Scripture reading for
Sunday, usually encountered through an open process of study, leads the
way to the exploration that follows.

Gordon Lathrop reminds us that, when it comes to the church's practice of making disciples, there is not just a single *ordo,* but plural *ordos.*
Not only is there an ancient ordering to the Sunday meeting, but the
church has given us orders intended for fullness of life, for example: seven
days and the eighth day; word and table; praise and beseeching; teaching
and bath; the year and *pascha.*[24] For the ancients, the catechumenate —
Christian initiation — was patterned by the preparation of Lent and the
new fire of *pascha,* the Passover of God, particularly of the Triduum. We
began to practice the liturgical season — and particularly the Three Days,

---

23. Gregory of Nyssa, *The Great Catechism,* chap. 35.

24. See Lathrop, *Holy Things,* for more on the seven days and the eighth day (p. 36),
word and table (p. 43), praise and beseeching (p. 55), teaching and bath (p. 59), the year
and *pascha* (p. 68).

in their fullness — about the same time that we instituted the catechumenate at St. Andrew.

The church's gift to Christian initiation is its *ordo* of teaching and bath, shaped by the Lent-Easter cycle, rooted in lectionary preaching. These things, set next to each other in a safe and generous space, provide a rich feast for immersion into the suffering and possibility of the world through orthopraxy, that is, reflection on the meaning of one's life in relationship to life that is immersed in the world: How did I find myself here? What brought me? What hungers and hopes are at work? Could what is rising within me be of God, and if so, in what way? What are the implications for me and for the world? What must I do to inherit eternal life?

We in the Pacific Northwest know particularly well that, though many left the church in reaction to the religious right described by Putnam and Campbell as a "second aftershock," it does not follow that interest in spirituality has waned. Putnam notes that the reaction was not theological or scientific: "[T]hey became unaffiliated, at least in part, because they think of religious people as hypocritical, judgmental or insincere. Large numbers also say they became unaffiliated because they think that religious organizations focus too much on rules and not enough on spirituality."[25] Jung Young Lee uses the image of ripples on a pond to reflect on a theology of marginality.[26] One day he was walking along a pond and saw the waves made from a fish surfacing in the center. The waves ebbed toward the margin, but then he noticed that they also were reflected back into the center. "Why did I not pay attention to ebbs returning to the center, but noted only the waves coming out to the edge? Why was I interested only in something happening at and from the center? Why did I neglect what happened at and from the margin?"

The end of the catechumenate process may lead to membership through baptism or its reaffirmation. At its most faithful, it always leads to deeper understanding and to the transformation of the church through the gifts God brings to its center from the margins and for its constant invitation to continue to make the liminal journey between the two locales.

25. Putnam and Campbell, *American Grace,* p. 131.
26. Lee, *Marginality,* pp. 29ff.

SCOTT ANDERSON

A Little Child Shall Lead Them

> Don't be afraid. My love is stronger. My love is stronger than your fear.
> Don't be afraid. My love is stronger. And I have promised, promised
> to be always near.[27]

Molly has become our go-to cantor for this poignant song from Iona that frequently sends out the assembly. The clear, uncomplicated quality of Molly's young voice and presence, we have perceived, is the fitting vessel to speak this powerful truth of the presence of God's faithful love for the world and for us, encountered in unexpected places and people. Over the years she has frequently climbed onto a step stool behind our pulpit to witness to the great courage that can be found in the least of these. Her presence has sent us out with hope for the future, strength for the journey, and joy in the presence of the mighty one who is our strength and our song.

Molly is an example of one of the most significant wellsprings of renewal for St. Andrew — its youth. In a culture that is increasingly polarized along generational lines, the church has too frequently mirrored and even exacerbated such trends by dividing itself similarly, and chronically subjecting us to the tyranny of our personal preferences. The invitation of the liturgy for the full participation of the whole assembly in its diversity has led us to pay closer attention to the waves ebbing from the margins to the center. And the invitation of the catechumenate to the full-throated conversations within the liturgy supports a deeper and more thoughtful engagement with the risen Christ and his message of good news.

Our youth, in fact, guided by Maggie's sensitivities to the formational power of the liturgy, have engaged most deeply and extensively in the cadences of the catechumenate. Our confirmation process is drawn from the same model as our adult catechumenate; yet the young are even more energetically engaged. Their process usually lasts between six and eight months during the year, culminating in the Easter season. Like the *ordo* of the liturgy itself, the confirmation process makes room for creativity, imagination, and deep exploration. Adults who are welcomed as sponsors engage fully in conversation and forge deep and lasting relationships across generations. Like travelers on a mission to a foreign country, they return surprised not by what they gave but by what they received. Many of the youth who have participated in previous years, rather than treating it as the last rite before leaving

---

27. "Don't Be Afraid," by John L. Bell. © 1995, GIA Music.

the church — as confirmation can all too often become — ask to participate again in the process, often serving as sponsors of new inquirers. It has become the heart of a generous life together. Through their conversations and the strong support of leaders within the church structure, our youth have found a springboard for meaningful leadership within worship. Children and youth — based on their readiness and the gifts they bring — are readers, cantors and musicians, choir members, and liturgical assisting ministers. They have found their voice among the assembly in the prayers of the people and in sharing in the life of the community at all levels.

We are preparing to say good-bye to Lydian and her family as they move across the country. It will be an excruciating separation. Lydian, we imagine, was born into and for this congregation as for the world. Her mother was hired to accompany our song; but through their engagement with the congregation, Lydian, together with her parents, was baptized on Pentecost.

Lydian has led us. She has invited us into the mystery of God through her sense of wonder in the sacrament of the bread and the cup. She has helped us think about hospitality as she struggled with the noises made by Jim, who is severely disabled, during worship. With loving guidance from caring adults, she has come to hear his sometimes loud and distracting groans as a heartbeat of our life together, and she has become his fierce protector. Whenever she asks questions about Jim, adults nearby pay attention, because they lack the unique gifts a child brings in being able to ask.

Birthing the catechumenate is a move of subversion. It is a calculated strategy to overthrow the world and evil. It is a way of giving priority to the outsider. It challenges us to join those on the margins in imagining different ways of relationships that point to God's intention to mend the whole of creation, beginning with ourselves.[28] It is a way of growing partnerships across generational lines so that the church will give away its faith for the next generations. *Other* becomes partner. The wolf lies down with the lamb.

A Singing Faith

> You, Lord, are both Lamb and Shepherd.
> You, Lord, are both prince and slave.
> You, peacemaker and sword bringer
> Of the way you took and gave.

28. Cf. Russell, *Just Hospitality*, p. 45.

You the everlasting instant;
You, whom we both scorn and crave.[29]

Sylvia Dunstan's haunting text has become a favorite of ours — especially as it is set to the spacious, lingering tune of "Let All Mortal Flesh Keep Silence." Our transition in the musical ministry that welcomes such wonders as Dunstan's hymn followed the path set by our renewal of worship. Stan had been the longtime choir director at St. Andrew, but he had retired (the first time) prior to my arrival in 2004. Particular aspects of his own story made him something of a seeker, even well into his retirement years. As Stan discovered that St. Andrew, where he had served so dutifully for years, could also be a place to ask the challenging questions that had resided within him, unresolved for so many decades, he found himself increasingly engaged. Soon he was standing once again in front of the choir, but with a fundamentally different job description than he had had for the preceding three decades.

Rather than simply preparing the choir to sing an entertaining anthem that might or might not have had anything to do with what else was happening on that particular Sunday, Stan was now being invited to lead a ministry whose primary role was to lead the congregation in the singing of its prayer.[30] Stan was a bellwether for me: he represented a significant portion of the congregation members who were both blessed and troubled by the reforms we were encouraging. Attending to his questions helped me to gauge the temperature of the congregation. He was an insider who found himself in that deeply unsettling in-between place that marginal people have experienced for so long.[31] He had glimpsed the implications of these reforms for the radical openness of this gospel even as he struggled with deeply held and rarely questioned assumptions of the dominant ecclesial culture that privileges personal preferences and maintains uniformity in so many American

29. "Christus Paradox." First verse of text by Sylvia Dunstan, © 1991, GIA Music.
30. See the *Constitution of the Presbyterian Church (USA), Part II: Book of Order* (Louisville: Office of the General Assembly, 2011), W-2:1004, on Music as Prayer: Choir and Instrumental Music: "To lead the congregation in the singing of prayer is a primary role of the choir and other musicians. They also may pray on behalf of the congregation with introits, responses, and other musical forms. Instrumental music may be a form of prayer since words are not essential to prayer. In worship, music is not to be for entertainment or artistic display. Care should be taken that it not be used merely as a cover for silence. Music as prayer is to be a worthy offering to God on behalf of the people."
31. Cf. Lee, *Marginality,* pp. 29ff.

worshiping communities. We can hear the echoes of the Nairobi statement in Donald Juel's summary of the dynamic possibilities and tensions:

[W]hat we celebrate in worship, perhaps more particularly at the Lord's Table, is the possibility of a primal — and eschatological — unity that transcends our differences. What we are to experience is an essential similarity that will develop as we become better acquainted. The reality is that in most congregations, the "essential similarity" is defined by a particular group, and those integrated into the congregation conform in terms of class and race. Genuine difference is often perceived as a problem to be overcome, and strategies are developed to accomplish this end.[32]

Stan's second retirement found us looking for someone new to work with the choir and to shape our music program to serve the liturgy. For nearly three years before that time, we had been hosting a conversation about the renewal of worship and its power to shape the people of God. We had also been given a great gift in that the Summer Institute for Liturgy and Worship had that year set its sights on the topic "The Sung Word: Congregational Music as Theology." A number of our members, including Stan, participated during that year.

If God was in Jesus-Christ,
the people of God must also be marginal people.[33]

Julie Kae was one of the assisting faculty and primary cantors of the institute, and had served on the board since the institute's inception. She was a 2002 seminary graduate and a certified candidate in the PCUSA, not to mention a well-trained and accomplished singer and instructor with a lengthy résumé.

I remember hearing an old saying about the art of preaching: If you think you're losing people, don't speed up, slow down. I understood it to suggest that, if a thing is important enough, you need to give it space and time to let people catch up. You need to emphasize it more, not less: that is, aim higher, not lower. We aimed higher in the shaping of the music position at St. Andrew. We advocated for a vision of transformative leadership. We

---

32. Donald Juel, "Multicultural Worship: A Pauline Perspective," in Brian K. Blount and Leonora Tubbs Tisdale, eds., *Making Room at the Table: An Invitation to Multicultural Worship* (Louisville: Westminster John Knox, 2001), p. 48.

33. Lee, *Marginality*, p. 4.

shaped a role in conformity to the centrality of worship in transcending our differences according to the essential unity in diversity of the triune God encountered in the juxtapositions of the liturgy. Even though our resources were limited, our vision was not. This was not an easy sell for some in that congregation, those who could not imagine that we were the kind of congregation that would attract talented people. Julie Kae was interested in that position, and in September 2008 she joined our work.

A House of Prayer for All Nations

"Every year," said Grandfather, "they run amuck. I let them. Pride of lions in the yard. Stare, and they burn a hole in your retina. A common flower, a weed that no one sees, yes. But for us, a noble thing, the dandelion."[34]

Suddenly I heard a familiar voice: "Daddy, Daddy." I was brought back to the present, then saw the yellow flower in my hand. I looked at it anew. It was no longer ugly. . . . Instead of throwing it away, I brought it into my house and put it in a plastic cup filled with fresh water. Like the golden sun, the flower shined on in my house for a long time. Several days later its head turned white. I took it outside, and blew on it as hard as I could. The white seeds sailed high and began to fall like parachutes all over the rich green yards. "Let them live — let them live anywhere they want. It is God's world, and they are God's creatures," I said as I watched them.[35]

After her graduation and the completion of the many requirements within the PCUSA for certification, Julie Kae continued to work with choirs and in liturgical leadership in multiple congregations. But she never found a path to ordination; indeed, by the time she came to St. Andrew in September 2008, she had let go of her deep sense that she was called to ordained pastoral ministry. Yet, as she became a part of our life together, and joined her wisdom and sensitivities to Maggie's and those of other paid and unpaid leaders, a seed of hope, once dormant, began to take root.

34. Ray Bradbury, *Dandelion Wine* (New York: Bantam, 1947; 1975), p. 12.
35. Lee, *Marginality*, p. 13.

First, Julie Kae turned her attention to the choir, which had such deep and nostalgic roots within the life of the congregation. This was both a gift and a challenge. Some of the deepest resistance to change had found a home in the choir. In week after week of practice and cajoling and intentional musical selection and nonanxious leadership, the choir transitioned from a small group of nonprofessional singers who prepared weekly anthems to a well of courage and musical leadership for an assembly that was quickly learning to sing its faith in new ways. Youth joined with adults in singing an increasingly diverse library of music that celebrated the faith present in all regions of the globe. Children led our song; youth accompanied music selected to accommodate their levels of ability. Thus has our practice intentionally and carefully demonstrated that there is no age that cannot proclaim the theology of the church. The people of St. Andrew began to get the sense that we were about something bigger than had been imagined. Through the more anxious early years of transition many carefully negotiated accommodations had been made to keep peace and promote love between various "camps" within the congregation. Our sanctuary, while not particularly beautiful, is modular. We rearranged seating to conform to liturgical seasons in ways that taught and formed us. The frequency of communion has been gradually increased over the years as we move toward weekly Eucharist. Various forms of midweek prayer were instituted. Service to local children was linked with a communal meal and evening prayer, at which we rehearsed some of the songs and psalms set for Sunday. The children became liturgical ministers in their own right. Dandelions sprouted among a people who were coming to celebrate their noble gifts. Slowly but surely, a congregation has emerged shaped around hospitality and openness to the stranger (see Heb. 12:28ff). And alongside these developments came the steady growth of a dream that had now taken root and sprouted. Julie Kae was ordained a "teaching elder," or "minister of word and sacrament."

Baptismal Theology/Marginal Theologies

A multicultural community is not one where otherness is obliterated. Rather, it is a community of hospitality in which the richness of individual gifts and the mystery of the other are celebrated.[36]

---

36. Blount and Tisdale, *Making Room at the Table* (Louisville: Westminster John Knox, 2001), p. xi.

The more closely marginal people want to identify themselves with central people, the more intensely they experience alienation. . . . The norm that validates their theology is not that of dominant-group people but of new marginal people who live in-beyond.

Postcolonial theologians are particularly aware that all theology is local. Our location shapes what we do, what we understand, what we articulate. There is a hermeneutic of suspicion that the multisightedness of theology has been nothing more than the cordial welcome of diversity. Unless we are willing to shift the center, to recognize and acknowledge that we have placed the canon of the dominant Western, Enlightenment theology at the center, rather than in its proper place in orbit, we will not move beyond this cordial welcome toward deeper truths and justice.

Perhaps we need a Copernican revolution of theology — a new orbit where words about God take the rightful center place and Western, white male theology moves from the center and takes its place among the other theological "planets."[37] Even though those traditions commonly referred to as "sacramental" are often associated with hierarchical ecclesial structures that preserve and protect a powerful class of Christians within a privileged "Copernican" theological center, liturgical theology understands that rooted in the ancient patterns of the *ordo* is a centrifugal force that resists all tendencies to privilege. Indeed, even as we are well aware of the relative lack of ethnic diversity at St. Andrew, and of the *metanoia* that must occur in order for authentically multicultural ecclesial communities to thrive, we do believe that the foundation has been laid for the kinds of evolution that speaks promise to a vision of an increasingly diverse worshiping community that reflects the diversity of the reign of God. For, at the heart of Christianity, after all, is its central figure, who was the ultimate marginal figure, one who bridges all divides and speaks to the radical welcome of God not only to all people, but to all creation.

If God was in Jesus-Christ,
the people of God must also be marginal people.[38]

37. Thanks to Charlene Jin Lee for these insights, which I gained in her class entitled "Self, Other, and Community," Summer 2011 Doctor of Ministry course at San Francisco Theological Seminary. Lee draws on Letty Russell's definition of theology as simply "words about God."

38. Lee, *Marginality*, p. 4.

Postscript: About St. Andrew Presbyterian Church's Logo

The inspiration to create an image representing St. Andrew was the Fiftieth Anniversary Celebration in November 2012, coinciding with the reorganization of St. Andrew's governing body, the Session.[39] The image background is comprised of four squares. They aren't perfectly square because as humans we are imperfect. We bring who we are to this place, and are reminded of God's absolute, unconditional love. The symbols represent more than just one category and are interchangeable.

- The white space and circle overlaying the squares represent a Celtic cross. When the squares are separated, part of the circle still appears in each square to signify that they are each part of a whole, one body.
- The four colors are liturgical colors: blue for Advent, purple for Lent, red for Pentecost, and green for ordinary time.
- The symbols in the four squares represent the four ministries of our governing body, the Session, and more broadly, represent part of who we are as St. Andrew.
  The green square represents *creation care and sustainability.*
  The red square represents *proclamation and evangelism.*
  The blue square represents *compassion, justice, and peace.*
  The purple square represents *worship and the arts.*
- The water image in the compassion, justice, and peace square reminds us of baptism. The three ripples of water evoke an image of us moving out into the world. The three water rings remind us of the Trinity.
- The three people in the worship and the arts square again remind us of

39. The color image can be seen at http://www.standrewpc.org/get-involved.html.

the Trinity. Their arms are raised in worship. And the different body forms represent diversity and inclusiveness of our congregation.

- The trunk and base of the tree of creation care and sustainability are made from the female figure from the worship and the arts symbol. The limbs of the tree are the same outstretched arms of the three figures in worship embracing different forms of creation — plant (an apple, pear) and animal (bird).
- The flames in the proclamation and evangelism square represent light and passion; an unquenchable spark of the divine that exists in us and among us. Sometimes it flickers and can be fragile, but when tended gives light and a way forward.

Dynamics of World Musics: A Methodology for Evaluation

Mark P. Bangert

Large-scale festivities for the Protestant Church of Bali normally involve Balinese dancing and the gamelan orchestra. Attending one of these events leaves one with the sense that here is the inculturated worshiping church at its best. In liturgies for churchwide festivities, young female dancers, usually about a dozen teenagers, offer their choreography through a sign language that is both understood by the worshipers and capable of carrying the message of the gospel. The fifteen or more members of the gamelan orchestra, all dressed in brightly colored costumes, sit to play their instruments, which include a variety of metalophones, xylophones, and gongs. Dancers and musicians carry on a dialogue, each group urging the other one on. Coming at the beginning of the liturgy, it is a kind of invitation to worship in an envelope that is recognizably Balinese, and, one suspects, appealing to the deep cultural roots of the people.

Experienced observers still thrill to the exotic sounds of the gamelan scale patterns, even as they cannot fail to be impressed by the musical and choreographic intricacies, all in a way reflective of Balinese life and faith. But if they stay around for more of the liturgy, they will hear all the people together sing hymns that are either Western in style or direct Western imports. With that, some of the exuberance over inculturation can dissipate. What goes on here among the more than sixty thousand people who belong to the Protestant Church of Bali lifts up a variety of opportunities and challenges facing churches both young and old. Like Christian churches all over the world, these Balinese worshipers use their own musical resources while they are simultaneously charmed by a hymnody from another culture. While the gamelan and its dancers are indeed marvelous examples of inculturated worship, they are never-theless performance-oriented and nonparticipatory. Does the gamelan really belong in the liturgy? If so, should it be balanced by other indigenous music that is more capable of carrying the assembly's song? Do the carvings that adorn the gamelan instruments, carvings that portray old Balinese under-standings of the yin-and-yang struggles between good and evil, represent a theology at odds with Christian teaching? Questions such as these are — or probably will be — asked by the Balinese Christians themselves.

Their struggles and joys in their own music give us all energy to search for those common dynamics that emerge when worship takes on musical form, no matter where one is in the world. To do that is a daunting, perhaps impossible, task, since the hundreds of micromusics across the world offer few universals.[1] Contrary to a popular adage, music is not a universal lan-guage. Work in micromusics around the world has taught us that. Common denominators are minimal, but a search for what can be said about all music, especially vocal music, can still be fruitful.

Before we begin such a search, there is time for happy wonder. Around the world Christians are breaking out in song that is birthed from the wombs of their own cultures. It is happening in Africa, in Bali, in India, in Thailand, in Taiwan, in Bangladesh, and in Latin America. When Martin Luther, fol-lowing Augustine's lead, boldly asserted that music was part of the creation, he probably was not thinking of bhajans from India, for instance, but his theology welcomes that new song, too. As younger churches explore their own musics, and as older churches reexamine assumptions about liturgy and music in a world grown musically complex, it is possible to lift up some common dynamics that can serve all Christians seeking to channel the mu-sical impulse in their worship. We begin with a concern for the ecology of music, will continue by exploring the inner connections between text and music, then propose a grid for structural analysis of music in worship while sorting out the possibilities and problems connected to meaning in music, and finally conclude with a word about the muse itself. It will become clear that individual parts of the plan take major facets of Luther's theology of music and apply them to the challenges and opportunities of worship set in the micromusics of the world.

---

1. The term "micromusic" refers to a musical system and repertoire belonging to a subculture. For instance, within the Western European musical culture one can distinguish Scandinavian music, but within Scandinavian music the music of the Sami people (formerly Laplanders) can be considered a micromusic.

Ecology

Music may not be a universal language, but it is present in one form or another in every culture on this earth. There is a wondrous array of micromusics across the globe, all related in one way or another to the world's five major musical systems: Greco-Roman/European, Persian, Chinese, Indian, and Indonesian. A major musical system is differentiated by a developed complex of notation and by a history of written theoretical materials. Each one of these systems has developed in its own way, and each displays some mutual influences. One of the Javanese scales systems, for instance, is based on an equidistant pentatonic division of the octave. That same octave division is thought by some to have shaped the scale systems of Eastern Africa, though Eastern African music also shares family traits with the Greco-Roman system.

In spite of these complexities, it can be said that all the world's peoples sing, that in all societies music is used in religious ritual, that in all cultures music is used to transform ordinary experience, and that, for all peoples, music is an emblem of identity.[2] Why one culture chooses a particular division of the octave, or why it sings in its own peculiar way, are matters influenced by a variety of factors, perhaps best summed up by the observation that a given society develops its music in accordance with the character of its social system.[3] None of the congruences mentioned so far represents some common technical building block. The musical products themselves will not yield common, unifying elements. Therefore, any search for commonality among musical systems is more promising when it is centered in the musical impulse itself. Among all peoples there is evidence for such a musical impulse. It is a human characteristic that invites us to think of it as part of God's design for creation. However, how that musical impulse is expressed — and, more importantly, why it works itself out — are matters that will also interest those of us who wish to explore the relationships between worship and music.

Because we have now intersected with one of Luther's principal theological observations, his view of music's origins is worth a closer look. Luther was trained in music at the University of Wittenberg. The study text for music there was written by Jean de Muris (fourteenth century), who was also a strong proponent of the universality of music. Muris, following the

2. Bruno Neill et al., *Excursions in World Music* (Englewood Cliffs, NJ: Prentice Hall, 1992), pp. 6-7.
    3. Neill et al., *Excursions*, p. 11.

medieval quadrivium of arithmetic, geometry, astronomy, and music, believed music to be founded on mathematical principles. He was only following Pythagoras, of course; yet Luther learned that number was at the base of everything. Therefore, music as audible number was universal, a part of creation, and since creation was good, music must also be a gift from God. That excited Luther, and the excitement has been with Lutherans ever since.

Whether one locates the universality of music in the musical impulse or in created numerical law, the point remains the same: music is a part of creation and is thus meant by God to be a good thing. Basing the origins of music in the musical impulse opens doors immediately to its many cultural manifestations. The musical impulse — that musical imagination that is present in all peoples — needs to be cared for as if one were caring for a good gift of creation meant by the Creator for the welfare of people. To lose any micromusic is to lose a manifestation of the musical impulse — as if losing a species of creation. Like other parts of the creation, the musical impulse suffers from the effects of sin. It can be made to serve perverse ends. Alert Christians will want to respond to attempts that threaten the fragile ecology of music in this world. In an article on the popular music industry, one Australian commentator issues this alarming observation:

> MTV: This giant advertising network has ensured that white Anglo-American popular music has consolidated its international hegemony visually as well as aurally.[4]

Most major record stores today offer a section containing "world music," a category that originated in 1987 and holds displays of recordings bringing together micromusics in a hybrid way. To some it might mean new and interesting combinations of sounds and systems; on another level, though, it means the mining of musics, as raw resources, from Latin America, Africa, and Asia, to serve the entrepreneurial hungers of pop-music producers. It would be one thing if this busy process of mining were producing some notable results; rather, this "commodity fetishism" has nothing more to show than a "shallow array of surfaces."[5] In the last century, missionaries delivered the gospel via cultural structures and methods that were, in retro-

---

4. Tony Mitchell, "World Music and the Popular Music Industry: An Australian View," *Ethnomusicology* 37, no. 3 (Fall 1993): 310.

5. Mitchell, "World Music," pp. 335-36. See also Marshall Blonsky, *American Mythologies* (New York: Oxford, 1992), pp. 17ff., for a lively discussion of "surface" in popular culture.

spect, blatantly imperialistic. That same kind of imperialism is at work again. This time its results are more insidious because current electronic gadgets enable the projection of Western musical will across time zones to any place in the world. Luther's basic insight about music, nature, and creation can and must be taken up anew in our midst. Care for the micromusics of this world should lead us to resist the profit-motivated plundering of earth's wondrous sounds, to tell the real story of MTV, and, above all, to nurture local musics inside and outside the church.

Text Longing for Melody

A baby's crying may not be music to its parents' ears, but it is clear that the body's mechanisms that facilitate crying are the very same mechanisms that the child uses for singing. The outcry, the shout, the acclamation, the amorous sighs of lovers, litanies of pleading, even children's games — they all seem to long for melodic expression. Heightened speech or zealous communication moves quickly to musical utterance. It is possible to speak of a self-contained continuum that moves from whispering on one end to song at the other. All oral communication occurs somewhere on that continuum, and, when impassioned, it advances to another place on the continuum. If, as some hold, liturgy is a repository of outcries, shouts, acclamations, and outbursts of love, then worship is never without music. Because it is sounded with pitches and can claim its own rhythm, spoken text is essentially musical, potentially melodic.

Spoken text often seems to yearn for melody as well. Why this longing occurs is not clear. Could it be that heightened speech is longing for a certain fullness, which melody can begin to provide? Or could it be that this longing occurs because melody is itself the tool by which the text, with some of its nuances, is preserved and remembered for further use? Perhaps all of that. Luther brilliantly recognized the unity of text and music as a pillar of theology. He wrote from a culture that was still essentially oral, but he seemed to anticipate the imminent revolution in printing when he differentiated between word/language/message, on the one hand, and tone/speech/voice, on the other. The former complex is about concept, grammar, and structure, while the latter refers to nuanced delivery, rhythm, and sound. A full and complete communication includes sound and is thus existential. Luther perceived that — theologically speaking — for the Word to become flesh at any time requires some kind of musical delivery.

Thus it was not without reason that the fathers and prophets wanted nothing else to be associated as closely with the Word of God as music. Therefore, we have so many hymns and Psalms where message and music [Sermo et vox] join to move the listener's soul. . . . After all, the gift of language combined with the gift of song was only given to man to let him know that he should praise God with both words and music, namely, by proclaiming [the Word of God] though music and by providing sweet melodies with words.[6]

Therefore, theology and music cannot be separated; a desire to articulate the gospel always leads to a musical expression. Music is also on the scene once the gospel is heard, for it is the primal and quintessential way by which one can express joy, the first response to the announcement of the gospel. In a very profound way, Luther understood music to be the natural form of the gospel.[7] For these reasons Luther exclaims that, next to theology, he "gives music the highest honor."[8]

We must take seriously once again the longing of gospel text for melody. It seems that there are no choices here, not *whether* the gospel will be dynamically inculturated musically, but *how* the gospel will be inculturated musically. This is at the heart of being Lutheran: that is, Word is taken to be an oral thing, an enfleshed event, seeking a voice *(vox)*, longing for fulfillment in song, hymn, or dance. As the musical impulse gives flesh to these longings within the world's cultures, a colorful array of musical possibilities emerges. Some examples follow to illustrate the variety of ways the gospel takes on musical form shaped by cultural inclinations.

First is an example of music that has transformed a bit of the text, from the liturgy used by a diocesan seminary near Arusha, Tanzania. At the conclusion of the Mass the priest dismisses the people, and they respond, in Swahili: *Asame, Bwana, Jesu, kwa mema vako* ("Thanks, Lord Jesus, for all your gifts"). Set to music in this Tanzanian example, the song is typically African as it uses the familiar call-response pattern. In this version, the call parts are improvised to highlight the occasion. Note that the song begins without any official signal.

---

6. Martin Luther, "Preface to Georg Rhau's Symphoniae iucundae," *Luther's Works,* American ed. (Philadelphia: Fortress; St. Louis: Concordia, 1955), 53:323-24. Hereafter, this edition will be referred to as *LW.*

7. Walter Blankenburg, "Luther und die Musik," in Erich Huebner and Route Steiger, *Kirche und Musik* (Göttingen: Vandenhoeck & Ruprecht, 1979), p. 23.

8. Luther, "Preface," p. 323.

A second example takes us back several centuries to the time of J. S. Bach. Most Lutherans have some allegiance to this great composer but do not know exactly why he figures so prominently within the Lutheran family. He and others of his contemporaries took seriously Luther's linkage of word and music and pressed the concept yet again by creating musical sermons, now known as cantatas. For the last section of such a cantata, which he wrote for Christmas Day, Bach chose to sum up his message with a stanza from Luther's Christmas hymn, *Vom Himmel hoch* ("From Heaven Above"): "Ah, Dearest Jesus, holy child/come, make a bed soft, undefiled/within my heart that it may be/a quiet chamber kept for thee." The four lines of the stanza are interspersed with trumpet and drum fanfares to make clear that this little child is at the same time a monarch.

A third example illustrates how prayer and meditation also long for melody. One form of popular religious music in India is the *bhajan,* a song that encourages meditation and contemplation through a loving rehearsal of God's names. Among Christians the *bhajan* is often used as music to be sung while the Eucharist is distributed.

Finally, text linked to melody is frequently used by Christians as a mode of private or small-group worship. In the area surrounding Udon Thani in northeast Thailand, Christians carry the memory of the assembly from meeting to meeting by singing and playing religious folk songs, some in a dialogical form (called *Maw lum*). These songs are group events: they encourage participation by several people at the same time.

Text longing for melody is more than a useful observation to explain what has happened among Christians in many times and in many places. As a theological insight it wants to be implemented as the mode for proclaiming the gospel in any culture and as faith's first response to the Holy Spirit.

Critical Impulses and Emerging Recipes

As soon as liturgical text finds melody, it seems, passionate guardians of the cult mobilize the critical impulse. Beginning jarringly with the prophet Amos (5:23f.), persisting doubts about music continued with Clement, Tertullian, and Augustine; appeared in the proceedings of ecclesiastical councils; appeared in the famous bull of Pope John XXII (*Docta sanctorum Patrum,* 1324-25); drove the very radical thought of Zwingli; hovered over the Council of Trent; preoccupied Lutheran orthodox theologians and Lutheran pietists; and influenced the worship practice of Lutheran missionaries. Reluctance about music has been fueled by a fear of syncretism; or by scruples regarding God's own appreciation of the music; or by a fear of being distracted from more important parts of worship; or by a fear that the liturgy will lose its purpose; or even by a fear of what was believed to be music's own seductive powers. Those who are awaking to the blessed possibilities of planting worship within the myriad micromusics of today's world often move with hesitation, slowed by the same old worries. Dare we ignore that critical impulse? Does it have substance? Is there something we should say about music in worship? Can it simply be given free rein? Is there some way it can be safely channeled?

For all of his enthusiasm about music, Luther himself responded critically to the impulse to receive music. He was vitally concerned about song and its influential role as the vehicle of life in the Christian worshiping community. For what else is his concern for the vernacular than to make it possible for all the people to mouth the word? For what else are his hymn paraphrases of the ordinary (*Kyrie, Sanctus,* etc.) — some of the very first hymns composed and much loved — than a way to get all the people together singing the liturgy? So he admonished parishioners: "Sing with the congregation and you will sing well."[9] When he sought to engage George Spalatin to write new hymns he advised: "In order to be understood by the people, use only the simplest and the most common words."[10] He knew instinctively that a reformed worshiping community needed a song that followed some overriding principles. That they should be anchored partly in the worshiping assembly makes him more contemporary than what we might at first think. But for him and for us, the development of critical principles rests on how we understand music to have meaning.

Given that the musical impulse shows up in human societies throughout the world, it should be possible to discover a common dynamic that escorts and energizes that impulse into musical event. As long as there might be agreement on the definition and meaning of music, such a supposition might hold promise. But there is no single and intercultural concept defining what music is. Definitions vary across the world, for music's contours are understood to range from noise to organized sound to language to game to dance and to social action.[11] If there is no consensus on music's contours, there can be little agreement on its meaning.

---

9. Luther, "An Exposition of the Lord's Prayer for Simple Laymen," *LW,* 42:60.

10. Luther, "To Georg Spalatin" (1523), *LW,* 49:69.

11. Jean-Jacques Nattiez, *Music and Discourse: Toward a Semiology of Music,* trans. Carolyn Abbate (Princeton, NJ: Princeton University Press, 1990), pp. 55, 58.

Attempts at finding universal meaning are instructive. Within Western musicological thought (and sometimes it seems as though *meaning* is a distinctly Western preoccupation), according to Leonard Meyer, meaning in music is thought to be delivered via one of two broad pathways. Some hold that there is no meaning in music outside of the musical structures themselves (e.g., a chord has meaning only as it relates to another chord, and it has no other meaning). If someone should claim meaning for music outside these purely analytical connections, such a one brings meaning to the musical event. Meyer identifies this category as "absolutionist."

The other approach — "referentialist," as Meyer labels it — holds that the structures and tools of a musical system innately bear extramusical meaning (e.g., upwards melodic movement implies tension and therefore excitement, anxiety, joy, etc.). [12] Within the referentialist camp there are smaller tribal gatherings, some worth mentioning because they are home for many who think and speak of church music. For one such subgroup, music is referenced to natural law, which then suggests that meaning in music is to be found in the cosmic laws that are held to be mirrored in the musical event. Beginning most clearly with Boethius (470?-525), this view concerning meaning dominated the church's thinking on music for over a millennium. Luther took on this tradition. We have noted his fondness for connecting music to the laws of the universe. Natural-law partisans, however, have struggled for years with the bothersome imperfections that acoustical principles impose — especially on the West's favorite way of dividing the octave. Using the interval of the perfect fifth as the primary interval, Western theorists derive the twelve pitches of the scale by building a series of fifths. Theoretically, this series should lead back to the original pitch, but instead it leads to an imperfect unison, one slightly off-key. That nagging imperfection mars a search for musical meaning in what one might suppose to be perfectly balanced law.

Another subgroup holds that the significance of music derives from its ability to reference an alternate time system, since musical time, or one's perception of it, usually differs from clock time — or one's perception of it. Music offers one a world of virtual time, which provides insight apart from clock time. [13] Insofar as music can offer such an experience, it becomes a means by which humans can symbolically transcend the strictures of the clock. This is its meaning, say some.

---

12. Leonard Meyer, *Emotion and Meaning in Music* (Chicago: University of Chicago Press, 1956), pp. 1-6.

13. Jonathan Kramer, *The Time of Music* (New York: Scribner's, 1988).

A third subgroup of referentialists seeks meaning in music through feelings that, many claim, accompany participation in the musical event. Victor Zuckerkandl, one contemporary proponent of this theory, explains that a melody has "something" that a random series of notes does not, and that "something" is a dynamic quality that creates a feeling over and above the simple existence of the notes.[14] Yet, for the sake of argument, if such a feeling does arise from a musical event (and some would say feelings are brought to the event), it is likely to be culture-bound. While perhaps not demonstrable, it is difficult to imagine that a given song will generate the same feeling in every human being.

While great debates about these matters continue among Western commentators in particular, a breath of fresh air has blown into the heated discussions from ethnomusicologists. Again and again, studies of world musics offer a way out of the absolutist/referentialist deadlock. Ethnomusicologists urge us to think of music as something much more than the sound event itself or notes on a page. Any usable definition of music, Alan Merriam proposed in 1964, must include its generating concepts, the actual product, and the behavior that accompanies and follows the sound event.[15] Especially with the inclusion of behavior in a definition of music, Merriam provides a way to think more universally about the micromusics of the world.

The far-reaching consequences of this comprehensive definition can be illustrated by John Blacking's study of music among the Venda people of Africa. "Music," he felt confident to summarize, "confirms what is already present in society and culture, and it adds nothing new except patterns of sound." Its chief function is to "involve people in shared experiences within the framework of their cultural experience."[16] Across cultures it serves "to promote soundly organized humanity by enhancing human consciousness." Music is "social text," John Shepherd has written.[17] It is to be understood through its sociological dimensions. This focus on behavior, as we revert to Merriam's tripartite definition of music, has gathered notable momentum, and, as if ignoring any forthcoming and telling criticism from the deconstructionists, proponents of the meaning-is-in-the-doing approach to music

14. This according to John Shepherd, *Music as Social Text* (Cambridge, MA: Polity Press, 1991), p. 63.

15. Alan Merriam, *The Anthropology of Music* (Evanston, IL: Northwestern University Press, 1964), p. 32.

16. John Blacking, *How Musical Is Man?* (Seattle: University of Washington Press, 1973), pp. 48, 54.

17. Shepherd, *Music as Social Text,* pp. 11-18.

have begun to look for meaning in the specific societal structures of the musical events themselves. The potentials and challenges of such a search are no more clearly seen than in the so-called Cantometrics Project, begun by ethnomusicologist Alan Lomax and his team about thirty years ago. Their discoveries beg for attention from anyone wanting to address the relationship of worship and music, for they take the conversation to a place that makes possible a reasonable methodology by which to critically evaluate the music of worship.

The Cantometrics Project has been most succinctly described by Jean-Jacques Nattiez:

> [Lomax's] objective is twofold: his first goal is to establish on a global scale, from a comparative point of view, stylistic characterizations of 233 specific musical cultures, belonging to 56 cultural areas. In pursuing his second goal he tries to relate the music-stylistic traits he inventories to cultural traits proper to limited areas, to arrive at an explanation of each style in terms of the culture to which it belongs.[18]

Or, as Lomax himself writes, "as people live so do they sing."[19] Song style, he discovered, responds to the following six variables:

1. Productive range [how people work]
2. Political level
3. Level of stratification of class
4. Severity of sexual mores
5. Balance of dominance between male and female
6. Level of social cohesiveness (p. 6)

If there is one single discovery that arises from the project, it is that a culture's favored song style reflects and reinforces the kind of behavior that is considered essential to its work habits and to its core and prevailing social institutions. Lomax and his colleagues concentrated their research efforts on performance characteristics, discovering further that there are several basic frameworks that are determinative:

18. For the influence of Claude Lévi-Strauss on Alan Lomax, see Nattiez, *Music and Discourse,* pp. 171, 169.

19. Alan Lomax, *Folk Song Style and Culture* (New Brunswick, NJ: Transaction Books, 1968), p. 4. Hereafter, page references to this work appear in parentheses within the text.

1. As a joint communication, song requires tacit agreement from its participants to abide by the musical formulas of the group. Performance organizes unity of purpose.
2. Music is socially louder than speech, and it tends to knit its participants together in a unified reaction or action; song, however, can silence an individual, or an individual singer can silence the group.
3. Basic to the whole study is the level of participation, particularly the ratio of group to individual or individual to group (pp. 14-15).

Song performances, researchers found, ranged on a continuum between the poles of individual and integrated (group deliveries). On the one hand, an individualized, group-dominating performance came about when a solo singer dominated the acoustical space, thereby in effect silencing the group. On the other hand, a highly cohesive group-involving performance made it possible for all to join in acoustically and socially. Each of the pole models displayed certain recurring musical characteristics:

Individualized	Integrated
Solo	Choral, multileveled, cohesive
Textually complex	Uncomplicated text
Metrically complex	Metrically simple
Melodically complex	Melodically simple
Ornamented	No ornamentation
Usually noisy voice	Usually clear voice
Precise enunciation	Slurred enunciation (p. 16)

Lomax and team arrived at their conclusions by sampling over twenty-five hundred songs and by using an elaborate coding book that permitted evaluations of thirty-seven characteristics. Among those characteristics are tempo, volume, rubato, glissando, melisma, tremolo, vocal width, nasality, raspiness, consonant production, phrase length, and so on. The project also included recognition of dance and movement style, phonemic patterning in sung verse, and conceptual patterns in sung verse. While instrumental accompaniment was included in the coding book when it was part of the song, instrumental music by itself was considered to be outside the focus of the project.

The study has demonstrated how closely linked music and behavior are and provides information concerning just what meaning music can have. Worship comprises much more than behavior, but how a worshiping assembly interacts and understands itself is a primary concern for worship leaders and liturgical agents. One way to utilize the project, then, would be to compile a list of characteristics that describe an ideal worshiping Christian community, and then to see what, according to the cantometrics study, that community's music might look like. Such a proposal immediately poses a problem: a worshiping community is not fully a culture; on the other hand, it does bear traits that suggest it has culture-like qualities. Besides, we are accustomed to describing the church as countercultural, implying that it is, in fact, a kind of culture. Here, then, are some characteristics that might describe an ideal liturgical assembly:

1. Energized by a message, purpose, hope, and power, all of which originate from outside the individuals of the assembly, the group thus does not look to itself for initiative.
2. Carries out its interchanges dialogically both when at worship and when not.
3. Affirms its unity while inviting into its midst a diversity of gifts because they are edifying.
4. Functions by recognizing the equality of male/female, young/old.
5. Embraces degrees of complexity regarding matters of social status, economic position, and educational levels of its members.
6. Provides information relative to the needs and abilities of its members.
7. Is action-oriented, that is, intends to translate worship into individual and corporate daily life.
8. Is conscious of living presently in two time systems — clock time and the "time to come."
9. Is determined to deal with contextual reality, and resists the inclination to escape from the world.
10. Encourages the "jazz factor" — the unpredictable presence of the Spirit.

Some predictable characteristics of song in such an assembly would be:

1. The song will be of the integrated type, that is, it will tend to be choral, multileveled, cohesive, textually repetitious, uncomplicated in melody and meter, with little or no ornamentation, favoring the clear voice and some slurred enunciation. Solo offerings will be welcome from time to time but only as they edify and support the group (1 Cor. 14). Because the Christian assembly depends on external initiative, its song will include little from individual claims to special insight; rather, it will incarnate what it corporately holds to be true (p. 14).

2. The integrated song of the assembly will include some degree of solo/group interaction. Lomax offers some ways this interaction might occur:

a. Interlock: leaderless song, often present in Africa, where songs are learned together with customary pitch
b. Simple social unison: someone may begin, but the part is soon swallowed up.
c. Overlap: song proceeds on the pattern of alternation between leader and group.
d. Simple alternation: this indicates a clear differentiation between group and leader.

3. Instrumental participation will be simple and supportive (but see no. 1 above). Pure instrumental sections within a song tend to silence the assembly. Basically, orchestral complexity reflects social rigidity and is thus not hospitable to the needs of the assembly (p. 154). If instruments are to be used, the ideal Christian musical expression may be heterophony: at least two sound producers delivering a melody simultaneously but with idiomatic variations.

4. Melodic embellishment, glissando, and other devices of ornamentation will occur rarely, because they are more characteristic of solo song. Elaborate songs are found in highly stratified societies where the fate of every individual depends on a carefully defined relationship to the superstructure (p. 151).

5. Vocal style will be free and clear. Vocal tension accompanies fear that is related to sexual mores. For example, women who must live according to sexual standards different from men will show tension in their voices (pp. 195-96).

6. In parishes of more complex social stratification, songs with heavy information loads will occur more frequently. Songs dense with information serve worshiping groups who are well educated, for instance, since the pieces are expected to define with precision the bonds that hold the group together. Where Christians are a minority within a larger culture, the same inclination will be at work, for Christians need to know how they differ from their neighbors (pp. 137-38).

7. Most songs will be delivered with two simultaneous voice parts (as in octaves) to reflect the equality of male/female, and young/old.

8. Song patterns will reflect the work patterns of the group. For instance, choir/people alternations on songs indicate a division of labor or a collabo-

rative approach to all tasks (pp. 195-96). Centralized authority in a single individual, or groups whose labor is delegated to a favored few, will tend to silence integrated group performance.

9. Worshiping groups that have a high sense of spatial freedom among the individual members will prefer songs with wide interval gaps.[20]

10. Some of the songs will incorporate an implicit invitation to dance, an invitation understood by the majority but not necessarily acted on in an overt fashion. Lomax observes that "dance functions to establish and renew consensus at moments when a society . . . is ready to act in concert."[21] African and African-American Christians readily use concerted physical movement in worship. Some Thai Christians, too, allow song to lead to dance. Evidence remains scant for this kind of linkage among Lutherans. One way to account for Lutheran reluctance may be that what is implicit is not automatically permitted. There may be a correlation between lack of dance and Lutheran hesitancy to act on belief. Within worship, dance should be understood to include all kinds of common movements and gestures.

These ten observations constitute a methodology for evaluating worship set in a musical context. The recurring emphasis on the prominence of assembly song, as opposed to individual offering, reiterates some of Luther's concerns. Should a parish lean toward a style opposite to what is described in the ten points, there is reason to examine its self-understanding of worship, perhaps providing a momentous opportunity to redirect its liturgical practice.

Two final observations accompany this attempt to offer a "Lutheran cantometrics." First, I submit these observations as guidelines for music within worship. Many Christians — and Lutherans in particular — also make religious music outside of the worship of the community. In such cases an entirely different set of descriptions could be developed to accommodate extraliturgical needs of both individuals and the community itself. Examples abound: for example, the sixteenth-century catechism songs designed to catechize the youth pleasantly and the folk-based narrative chants currently used in northeast Thailand to teach Old Testament stories.[22]

---

20. The Sami people, formerly known as Laplanders, inhabit areas of the far north in Norway, Sweden, Finland, and parts of Russia. Historically, the economy of the Samis has been tied to the reindeer herds, which necessitates a considerable willingness for mobility on their part.

21. Lomax, *Folk Song Style,* p. 224.

22. These presentations, called Leh, follow the pattern of old Thai chants that recount the deep stories of the culture and are punctuated by acclamations from the listeners.

Second, the influential French politician/philosopher Jacques Attali believes that it is helpful for us to understand that music, together with all its other characteristics, is also noise.[23] Because music is channeled or controlled noise, it can exert power over uncontrolled noise. Uncontrolled noise is destructive — and therefore violent. But music can overcome such noise, can exercise control, and thus it is powerful. People who make music actively join forces to silence the violence, and this is, according to Attali, one of music's chief functions. Whenever people are silenced, they are victims of noise and those who manipulate it. MTV, insofar as it silences the individual, is a world of noise. But there is hope. In the midst of society gone mute, there is an occasional commuter who hums along with the Walkman, and more and more people line up to sing along with the Karaoke machine, especially in certain areas of southeast Asia. If music as channeled noise muffles the power of noise (violence), then — in a most profound way — sung words of the gospel are both song and a means of God's saving work in the world. To sing in worship, therefore, is to participate in the saving power of the paschal mystery, the death and resurrection of Christ.

The Last Word

I have proposed that a focus on the musical event as behavior releases us from aesthetic theories as a base for evaluating worldwide musical expressions of worship. Behavioral dimensions, especially as they have been broadly studied by Lomax and coworkers, provide a set of expectations for the shape of music in worship. These expectations can serve partially as critique; they can offer some direction; they can even become a kind of emerging recipe. But they can never become a rigid mold, simply because there are too many variables from culture to culture, from assembly to assembly.

One of those variables is the musical impulse itself. Earlier I listed the "jazz factor" as a characteristic of the worshiping community. In jazz music, players and singers best practice the style when they "swing" the beat and/or bend the intonation of selected pitches. Square beats (clock-like pulses) invite and enforce conformity, according to certain Western understandings of rhythm. But the jazz musician, in search of alternative visions, addresses

23. Jacques Allali, *Noise: The Political Economy of Music,* trans. Brian Massumi (Minneapolis: University of Minnesota Press, 1985).

them with a kind of anticipatory or delayed freedom, which attains significance only because of continued recognition of the pulse. Bent intonations are similar in that expected pitches are lowered for effect. Both examples push the edges of accepted musical convention, and are likewise manifestations of the basic musical impulse.

This propensity to push the edges provides any musical system with a continued livelihood, and it is usually sanctioned by its constituents. For they are the ones who have learned to know the "language" as a series of recognized and accepted units of melody, harmony, rhythm, vocal style, and so forth, each of which is combined as a matrix with others in new and creative ways, which results in what we know as a composition or improvisation.[24] Occasionally, a composer or improviser will come along who will push the edges in such a way as to elicit either great admiration or reactionary disapproval. Usually such a matrix reorganization brings with it new insight and behavioral empowerment. A new vision has then emerged. When the musical impulse is encouraged fully to unfold within the worshiping community, the liturgy may be given a way by which to incarnate its own internal creative urge, an urge that Anscar Chupungco holds as a life-giving, inherent imperative.[25] But that can be frightening to some, for it then seems as if the liturgy has lost its hold on the event, leading all too easily to a kind of ritual anarchy driven by the musical impulse. Then one is tempted to apply shackles. However, the muse will not be muzzled. It has been said in many ways. When text leads to melody, the dynamics will hold liturgy and music in tension, making it necessary to place equal emphasis on both church and music.[26] Ultimately, when all is sung and done, this dynamic tension may be the best icon of the Spirit's presence the community can have.

24. Peter van der Merwe, *Origins of the Popular Style* (Oxford: Clarendon Press, 1989), pp. 93-100.

25. Anscar Chupungco, *Liturgical Inculturation* (Collegeville, MN: Liturgical Press, 1992), p. 54.

26. Oskar Soehngen, "Theologische Grundlagen der Kirchenmusik," in Karl Ferdinand Mueller and Walter Blankenburg, eds., *Die Musik des evangelischen Gottesdienstes,* vol. 4 of *Leiturgia* (Kassel, Germany: Johannes Stauda, 1961), pp. 216-17.

The Last Word? Dynamics of World Musics
Twenty Years Later

Mark P. Bangert

There is more to write, of course, even though the methodology proposed above carries fundamental observations about which I still have considerable passion and in which one should still be able to find sentiments useful for evaluating music and worship.

Essential things to be appended require two preliminary notices. In its first published version, this methodology limped along without the benefit of the musical examples that were meant to entice the word-laden Hong Kong study team into alternative means of perceiving the tasks before them. Alas, the limping understandably remains with us, and, as refreshing as they might be, the examples can still only be imagined.

Second, the reader needs to be reminded that a Lutheran compiled this methodology for other Lutherans. While anybody can benefit from consulting with Luther on music, a broader address of the subject, taking into consideration ecumenical interests and commitments, might want to draw in other churchly voices, but surely has plenty of other grounds on which to stand, including a refreshing array of emerging areas of music study. Some of those will emerge in what follows, as we turn now to a tuning of the 1994 proposal.

Here are four points that can benefit from further conversation: (a) the musical impulse, (b) the focus on music as event or behavior, (c) the critical impulse, and (d) ecology. Even though words like "transcultural" and "countercultural" were bandied about in Hong Kong, they were not yet part of a more official vocabulary of the study team. That recognition happened months later, in Nairobi. Perhaps not surprisingly, the four points do find their way easily into the spaces created by the quartet of "cultural" words; in fact, the new surroundings provide insight.

Transcultural

By proposing a kind of universal musical impulse, I sought to accomplish two things: (a) to deflect attention away from the notion of music as a "thing," or object, a typically Western habit that easily ends in commodifying and the inevitable dead-end ranking of cultural artifacts; and (b) to slightly bend Luther's understanding of music as *creatura dei* (creature of God). As indicated in the initial essay, the *creatura dei* approach, while enjoying a long history among Christians, raises problematic questions about cosmology and is, frankly, difficult to defend. Of course, it is fun to ponder and a seemingly handy tool for convincing those who balk at the proposed importance of music in worship.

To be sure, a deity who envisions music as part of the divine creative project is a God who resonates with nearly every Christian worshiper. Hence, what if one were to posit as the *creatura dei,* not a cosmology of numbers, but rather a kind of universal human musical impulse? Is it possible to defend such a thing? That was the 1994 proposal; frankly, though, it was offered without much supporting evidence.

Twenty years later the scene has changed. A handful of scholars have embarked on a study of the neurological and neurophysiological origins and purposes of music, proposing that music's origins lie deep in the brain, that they probably precede language, and that they were manifested in the shouts of animal herders, thereby serving strong social urges.[1] Compatriots in a way are those who, because of the current ease and precision of brain scans, have begun to map brain waves induced by musical stimuli. Results of these ventures have been dubbed as "endlessly stimulating," even as they have been subjected to various popular theories that are not altogether substantiated. What does seem to be sure is that "humans need social linkages to make society work, and music is one of them."[2]

Two additional studies have lent energy to thinking about music (the

1. Nils L. Wallin, *Biomusicology* (Stuyvesant, NY: Pendragon Press, 1991), p. 424, passim. See also Wallin, Björn Merker, and Steven Brown, eds., *The Origins of Music* (Cambridge, MA: MIT Press, 2001).

2. Daniel J. Levitin, *This Is Your Brain on Music* (New York: Penguin Group, 2006), p. 258.

musical impulse) as transcultural. Seeking new ways to understand how music is learned, music psychologist and educator Edwin T. Gordon has proposed a theory of "audiation" (the process of translating sounds in our mind and of giving them meaning), which, he has discovered from his research, is a "matter of musical aptitude which comes naturally" and needs to be nurtured at an early age.[3] In a similar vein, developmental psychologist Howard Gardiner theorized more than thirty years ago that human beings have multiple intelligences, that is, skills or abilities of learning, and among the six he outlines is musical intelligence. He has concluded that musical intelligence, though appearing in a variety of strengths, singularly provides an individual with the ability to perceive and apprehend aspects of feeling, as well as knowledge about feeling, that are unavailable through other intelligences.[4]

For anyone searching for common ground on which to shape the playing field for music and worship, these more recent forays provide fresh nourishment. Furthermore, these scholars almost take for granted that there is something about music that is universal and that something is located in people — in the person. To the study team's Nairobi list of transcultural elements, then, ("One Lord, one faith, one baptism, one Eucharist") could be added the one assembly consisting of individuals, each of whom is blessed with the musical impulse.

Contextual

Christian worship, according to the Nairobi Statement, will be "rooted in diverse local cultures." To assist that process, authors of the document offer two operating principles; (a) dynamic equivalence, which is to reexpress components of Christian worship with something from a local culture; and (b) creative assimilation, which is to add pertinent components from a local culture in order to enrich the local gathering. While these operating principles of contextualization seem to work best in the areas of text, ritual act, and visual art, there are abundant examples demonstrating their generating forces in music, such as the use of the Balinese gamelan orchestra that I described above.

3. Edwin T. Gordon, *Learning Sequences in Music* (Chicago: GIA Publications, 2012), p. 3.

4. Howard Gardner, *Frames of Mind* (New York: Basic Books, 2011), p. 131. Gardner and Edwin Gordon have been creatively placed in dialogue with each other by Lisa M. Hess, *Learning in a Musical Key: Insight for Theology in a Performative Mode* (Eugene, OR: Pickwick Publications, 2011).

Simply to introduce cultural musical niceties, however, misses the more profound issues inherent in these two principles. More to the point would be questions like: How does music come to be in this culture? How does music mean something? What role does music have in preserving the integrity of this culture? And, of course, lurking behind these questions is the suspicion that maybe there are answers to these questions common to all cultures. That's why the Lomax system of cantometrics was and still is so attractive, even though more recently it has been shelved as an interesting but imperfect relic of comparative musicology, a discipline that has largely imploded. Nevertheless, Lomax's research and theories live on in part and in slightly metamorphosed existence through his focus on the behavioral aspects of all music-making. Understanding music as *activity* has become widespread and lends the methodology continuing promise.

Consider the work of Christopher Small, who has invented the word "musicking" to describe what he believes to be at the center of all music. "Music is not a thing at all but an activity, something that people do." "For performance does not exist in order to present musical works, but rather, musical works exist in order to give performers something to perform." "The act of musicking establishes in the place where it is happening a set of relationships, and it is in those relationships that the meaning of the act lies."[5] In a compelling way, Small redirects any discussion of music to factors usually considered tangential. When music is happening, look for what's going on, he would urge. The social dynamics of musical activity reveal deep, often otherwise unexpressed bonds and meanings, so that Simon Frith observes that making music provides a way of being in the world, a way of making sense out of it.[6] Each culture will have its own "way" of being and making sense. Once discovered and described, such a "way" benefits from being put into dialogue with the Christian gospel, a process that might be described as first steps along the way to contextualization.

Sometimes, as is foreshadowed in the Nairobi Statement, the quest for contextualization results in the need to find alternatives to what was first thought useful. But the discipline of seeking out behavioral and social meanings can just as surprisingly lead to a more profound embrace of the musical impulse as it is culturally tuned. As popular as gospel music has become

---

5. Christopher Small, *Musicking: The Meanings of Performing and Listening* (Hanover, NH: University Press of New England, 1998), pp. 2, 8, 13.

6. Simon Frith, *Performing Rites* (Cambridge, MA: Harvard University Press, 1996), p. 272.

recently for a broad spectrum of worshiping Christians, its contemporary incarnations have drawn criticism from some of its practitioners and have elicited guarded dismay from some not happy with its thoughtless cross-cultural usage. Grumblings might cease, however, if all concerned were to return to its contextual roots in the ring shout. Here's what I wrote about the ring in 2004:

> The ring *enacts* the community its members both deeply remember and presently seek. It is flexible. The ring can always expand — easily. It welcomes the individual and the individual's gifts. Its very movement inscribes the changes that are forced upon it, but it does so by creative adaptation while being sustained by its own power. The ring does not exclude because of heterodox station but rather expects some to have a part by being outside the ring; yet even those in such liminal space are needed for the enactment, too. . . . The ring enacts and in some respects suspends the tensions and negotiated resolutions that exist between the individual and the larger cultural community. The ring is therefore a metaphor for the worshiping Christian assembly.[7]

Countercultural

What may in fact be the most important thing about music, writes Wayne Bowman, is "the ways it shapes and defines human society."[8] Grasping music's significance via its social and behavioral dimensions not only frees one from dealing with it as "thing," language, or emoting tool, but can also serve to invite custodians of Christian worship from every culture and denomination into rethinking the function of music in individual assemblies. It feels like that's not happening much today. Apart from a few brave advances, such as Dan Lucarini's *Why I Left the Contemporary Christian Music Movement,* hesitancy reigns among us, perhaps for lack of a rhetoric, perhaps for fear of hurtfully stomping all over someone else's tastes.[9] However, the Nairobi Statement sets a bold and ambitious pace, cautioning against the easy adop-

---

7. Mark Bangert, "The Gospel about Gospel — The Power of the Ring," *Currents in Theology and Mission* 31, no. 4 (August 2004): 257-58.

8. Wayne D. Bowman, *Philosophical Perspectives on Music* (New York: Oxford University Press, 1998), p. 304.

9. Dan Lucarini, *Why I Left the Contemporary Christian Music Movement* (Webster, NY: Evangelical Press USA, 2002).

tion of cultural signs and practices that are "dehumanizing," or encourage "oppression," or "idolize the self," or glorify the "acquisition of wealth." The health of any worship assembly depends on its musical systems. Those invested in caring for assemblies will benefit from following the advice from Nairobi, and will ask questions such as: What does the "how" of our music-making mean or signify? Who are we as music-makers? Who are we as worshipers? Who do we want to be? Does our music prevent us from being who we want to be? In our music-making, who is doing what, from where, and who is silent and why?

In addressing such questions these days, serious assembly custodians will inevitably have to weigh the influence on our gatherings of the "star" culture inherent in popular music (also called "Christian contemporary music") and in surprising ways also in the classical music scene.[10] Far more importantly, contemporary critique must account for the noise factor Jacques Attali has identified. For him, it is to be recalled, noise is more metaphor than acoustical phenomenon, but the two are closely related. By definition, noise invades silence as unwelcome guest. Insofar as music speaks louder socially than speech, any sound event or music event can turn into noise, thus possessing power — and too often power over another. As power, noise easily turns into violence. And in subtle ways music, even church music, can be violent.

In a broader sense, then, what are the conditions by which even worship music, by virtue of how it is done, enacts postures of power that are detrimental to the nature and function of the worshiping assembly? The conditions may be acoustical, they may be matters of privilege, they may be financial matters, they may, in fact, be musical matters. In any case, noise is rarely neutral and serves as a useful way to focus on music as an event that brings relationships to the surface and exposes the power issues residing in those relationships.

Cross-Cultural

Hymn collections of recent vintage witness an energetic undertaking on the part of the churches to share with one another their cultural musical resources. The European embrace of gospel music and spirituals, for instance,

10. The work of Simon Frith is helpful in these matters.

is a sign of the amazing progress the cross-cultural goals of the Nairobi Statement have initiated.

While calling for the sharing of gifts among the churches, the statement urges simultaneously both respect for the cultures from which these gifts come and an empathetic understanding of the gifts themselves. Amid the laudable successes there remain these two challenges for the future. Respect, on the one hand, entails a posture of reception that rules out (especially) Western tendencies to plunder other musical cultures for artifacts that titillate or reward a thirst for the exotic. An unwitting sense of superiority frequently accompanies such tendencies, which can be countermanded with an honest desire to encourage in whatever way possible the continuity of local church musics. It becomes necessary to suggest this because the gargantuan enterprise of Western musical traditions is engulfing the entire globe, and many local cultural traditions suffocate. It can be argued that it's always been that way, or that inducing the larger churches to look after the younger churches is one more example of colonialism. Yet care for the ecology of the dance-based national tunes (and hymns) of East Africa or support for the continuing development of East Indian Christian poetry and music, for instance, may well be crucial components of the church's cross-cultural commitment and in need of immediate attention.

Truly caring for the ecology of local church musics means also caring for the way the music, when it is borrowed or received, is done. Some provide a rhythmic base for East African hymnody by using an electronic drum machine or, better, the all-pervasive *djembe,* a West African drum designed to deliver several rhythmic "lines" at once. But nothing compares to many people playing many drums at the same time, each offering his or her line to the whole — bringing back the idea of music as behavioral event. In any event, there are many ways for everyone to be ecologically aware and active.

On the other hand, understanding calls for a desire to get beyond a kind of acoustical voyeurism or to resist the repurposing of music designed for a specific set of relationships (cross-cultural adaptation) by first joining the original musical event itself. To say it another way, understanding ultimately means allowing the music to lead one to the people whose it is, to their joys and sorrows, their unique insights into God's love for them and for the part of the earth they inhabit. We can be thankful that more and more worshipers across the world have access to the raw material of local church musics. Within these texts, melodies, rhythms, and accompaniments lies a promise for an even greater gift: the far-off sound of the choirs of singers and players on their way to the city of God.

A Model Hymn from Africa: "Christ Has Arisen, Alleluia!"

To lift up a "piece" of music for modeling purposes subverts the above crusade to find the true meaning of music in its delivery. Yet some examples serve well as a kind of old-time piano roll, its sundry holes serving as the means to the sounding of captivating tunes in real life. Numerous songs have the right mixture of characteristics to elicit assembly music that sonically lifts the veil for a brief experience of what the body of Christ is and does. Let us examine here one such piece, the Swahili hymn *Mfurahini, Haleluya* ("Christ Has Arisen, Alleluiah").

The text of this hymn was first written in 1966 by Bernard Kyamanywa (b. 1938), a pastor of the Evangelical Lutheran Church of Tanzania. Kyamanywa was a student at the Makumira University College when he wrote this hymn at the suggestion of his mentor and teacher, Howard S. Olson, who in 1969 translated it into English. A year later it appeared in *Laudamus,* a service book for the Lutheran World Federation, and subsequently in many other collections, including the World Council of Churches' *Cantate Domino,* as well as in several editions of Olson's own pathbreaking *Tumshangilie Mungu,* a collection of East African hymns for use in Tanzania.[11] Though there are other translations of the original text, Olson's version continues to be the most broadly used.

Following principles enunciated by Olson for his mission of developing an original corpus of East African hymnody, the tune Kyamanywa chose for this hymn comes from his own Haya nation. How it was used before is unknown, but it fits a pattern of similar Haya tunes for four other hymns of his that appear in Olson's collection. The Haya people are located in northwest Tanzania, and they have roots in areas now parts of Uganda and Burundi. Haya society is traditionally hierarchical with clear patterns of authority and power, most of which centered ultimately in the king, who announced his station at appropriate moments via the royal drums *(ngoma).*

In most presentations of the hymn, there are distinct parts for a leader (solo, or *Kiongozi*) and for the assembly (people, or *Wote*). This call and response form yields to the leader the first line (with two parts), A(ab), and its repetition, A(ab), each line with its own text. Then the assembly part follows, always the same for all six verses: a new melodic fragment that is repeated with new text, B(cc), and a repeat of the music for the leader with

---

11. In the sixth edition of *Tumshangilie Mungu* (Nairobi: Printfast Kenya Limited, 1987), the translator is identified as Mudimi Ntando.

new text, A(ab). Explaining the form makes it appear more complicated than it is. In fact, the tune is simply and economically constructed, making it possible for the leader to be responsible for the changing textual material while foreshadowing most of the people's music in the leader's part.

This song is multilevel, choral with textual repetition. It provides for solo/group presence and thus reflects the ideal makeup of the assembly. While keyboardists often lead the song north of the equator, the song is by design independent of instrumental accompaniment, save for drums and rattles, whose involvement is nearly mandatory. Ornamentation is ostensibly nonexistent, though improvisatory moments on the part of the leader are conceivable. Finally, the song does carry considerable information, but its "load" consists of narrative, a narrative readily familiar to any Christian assembly and hence not out of reach for the majority of Christian gatherings.

These characteristics not only explain the current popularity of the song, but also advance it as a model of what ideal assembly music looks like. An expanding collection of choral settings of the song suggests that the tune stands up to alternative harmonizations and treatments, a sign, finally, that this piece of assembly music invites invention and playful improvisation, gifts that have traditionally built up Christian communities.

Christ Has Arisen, Alleluia![12]

1. Solo: Christ has arisen, Alleluia!
   Rejoice and praise him, Alleluia!
   For our Redeemer burst from the tomb,
   Even from death, dispelling its gloom.

   All: Let us sing praise to him with endless joy.
   Death's fearful sting he has come to destroy,
   Our sins forgiving, Alleluia!
   Jesus is living, Alleluia!

2. Solo: For three long days the grave did its worst,
   Until its strength by God was dispersed.

---

12. Hymn Text by Bernard Kyamanywa, trans. Howard Olson. © 1968 Lutheran Theological College, Makumira, Tanzania; admin. Fortress Press. Music: Tanzanian Traditional © 1977 Olson; admin. Fortress Press. In *Evangelical Lutheran Worship* (Minneapolis: Augsburg Fortress, © 2006 Evangelical Lutheran Church in America), pp. 364-65.

He who gives life did death undergo,
And in its conquest his might did show.
All: Let us sing praise to him with endless joy. . . .

3. Solo: The angel said to them, "Do not fear,
You look for Jesus who is not here.
See for yourselves, the tomb is all bare.
Only the grave cloths are lying there."
All: Let us sing praise to him with endless joy. . . .

4. Solo: "Go spread the news, he's not in the grave.
He has arisen all folk to save.
Jesus' redeeming labors are done.
Even the battle with sin is won."
All: Let us sing praise to him with endless joy. . . .

5. Solo: He has arisen to set us free.
Alleluia, to him praises be,
The pow'r of Satan no longer binds,
Nor can it enslave the thoughts of our minds.
All: Let us sing praise to him with endless joy. . . .

6. Solo: Jesus is living, let us all sing.
He reigns triumphant, eternal King.
And he has promised those who believe
Into his kingdom he will receive.
All: Let us sing praise to him with endless joy. . . .

PART II

CHRISTIAN WORSHIP:
UNITY IN CULTURAL DIVERSITY

The Nairobi Statement on Worship and Culture

Lutheran World Federation, 1996

This statement is from the third international consultation of the Lutheran World Federation's Study Team on Worship and Culture, held in Nairobi, Kenya, in January 1996. The members of the study team represented five continents of the world and had worked together with enthusiasm for three years. The initial consultation, held in October 1993 in Cartigny, Switzerland, focused on the biblical and historical foundations of the relationship between Christian worship and culture, and it resulted in the "Cartigny Statement on Worship and Culture: Biblical and Historical Foundations." (The text of this Nairobi Statement builds on the Cartigny Statement; in no sense does it replace it.) The second consultation, in March 1994 in Hong Kong, explored contemporary issues and questions of the relationships between the world's cultures and Christian liturgy, church music, and church architecture and art. The papers of the first two consultations were published as *Worship and Culture in Dialogue.*[1] In 1994-1995, the study team conducted regional research and prepared reports on that research. Phase IV of the study commenced in Nairobi and continued with seminars and other means to implement the learnings of the study, as LWF member churches decided would be helpful. The study team considered this project essential to the renewal and mission of the church around the world.[2]

1. *Worship and Culture in Dialogue* (Geneva: LWF, 1994). Also published are complete translations in French and Spanish, and a partial translation in German. The Nairobi papers appear below in this volume.

2. Parallel to the LWF Worship and Culture Study has been work by the WCC Commission on Faith and Order, on the relationship between worship and church unity. A part

1. Introduction

1.1. Worship is the heart and pulse of the Christian church. In worship we celebrate together God's gracious gifts of creation and salvation, and are strengthened to live in response to God's grace. Worship always involves actions, not merely words. To consider worship is to consider music, art, and architecture, as well as liturgy and preaching.

1.2. The reality that Christian worship is always celebrated in a given local cultural setting draws our attention to the dynamics between worship and the world's many local cultures.

1.3. Christian worship relates dynamically to culture in at least four ways. First, it is transcultural: the same substance for everyone everywhere, beyond culture. Second, it is contextual: it varies according to the local situation (both nature and culture). Third, it is countercultural, challenging what is contrary to the gospel in a given culture. Fourth, it is cross-cultural: it makes possible sharing between different local cultures. In all four dynamics there are helpful principles that can be identified.

2. Worship as Transcultural

2.1. The resurrected Christ, whom we worship and through whom, by the power of the Holy Spirit, we know the grace of the triune God, transcends — indeed, is beyond — all cultures. In the mystery of his resurrection is the source of the transcultural nature of Christian worship. Baptism and Eucharist, the sacraments of Christ's death and resurrection, were given by God for all the world. There is one Bible, translated into many tongues, and biblical preaching of Christ's death and resurrection has been sent into all the world. The fundamental shape of the principal Sunday act of Christian worship, the Eucharist (or Holy Communion), is shared across cultures: the people gather, the word of God is proclaimed, the people intercede for the needs of the church and the world, the eucharistic meal is shared, and the

---

of that work has necessarily examined contextual questions as well as questions of the essential shape or *ordo* of Christian worship. The work of the two projects has been mutually informative. See Faith and Order's Ditchingham Report, reprinted in Thomas F. Best and Dagmar Heller, eds., "So We Believe, So We Pray: Towards Koinonia in Worship, Faith and Order," Paper No. 171 (Geneva: WCC, 1995); and "Concerning Celebrations of the Eucharist in Ecumenical Contexts: A Proposal from a Group Meeting at Bossey," in *Ecumenical Review* 47, no. 3 (July 1995): 387-91.

people are sent out into the world for mission. The great narratives of Christ's birth, death, resurrection, and sending of the Spirit — and our baptism into him — provide the central meanings of the transcultural times of the church's year, especially Lent/Easter/Pentecost, and, to a lesser degree, Advent/Christmas/Epiphany. The ways in which the shapes of the Sunday Eucharist and the church year are expressed vary by culture, but their meanings and fundamental structure are shared around the globe. There is one Lord, one faith, one baptism, one Eucharist.

2.2. Several specific elements of Christian liturgy are also transcultural, for example, readings from the Bible (though the translations vary, of course), the ecumenical creeds and the Our Father, and baptism in water in the triune name.

2.3. The use of this shared core liturgical structure and these shared liturgical elements in local congregational worship, as well as the shared act of people assembling together and the shared provision of diverse leadership in that assembly (though the space for the assembly and the manner of the leadership vary), are expressions of Christian unity across time, space, culture, and confession. The recovery in each congregation of the clear centrality of these transcultural and ecumenical elements renews the sense of this Christian unity and gives all churches a solid basis for authentic contextualization.

3. Worship as Contextual

3.1. Jesus, whom we worship, was born into a specific culture of the world. In the mystery of his incarnation are the model and the mandate for the contextualization of Christian worship. God can be and is encountered in the local cultures of our world. A given culture's values and patterns, insofar as they are consonant with the values of the gospel, can be used to express the meaning and purpose of Christian worship. Contextualization is a necessary task for the church's mission in the world, so that the gospel can be ever more deeply rooted in diverse local cultures.

3.2. Among the various methods of contextualization, that of dynamic equivalence is particularly useful. It involves reexpressing components of Christian worship with something from a local culture that has an equal meaning, value, and function. Dynamic equivalence goes far beyond mere translation; it involves understanding the fundamental meanings both of elements of worship and of the local culture, and enabling the meanings and actions of worship to be "encoded" and reexpressed in the language of local culture.

3.3. In applying the method of dynamic equivalence, the following pro-cedure may be followed. First, the liturgical *ordo* (basic shape) should be examined with regard to its theology, history, basic elements, and cultural backgrounds. Second, those elements of the *ordo* that can be subjected to dynamic equivalence without prejudice to their meaning should be deter-mined. Third, those components of culture that are able to reexpress the gospel and the liturgical *ordo* in an adequate manner should be studied. Fourth, the spiritual and pastoral benefits our people will derive from the changes should be considered.

3.4. Local churches might also consider the method of creative assimi-lation. This consists of adding pertinent components of local culture to the liturgical *ordo* in order to enrich its original core. The baptismal *ordo* of "washing with water and the Word," for example, was gradually elaborated by the assimilation of such cultural practices as the giving of white vestments and lighted candles to the neophytes of ancient mystery religions.[3] Unlike dynamic equivalence, creative assimilation enriches the liturgical *ordo* — not by culturally reexpressing its elements but by adding new elements from local culture to it.

3.5. In contextualization the fundamental values and meanings of both Christianity and of local cultures must be respected.

3.6. An important criterion for dynamic equivalence and creative assim-ilation is that sound or accepted liturgical traditions are preserved in order to keep unity with the universal church's tradition of worship, while progress inspired by pastoral needs is encouraged. On the side of culture, it is under-stood that not everything can be integrated with Christian worship, but only those elements that are connatural to (i.e., of the same nature as) the litur-gical *ordo*. Elements borrowed from local culture should always undergo critique and purification, which can be achieved through the use of biblical typology.

4. Worship as Countercultural

4.1. Jesus Christ came to transform all people and all cultures, and he calls us not to conform to the world, but to be transformed with it (Rom. 12:2).

3. *Worship and Culture in Dialogue*, pp. 39-56.

In the mystery of his passage from death to eternal life is the model for transformation, and thus for the countercultural nature of Christian worship. Some components of every culture in the world are sinful, dehumanizing, and contradictory to the values of the gospel. From the perspective of the gospel, they need critique and transformation. Contextualization of Christian faith and worship necessarily involves challenging of all types of oppression and social injustice wherever they exist in earthly cultures.

4.2. It also involves the transformation of cultural patterns that idolize the self or the local group at the expense of a wider humanity, or give central place to the acquisition of wealth at the expense of the care of the earth and its poor. The tools of the countercultural in Christian worship may also include the deliberate maintenance or recovery of patterns of action that differ intentionally from prevailing cultural models. These patterns may arise from a recovered sense of Christian history, or from the wisdom of other cultures.

5. Worship as Cross-Cultural

5.1. Jesus came to be the Savior of all people. He welcomes the treasures of earthly cultures into the city of God. By virtue of baptism, there is one church; and one means of living in faithful response to baptism is to manifest ever more deeply the unity of the church. The sharing of hymns and art and other elements of worship across cultural barriers helps enrich the whole church and strengthen the sense of the *communio* of the church. This sharing can be ecumenical as well as cross-cultural — as a witness to the unity of the church and the oneness of baptism. Cross-cultural sharing is possible for every church, but is especially needed in multicultural congregations and member churches.

5.2. Care should be taken that the music, art, architecture, gestures and postures, and other elements of different cultures are understood and respected when they are used by churches elsewhere in the world. The criteria for contextualization (above, sections 3.5 and 3.6) should be observed.

6. Challenge to the Churches

6.1. We call on all member churches of the Lutheran World Federation to undertake more efforts related to the transcultural, contextual, countercultural, and cross-cultural nature of Christian worship. We call on all member churches to recover the centrality of baptism, Scripture with preaching, and the every-Sunday celebration of the Lord's Supper — the principal transcultural elements of Christian worship and the signs of Christian unity — as the strong center of all congregational life and mission and as the authentic basis for contextualization. We call on all churches to give serious attention to exploring the local or contextual elements of liturgy, language, posture and gesture, hymnody and other music and musical instruments, and art and architecture for Christian worship, so that their worship may be more truly rooted in the local culture. We call on those churches now carrying out missionary efforts to encourage such contextual awareness among themselves and also among the partners and recipients of their ministries. We call on all member churches to give serious attention to the transcultural nature of worship and the possibilities for cross-cultural sharing. And we call on all churches to consider the training and ordination of ministers of word and sacrament, because each local community has the right to receive weekly the means of grace.

6.2. We call on the Lutheran World Federation to make an intentional and substantial effort to provide scholarships for persons from the developing world to study worship, church music, and church architecture toward the eventual goal of enhanced theological training being led by local teachers in their churches.

6.3. Further, we call on the Lutheran World Federation to continue its efforts related to worship and culture into the next millennium. The tasks are not quickly accomplished; the work calls for ongoing depth-level research and pastoral encouragement. The Worship and Culture Study, begun in 1992 and continuing during and past the 1997 LWF Assembly, is a significant and important beginning, but the task calls for unending efforts. Giving priority to this task is essential for the evangelization of the world.

A Fragile Future for the *Ordo?*

Stephen Burns

There is no such thing as "theology"; there is only contextual theology.[1]

Distillations

The Nairobi Statement suggests that contextual dimensions of worship are grounded in and modeled on the mystery of Christ's incarnation: thus recognition that "Jesus whom we worship was born into a specific culture of the world" means that "God can be and is encountered in the local cultures of our world" (3.1). As the statement's contextual focus is allied to the doctrine of the incarnation, so the statement centers on the doctrine of resurrection with respect to its transcultural category. It conceives the "source" of the transcultural dimensions of Christian worship to be in the mystery of Christ's resurrection (2.1), identifying the "principal transcultural elements" of worship as "baptism, Scripture with preaching, and the every-Sunday celebration of the Lord's Supper" (6.1). What makes them transcultural is that "Baptism and Eucharist, the sacraments of Christ's death and resurrection, were given by God for all the world. There is one Bible, translated into many tongues, and biblical preaching of Christ's death and resurrection has been sent into all the world" (2.1).

This focus on Scripture and sacraments accounts for the Nairobi State-

1. Stephen B. Bevans, *Models of Contextual Theology,* 2nd ed. (Maryknoll, NY: Orbis, 2002), p. 3.

143

ment's interest in the notion of "the *ordo*," the so-called fundamental pattern or "shared core liturgical structure" (2.3) of eucharistic worship, which the statement promotes (at 3.3; cf. 2.1). Like the statement itself, this *ordo* is "greatly influenced" by Gordon W. Lathrop,[2] one of the members of the Lutheran World Federation (LWF) team working on *Christian Worship: Unity in Cultural Diversity* and its companion volumes, as well as on the Ditchingham Report of the World Council of Churches (WCC)[3] and the WCC's *Eucharistic Worship in Ecumenical Contexts*.[4] In the WCC's work, that *ordo* is said to be:

GATHERING of the assembly into the grace, love, and koinonia
of the triune God

WORD-SERVICE
Reading the Old and New Testament scriptures
Proclaiming Jesus Christ crucified and risen as the ground of our hope
(and confessing and singing our faith)
and so interceding for all in need and for unity
(sharing the peace to seal our prayers and prepare for the table)

TABLE-SERVICE
Giving thanks over bread and cup
Eating and drinking the holy gifts of Christ's presence
(collecting for all in need)
and so

BEING SENT (DISMISSAL) into mission in the world.

At the center of the *ordo* are, of course, word and table, elements that are in some sense transcultural, according to the Nairobi Statement. This *ordo* is a considerable development of the WCC's earlier document *Baptism, Eucharist and Ministry* (BEM),[5] "the most important multilateral document on

2. Maxwell E. Johnson, ed., *Sacraments and Liturgy* (Louisville: Westminster John Knox Press, 2012), p. 76.

3. Thomas F. Best and Dagmar Heller, eds., *So We Believe, So We Pray: Towards Koinonia in Worship* (Geneva: WCC, 1995). Note a distillation of the Ditchingham Report as an appendix in Gordon W. Lathrop, *Holy People: A Liturgical Ecclesiology* (Minneapolis: Fortress, 1999), pp. 229-32.

4. Thomas F. Best and Dagmar Heller, eds., *Eucharistic Worship in Ecumenical Contexts: Beyond the Lima Liturgy* (Geneva: WCC, 1994).

5. *Baptism, Eucharist and Ministry* (Geneva: WCC, 1981).

worship of our age,"[6] which spoke of the eucharistic liturgy as "essentially a single whole" but one that "consist[s] historically of the following elements in varying sequence and of diverse importance."

BEM simply listed those elements as

- hymns of praise;
- act of repentance;
- declaration of pardon;
- proclamation of the Word of God, in various forms;
- confession of faith (creed);
- intercession for the whole church and for the world;
- preparation of the bread and wine;
- thanksgiving to the Father for the marvels of creation, redemption, and sanctification (deriving from the Jewish tradition of the *berakah*);
- the words of Christ's institution of the sacrament according to the New Testament tradition;
- the anamnesis, or memorial, of the great acts of redemption, passion, death, resurrection, ascension, and Pentecost, which brought the Church into being;
- the invocation of the Holy Spirit *(epiklesis)* on the community, and the elements of bread and wine (either before the words of institution or after the memorial, or both; or some other reference to the Holy Spirit which adequately expresses the "epikletic" character of the Eucharist);
- consecration of the faithful to God;
- reference to the communion of saints;
- prayer for the return of the Lord and the definitive manifestation of his kingdom;
- the amen of the whole community;
- the Lord's Prayer;
- sign of reconciliation and peace;
- the breaking of the bread;
- eating and drinking in communion with Christ and with each member of the church;
- final act of praise;
- blessing and sending.[7]

6. David Holeton, "Anglican Worship: An Evolution from Imperialism to Ecumenism," in Thomas F. Best and Dagmar Heller, eds., *Worship Today: Understanding, Practice, Ecumenical Implications* (Geneva: WCC, 2004), pp. 61-68, 64.

7. *Baptism, Eucharist and Ministry,* E. 27.

The *ordo* brings them to much greater coherence.

The following reflections consider aspects of the *ordo* with respect to the Nairobi Statement's own categories of the transcultural and the contextual, and relate both to a number of recent theological studies. In particular, I explore intersections between the Nairobi Statement's concerns and the *ordo:* first, academic debate; then, growing conversation about the emerging church; and, most importantly, subalterns speaking for themselves.

The Growing Strength — and Fragility — of the *Ordo*

In the first place, however, it should be noted that the efforts of the LWF and the WCC to promote the eucharistic *ordo* have been rewarded insofar as the *ordo* has been widely adopted across a very wide spectrum of Christian traditions and has clearly shaped a diverse spread of contemporary ritual books. The *ordo* is now echoed in all kinds of liturgical resources across many Christian traditions. It shapes the structure of rites and is narrated in compelling ways, such as in the Church of England's framing statement for its *Common Worship* materials: "The journey through the liturgy has a clear structure with signposts for those less familiar with the way. It moves from the gathering of the community through the Liturgy of the Word to an opportunity of transformation, sacramental or non-sacramental, after which those present are sent out to put their faith into practice."[8] The contemporary embrace of the *ordo* includes numerous traditions that had previously patterned their liturgical life in other ways, including both those in old-line traditions in the West and the heirs of more recent missionary legacy.[9]

At the same time, though, we must acknowledge that the *ordo* has been, by some — and from a range of perspectives — ignored, questioned, suspected, and rejected, which may signal a fragile future for the *ordo,* at least in some traditions. This is to say that the *ordo*'s coherent pattern of Christian assembly is by no means always to be found. Note, for example, remarks made by Alistair McRae, a former president of the Uniting Church of Australia, speaking in his outgoing address as he passed on his office:

8. *Common Worship: Services and Prayers for the Church of England* (London: Church House Publishing, 2000), p. x.
9. An interesting example is the Presbyterian Church of Korea, whose 2008 liturgical resource reflects contemporary ecumenical patterns. See Kyeong-Jin Kim, "The Context, Contour and Contexts of Worship of the Korean Church: Focused on the Presbyterian Church," *Korea Presbyterian Journal of Theology* 44, no. 3 (2012): 65-93.

I have wondered on occasions if we are in danger of losing connection with the catholicity and apostolicity of the church in our gatherings. Some of the markers of continuity with the church in time and space have practically disappeared in some places and the local and the contemporary seem the only note. The broad horizons of Christianity have closed in. I have been at baptisms where some alternative to the Apostles' Creed has been used. Why not use a contemporary creed and one that links us with the church catholic across time? I have been at celebrations of Holy Communion that are scarcely recognisable in terms of the meal at the heart of Christian life for 2000 years. Friends, we have only got two official sacraments in our church, let's not mess with them. Is it so hard to keep them aligned with the church ecumenical and historical, and contextual and contemporary? That's what we do every time we preach from ancient scriptural texts.[10]

Set this alongside comments by Steven Croft, an English Anglican bishop — and notable in terms of the ground these reflections go on to traverse, the English Church's archbishops' missioner — writing about the Church of England:

It is becoming quite common to experience main Sunday services in Anglican churches where the Lord's prayer is not used; where there is no time of intercession for the needs of the world; where there is no formal structured confession and absolution; where the only words spoken by the congregation are in the songs or the Amen; where the reading of the scriptures is brief and perfunctory; where the mood and tone are set by the celebratory worship and by the upbeat style of worship leaders and there is little space for the minor key; where, when a set liturgy is used for baptism, confirmation, or even the Eucharist, it feels [like] an unfamiliar intrusion into the normal worship style.[11]

Neither Croft nor McRae refer specifically to an *ordo,* and they do not necessarily reveal that the *ordo* was not in place in the scenarios they describe, though minimal Scripture readings, somehow oddly discontinuous commu-

10. http://assembly2012.uca.org.au/proposals-and-reports/reports/item/207-retiring-president

11. Steven Croft, "Searching for Simplicity Beyond the Complexity: Developing Liturgy for a Mixed Economy Church," in Stephen Burns, ed., *The Art of Tentmaking: Making Space for Worship* (Norwich, UK: Canterbury Press, 2012), pp. 159-73, 165.

nion practices, the absence of intercession, and concern about apostolicity and catholicity might seem to give the clue. Perhaps, one might wonder, if these church leaders had framed their reflections through the interpretative categories of the Nairobi Statement, they might have added sharpness and specificity to their concerns. In any case, they both refer to ecclesial traditions whose central authorities clearly advocate the ecumenical *ordo* as the WCC has commended it, holding flexible patterns of worship within what the Uniting Church of Australia calls "standards" and "norms" for liturgical expression.[12] At the very least, their testimony gives pause to any sanguine notions of widespread reception of the *ordo.*

No doubt there are many different reasons for the situations Croft and McRae relate, but it is fair to assume that it involves critique, reserve, or opposition to the *ordo,* as well as sheer ignorance of it. The linking of the *ordo* to talk of the category of the transcultural may well be at the heart of at least some people's unease with it, and this is — notably — an unease that, since working on the LWF's project, Gordon Lathrop has expended considerable energy attending to.

Weighing the Academic Debate

The *ordo* is indeed a construct, though it is at least to some extent constructed from ancient sources, Justin Martyr's *1 Apology* (67 CE) being key. Turning to ancient sources has had its attractions in ecumenical conversation, at least for navigating toward a center away from Reformation-era roadblocks. But turns to ancient sources are problematic for reasons of their own, which have been highlighted in liturgical studies in the period contemporaneous with the LWF's work on culture, especially by Paul F. Bradshaw. Bradshaw's work on liturgical history has pressed the point that the search for the origins of Christian worship is more akin to searching for faint dots on a blank page than it is like finding straight lines of development that can easily be joined up.[13] In this light, Justin's witness is just one such dot, more or less dim, quite possibly disconnected from other dots representing impressions — if not necessarily actual practice — from elsewhere in other early churches.

12. See the Uniting Church in Australia, *Uniting in Worship 2* (Sydney: Uniting Church Press, 2005), pp. 8-9.

13. Paul F. Bradshaw, *The Search for the Origins of Christian Worship: Sources and Methods for the Study of Early Liturgy,* 2nd ed. (London: SPCK, 2002), p. 20.

Therefore, some suspicion of how much continuity should be admitted between Justin's description and any actual lived experience of liturgy in Justin's community, let alone other communities, may be apt.

This point, in turn, unfolds the implication that advocates of liturgical uniformity in any age may simply have forgotten (or may be ignorant of) the sheer diversity of the early churches. This point can be brought to bear on the transcultural category, and on the *ordo,* via Bradshaw's scolding of liturgical scholars who have trusted in what Bradshaw has called "imagined archetype[s] of the early church." Notably, however, Bradshaw specifically distances Lathrop from those scholars as taking "a rather different and more minimalist stance than do other liturgical theologians with regard to the 'deep structures' that liturgy is supposed to possess." Perhaps because it tends more to theological — as opposed to historical — construction, Bradshaw deems Lathrop's conviction "a little too neat and tidy, a little over-systematised to fit the full facts of history, yet [offering] a promising avenue for future exploration."[14] Lathrop's own response to Bradshaw's position involves acknowledgment of Bradshaw's "cautions about evidence and too easy harmonization" while also "assert[ing] that there is a core Christian pattern which, in its largest outline, can be explored in early sources," a sensibility that evidently influences the *ordo.*[15]

The communities whose practice Croft and McRae speak of may or may not know of this debate, or the reasons these interlocuters give for their convictions about early Christian "dots," whatever their weight and visibility, and "outlines" — large or small. But the question of how their practice might be educated by such debates remains an important one for church leaders to find ways of representing if the *ordo* is not to be lost to arguments that are less reflective.

A couple of ancillary points may be brought up here. First, it is interesting that Bradshaw's last-published work prior to his retirement was a reflection on the diversity of worship in the contemporary Church of England, his own ecclesial communion and the body about which Croft also speaks. In that piece Bradshaw appeals for greater resemblance in English Anglican worship, so as to enable "Christians of different theological persuasions" to "recognize one another as members of the same Church." While not arguing

14. Paul F. Bradshaw, "Difficulties in Doing Liturgical Theology," *Pacifica* 11 (1988): 181-94, 185-86.
15. Gordon W. Lathrop, *Holy Things: A Liturgical Theology* (Minneapolis: Fortress, 1993), p. 35.

"for a return to a rigid uniformity of practice," he does wish to recognize the great importance of some sort of liturgical bond to a church, and especially to an Anglican Church with all its other varieties, something that has been rather overlooked in a generation when individuality, freedom, and creativity have become the watchwords.[16]

This is a fascinating last word, at least of sorts, given the work for which he has justifiably become so well known — with its strong insistence on diversity. For, as Ruth Meyers says, Bradshaw's work challenges contemporary churches "to recognize the pluriformity of early Christian liturgical practice and so to be open to the possibility of a greater diversity of contemporary practice."[17] In his latest writing, Bradshaw is neither making an appeal to a particular *ordo* nor stating a transcultural conviction; nor should he be read as renouncing his strident advocacy of the early churches' plurality. But he is clearly not arguing for unbridled contemporary diversity. At the same time, it is notable that he does not mention, or expound on, or evaluate what the Church of England, through its Liturgical Commission — of which he has been a longtime member — has identified as marking the "common core" of its contemporary rites gathered together as *Common Worship:*

- a recognizable structure for worship;
- an emphasis on reading the word and on using psalms;
- liturgical words repeated by the congregation, some of which, like the creed, would be known by heart;
- using a collect, the Lord's prayer, and some responsive forms of prayer;
- a recognition of the centrality of the Eucharist;
- a concern for form, dignity, and economy of words;
- . . . a willingness to use forms and prayers that can be used across a broad spectrum of Christian belief.[18]

16. Paul F. Bradshaw, "Liturgical Development: From Common Prayer to Uncommon Worship," in Stephen Platten and Christopher Woods, eds., *Comfortable Words: Polity, Piety and the Book of Common Prayer* (London: SCM Press, 2012), pp. 121-31, 130-31.

17. Ruth A. Meyers, "Introduction: Learning the Lessons of History: The Contributions of Paul F. Bradshaw to the Study and Practice of Liturgy," in Maxwell E. Johnson and L. Edward Phillips, eds., *Studia Liturgica Diversa: Essays in Honor of Paul F. Bradshaw* (Portland, OR: Pastoral Press, 2004), pp. xii-xix, xvi.

18. Paul F. Bradshaw, *Patterns for Worship* (London: Church House Publishing, 1989), pp. 6ff. See also Stephen Burns, *Worship in Context: Liturgical Theology, Children and the City* (Peterborough, UK: Epworth Press, 2007), chap. 2, "Patterns for Worship in the Church of England."

Of course, such a common core is not the *ordo*. But Bradshaw's appeal for resonance is related neither to transcultural nor what might arguably be categorized as more contextual, tradition-specific but *shared,* considerations. One might well wonder what kind of structures, deep or otherwise, he would now recommend for generating the "shared liturgical experience" he seeks for ecclesial formation.[19]

Second, Bradshaw's former student Maxwell Johnson makes a further fascinating reference point with respect to approaching the transcultural category. Johnson is an avid editor and compiler of texts for liturgical study (many with Bradshaw); his recent collection *Sacraments and Liturgy* is an update of James F. White's *Documents of Christian Worship*.[20] It includes, along with its chapter on "modern theological theology," an extract from Gordon Lathrop as well as from Bradshaw, and another from the Nairobi Statement. In that regard it may be the kind of resource that communities Croft and McRae describe could use to map out some theological positions between which to locate their own practice. At the same time, Johnson's book generates some problems of its own, for while Johnson's sourcebook — a contender for a major curriculum resource in liturgical studies — claims to be "extensive," it is extensive in some ways and not in others. It is not just that women's perspectives are minimal in Johnson's historical trajectories, with the absence of Teresa Berger's *Gender Differences and the Making of Liturgical History* as just one kind of study that should rightly invite some suspicion of the history that is collated in Johnson's sourcebook.[21] It is also that, when Johnson makes suggestions of further reading, citing dozens of studies, studies by contemporary women are markedly missing: all but a very paltry few are the works of men. This is a problem that has plagued not just liturgical studies but Christian theology at large, but the fact that Johnson's mainstream is a "manstream" also reveals that a similar critique could be developed concerning other issues of diversity that are a growing part of contemporary liturgical studies.[22] Johnson's book shows that one does not

19. Bradshaw, "Liturgical Development," p. 131.

20. James F. White, ed., *Documents of Christian Worship* (Edinburgh: T&T Clark, 1994).

21. Teresa Berger, *Gender Differences and the Making of Liturgical History: Lifting a Veil on Liturgy's Past* (Farnham, UK: Ashgate, 2011). For a discussion of this book in relation to Berger's earlier work, see Stephen Burns, *Worship and Ministry: Shaped Towards God* (Melbourne: Mosaic, 2012), chap. 10, "Mission-Shaped Women-Church: Feminist Christian Assembly and Feminist Cultural Exegesis."

22. Feminist, postcolonial, and queer perspectives on liturgy, for example, are not yet

need to invoke notions like the transcultural to be exposed to a welter of critiques that cluster around the descriptor "postmodern."

Postmodern questions are key to making an assessment of the Nairobi Statement's transcultural convictions. It is notable, therefore, that Gordon Lathrop, as a key member of LWF also engaged in the WCC's liturgical work, has engaged deeply with a range of possible postmodern critique of the *ordo*. In an essay at the end of the festschrift for him, entitled "Bath, Word, Prayer, Table . . ." Lathrop is acutely alert to the challenge of postmodern perspectives to any proposed ecumenical shape of worship. He names suspicion of "liturgical imperialism"[23] and of "unwarranted 'meta-narrative' " (p. 219) as causes of suspicion. He asks: "How does *ordo* avoid becoming ideology?" (p. 219). And he echoes the Ditchingham Report's insistence that "compulsion in worship always distorts the thing it seeks to reform" (p. 220). Lathrop suggests that, in the face of postmodern challenges,

> an open meeting around a multivalent pool, around an interesting set of words and around an inviting supper is not, in the first place, designed to compel. Healthy liturgy, focused on strong central signs and not on individual personal decisions, makes a way of ever deeper significance available to its participants, but it also lets those participants be free. (p. 221)

In a piece entitled "*Ordo* and Coyote," Lathrop goes further. He identifies pool, word and supper — "certain classic things" — as "the most likely candidates to create space" for "hold[ing] us, our losses and our dreams, and, from that place of holding, to propose to us both re-readings of the world and consequent actions for justice." The *ordo* is "the scheduling of that space," but its order is in a certain way crooked, indirect, a way that makes it also able to be open.[24]

---

as "central" as they should be. See Stephen Burns, *Liturgy,* SCM Studyguide (London: SCM Press, 2006), chap. 5, "Styles and Substance: Celebrating Diversity"; see also Michael N. Jagessar and Stephen Burns, *Christian Worship: Postcolonial Perspectives* (Sheffield, UK: Equinox, 2011).

23. Gordon W. Lathrop, "Bath, Word, Prayer, Table: Reflections on Doing the *Ordo* in a Postmodern Time," in Dirk Lange and Dwight W. Vogel, eds., *Ordo: Bath, Word, Prayer, Time: A Primer in Liturgical Theology in Honor of Gordon W. Lathrop* (Akron, OH: OSL Publications, 2006), pp. 216-28, 219. Hereafter, page references to this essay appear in parentheses within the text.

24. Gordon W. Lathrop, "Berakah Response," *Proceedings of the North American Academy of Liturgy* (2007): 26-40, 32. A version of this address also appeared as "*Ordo* and Coyote: Further Reflections on Order, Disorder and Meaning in Christian Worship," *Worship*

Lathrop expounds this in some resistance to the recognition that "every structure . . . is constituted and maintained through acts of exclusion" (p. 33)[25], and he does so by means of reflecting on the role of the symbol of the coyote in Najavo culture, and related figures — those perceived as trick-sters, unbalancers, boundary-crossers, even sneaks and fools — in other cultures.[26] In liturgical contexts, he suggests, Coyote represents "instances of ceremonial breaking, instances of the ritual order unable to contain the whole world of experience, lest it become false order and prison" (pp. 36-37).

> You have encountered Coyote when, in your most beautiful liturgical mo-ment, your voice broke, you lost your place, the wrong sermon really was before you on the ambo, as you feared. Or your community has encoun-tered Coyote when that homeless man who is frequently on the street outside of the building, actually came inside, sort of joining in the singing, speaking an odd petition in the prayers, presenting himself for commu-nion, none of it in the way you ordinarily do these things. (p. 37)

Most importantly, Lathrop identifies Coyote with the figure of Jesus, partic-ularly in the depictions of the royal parable of Matthew 25.

> At best, the center of a Christian meeting can be continually eccentric, the one at the center of the meeting, encountered in word and sacrament, being the one who identifies with the wretched, the disordered, the war-torn, the unincluded and the poor, who shares all still-hidden trauma, outside of this meeting. . . . (p. 38)

The *ordo,* as Lathrop comes to expound it, is "a focused, ordered meeting, with disorder and away-from-here at its heart," "those left out as part of its essential character," an always open order (p. 38).

It is clear in these elaborations on the *ordo* that Lathrop is invested in much more than historical reconstruction, that his moves are essentially theological. Indeed, the *ordo,* for him, is a way of "critical and re-orienting

---

80, no. 3 (2006): 194-213. Hereafter, page references to this essay appear in parentheses within the text.

25. Lathrop, citing Mark C. Taylor.

26. See, e.g., Michael N. Jagessar, "Spinning Theology: Trickster, Texts and Theology," in Michael N. Jagessar and Anthony G. Reddie, eds., *Postcolonial Black British Theology: New Textures and Themes* (Peterborough, UK: Epworth Press, 2007), pp. 124-46.

association with Jesus" (p. 39), even "the enacted doctrine of the Trinity" (p. 38) and "received from the tradition as if from God" (p. 32). Such statements are admittedly a jump from — but not necessarily incompatible with — Paul Bradshaw's "acknowledg[ment] that liturgy is as much a human artifact as a divine creation." For Bradshaw seems to concede that there may be a "divine contribution" (p. 185), albeit while wishing to destabilize inherited notions of what might constitute that divine aspect. But as I have already noted, he neither appeals to it in his desired latter restoration of shared forms for the Church of England, nor aligns himself with a Lathropian theological turn.

Yet, while much of Bradshaw's work might serve postmodern suspicion, the lynchpin of postmodern negotiation of the *ordo* might well rest on the capacity or appetite to explore the construct with careful attention to Lathrop's commendation of it. For in his "*Ordo* and Coyote" piece, Lathrop commends the transcultural aspects of the *ordo* not necessarily as divine gift, but as if so given. This rather subtle, somewhat muted, shift may be given more or less weight, but for some it may prove crucial to their being convinced that that *ordo* is not "designed to compel." At least some of those who have rejected the *ordo* — those who might be regarded as conscientious objectors to its vulnerability to unwarranted metanarrative — might be asked to weigh for themselves the arguments Lathrop advances.

Joining the Emerging Conversation

Perhaps, however, some of those who downplay the *ordo* — in fact, perhaps, the lion's share of what both McRae and Croft think they see in their respective churches — embody less ideologically conscious questioning of postmodern culture, and may be for one reason or another theologically embedded or missionally savvy about it. In any case, a variety of liturgical expressions may be sheltered in such cultural engagement, though most are likely to take a dim view of any "one-size-fits-all" approach to worship.[27] Of course, it can be flatly declared that an embrace of the *ordo* means no such thing.[28] The *ordo* is compatible with and commendable to, for example, the

27. This important clarifying phrase appears in Pete Ward, *Liquid Church* (Carlisle, UK: Paternoster Press, 2002), p. 19.
28. See Stephen Burns, "Heaven or Las Vegas? Engaging Liturgical Theology," in Pete Ward, ed., *Mass Culture: The Interface of Eucharist and Mission* (Oxford: BRF, 2008), pp. 95-112.

kind of emerging church perspectives that continue to receive powerful advocacy, not least from ecclesial leaders, Anglican bishops Mary Gray-Reeves and Michael Perham being some recent examples.[29] It is thus important that reflections on the *ordo* attempt to engage the many groups who consider themselves part of the emerging church.

In the British context at least, one of the first people to write about the liturgical dynamics of so-called emergent worship was Doug Gay. Using the term "alternative worship" (as has been common in the UK), he and colleagues wrote about what happens in the emerging church as a selective kind of reception of liturgical tradition. Indeed, they asserted that, given that communities practicing this kind of worship tended to come from the kind of low-church Protestant background in which written liturgical forms, congregational responses and intentional ritual gestures were often eschewed, this involved a "revival of interest in the worship traditions of the church." Gay and others likened the selective reception of such things to the kind of "sampling" techniques used by musicians playing electronic instruments, in which "a slice of music is extracted from its original setting" and "inserted into a new musical context, where it combines with other elements to form a new whole."[30] What may have sometimes or often been absent in such early experiment was "reflect[ion] on the principles that might guide such techniques," whereas principles shaped around the Nairobi Statement's categories of the transcultural and contextual, and around the *ordo* (especially perceived as allied with the coyote and always open), might have been very helpful.[31] However, in a later work, *Remixing the Church,* Gay not only provides some complementary images — "catholic tradition is to be approached as a kind of massive dressing-up box, a huge CD collection, a sprawling image bank, a compendium of stage directions, a liturgical lending library" — he also begins to sketch out a series of techniques (what he calls auditing, retrieval, unbundling, supplementing, and remixing) that may all play a role in an emerging ecclesiology.[32]

In *Remixing the Church,* while Gay oddly and without explanation drops

29. Mary Gray-Reeves and Michael Perham, *The Hospitality of God: Emerging Worship for a Missional Church* (London: SPCK, 2010). Gray-Reeves is an Episcopal Church bishop, Perham an English Anglican bishop.

30. Jonny Baker, Doug Gay et al., *Alternative Worship* (London: SPCK, 2003), p. xiv.

31. Burns, "Heaven or Las Vegas?" p. 96.

32. Doug Gay, *Remixing the Church: Towards an Emerging Ecclesiology* (London: SCM Press, 2011), p. 51. Hereafter, page references to this work appear in parentheses within the text.

the word *ordo* into his proposals (without making any link to the WCC's or LWF's work), he writes articulately about "critical and partial reception of 'catholic' tradition" (p. 38), crediting the Iona and Taize communities as "among the most important bridging and mediating influences within the UK" (pp. 37-38), between aspects of what he calls " 'catholic' liturgical tradition" and those from "low church traditions": Baptists, Brethren, Congregationalists, independent evangelicals, Pentecostal denominations, and independent Pentecostal churches, new "charismatic" churches and networks, as well as many conservative and charismatic evangelical congregations within Anglican, Methodist, and Presbyterian churches, to whom catholic traditions such as written liturgies, congregational responses, and forms of intentional ritual, were "deeply alien" (p. 37). Through Taize, Iona, and other experiences, low-church Protestants have come to find "portals" into the catholic tradition, he suggests, and so they have come to pick up interest in the church year, ritual action, images and icons, set prayers, and — significantly for a discussion of *ordo* — "classic shapes" (p. 40). Of particular interest is his suggestion that "a renewed appreciation of and attentiveness to liturgical traditions among emerging groups is often rooted in what I would term a 'wisdom' perspective, rather than a 'mandate' perspective" (p. 40), albeit in their wisdom, "without fully understanding the liturgical codes and conventions within which these 'old tricks' were previously embedded" (p. 41).[33] Specifically, Gay calls for "gracious conversation with those who are discovering the riches of 'their' tradition" from "the high church side of the equation" (p. 41).

The *ordo* is much more inclusive than notions of high or low church, but Gay's call for others' engagement with emerging communities is one that advocates of the *ordo* can and should take up, to encourage and educate and, no less, to learn. Indeed, the emerging church constituency has a major capacity to reverse what might otherwise be a fragile future for the *ordo,* as well as perhaps having most to gain from serious engagement with notions of the *ordo* and the categories of the transcultural and contextual in all their obvious resonance with missional concerns. And the gain may be greatest with respect to those parts of the "worldwide phenomenon" of the emerging church that form what Steven Croft describes as the "international move-

---

33. Gay's allusion to "old tricks" is to Martyn Percy's essay "Old Tricks for New Dogs? A Critique of Fresh Expressions," in Louise Nelstropp and Martyn Percy, eds., *Evaluating Fresh Expressions: Explorations in Emerging Church* (Norwich, UK: Canterbury Press, 2009), pp. 27-39.

ment" of "fresh expressions of church."[34] This movement, unfolding from the British Anglican report *Mission-Shaped Church,* quickly became not only international but also ecumenical. It has gone on to define a fresh expression of church as being "established primarily for the benefit of people who are not yet members of any church." Interestingly, though, fresh expressions of church are further defined as coming into being "through principles of listening, service, contextual mission and making disciples," and as having potential to become "a mature expression of church shaped by the gospel and the enduring marks of the church and for its cultural context."[35]

There is much even in this threefold definition to resonate with Lathrop's notion of the *ordo,* not only as something that makes for "association with Jesus" but also the Nairobi Statement's intersecting assertions about transcultural and contextual dimensions of worship. Just as with many circles of emerging church, there may be, with respect to fresh expressions of church, a great possibility for what Doug Gay calls "gracious conversation." Note Steven Croft's call for clarity that fresh expressions are not to be confused with charismatic evangelicalism, to which his comments cited at the opening of this essay were directed: "The movement to form fresh expressions of Church is not in my observation, un-liturgical. In some ways it is by instinct and intention a profoundly liturgical movement. It recognizes the need to contextualize liturgy and match it closely to the needs of the emerging community."

Notably, he goes on to add: "[B]ut in any case that principle is at the

---

34. Croft, "Searching for Simplicity," p. 162. At the same time, it is salutary to recall that the Anglican-Methodist document giving rise to fresh expressions, *Mission-Shaped Church* (London: Church House Publishing, 2004), draws a certain line between the emerging church and fresh expressions of church — or at least between fresh expressions and notions of "emergent"/"alternative worship." *Mission-Shaped Church* identifies a series of problems with alternative worship: "Because it is significantly populated by people departing from existing church, [it] contains a strong desire to be different and is among the most vocal in its repudiation of existing church. The firmness of this posture means it is less clear about its own self-identity beyond what it is not . . ." (p. 44). It links this view to a criticism of alternative worship for "lack of ongoing engagement with mission — either social involvement or evangelism." *Mission-Shaped Church* reckons that alternative worship "tends to act more as a safety net for those falling out of existing church," while "finding it difficult to act as a fishing net for those still outside the church" (p. 45). Such a view of worship in emerging churches needs to be revised.

35. http://www.freshexpressions.org.uk/guide/about/whatis. See also Steven Croft, "What Counts as a Fresh Expression of Church and Who Decides?" in Nestropp and Percy, *Evaluating Fresh Expressions,* pp. 3-14.

heart of *Common Worship*," a perspective that Bradshaw seems to have become less sympathetic toward. And while there may not always be the same depth of openness in charismatic evangelical circles (though this should not be simply assumed), clarification of the *ordo* may have a strong role in helping groups within old-line churches that have rejected complex versions of liturgical provision for "thrifting and pruning and reducing what is there to allow the shape and character of our liturgy to be seen more clearly and understood more deeply."[36]

Listening to Subaltern Voices

But I believe that there is a need for other kinds of gracious conversation. We might perceive the need for that if we connect these strands from the preceding reflections: with LWF, Gordon Lathrop locates Scripture within the transcultural category; Doug Gay names "the church year" as something that "emergers" have (re)discovered; and because the catholic tradition ties calendar and lectionary, the transcultural and contextual cannot always be disentangled — at least if we take a broad view. While Scripture may perhaps, in some complicated way, be deemed to be sometimes above culture, lectionary disciplines are another matter, and these are firmly embedded in seasonal and climatic patterns of some parts of the world and tenuously connected to other parts. In the so-called global South, for example, Easter is not in spring; Lent may not be an experience of lengthening days — in fact, the opposite; and Advent may not be a time of darkness and shadows but the height of summer.[37] These disjunctions may or may not be trivial, depending on where one is located, nor may they be entirely unwelcome. Therefore, in the intensity of an Australian summer, for example, a snow-covered Christmas card "may just be a plea for relief."[38] But because calendar and lectionary mediate the Scripture,

36. Croft, "Searching for Simplicity," p. 164.

37. See Clare V. Johnson, "Inculturating the Easter Feast in Southeast Australia," *Worship* 78 (2004): 98-117; Clare V. Johnson, "Relating Liturgical Time to 'Place-Time': The Spatiotemporal Dislocation of the Liturgical Year in Australia," in Stephen Burns and Anita Monro, eds., *Christian Worship in Australia*, pp. 33-45; see also Carmel Pilcher, "Poinsettia: Christmas or Pentecost — Celebrating Liturgy in the Great South Land that is Australia," *Worship* 81 (2007): 508-20; see also Pilcher, "Marking Liturgical Time in Australia: Pastoral Considerations," in Burns and Monro, eds., *Christian Worship in Australia*, pp. 47-58.

38. Anita Monro, "A View from the Antipodes, Juxtaposing Dingo and Baby: A Con-

which is central to "association with Jesus," we may not consider the disjunction inconsequential.

What Gay calls "'catholic' liturgical tradition" is allied to certain kinds of Northern experience. And it is allied not only to particular natural cycles but also to cultural values, such that transmuting — perhaps settling into — cultures to which it is transported is no simple thing, not least because such "settlement" can be as much the result of destructive invasion as it is of missionary benevolence. In any case, these two are themselves deeply entangled. A lectionary-related example emerges from Jione Havea's consideration of the Revised Common Lectionary (RCL) from the perspective of his native Tongan culture. He suspects that, "if the RCL had tellers — as opposed to preachers and readers — in mind, the selection of biblical passages would be different."[39] He calls this an "over-sight," and he charges that "the RCL cannot have the same impact at all geographical sites during any given Christian season." But he also names its being "dislocating in its patriarchal and pro-Israelite orientations" (p. 120), a dynamic he coins as "oversites." Likewise, he suggests, the RCL may not encourage critique of offensive behaviors in native cultures that uncritically reflect bias in biblical narratives about Israel and the church. To counter such proclivities, Havea wishes to turn to a notion of a "commoners' lectionary" that can expose the RCL selection of texts favoring "dominant people and their mainline ways" (p. 122). Havea calls this "over sighs," which make room for the clash of seasons at different locations (p. 123), are biased in the interests of local commoners, and require supplementation of Scripture with other ancient texts, local instructions, and popular narratives (p. 124). Only in such ways could a lectionary be genuinely "sited," Havea says.

The force of Havea's comments may be more readily felt by cross-reference to his notion of "kontextuality," or what he calls the "cons of contextuality."[40] In a separate essay he challenges the "growing claim" that the center of gravity of Christianity has shifted to the global South:

---

sideration of the Cycle of Light in the Australian Summer," *Studia Liturgica* 40 (2010): 94-101, 99.

39. Jione Havea, "Local Lectionary Sites," in Stephen Burns and Anita Monro, eds., *Christian Worship in Australia: Inculturating the Liturgical Tradition* (Strathfield, New South Wales: St Pauls, 2009), pp. 117-28, 118. Hereafter, page references to this essay appear in parentheses within the text.

40. Jione Havea, "The Cons of Contextuality . . . Kontextuality," in Stephen B. Bevans and Katalina Tahaafe-Williams, eds., *Contextual Theology in the Twenty-first Century* (Eugene, OR: Wipf and Stock, 2011), pp. 38-52.

There surely has been a demographic shift, for the majority of Christians now live in South America, Asia, and Africa, but the political gravity is still located in the North. . . . We in the South have numbers but they/you in the North have power and means. . . . It does not really matter that the Bible is in the hands of Africans, and of Asians and Islanders, and so forth, if they are to interpret it according to the teachings of white men.

In particular, he insists that far too much the North still determines "how we contextualize."[41] Furthermore, Havea contends that he is suspicious when he hears *essentialist people doing the contextual talk* because the context for them is just a shelter for their essences."[42] In Havea's view, contextual theologies need to be much more clearly in the interest of the context before they are contextual enough. His articulations cast shadows on easy notions of the transcultural — as if to suggest that there is no such thing.

Havea's critique is more striking and more complex than I have space to try to represent, but perhaps what I have sketched of it already conveys the point that reserve about the transcultural category and how it is manifest in the notion of the *ordo* can arise from serious concern about how power flows from missionary legacies that alienate some while leaving some others — in Havea's categories, "preachers and readers" and their cultures — more secure. The postcolonial question ("Can the subaltern speak?"[43]) is one that is yet to be adequately addressed with respect to the LWF project, for all that the conversation unfolding from that project has become increasingly sensitive and open to a range of postmodern challenges. Alongside various kinds of "gracious conversation" there may also need to be, in fact, more space made for what postcolonial theorists call "contrapuntality,"[44] or — perhaps more accessibly expressed — something like what the feminist theologian Letty Russell calls "talking back to the tradition."[45] Until that happens, and

41. Havea, "Kontextuality," p. 41.

42. Havea, "Kontextuality," p. 44.

43. This question is the title of Gayarti Chakrovorty Spivak's famous article, in Cary Nelson and Lawrence Grossberg, eds., *Marxism and the Interpretation of Culture* (Basingstoke, UK: Macmillan, 1988), pp. 271-313.

44. For further discussion, see Jagessar and Burns, *Postcolonial Perspectives*, pp. 76-79, 83, passim.

45. See Letty Russell, *Church in the Round: Feminist Interpretation of Church* (Louisville: Westminster John Knox, 1993), p. 33. For discussion, see Stephen Burns, "Over the Ocean," in Burns and Monro, eds., *Christian Worship in Australia*, pp. 17-29, 18, 29, passim; see also Stephen Burns, " 'Four in a Vestment': Feminist Gesture for Christian Assembly," in Nicola Slee and Stephen Burns, *Presiding Like a Woman* (London: SPCK, 2010), pp. 9-18.

is heard where political power is still located in the North, I am not sure that we can know about the future of the *ordo*.

Conclusion: Knowing Our Place

In this chapter I have suggested three avenues for further reflection on the Nairobi Statement and its alliance with the *ordo*. Postmodern questions need to be negotiated with a Lathropian "as if," or by other means. Emerging church circles have much to offer to conversation about the missional merits of the *ordo*, from which they and others with them stand to gain. And subaltern voices need to be welcomed to unsettle any essentializing projections about how the transcultural and contextual may intersect. How central are word and table? And how do emerging and subaltern voices find "a place at the table" of discussion of the Nairobi Statement's categories and concerns? Each of these avenues is challenging, but all are worth pursuing and, to borrow from Australian indigenous literature, each for its own reasons:

How deprived we would have been
if we had been willing
to let things stay as they were.
We would have survived
but not as whole people.
We would never have known our place.[46]

46. Sally Morgan, *My Place* (Freemantle, Western Australia: Freemantle Arts Centre Press, 1987).

Worship: Translating the Untranslatable

Dirk G. Lange

Acknowledgment and Question

Many have studied and applied the Nairobi Statement since it was first published in 1996, the fruit of extensive regional negotiation and focused ecumenical effort. S. Anita Stauffer admirably organized, inspired, and collated the work — and then went on equally well to introduce the statement to international and ecumenical audiences.

In her own published introduction, Stauffer notes that the most challenging fact that the Nairobi Statement has attempted to address is the "relationships between worship and culture." In the same breath, she points out that dealing with the relationships between worship and culture "is at once to deal with the heart of Christianity, and with a deeply complex subject. It affects people's primary Christian experience, their spirituality, and it can therefore be very controversial. It is a subject on which everyone has an opinion and many emotions."[1]

We have all known and experienced the divergent opinions and the many (sometimes far too intense!) emotions concerning these relationships and how they are to be negotiated. One question will always arise: Is there a unifying pattern? Is there a code, so to speak, that can be applied across cultural contexts? These questions are continually debated, particularly in

---

1. S. Anita Stauffer, "Worship: Ecumenical Core and Cultural Context," in Stauffer, ed., *Christian Worship: Unity in Cultural Diversity* (Geneva: LWF, Department for Theological Studies, 1996), p. 7.

the academy and in theological schools. Today's students pursuing a theological education come to divinity schools or seminaries from vastly different contexts and with vastly different goals in view (not all seminarians wish to pursue a career in ordained ministry, for example, but seek a theological degree to work in other organizations — governmental and nongovernmental). As I work with them, I encounter, on the one hand, people for whom nothing can be "transcultural" (or "central") and, on the other hand, persons who fall back with extreme rigidity on precisely the "universally valid" forms of worship, wishing to reclaim and impose. This observation of student behavior states nothing new, but the lines of demarcation seem to be ever stronger and more clearly drawn.

But why would Stauffer write that this question of the relationships between worship and culture is both the heart of Christianity and a deeply complex subject? She immediately states what is at stake: this question shapes a Christian experience and defines a spirituality.[2] We are beyond the realm of simply asking how a particular form of worship is received or becomes communicable or finds a representative form. What Stauffer is suggesting, I believe, relates directly to the experience of faith. Worship does not exist as an ideal, in some platonic realm, that is then received into the local community. Instead, worship emerges as a translation of the gospel's own embeddedness within the languages, within the cultures, of any given faith community.

The complexity of embeddedness is entangled with its multidimensional character. Stauffer's use of the plural in itself destabilizes the neat categorization of the term "relationship" that most would like to uphold. There is not just one relationship between worship and culture; there are a multitude of relationships. The Nairobi Statement speaks of four dimensions: transcultural, contextual, cross-cultural and countercultural. In these four dimensions, however, "worship" is assumed as one entity and "culture" as another. The question then focuses on how these two entities interrelate. How are the pattern of worship and the characteristics of a particular culture to intermingle (in, with, for, against, etc.)? But doesn't Stauffer's use of the plural imply something more? The "complex" nature of the question becomes apparent. It resides in the fact that worship and culture are not two distinct entities; rather, they are codependent and cannot be thought of separately. The relationship*s* of worship and culture imply organic, material, earthy, incarnational dimensions — the complexity of living things, not static entities. Neat categorization becomes impossible.

2. I leave this term as it is in Stauffer's text with a fairly wide-open definition.

In this regard, *embodiment* is a better word than "embeddedness" for the purposes of this task of analysis of the Nairobi Statement and the implications of this analysis for the pattern of worship. With the word "embedded," a hint of metaphysical ordering lingers, maintaining the identity split between worship and culture. Is worship an independent reality that must be planted within the soil of culture?

Such metaphysical ordering hovers over much of the worship debate focused on pattern(s). It is exemplified already in the first lines of the LWF volume being celebrated: "The problem of how the Gospel relates to various cultures is one which has acquired special importance as we approach the end of the twentieth century. We have learned to respect the rich diversity of cultural expression around the globe, while understanding that the Gospel can only be fully comprehended and accepted once it has taken root in any given culture."[3] Is the gospel something "out there" that must find a way to relate to — or be represented in — cultures? Is the gospel a structure of being, an "original" that is simply to be copied? Is the gospel to take "root" before it is comprehended and accepted? This form of relating — original to copy — is not what is espoused by the Gospel of John. In that Gospel, the Word does not take root but becomes flesh, that is, the Word takes on a body, in a particular cultural context and at a particular time. It does not take on flesh, but becomes flesh. The Word takes on the precariousness of the body, the vicissitudinal characteristics of the body, allowing itself to be shaped by the body, God, the gospel itself (the original) shaped by a body (its translation).

The issue that has inspired theologians to ask about Christian worship and what the basis of unity within cultural diversity might be rests primarily on the assumption that the gospel can be represented by a particular communicable code. However, Stauffer's statement in her introduction already questions this assumption. Is not the complex character of the relationships between worship and culture due to the fact that worship, in itself, is not a "unifying" activity (as a type of Christian universal)? What is unifying is precisely what worship attends to, what Stauffer calls, as the primary Christian experience, "spirituality," and what the Lutheran confessional writings more simply call faith? The complex subject matter that elicits so much emotion does so because it touches the nerve center of Christian experience: the new creation, faith itself.

---

3. Viggo Mortensen, preface to Stauffer, *Christian Worship*, p. 5.

Translation and Untranslatability

Can we engage in a critique of worship as a universally agreed-upon code that unifies the Christian people without questioning the very heart of worship, namely, word and sacrament? Can we engage in a critique of the "transcultural" character of Christian worship? I believe that we can when we recognize, as I began to express above, that terms such as "transcultural," "contextual," and "cross-cultural" may betray a "metaphysical prejudice."[4]

Metaphysical prejudice is fixing the meaning of revelation as if it were eternally valid. Meaning can be fixed by science, or by a certain vision of history, or, of course, by ecclesial authorities and hierarchies. That type of metaphysical fixing, Gianni Vattimo argues, is simply an example of the power of "natural religion" to help us define who God is and thus who we are. In rather scandalous words, Vattimo declares that there is no sole truth "out there" in some metaphysical heaven: "[T]he sole truth of Christianity [as Jesus taught] is the one produced again and again through the 'authentication' that occurs in dialogue with history, assisted by the Holy Spirit."[5] Or, as he also formulates it: "[S]alvation takes place through interpretation."

Interpretation is to be understood not as the work of communication, as if salvation could be represented and thus simply inserted into any given context. The interpretation Vattimo writes about is a translation that arises out of a continual dialogue with history, with the events of human living, assisted by the Holy Spirit. An "original" per se is absent. The Holy Spirit ensures, when and where it pleases, that this "translation" is always gospel, that is, proclamation anew that embodies the Word anew in people's hearts, faith alone. Worship, as proclamation, is itself an embodiment of this translation as iterated original.

An understanding of this kind of translation depends on the realization that there is, in fact, no original to translate. Or, more precisely, the original and the translation are never distinguishable. Jacques Derrida puts it this way: "If the translator neither restitutes nor copies an original, it is because the original lives on and transforms itself. The translation will truly be a moment in the growth of the original, which will complete itself in enlarging itself." The original, in other words, is not complete and never will be. It calls

4. Gianni Vattimo, *Belief,* trans. Luca De Isanto and David Webb (Stanford: Stanford University Press, 1999), p. 60.

5. Vattimo, *Belief,* p. 59.

for translation: it calls for a multitude of translations, and those translations all become part of the original — extensions, developments, completions, each shaping the other and the original. The surprising thing, Derrida says, is that "at the origin [the 'original'] was not there without fault, full, complete, total, identical to itself."

Within the original, there is something that fascinates the translator, which Derrida describes as the intangible and untouchable. This something in the original is what precisely cannot be translated but calls for continual translation that "orients" the work of the translator.[6] In a book entitled *Trauma Recalled,* I have argued that worship is such a work of translation.[7]

Worship is a peculiar form of translation. It is the translation, not of an original idea, or work, or doctrine, but of an event that is never captured in its happening. Worship as translation is itself a living event. Worship arises out of that demand to say the "unsayable," to express the inexpressible, to name what is impossible to name, what always remains inaccessible, intangible in an event.

According to trauma theory, the event that is unceasingly repeated — the traumatic event — is not the event itself but what made the event traumatic in the first place. What is repeated is the fact that the traumatic event was not known in its happening or was not fully experienced in its happening. As Cathy Caruth says, it is an awakening one moment too late: "Trauma . . . does not simply serve as record of the past but precisely registers the force of an experience that is not yet fully owned."[8]

For the faith community, the traumatic event is the Christ event. And the question raised is then: How is this traumatic event, an event that we cannot fully grasp, an event that is only "registered" as a force of experience, a force that continually returns — how is this traumatic event remembered, repeated, and thus, of course, ritualized? Worship, then, is not simply translating a pattern into various contexts; rather, within each context, in all the multicultural characteristics of each context, worship registers the force of an experience, the dynamic of the gospel, the continual return and irruption of the Holy Spirit. Worship arises out of the dialogue with history, assisted by the Holy Spirit. The rituals of worship and their ordering are not tools for

6. Jacques Derrida, "Des Tours de Babel," in *Acts of Religion* (New York: Routledge, 2002), pp. 121, 124.

7. Dirk G. Lange, *Trauma Recalled: Liturgy, Disruption, and Theology* (Minneapolis: Fortress, 2009).

8. Cathy Caruth, ed., *Trauma: Exploration in Memory* (Baltimore: Johns Hopkins University Press, 1995), p. 151.

the mastery of Christian life but rather an incessant questioning: How does the gospel, the Christ event, become for us?

When Martin Luther asks the question "How do we remember this event?" he is pushed to find a language for this force of a return, and he finds it in the liturgy — specifically in the eucharistic liturgy.[9] In worship, and particularly in the sacraments, the force of a return — what cannot be captured, known, represented, or memorialized by ritual — is not some abstract notion of grace or forgiveness of sins or other theological construct, but is the irruption of the Holy Spirit as "other," as body, as that which resists all human attempts at control, manipulation, mastery. At the heart of worship is this action of the Holy Spirit: a body continuously returns in the body of Christ, the body of our suffering neighbor.

Since that body cannot be systematized, classified, controlled (except through tyranny), and since the inaccessible in the Christ event cannot be grasped, it is repeated; but this repetition is not just blind, compulsive repetition. The inaccessible is "grasped," but only indirectly through what I have been calling a "translation." The inaccessible calls for translation: translation understood as living, marked by what is inaccessible in the Christ event, exercising and deepening Christian experience — in other words, a spirituality. The inaccessible asserts itself not through what it communicates (an idea) or represents (an image) but in a continual return (repetition) of a body, the Word made flesh.

Translation of the inaccessible (Luther calls it the *unaussprechliche*, the "unsayable," even the "absent thing") into the intracultural reality of communities sets up a confrontation between what is not fully perceived and the self-contained identities of individuals and communities. This confrontation pushes individuals and faith communities to a response, a "holy" or ethical response. The inaccessible in the Christ event, the gospel, necessitates or calls on translation that will always be, in itself, a displacement, but a displacement in which something is added, something that embodies the call to responsibility, something that strangely directs identity beyond itself to the neighbor — the other, both familiar and unknown.

The juxtaposition of word and sacrament continually introduces the body, Christ's body, the neighbor's body, and thereby confronts us with a failure of meaning, with the failure of the self — the individual — to define meaning alone, by oneself. It confronts us with the failure of all metaphysical constructs designed to capture the gospel in a system. The *ordo*, the pattern

---

9. See Lange, *Trauma Recalled,* chap. 5.

of worship, is meant to confront us with the failure of systematization. The Word — in worship, beyond systematization, through the sacrament — reveals to us the depth of our need and God's immeasurable goodness.

Translating word and sacrament within every context has no goal other than to proclaim this immeasurable goodness to a needy world. This translation is not rendering an abstract notion specific; it is not rendering a universal particular. This translation is itself a continual iteration of God's promise that is always spoken and distributed to individuals and within local communities. It is a living translation.

Martin Luther, already in his time, hesitated to note down how the Christ event — how Christ's life, death, and resurrection, indeed, how the gospel — is translated ritually because he realized that every local community is unique, in its gifts and in its need, in its death and in its life. Luther didn't want to establish one order of worship that might then be misused. He didn't wish to imprison the Spirit in one form. He knew very well that if he were to write an order of service, people would appropriate it as eternally valid, would turn it into gospel itself, and would worship the order rather than be admonished and brought to faith. Despite all his warnings, an absolutizing of order is precisely what happened! Even today, some idolize or attempt to reclaim the form, the rites above and beyond the event they seek to embody.

The first thing Luther writes, in the very first sentence of the preface to the German Mass, is this: "Do not make it a rigid law. . . ."[10] When we study worship, we are not studying an eternal law that must be imposed in the same way in every place for everyone. In fact, when we make it a law, we destroy the whole purpose of worship, and the gospel becomes superstition.

This is the "complex subject" that Stauffer describes. Contextual and cross-cultural, even transcultural, may all risk creating a superstitious approach to the gospel. As a particular code of translation, they may edge toward becoming a new form of law. Codifying an approach to the gospel can quickly become law, particularly as culture is engaged. Every culture will want to embed, render sacred, make eternally valid a given historical moment. Luther understood this very human tendency. He realized that even his order of service, firmly rooted in word and sacrament, could be abused. What does this mean? That word and sacrament themselves could be questioned? No, word and sacrament remain central for Luther and for the Lu-

10. *Luther Works* (hereafter cited as *LW*), 53:61.

theran confessional documents because these are the means (AC 5) that God has chosen as a place of promise. But this word and these sacraments (baptism and Eucharist) will proclaim or translate the gospel, will speak it and distribute it, differently from place to place, including, I would argue, within a culture.

But there is another word that Vattimo also uses when describing the dialogue that ensues with history, assisted by the Holy Spirit. It is the word "authentication." The dialogue produces authentication. Authentication is not a measuring stick, or a code, to which worship in any given context must comply. It is a truth that emerges in the worship moment itself.

This authentication should perhaps be the center of our concern. This authentication is a freedom from the finding the perfect memorial of the Christ event. It is a freedom from the temptation to immortalize a particular ethnic or cultural representation of worship. On the contrary, liturgy (the ceremony and rites) is to be an action where the Holy Spirit continually returns or irrupts to reveal both human need and proclaim God's promise, that is, consolation, comfort beyond all memorials and representations and identities.[11] The Lutheran confessional writing declares as much in the Augsburg Confession, Article 24, "Concerning the Mass": "Our people have been unjustly accused of having abolished the Mass. But it is obvious, without boasting, that the Mass is celebrated among us with greater devotion and earnestness than among our opponents."[12] The statement that the parishes/communities of the Reformation celebrate liturgy "with greater devotion and earnestness" opens up for us today the possibility of discussing worship, not from the perspective of specific well-controlled or -maintained rituals, but from the perspective of the work of the Holy Spirit within different worshiping traditions and ethnicities — contextually, cross-culturally, transculturally, but even more, counterculturally.

The point here is that word and sacraments are not transcultural, as if they belonged to an order, a hierarchy, an institution (even if that institution is named "worship"). When we refer to an overarching system, concept, or idea that demands application by using the word "transcultural," we are reasserting a certain control over what we name. A concept can be neatly

---

11. Dirk G. Lange, "Confessions, Ecumenism, Ethnicity: A Lutheran Charism," in *Theological Practices That Matter: Theology in the Life of the Church*, vol. 5 (Minneapolis: LWF, Lutheran University Press, 2009).

12. The Augsburg Confession (hereafter AC), Article 24 (German text), in Robert Kolb and Timothy J. Wengert, eds., *The Book of Concord: The Confessions of the Evangelical Lutheran Church* (Minneapolis: Fortress, 2000), p. 68.

defined; the living tension in word and body cannot. Word and sacrament are not transcultural entities, but are living things happening in the midst of an assembled people. They are made alive — that is, they are "living things" — by the action of the Holy Spirit alone, who is continually interpreting anew God's promise in every context.

Word and sacrament are not "marks" that are quantifiable or, if you will, given to representation. Of course, Luther does use the term "marks," but these marks are very surprisingly defined as possessions that we do not actually possess. On the contrary, they are "holy possessions" that possess us! They are living things, living in a community. Martin Luther puts it this way: "This word preached, professed, believed and lived. . . ."[13] These "living" marks unsettle us. The ways in which the Holy Spirit is "lived" is not something that can be "represented" and therefore made "visible." Something remains inaccessible in these "marks," which makes them precisely "living." They demand live translation. Word and sacrament are constantly opening up a worshiping assembly, a faith community, to what cannot be captured, verified, represented within its midst — or within its society and culture.

When the Reformers write about keeping all the ceremonies and rites with greater devotion, I believe that they mean precisely this "living" aspect. Word and sacrament are the place of the Spirit's in-breaking. Devotion here is not evoking emotionalism or pietism but a radical living in the Word. The liturgy is translated in such a way that the Spirit is continually interpreting context and culture and pushing it toward the gospel, that is, disrupting it in what we might call a countercultural move.

The Nairobi Statement

The countercultural character of worship has been the missing player throughout most of the church's history. This is understandable because it is difficult to remain open to the constant disruption of the Holy Spirit; it goes against the stability human beings so desperately seek. A concern for transcultural and contextual is far simpler to grasp. One well-known Lutheran example can serve to demonstrate this point.

Dietrich Bonhoeffer was perplexed and disturbed by the situation of the church in the 1930s. He looked at it and observed:

13. *LW*, 41:149.

We gave away preaching and sacraments cheaply; we performed baptisms and confirmations; we absolved an entire people, unquestioned and unconditionally; out of human love we handed over what was holy to the scornful and unbelievers. We poured out rivers of grace without end, but the call to rigorously follow Christ was seldom heard. . . . Blessed are they who, in the knowledge of such grace, can live in the world without losing themselves in it. In following Christ their heavenly home has become so certain that they are truly free for life in this world.[14]

Here Bonhoeffer asks our question in his own time. Giving the sacraments away "wholesale" is giving them away to that self-contained, boundaried self, the self that relishes its own identity, success, culture, language, and so on, living in an enclosed, overcast place. Giving the sacraments away wholesale is strengthening the divide between the private and the public, communal self. For example, his comment that we should all sing in unison rather than four-part harmony — which has had so many of us perplexed, especially musicians — goes directly to this point. It's as if he were saying, "You regale yourself in your harmonization! It has more value to you than God and neighbor do!" His comment is not a comment on musical aestheticism but a countercultural comment on the use of music.

We are challenged in every age, in every context, by this very question: Have we given word and sacrament away wholesale? Have we catered to the buffered self, as Charles Taylor defines that self?[15] Have we used worship for other purposes than that for which worship has been given to us: to proclaim the mercy of God in the midst of a violent world; to show forth the immeasurable goodness of God in a world burdened, in a world brought down by thousands of conflicting desires and options?

And there are still more questions that arise as we consider the deeply countercultural character of worship, for example:

(1) Has the gospel, through the discipline of worship, opened the doors of hearts and lives and communities so that the narrow way of Jesus is heard?
(2) Has confession and forgiveness led us into the depth of God's mercy, reshaping the life of a community around the truth of baptism, a community participating in the suffering of the neighbor?

14. Bonhoeffer, *Discipleship*, vol. 4 (Minneapolis: Fortress, 2003), pp. 53-54, 55-56.
15. Charles Taylor, *A Secular Age* (Cambridge, MA: Belknap Press of Harvard University, 2007), pp. 37-42.

(3) Has the word read and preached brought us to prayer for the other, for the world, for God's reign to appear?

(4) Has the meal that we distribute welcomed broken bodies and formed us into a communion that in turn is always welcoming, where young and old, abled-bodied and other-able-bodied, are together in lament and praise?

(5) Is this "our" vision?

As we consider these questions afresh in this book, and as we once again take up the challenge of the Nairobi Statement, we enter more fully into the complexity that Stauffer hinted at. One other danger (besides the metaphysical prejudice) of the neat quadilateral formula (worship as transcultural, contextual, countercultural, and cross-cultural) is, of course, the fact that today there truly is not one homogeneous culture in relationship to other cultures.

The American cultural context, where I currently reside, is itself fraught with fissures. It is defined as much by dominant white experience as by an ever-new frontier mentality, and an individualism rarely as highly exalted in history. At the same time, it bears in it — or rests on — the slave experience of millions of African-Americans, who continue to be excluded from the typical white American cultural definition. They have experienced word and sacrament as oppressions from the ruling powers, identity markers from which they were excluded. What, then, does it mean to claim an ecumenical value if we ignore their experience? How can a transcultural value be anything but oppressive to a continually exploited group?

I raise these questions not to undermine the centrality of word and sacrament; I raise them to sharpen our attention toward the danger of conceptualizations, such as the designation, for example, of "transcultural." By asking the transcultural question, I am raising the issue of normativity. Even word and sacraments can too quickly be imposed in a particular normative form rather than as living actions arising from a culture's practice of storytelling and meal-sharing.

The quadrilateral framework that the Nairobi Statement proposes can invite faith communities toward countercultural reflection. It can invite them to self-reflection, reflection, first of all, on one's own multicultural context, including the cultures of the neighbor — not only the neighbor far away but especially the neighbor around the corner. Rather than imposing a normative guide, word and sacrament can be translated in terms of a disarticulation that breaks open a space — a space of cultural and religious contexts and subjects — toward something of God.

A predecessor document to the Nairobi Statement names this tension. The Ditchingham Report (1994) clearly names the danger of power dynamics within worship in one of its most significant paragraphs:

> 5. This pattern of Christian worship, however, is to be spoken of as a gift of God, not as a demand or as a tool for power over others. Liturgy is deeply malformed, even destroyed, when it occurs by compulsion — by civil law, by the decisions of governments to impose ritual practice on all people, or by the forceful manipulation of ritual leaders who show little love for the people they are called to serve. At the heart of the worship of Christians stands the crucified Christ, who is one with the little and abused ones of the world. Liturgy done in his name cannot abuse. Rather, it must be renewed by love and invitation and the teaching of its sources and meaning. Jesus says: "And I, when I am lifted up from the earth, will draw all people to myself" (John 12:32). The liturgy must draw with Christ, not compel.[16]

At the heart of Christian worship stands the crucified Christ. The crucified and risen one is present, not on that cross on a wall, but in the people gathered and the things that they are engaging. The Christ event — and our participation in that event, dying and rising — is present today in the waters of baptism, in confession and forgiveness, in the reading of Scripture, in the preaching, the praying, and the sharing of a meal. In these things we encounter Christ, both the neighbor in our midst and the stranger knocking.

The Christ we gather around, however, the Christ who stands in the midst of our worshiping assembly, is not the romantic or heroic Christ that any culture might construct and adore. The Christ who stands in the midst of our assemblies is the one we encounter in the little and abused ones of this world, the excluded and the marginalized neighbors, those who do not regularly (if at all) attend celebrations of word and sacrament.

James Cone challenges the ecumenical movement when he says, "The acid test of any ecclesiological statement is whether it has taken sufficient account of the actual world in which liturgical confessions are made."[17] As our liturgical confession, word and sacrament are means — God's voice and

---

16. "Towards Koinonia in Worship: Report of the Consultation," held in Ditchingham, England, August 1994; published in Thomas F. Best and Dagmar Heller, eds., *So We Believe, So We Pray: Towards Koinonia in Worship,* Faith and Order Paper 171 (Geneva: WCC, 1995).

17. James Cone, *Speaking the Truth: Ecumenism, Liberation and Black Theology* (Maryknoll, NY: Orbis, 1986), p. 115.

body — in the assembly, inclining the assembly toward the neighbor. Only in light of such a confession is it possible to understand how word and sacrament can be designated as gift. When we call "baptism" and "Eucharist" gifts of God to the people of God, we understand them not as possessions or assurances of salvation (which they certainly are) but as call.

Baptism into the death and life of Jesus Christ, into the suffering of Jesus Christ in order to participate in the resurrection of Jesus Christ, is baptism into the suffering of the world. The sharing of the body and blood of Christ in the Eucharist becomes a lived-out example of our baptism. In the simple sharing of bread and wine we acknowledge and engage in a different form of living in the world — a way of simplicity and not of excess. Word and sacrament are not a privilege that reassures a community, but a call toward dissemination within the world. The faith community belongs totally to the world.[18] It is a community where all barriers fall away.

But as long as our practice of baptism and Eucharist remain captive to a metaphysical prejudice (something neatly disguised as a form of systematic theology), as long as these liturgical practices simply reflect a fossilized form of ecclesiology, where the "body of Christ" is envisioned as a mystical, "preexisting form," a kind of preexisting church that hovers above or around us or where it is conceived simply as a sporadic event that has no historical continuity, practices will always remain cut off from the complexities of the social matrix where most people live their lives.

Rather, what is demanded of us is a struggle to define our identity as we are immersed in the struggle of others to define their identity. There is boundary crossing. Our identities are always formed in the struggles we encounter in daily living, in our struggle with the forces of powers around us. This is why James Cone continually insists on first analyzing the social contexts of local congregations.

Is this not what it means to be countercultural? It is the basic gospel turn toward an outward focus. The attentiveness to context, social context, and the neighbor — especially the neighbor who does not look like me — implies the following: a provisionality with regard to one's self-determined identity is, to a certain extent, an openness to the reality of death in all life. Even the welcome of the stranger at our door signifies for us a judgment about who we think we are. The neighbor always challenges those identities that we self-construct. But that welcome, and that judgment, is not met in fear, be-

---

18. Bonhoeffer, *Letters and Papers from Prison,* Dietrich Bonhoeffer Works, vol. 8 (Minneapolis: Fortress, 2010), pp. 280-81.

cause in daily dying we know, as baptized people, that the Spirit works, raising us always to new life. This faith, engendering provisionality, knows that the God of life is always stronger than death and in fact has this habit of actually rising from the dead.

Yet it is too often the case that our worship actually closes the door or fortifies the walls, reinforcing patterns inherited from the past or inculcated by cultural milieu. This tendency is known in that most classic and common response given in discussions about worship: "But we've always done it this way!" We can hear this response made in reaction to change in any context, whether so-called traditional or contemporary, or contemplative, or relaxed, or emergent — or any type of worship. We fall too quickly back into maintaining our self-determined identity. We prefer to avoid judgment. We avoid dying, because we are afraid.

Even when, in our worship, we appeal or connect to the sensitivity of the worshiper or seeker, another question must be asked: To what extent is our worship limiting the horizon, closing worshipers off into their own expectations, exerting even a certain power over an individual's emotional landscape? To what extent are our words and music — perhaps especially our music — focusing the worshiper on the self rather than on the community and the neighbor? Is the novelty experienced in a small circle or in a megachurch only reinforcing the walls, creating self-contained communities, look-alike communities? In such a scenario, it does not matter what style of worship we engage in, people probably will not come. Young people did not go to Taizé, for example, because of the worship style but because their deep need was heard, welcomed in prayer, and transfigured in community. They experienced judgment and new creation, death and life — these two, held together. The world of simple narratives, of easy meaning, of finite symbols, of simple correspondence between need and satisfaction, of power dynamics — this deciphered world, with no empty spaces, gave way to silence. In worship, are we opening this space of silence or simply filling in, fabricating something like new convent-like structures of medieval times, new self-enclosed communities turned in upon ourselves?

For faith communities, the call of faith, the call to continually exercise faith, will always result in a countercultural relationship with the world around them. The countercultural move always places the neighbor alongside God. The self is not initially part of the equation. This orientation is not new: the gospel already embodies it. Luther defines it in this way: worship is "for the glory of God and for the good of our neighbor and not for our own advantage and pleasure."[19] The movement of faith, this countercultural movement, will continually resist all hegemonies but will not withdraw from the world. It will equally engage creation and the world of neighbors.

Lutheran Confessional Witness

I have attempted, at the beginning of and throughout this chapter, to define what Anita Stauffer called "the deeply complex subject": the relationships between worship and culture. Deeply complex, as we have seen, because worship and culture are not self-contained entities that can be set side by side and easily "related." Worship in this life does not exist without culture. Worship arises from that dialogue with history, assisted by the Holy Spirit — finally, a dialogue between the Holy Spirit and history, between the Spirit and faith communities and the events of human lives.

Luther's own hesitation about defining worship is now perhaps better understood. Beyond his fear that human beings turn a worship order into law, Luther is motivated by perhaps an even greater (and finally unanswerable) concern: that worship, when standardized, becomes simply self-expression rather than the spontaneous irruption of new creation, rather than that profound thanksgiving that overflows and constitutes new life. A tension exists between this movement of thanksgiving and a basic characteristic of human life, namely, that it is lived in creation, as created beings. Human beings as bodies will always need to cling to something, and they will always be pushed — in their experience of the sacred and the inaccessible, in their experience of the Christ event — toward translation. The need to cling or grasp something is not the result of human depravity as has too often been assumed (or mistranslated), as though the body weighed down the upward movement and struggle of the human spirit. That human beings are compelled to translation resides in this realization: human beings stand, in all their fullness, as an integral part of God's good creation.

As part of this good creation, God gives living means by which God is present, means by which the human beings can grasp, hold on to, cling to. These are known as word and sacrament. The Augsburg Confession states that it is enough *(satis est)* for a faith community to be constituted as *ecclesia,* as a gathering of the called. It is, I believe, this word and sacrament as *living* things in a faith community that help us answer one of Gordon Lathrop's

19. *LW,* 53:61.

questions: "[W]hat is the other thing that might be juxtaposed to *ordo* itself? How does *ordo* avoid becoming ideology?"[20]

The Lutheran Confessional writings clarify how word and sacrament become living things rather than programmatic criteria or organizing principles of worship. Word and sacrament engage people, engage faith communities, within the radical dynamic of the gospel. Word and sacrament are here considered, not as representations of some ideal, as if harking back to a Gospel as a written text. They are not a resystematization of speech, as if they would have a particular meaning, controllable and communicable in every situation, irrespective of context or time. In such a case, word and sacrament would be once again a human activity of control, though controlling the Holy Spirit itself! Michel de Certeau speaks of a "testimony of negation." Taking on the task of translation myself for a moment, I will, considering this testimony, claim that word and sacrament are not meant to be equated with power but with power's negation. Word and sacrament are meant to shatter power structures and all forms of categorization. This testimony, which I have called disruptive, redefines relationships and the fabric of living, opening up new and different levels of community, of solidarity. According to de Certeau, this testimony is creative: "a throng became poetic." Might we say that an assembly, or a gathering, becomes poetic, reconfiguring culture and language and human relationships, discovering "unforeseen bonds of solidarity" with the neighbor?[21]

Word and sacrament are such a testimony of negation, creating a poetic of faith that renders individuals of a faith community living members of a body. Lathrop has consistently pointed out this dimension: worship introduces us to some basic, biblical things that we use in order to tell and retell the story. These central things are not earth-shattering, nor are they esoteric. They come from daily living, from everyday practices: there is a bath and water; there are words and prayers; there is a table and meal-sharing. As living things, word and sacrament distill the reality of the created order. Word and sacrament hold together word and body — hearing, yes, but also seeing, tasting, touching.

We seek to hold these together in juxtaposition, and they simultaneously disrupt the easy meanings or the hegemonic control human beings wish to

20. Gordon Lathrop, "Bath, Word, Prayer, Table: Reflections on the Liturgical *Ordo* in a Postmodern Time," in Lange and Vogel, eds., *Ordo: Bath, Word, Prayer, Table* (Akron, OH: OSL Publications, 2006), pp. 216ff.

21. Michel de Certeau, *The Capture of Speech and Other Political Writings* (Minneapolis: University of Minnesota Press, 1998), p. 13.

exert. At the very heart of worship, in its most fundamental components, word and body are one. "Word and rite have the same effect. . . ."[22]

The body continually knocking at the door of representation prevents, or should prevent, any form, any system, from imposing itself. The neighbor, the stranger knocking at the door of our sanctuaries asking for some bread, redirects our stories from ourselves to the other. Worship cannot be merely narrating a story; it is doing much more. If worship merely tells a story or teaches a narrative, even a biblical one, it risks simply repeating a historical story, one that people quickly forget, as Luther notes. He also notes that simply knowing the story is something the devil does much better than we ever will! The whole point, of course, is that the devil does not understand that the story is for him, that the hearing is accompanied by tasting, touching, seeing — that story is really an event that is engaging all of us directly in death and in life.

Worship, the whole liturgical event, moves us always deeper into the story as event: it moves us deeper into the "for you." And this "for you" is both individual and communal, both mind and body. Worship, grounded in Scripture, is not just secondary literature, mere representation, or simply commentary on particular texts. The *ordo* of worship is not a rule to be applied. It is a dynamic — word and sacrament — that maintains a continual poetic tension.

As we can read in the Lutheran confessions, "ceremonies should be observed both so that people may learn the Scriptures and so that, admonished by the Word, they might experience faith and fear and finally even pray."[23] The rituals of worship engage us in an event. We are admonished so that we might experience faith, that is, so that we are gripped by faith, confronted, disputed, and transfigured by faith so that in this experience we fear God: the deep awe about and dependence (yes, dependence) on God alone, the fulfillment of the First Commandment. All this brings us to another activity that in many places defines us, for Luther, as human beings: it brings us to finally even pray.

Proclamation is event, not just a story, and worship enacts this event. It attempts to express something of the inexpressible, to say something about the unsayable. And it does so primarily without words! This exercise of faith that we name worship, this impossible task of translation, calls for, requires,

---

22. Apology of the Augsburg Confession (AP), Article 13: The Number and Use of the Sacraments, *Book of Concord*, pp. 219-20.

23. AP Article 24: Mass, p. 258.

even demands constant renewal. Translation is an ongoing task. This necessity is already evidenced in the simple fact that the gospel is in dialogue with a local community and its culture(s), always breaking local cultures open to the neighbor, to the one who is not part of the "established" culture. If such a dialogue is not happening, worship can become esoteric or otherworldly, performance or entertainment, too quickly engaging a story different from that of the cross. (The most blatant example, perhaps, is when the flag or some other cultural value is equated or set side by side with the gospel.) Without this attentiveness to the neighbor, worship becomes submission to a rule. Worship, on the other hand, is always to take us to the cross in everyday life, in the world around us, not to the cross as we might imagine it two thousand years ago.

The citation above from the Apology of the Augsburg Confession, "Ceremonies should be observed both so that people may learn the Scriptures and so that, admonished by the Word, they might experience faith and fear and finally even pray," offers a succinct definition of worship. The ceremony (worship itself and the pattern, *ordo,* that forms it) has no other goal than that faith be exercised and that the assembly finally come to prayer. That the *ordo* itself is not the goal needs not even be stated. But what is sometimes less obvious is that the *ordo* is not the source of Christian unity. Our unity does not depend on having an *ordo* that is celebrated in the same way across the globe. Our unity as faith community resides in what the *ordo* exercises: faith. Our unity resides, first of all, in our baptism. Faith is our worship.

> However, the church is not only an association of external ties and rites like other civic organizations, but it is principally an association of faith and the Holy Spirit in the hearts of persons. It nevertheless has its external marks so that it can be recognized, namely, the pure teaching of the gospel and the administration of the sacraments in harmony with the gospel of Christ.[24]

The church is an association of faith and the Holy Spirit. In this "association," the believers are living members of a living body. The word "living" (*vivum* and *viva*) is used twice in a few short lines. The body of Christ, the faith community gathered around word and sacrament, is living through the righteousness of the heart that the Holy Spirit alone gives. The body is living through the gifts of the Holy Spirit. This is the true unity, the spiritual unity,

---

24. AP 4: Justification, p. 128.

for which "it is not necessary to have similar human rites, whether universal or particular, because the righteousness of faith is not a righteousness tied to certain traditions. . . ."[25]

Because of statements like this one in our own confessional heritage, many have dismissed, downplayed, or even rejected a pattern for worship — or the *ordo* as I have defined it here.[26] However, that position would miss the point of the confessional witness. The Reformers clearly declare that unity is a unity grounded in faith, but this faith is exercised by the "ceremonies" that the assembly engages in. This exercise consists in teaching, in admonition, leading to "fear" (both as a result of our inability to fulfill God's law and as total dependence on God's immeasurable goodness), to faith, and finally even to prayer, which engages us again fully in the world. To describe this "leading" to fear and faith, the Reformers use the words *concipiant fidem* (to "receive," "catch," or "grasp faith"). The ceremonies, the *ordo*, that is, the holding together of word and sacrament, embody proclamation of the gospel in such a way that the community and believers not only hear the word but catch and grasp it. The body is never absent, even in the *concipiant fidem*.

This is further underscored by the Augsburg Confession in Article 24: "For to remember Christ is to remember his benefits and realize [*sentire*] that they are truly offered to us."[27] The remembering and the realizing are unique. To remember Christ is to encounter Christ today, not imagining Christ or the cross of two thousand years ago. To "remember Christ" is to go to the cross in the world today. And to realize Christ's benefits *(sentire)* is to feel, hear, even smell them! *Sentire* is not cognitively bound.[28] It is this radical presence of the body — at the very heart of proclamation, at the very heart of worship — that pushes worship outside of itself and disrupts all our attempts at systematizing worship. It is the presence of the body that continually demands translation. The *ordo* is this attempt at translation that the Holy Spirit engages in with history and with our lives, which, however, is not meant to define our worship pattern eternally or universally, but is to continually exercise faith and prayer in the community — in us.

The *ordo* is a curious word that exists in multiple forms and in many languages; and yet, on another level, as a word per se, it does not belong to

25. AP 7 and 8: The Church, pp. 174, 179.

26. Despite their rejection of *ordo*, they simply replace it with another pattern, to which they demand equally strict adherence!

27. AP 24: Mass, p. 71.

28. Gláucia Vasconcelos Wilkey perfectly captured the meaning of *sentire* with that sentence.

any one language, other than an ancient one that is no longer spoken. Strangely, as a word without a context and yet surfacing in a multitude of contexts, it points itself to a desire for God's ordering. It points to God's own work, to creation.[29] It points to the body, that most local of all things, to Word made flesh.

As such *ordo* stands for the impossibility of a universally applied, humanly constructed form, opening up rather to an equally impossible task and responsibility, a call to translate the untranslatable, yet continually beginning anew every Sunday — or whenever word and sacrament are celebrated.

29. The Lutheran Confessional writings use *ordinatio* only in this sense; see, e.g., AP 7 and 8: The Church, p. 183.

Inculturation: God's Mission and the Crucian "Old Year's Night" Liturgy

Joseph A. Donnella II

Jesus and Commensality: Context

The community that bears the name of Jesus is also the community gifted with the mandate to share the gospel of Jesus, as Jesus shared God's word and is the very incarnate Word of God. At the outset let me say that the focus of this report has to do with the question of how we are to continue and extend God's mission in our contemporary world. To be more precise, if the mandate to incarnate God's mission as given to us in Jesus Christ is the mandate we now share as the embodied people of God in word, baptism, and Holy Communion, what implications arising out of this mandate are to be drawn as we strive to extend the gospel in local and global communities, as we strive to inculturate worship and missiology?

To assure that we are beginning on common ground, I would cite two principles. These principles are derived from *The Use of the Means of Grace: A Statement on Practice of Word and Sacrament,* which was adopted by the Evangelical Lutheran Church in America (ELCA) in the fall of 1997. In response to the question "What is the Word of God?" principle 5 declares: "Jesus Christ is the Word of God Incarnate. The proclamation of God's message to us is both Law and Gospel. The canonical Scripture of the Old and New Testaments are the written Word of God. Through this Word in these forms, as through the sacraments, God gives faith, forgiveness of sins, and new life."[1] The principle underscores the significance of our understanding

1. *The Use of the Means of Grace: A Statement on the Practice of Word and Sacrament*

of the gospel as a reality that is alive, discernible, and knowable in any cultural context. We see in Jesus Christ the visible presence of the healing mercy of God enfleshed in a human being whose purpose in life was to make known to us God's redeeming will. In history and time, Jesus reveals to us God's desire that this world, our world, might be reconciled to God. For us to encounter Jesus, then, is to encounter in visible form the personal incarnation of God's redeeming love.

This is my understanding of the above, and this is how I would express it in language that is as clear as possible: The gospel that Jesus Christ communicates is a gospel that is uniquely embodied in Jesus. This gospel is known in Hebrew Scripture and community; this gospel is also encountered in the ecclesial communities bearing the name of Jesus Christ and in sacred Scripture and sacramental activities, those sign acts that make visible in outwardly perceptible forms the inward workings of God's grace given by the Holy Spirit to the church to form and empower it to carry on the godly work of Jesus.

The dynamic of the incarnation is pivotal for our understanding. God's redemptive intervention on behalf of humanity and the cosmos is made visible through the encounter we have with the Son of God, Jesus Christ, and God's offer to us of healing mercy is made known through the totality of Christ's life. The incarnation of Christ Jesus is the foundational basis for the missiological work we are called to do as Christians.

As Jesus incarnated the redemptive will of God for us and for the cosmos, we are called in mission to incarnate the mission of Jesus for us and for all the world. We find affirmation of this in Jesus' priestly prayer: "Now they know that everything you have given me is from you: for the words that you gave to me I have given to them, and they have received them and know in truth that I came from you; and they have believed that you sent me" (John 17:7-8a, NRSV).

The work of spreading the gospel involves us, engages us, in revealing to the world that God has opened God's self to us so that we might share in the life of God in the here and now (as well as in the hereafter). How do we know this? And how is this related to issues of worship and inculturation? To get at this, we need to highlight two other principles from *The Use of the Means of Grace*.

Principle 6 establishes that "Sunday, the day of Christ's resurrection and

---

(Minneapolis: Augsburg Fortress, 1997), Principle 5, p. 12. Hereafter, section and page references to this work appear in parentheses within the text.

of the appearances to the disciples by the crucified and risen Christ, is the primary day on which Christians gather to worship. Within this assembly, the Word is read and preached and the sacraments are celebrated" (6:13). This principle needs to be considered in conjunction with Principle 32: "The Lord's Supper was instituted by Jesus Christ on the night of his betrayal" (32:36). Implicit in the Augsburg Confession is an understanding that Holy Communion, consisting of two principle parts, would continue as the chief act of worship on Sundays and festivals of the church. Principle 6 and Principle 32 of *The Use of the Means of Grace* serve to ground the present-day work of the church by linking it with the early Christian community.

> For I received from the Lord what I also handed on to you, that the Lord Jesus on the night when he was betrayed took a loaf of bread, and when he had given thanks, broke it and said, "This is my body broken for you. Do this in remembrance of me." In the same way he took the cup also, after supper, saying, "This cup is the new covenant in my blood. Do this, as often as you drink it, in remembrance of me." (1 Cor. 11:23-25, NRSV)

When the task force responsible for *The Use of the Means of Grace* proposed principles for the Evangelical Lutheran Church in America (ELCA) to adopt, the initial statement regarding the institution of Holy Communion was much fuller. The application to principle 32, listed as background item 32a, hints at the fullness the task force originally had in mind: "In numerous places in the Gospels, the early Church also recognized the Eucharistic significance of other meals during Christ's ministry and after his resurrection" (32:36; see Mark 6:30-52; Luke 24:13-35).

Contemporary New Testament scholars attest that it is the meal practices or open commensality of Jesus during his life, rather than the Last Supper before his death, that lies at the root of any later ritualization of Jesus' presence. Without this far-reaching understanding afforded by seeing the institution of the Eucharist as not strictly limited to the Last Supper — but in the expansive light of the actions and behavior of Jesus while at meals during his lifetime — our ecclesial communities continue to suffer from a narrowness that may be antithetical to the very nature of the gospel itself.

The meal practices of Jesus provide a propitious map guiding us to challenging and transforming perceptions of God's realm or kingdom as envisioned by Jesus. Contemporary anthropologists believe that language developed as a result of the desire for human beings to share food. Peter Farb and George Armelagos summarize the implications of commensality:

In all societies, both simple and complex, eating is the primary way of initiating and maintaining human relationships. . . . To know what, where, how, when, and with whom people eat is to know the character of their society.[2]

For human beings, *commensality,* the rules of tabling and eating, resulted in an intensely complicated web of interconnections and mutual obligations as humanity evolved. In the distinctively sharp social climate of Roman-occupied Palestine at the time of Jesus, conventions about the meaning and circumstances, about the when and where and with whom one shared food, abounded. According to Marcus J. Borg, "the simple act of sharing a meal had exceptional religious and social significance in the social world of Jesus."[3]

Although, we know very little ritually about the meal practice of Jesus, we do know something about the meaning of that meal practice *as an act.* The act of Jesus' meal practice provoked strong negative comment. Several times the Gospels report that Jesus "eats with tax collectors, outcasts and sinners" (see Mark 2:15; Luke 19:7; Matt. 11:19, as well as Luke 7:34).

Our modern sensibilities may render us immune to the social implications of these negative statements. Our common parlance affirms that "all have sinned and fallen short of the glory of God," so that we are accustomed to thinking of all people as sinners. It was not so in the ancient Palestinian world. When criticizers accused Jesus of being a friend of sinners, tax collectors, prostitutes, drunkards, and gluttons, they were pointing to those considered way outside the pale of social respectability. In first-century Palestine, sinners meant outcasts, and the "outcasts" that the criticizers of Jesus had in mind were the poor and traditionally nonobservant Jews, Samaritans and others, including orphans, widows, and foreigners.

The practice of open commensality engaged in by Jesus shattered the barriers of social conventionality. By doing what he was doing, Jesus was enabling "outcasts" to see themselves as belonging, as acceptable to and accepted by God. By doing what he was doing, Jesus was symbolizing and embodying the realm of God as radically egalitarian and compassionate. The open commensality of Jesus during his life became the basis by which the community that bears the name of Jesus anamnestically remembered and

---

2. George Armelagos and Peter Farb, *Consuming Passions: The Anthropology of Eating* (Boston: Houghton Mifflin, 1980), pp. 4, 211.

3. Marcus Borg, *Jesus: A New Vision* (San Francisco: HarperSanFrancisco, 1987), p. 132.

ritualized his presence through his incarnation, life, death, resurrection, and ascension.

There are myriad implications to this, two of which have stunning significance. First, that the meal practice of Jesus challenged conventional social boundaries that delineated the roles between men and women cannot be reasonably doubted. This challenge continues to remain taxing to some ecclesial bodies even today. Second, children in the Roman world were regarded as almost nothing, and a young child's life hung in the balance. This was particularly true for a female child, depending on whether or not that child was perceived as desirable and acknowledged as legitimate. A child's father literally had the right to determine the life or death of that child. Thus the statement attributed to Jesus regarding discipleship — "Let the children come unto me, for to such as these belongs the kingdom of God" — is an extraordinary statement about God's radical inclusiveness.

Contemporary New Testament scholars see continuity between the open commensality of Jesus during his lifetime and the institution of the Eucharist in four key actions highlighted in Dom Gregory Dix's liturgical classic *The Shape of the Liturgy*. Dix reduced the shape, or *ordo*, of eucharistic activity from seven to four principle actions: *took, blessed* (or gave thanks), *broke,* and *gave.*[4] These four actions appear not only in the Last Supper but in the Emmaus meal, plus in the several stories of Jesus feeding the crowds in Mark and John. These actions also materialize in the bread-and-fish Eucharists, or "appearance narratives," at the end of John's Gospel.

These actions, as ritualized embodiments of Jesus' open commensality, startle us when we realize how easy it is for us to miss the dynamic process of Holy Communion when we simply refer to the material elements of the Meal — the "bread and wine" — but not to the receiving community at Holy Communion. The symbolic connotations of *took, blessed, broke,* and *gave* imply, first and foremost, equality of sharing: whatever food there is, is to be shared by all. Incidentally, this is what Paul meant when he chided the Corinthian community for not discerning the body of Christ (see 1 Cor. 11:16): that some people at this meal, or at a meal similar to this, were acting like gluttons and not sharing, that is, they were continuing to maintain the conventional distinctions of class, caste, nationality, and gender (for a fuller context, see 1 Cor. 11:18-29). But there is more: *took* and *blessed* are verbs indicating the actions of a host or master;

---

4. Gregory Dix, *The Shape of the Liturgy* (London: A. & C. Black Ltd., 1945; 1978), pp. 48-49.

broke and *gave* are the actions of a servant. In the most common experiences of males in the world of Jesus and among Jesus' followers, these were the actions of the females of the household, the preparers and servers of the family's food. Dare we suggest that, in his meal practice, Jesus took on the role of both the host and the servant, the gendered roles of both female and male?

The radicality of Jesus' open commensality is manifest in the fact that, at table, Jesus did not simply recline and be served. Jesus did what both host and servant would do out of hospitality and compassion. Like any host at home, Jesus served everyone the same meal, including himself.

Context: Inculturation as a Theological Imperative

With this hermeneutic undergirding our understanding of Jesus' meal practice, we can see that our Eucharists are derived from the meal practices of Jesus. Likewise, we are able to see that the *ordo*, or shape, of the liturgy in the Western world is a derivative rite combining the Word with the sense of open commensality and radical hospitality from the life of Jesus in the commemoration of his death and resurrection. Thus we can now consider issues of inculturation and worship in a particular liturgical and *missiological* context.

"Culture mediates reality; culture is a given," says Louis-Marie Chauvet, professor of sacramental theology at the Institut Catholique in Paris. Theology, as such, can only be contextual; without context there can be no theology.[5] The traditional understanding of classical theology tended to conceive of the theological enterprise as a type of objective science of faith. Indeed, the classic definition that theology is *fides quaerens intellectum* ("faith seeking understanding") gave little to no consideration of how *intellectum* is formed by local context and the "mediation of meaning." Theology is, in and of itself, deeply colored by cultural context. Not paying attention to local context resulted in traditional Western theologies that were unconscious of their own specificity and limitation.

According to Steven Bevans, "reality is not just 'out there,' [reality] is mediated by meaning," a meaning that we give in the context of our culture or historical situation, interpreted from our own particular horizon and in

5. Louis-Marie Chauvet, *Symbol and Sacrament: A Sacramental Reinterpretation of Christian Existence* (Collegeville, MN: Liturgical Press, 1995), pp. 426-27.

our own particular thought forms.[6] Epistemological forms and methods for understanding have strong cultural tints. Robert J. Schreiter reminds us that starting with a "universal" anthropology means starting with a local anthropology extended beyond its cultural boundaries.[7] We cannot get around it; we do not have access to the gospel apart from some kind of human formulation. The reality in our modern world is that the locus of theology is always contextual. This has at least two implications: (1) the message of Christianity is always inculturated/contextual); and (2) cultural patterns that can be used in an attempt to contextualize/inculturate/incarnate the gospel's Christian meaning and existence must be carefully engaged. This is true in spite of the fact that most theologians point to three loci or sources of theology: Scripture, tradition, and the present human context.

The 1996 Nairobi Statement on Worship and Culture of the LWF highlights the interplay of Scripture, tradition, and present human context in the missiological task of inculturation. The statement underscores the fact that worship always involves saying yes and no to any given local culture, and that there is an essential gospel core that supersedes both culture and context. For example, Nairobi declares:

All Christian worship . . . relates dynamically to culture in at least four ways. First, worship is *transcultural,* the same substance for everyone everywhere beyond culture. Second, worship is *contextual,* varying according to local and natural contexts. Third, worship is *counter-cultural,* challenging what is contrary to the gospel in any given culture. Fourth, worship is *cross-cultural,* making sharing possible between different local cultures.[8]

There is much to celebrate in Nairobi's framework of recommendations: (1) The particularity of the cultural setting of the gospel itself is taken seriously; (2) the recognition that the gospel was born into the specificity of a particular Israelite culture; (3) that God can be and is encountered in the various local cultures of our world; (4) that it is possible to share meanings across cultures; (5) that every culture remains subject to the scrutiny, cri-

6. Stephen B. Bevans, *Models of Contextual Theology* (Maryknoll, NY: Orbis, 1992), p. 3.

7. Robert J. Schreiter, *Constructing Local Theologies* (Maryknoll, NY: Orbis, 1986), p. 75.

8. Anita Stauffer, ed., *Christian Worship: Unity in Cultural Diversity* (Geneva: LWF, 1996), pp. 23-28 (italics added).

tique, and transformation mandated by the gospel; and (6) that not everything within a given culture may be seen as connatural in meaning with the essential core of the gospel. These are all good and positive attributes inherent within this missiological method.

This method itself, however, must be subject to critique. And the most ardent critique I have discovered is found in Bevans's *Models of Contextual Theology*. Bevans contends that the weakness in this method is that it has as a starting point the presumption of a supracultural and supracontextual essential doctrine. As Robert McAfee Brown has succinctly put it, gospel content affects cultural and social context.[9] Am I, as a person of African heritage, a *black* Christian Lutheran, or am I a *Christian Lutheran* black? Are the people of the Lutheran churches in the former Danish West Indies *Afri-Caribbean/West Indian* Lutheran Christians, or are they *Christian Lutheran* West Indian/Afri-Caribbean people? Or, given cultural hybridity and migration patterns, could we say that all of us are multiculturally layered, often defying even such ethnologically specific characterizations? But then, how about locality as a gift to be shared, context itself proposing modes of gospel inculturation?

Experience, culture, social location, and social change in this methodology are elements that are always ancillary or subordinate to the supracultural, "never changing" gospel core. Context is always secondary. Ultimately, the gospel is the judge of all contexts, even though the gospel seeks to work with and within every contextual particularity. Both the propositional and quantitative understanding of divine revelation implicit in such a methodology may also be seen as problematic. Revelation is primarily conceived of as a communication of certain truths or doctrines from God, and because such truths are from God, they are perceived with an aura of neutrality, wholly culturally free or clothed in a culture that is divinely sanctioned.

Considering these matters from a missiological perspective, Aylward Shorter asks this question:

> Is inculturation possible . . . as long as Africans are not in control of their own lives and destinies?[10] Is inculturation to be the work of outsiders? Clearly, the answer is "No". . . . Inculturation is not antiquarian, but liber-

---

9. Robert McAfee Brown, "Context Affects Content: The Rootedness of All Theology," *Christianity and Crisis* 37 (July 1977): 170-74.

10. In the context of St. Croix, we would substitute "Crucians" for "Africans."

ational. Missionaries cannot carry out inculturation. They are merely at the start of inculturation, as long as they are in cultural and socio-economic bondage to non-Africans. They are not free to be themselves.[11]

"Liberation of the poor and the oppressed is the fundamental condition for authentic inculturation," Shorter goes on to say. The implicit end of inculturation as a missiological task has to be the creation of something new: a local form of inculturated Christianity. Local cultural experimentation must be allowed in order to achieve this. Without experimentation, the process of inculturation is denied or too long delayed. But how much experimentation, how wide a scope of diversity, can a communion or ecclesial body handle without fear of dissolving? Shorter believes that the process of inculturation must be a reciprocal dialogical process: "Ultimately, inculturation is a community project. The community provides the criteria of authenticity and success, because it is the life of the community that is in question. The community also provides the means of implementation."[12]

What follows is a case study describing an Afri-Caribbean/West Indian community's dialogical engagement regarding a highly local and unique celebration of New Year's Eve, known as "Old Year's Night." My hope in exploring this particular instance of inculturation is to see whether the implications of this case study might also serve as a basis for raising similar questions regarding the process of inculturation among contemporary young people in North America, my own field of ministry at this writing.

A West Indian Liturgical and Contextual Celebration: Old Year's Night

It is customary in the Danish West Indies (now the U.S. Virgin Islands) for the community to gather in prayer on what we in North America call New Year's Eve, but what is known there as Old Year's Night. The final hour of Old Year's Night must be spent with all able-bodied members of the community in prayer, reflection, and reconciliation. The derivation of this ritual practice is unknown. However, the word "inculturation" is a good descriptor here, since the presence of night-watch services or vigils in the Moravian

---

11. Aylward Shorter, *Toward a Theology of Inculturation* (Maryknoll, NY: Orbis, 1994), p. 247.
12. Shorter, *Theology of Inculturation*, pp. 248, 254.

tradition was probably shared and handed on to Lutherans with Afri-Caribbean/West Indian backgrounds.

The two congregations of Center Island Lutheran Parish, Kingshill Lutheran Church and LaVallee's Christus Victor Lutheran Church join in a combined rite of public or corporate confession with a celebration of Holy Communion. This, I learned, is an island custom. The community gathers one hour before midnight. The atmosphere usually is a charged mixture of hushed chatter and quiet resolution. Candles are lit, and they mark the entryway to the sanctuary, where the baptismal font is placed, signaling the light of Christ. The paschal candle is also lit as the pastor calls the community to recollection by sharing the significance of this night.

A corporate rite of confession, prayer, and absolution, complete with Scripture readings, a sermon, hymns, and the laying on of hands makes up the first half of the worship experience. The readings are chosen with care to emphasize the communal nature of the brokenness felt in the Christian community whenever there is discord and pain. In the colloquial language of the Crucian community, the people of the community are asked to remember what "vexes them." What causes them to be at odds with one another? What leads them to dissociate from or shun one another? There is one particular Gospel pericope customarily associated with this night. It is the parable of the barren fig tree found in Luke 13:6-9:

> Then [Jesus] told this parable: "A man had a fig tree planted in his vineyard; and he came looking for fruit on it and found none. So he said to the gardener, "See here! For three years I have come looking for fruit on this fig tree, and still I find none. Cut it down! Why should it be wasting the soil?' [The gardener] replied, "Sir, let it alone for one more year, until I dig around it and put manure on it. If it bears fruit next year, well and good; but if not, you can cut it down" (Luke 13:6-9; NRSV).[13]

I did not initially understand the significance of this parable to the Crucian community. It seemed harsh, unyielding, hardly appropriate as a way of beginning something new. So, when I asked why this would be the reading, members of the local community responded that it is because it's about being given another chance at life. It's about being given one more year. It's about

---

13. Michael D. Coogan, Marc Z. Brettler, Carol A. Newsome, and Pheme Perkins, eds., *The New Oxford Annotated Bible: New Revised Standard Version with the Apocrypha* (Oxford: Oxford University Press, 2010), p. 1856.

the mercy and graciousness of God. On Old Year's Night we ask forgiveness of everyone we know we have offended in the hope that we may begin the New Year with a clean slate. Old Year's Night is an opportunity to get rid of grudges — to start again.

The somberly reflective tone of Old Year's Night stands in stark contrast to the normally jubilant directness of the Crucian community, as members of the community are asked to quietly recall and reflect on destructive, neglectful, or self-indulgent behaviors engaged in during the past year. They are also asked to think of ways to effect active reconciliation between estranged family members, neighbors, and/or other community members. The presider/preacher's understood objective during this time is to encourage honest self-recollection and consolation: to move the community away from apathy, indifference, despair, neglect, or violent destructiveness. In the context of the island, this meant that allowance had to be made for spontaneous prayer, for coming with whispered voice to hear the mercy of God proclaimed individually through prayer and the laying on of hands. While confessing burdens of the heart, mind, and soul, it was important to members of the Crucian community that their confessor be nonjudgmental. In small communities, people often know what has been done that has caused feelings to be rubbed raw. Salt on open wounds only hurts more. Hence, the public order of confession is acknowledgment enough of the desire to turn life in a new direction. The public rite culminates in a private and personal declaration of absolution.

Once all who desire it have received personal absolution and consolation, the rite of Old Year's Night reaches its first climactic peak, as the peace of Christ is exchanged and those within the community who formerly have been estranged begin anew the process of accepting one another. Life in community is restored. The community then turns to its celebration of belonging as the reconciled body of Christ in the thanksgiving (Eucharist) of Holy Communion.

An outline of the rite as customarily practiced in the Center Island Lutheran Parish, one that reflects both the heritage of the past and the local context, follows:

The Liturgy of the Word
Sign of the Cross [sign of Baptism is made]
Gathering hymn: "Abide With Me"
Confessional Collect: "Father of mercies and God of all consolation . . . ."

Silence
Old Testament reading: Jeremiah 31:31-34
Psalm 51 (recited or sung responsively)
New Testament reading: Romans 7:14-25
"Alleluia" (verse or sentence)
Gospel reading: Luke 13:6-9
Sermon
Hymn: For example, "The Day You Gave Us"
Confession (corporate)
Absolution
Laying on of hands (individually)
Intercessions
The sharing of peace

The liturgy of the meal
The offering: Presentation of gifts
Offering prayer
The great thanksgiving
Dialogue
Proper preface
Sanctus
Eucharistic prayer
Lord's Prayer
Fraction: Breaking of the bread
Agnus dei: Lamb of God
Communion (during distribution, singing of hymns, for example, "Let Us Break Bread Together," "Come. Let Us Eat." or "Let Us Ever Walk with Jesus")
Post-Communion table blessing
Post-Communion canticle
Post-Communion prayer (led by assisting minister)
Benediction and dismissal

Reflections on Old Year's Night

Pastors of souls must therefore realize that when the liturgy is celebrated, more is required than the mere observance of the laws governing valid and licit celebration. It is their duty to ensure that the faithful take part knowingly, actively, and fruitfully.[14]

Good pastoral practice begins by listening, by taking seriously the concerns and witness, the authenticity of the community. Center Island Lutheran Parish at that time had not yet fully entered into the present contemporary technological world of possibility and malaise. The culture of the islands was a strong culture of belonging with permeable boundaries; surviving required a certain sense of permeability. An anthropologist or sociologist would probably have said that the culture of the islands had not yet entered into modernity. Mary Douglas writes:

> In a culture of modernity people have a weak sense of belonging or of obligations to the group. Individuals form alliances with one another to provide better opportunities for competitive success, but such bondings are very fragile since they are held together only by the self-interest of the individuals themselves. They break apart as soon as more profitable inter-relationships appear.[15]

David Power tells us that "a perception as old as Christianity is that faith in Jesus Christ brings freedom."[16] Though the basic idea of an end-of-the-year service came through mission work from the outside, the Old Year's Night service was created not by outsiders but by the Crucian people of the islands themselves. Perhaps even in their designation of this celebration, the Crucian community expressed an essential struggle that they experienced internally as their community tried to rid itself of what was stopping them from empathetic and sympathetic regard. For instance, the language of the Crucian community regarding "vexing, melee [gossip], straf [strife], untruth and withholding" is understood to be the language of life and death.[17] The pattern of worship was established with a view toward communal reconciliation. Seldom was the verbiage the continental language of sin and guilt. While

14. Walter M. Abbot, ed., *The Documents of Vatican II,* Constitution on the Sacred Liturgy, Article 11 (New York: The America Press, 1966), p. 143.
15. Mary Douglas, *Purity and Danger: An Analysis of the Concepts of Pollution and Taboo* (London: Routledge and Kegan Paul, 1966), pp. 41-57, 95.
16. David N. Power, *Worship: Culture and Theology* (Washington, DC: Pastoral Press, 1990), p. 68.
17. See Joseph A. Donnella II, *Like Other People's Children* (Saarbrucken: LAP Lambert Academic Publishing, 2010), pp. 186-93.

there were Western and Northern theological understandings present, the communities of LaVallee and Kingshill were more keenly aware of everyday life struggles and the necessity of interdependent reliance from person to person. When the community was broken, the future remained uncertain.

Old Year's Night was about letting go, being liberated, understanding and reverencing one another in community and communion. Elochukwu Uzukwu describes ritual action and indicates that "every ritual is a gesture, though not every gesture is a ritual." Groups use ritual as a means of communication and as a source of identity and belonging. Ritual gestures are symbolic actions — ritual symbols. Rituals are, in fact, generative action signifying initiation into a group. At the heart of any society are ritual behaviors that reveal who a people understand themselves to be. "Ritual behavior is a laying down of patterns that are normative and creative for existence (ethical and aesthetic)."[18] The way things *were* controls the way things *are*. Artistic expression and creativity leads ritual to also indicate the way things *should be*. Normative dynamic and transformative aspects of ritual life are thereby indicated. Religious and spiritual practices have implied moral and ethical behavioral consequences. This is why oppressed peoples across the globe are suspicious when the practices of religious and spiritual life seem to lead to little or no social transformation, liberation, or change in the way a society structures dynamics of power. What was and what is of necessity yield to what ought to be.

The ritual of Old Year's Night on the island of St. Croix connects the community to its core. The coherence of the community is reestablished as the people of the community acknowledge ways they have contributed to the collapse of social cohesiveness. In a world where survival is dependent on mutual interdependence and belonging, the reconciling nature of the Old Year's Night celebration re-creates the community, anchoring the community's existence in a relationship of transcendence. The conciliatory nature of Old Year's Night centers on the recognition that, by entering a transcendent relationship with God and one another, the community restores its life. The Crucian community attempts to overcome the limits of human brokenness by participating in this rite: reconciliation and peacemaking lead to renewed communal self-discovery, and the community is reborn, reformed, and reconstituted. Participation in the Old Year's Night rites of public confession, individual and corporate absolution within the community, and

18. Elochukwu E. Uzukwu, *Worship as Body Language* (Collegeville, MN: Liturgical Press, 1997), p. 41.

sharing the breaking of bread (the Eucharist) — with the pivotal movement of the community actualized at the center of ritual life — leads to the embrace of peace. Thus does the gospel lead us:

> So when you are offering your gift at the altar, if you remember that your brother or sister has something against you, leave your gift there at the altar and go; first be reconciled to your brother [or sister], then come and offer your gift. (Matt. 5:23-24; NRSV)[19]

The Old Year's Night celebration brings the Crucian community to awareness of "how it is" in the world, how God is calling them to be their most authentic selves at the same time that God is asking them to "let go" of the stresses that lead to untruth and annihilation. Old Year's Night celebration allows the re-created community to continue. The ritual activities of Old Year's Night thus bring the community of Center Island Lutheran Parish to a moment in time that takes them beyond time to what they, the community, are called to be in the future as the community of God's people. Reconciliatory rites re-create not only by restoring stability and a sense of belonging; they also bring the promise of material and spiritual healing.

A predominant theological motif in recent years has been to see the connection between rites of reconciliation and baptism. There is something in the public pattern of reconciliation and renewal of baptism adopted by the Crucian community that may well serve to deepen the understanding of all Christian communities — that is, the power of lamentation. At the font of baptism, we may pour out our hurt, our grief, our anguish, our woeful "why" when the world's existential injury touches our brokenness at the same time as we express longing for God and desire for unity with one another. Lamentation needs to be more regularly incorporated into rites of reconciliation. Oppressed people seem to be more adept at recognizing the social and communal aspects of sin than are their more materially privileged colonial brothers and sisters. Still, reconciliation includes everyone.

Crucian communal life has been radically inclusive when left to flourish apart from colonial influence. In baptism God sets us free both as individuals and as the people of God. Free from sin, free from oppression, free from the weight of colonial or spiritual dominance. The ritual activities of Old Year's Night are carefully scheduled so as to be completed by midnight. At mid-

---

19. *The Oxford Annotated Bible: The New Revised Standard Version, New Testament*, p. 12.

night, church bells are tolled, the entire island community moves from ecclesial gatherings into the streets and public squares of the towns. The celebration of the New Year takes on a carnival-like atmosphere as rhythms of calypso, reggae, salsa, jazz, and contemporary song fill the night air. Dance, food, and drink are plentiful as the celebration continues till the light of dawn. Hybridization is the norm here. Harmony exists when all God's children share life together. Thank God! A New Year has been granted. Life continues!

Inculturation and Worship with Today's Young: Taizé's Model

In light of contemporary sensibilities, it seems that the advance of Christian life in the postmodern West has come to a still-point in which diminishing returns are more than likely the wave of the future. Rapid growth in the last five years of new college students who declare that they have no religious affiliation is a certain sign that there is a problem. Is there any insight to be gained from the missiological work of the Crucian community with regards to inculturation? Inculturated liturgies are ritual experiences of the transcendent evoking local culture in such a way that the community may claim the liturgy as its own. Is there, then, anything in the Caribbean framework of Old Year's Night that may be translatable to places and situations that focus on Christian formation, such as college campuses or seminaries? Many North American young people (ages eighteen to twenty-two years) characterize their religious lives and spiritual tradition as "none." If ritual generates community, is there something about the way ritual is engaged that does not work? Is there something about the way communities participate in ritual life that strikes the young as unreal, as inauthentic? Or are we ritually enacting what seem to them to be experiences of cognitive dissonance?

In January 2013, I led a small group of college students on an experiential pilgrimage to the Taizé community in Macon, France. Since 1962, thousands of young people from all parts of the globe have flocked to that place. There they are welcomed, invited to dialogue, sing, pray, share in small groups, and experience silence as they join the daily and weekly life cycle of work and prayer that characterizes this ecumenical community. The Taizé community's simplified Benedictine rule of prayer, study, and work appeals to young people who are searching, trying to discern what they believe and whether or not they believe. Here young people witness a community of people formed of varied religious backgrounds — Protestant, Catholic, Maronite, and Orthodox — who are faithfully committed to monasticism as a way of living out the gospel. Christ's life as this community fleshes it out, incarnates it, is experiential reconciliation and communion. East and West, North and South, male and female, lay and ordained — people come from all across the globe.

Just as Jesus bore witness to God's radical inclusiveness, the Taizé community seeks to model God's way of life in persons, art, prayer, and lifestyle. Taizé and the Crucian community share at heart an experience of ritual re-creating community. Why do young people come to Taizé? "Because," as those who sojourned at Taizé informed me, "Taizé is not like any other place in the world. Young people flock to Taizé because they seek belonging and communities where they may authentically be themselves." How does this happen? Through silence and the singing of simple chants, through reflective engaged reading of sacred Scripture, by sharing and listening and by being listened to, young people experience transformation and transcendence.

Young people who develop in communities of material privilege often are misinformed concerning ways that help them to experience belonging. What they have known and felt are experiences of disharmony and disintegration. Sometimes, in order "to deaden the pain of not belonging," young people resort to different kinds of behavioral addictions. Sometimes, like their families of origin, young people look for meaning and purpose by acquiring more and more in the way of the material aspects of life, not realizing that conspicuous material consumption rarely conveys the deep satisfaction one feels through relational connections in a community of belonging. The Taizé community provides a countercultural experiential alternative to a life centered in a preoccupied material existence. But can that ethos be transported elsewhere — and should it be? Or is there an invitation for church leaders to reflect on the basic principles taken into account on liturgical preparation in Taizé?

Sensing welcome from the brothers as unconditional as can be known among human beings, young people experience connectedness and the beginning groundswells of belonging. Is this not possible on Sunday services in each place and time? At Taizé you don't have to worry about whether or not you fit in. You belong — as a seeker. You are welcomed to explore life in a better way. In this safe space, you are free to be who you are. But then, all of us are seekers.

Ritual re-creates God's better way. On St. Croix the Old Year's Night ritual re-creates the community of belonging, the community of the baptized. What Taizé and the cultural community ritual of reconciliation and communion on the island offer in common is a hopeful recasting of the future — a sense of what life may be like in God's kingdom — in a community in which all belong. What young people seek today is a better way to experience what it is to belong. Liturgy that is truly inculturated models this better way.

Worship: Ecumenical Core and Cultural Context

S. Anita Stauffer

To deal with the relationships between worship and culture is at once to deal with the heart of the Christian life and with a deeply complex subject. It affects people's primary Christian experience, their spirituality, and it can thus be very controversial. It is a subject on which everyone has an opinion and many emotions.

The subject of worship and culture includes church music and church architecture and art, as well as preaching and liturgy. Its foundations are in the overall relationship between the gospel and culture, but it also relates to a wide variety of particular disciplines, among them biblical studies, theology, cultural anthropology, church history, liturgics, homiletics, ritual studies, topistics, ethnomusicology, aesthetic philosophy and theology, and architecture and art.[1] Although an enormous body of literature has already been published on the matter, in most congregations all over the world, either local culture is ignored in worship or it has been reflected in shallow and unexamined ways.[2]

---

1. Topistics is "the holistic study of places" and human experience in those places. See E. Victor Walter, "The Places of Experience," *The Philosophical Forum* (Winter 1980-81): 163.

2. For a select listing, see the bibliography in the back of this book.

An earlier — and quite different — form of this article appeared as "Culture and Christian Worship in Intersection," *International Review of Mission* 84, nos. 332/333 (January/April 1995): 65-76.

It is on the basis of this situation that the Lutheran World Federation (LWF) initiated a long-term interdisciplinary study of the relationships between Christian worship and the diverse cultures of the world. An ongoing study team was formed, consisting of about twenty-five people from five continents, with Anglican, Roman Catholic, and Methodist participant-observers. Two eminent scholars were enlisted to serve as resource persons: Gordon W. Lathrop, professor of liturgy at the Lutheran Theological Seminary in Philadelphia; and Anscar J. Chupungco, OSB, director of both the Paul VI Institute of Liturgy in the Philippines and at the Pontifical Liturgical Institute in Rome. The ecumenical involvement was deemed vital from the beginning, for the subject itself is ecumenical in fundamental ways.

The team first met in October 1993 in Cartigny, Switzerland, for an exploration of some of the biblical and historical foundations of the topic, particularly with regard to baptism and Eucharist in the New Testament era, the early church, and the Lutheran Reformation. Concentrated attention was given to how worship (liturgy, music, and architectural setting) in the early church was contextualized in the Jewish and Hellenistic milieus. In March 1994, the study team gathered again, this time in Hong Kong, to explore contemporary issues and questions, including discussions of case studies from all over the world. The differing dynamics of monocultural, bicultural, and multicultural societies were considered, as were such realities as cultural evolution and cultural diffusion. The major essays and reports from both of those consultations appeared in the previous LWF Studies volume, entitled *Worship and Culture in Dialogue*.[3]

From mid-1994 through the end of 1995, the study was in a regional phase, during which regional study teams identified and explored the particular issues related to worship and culture in their parts of the world, using different methodologies and involving a wide variety of laity, pastors, bishops, professors, musicians, and artists/architects. The regional teams were encouraged to do their research ecumenically to the greatest possible extent, though in the end we had to admit that that did not happen.

Among the questions listed for the regional teams to explore were the following:

3. S. Anita Stauffer, ed., *Worship and Culture in Dialogue* (Geneva: LWF, Department for Theology and Studies, 1994) (hereafter cited as *WCD*). There are also editions in German: *Gottesdienst und Kultur im Dialog;* French: *Culte et culture en dialogue;* and Spanish: *Dialogo entre Culto y Cultura.* Quotations in this chapter are from the English edition, hence *WCD*.

General Areas for Inquiry

1. What is the cultural situation in a given region/subregion of (a) the population as a whole, and (b) of the Lutheran church(es)? To what extent is the situation homogeneous and monocultural, heterogeneous, indigenous, immigrant, and so forth? What are the cultural values and patterns?[4]
2. What cultural patterns might be brought into Christian worship? Why?
3. In what regards should Christian worship in this region/subregion be countercultural? Why? In what sense should worship (a) contradict the culture or (b) reinterpret the culture?
4. What resistance is there to (a) contextualization and (b) the countercultural? Why?
5. What are the questions regarding the liturgical core (Cartigny Statement, 3.7) to be explored in this region[5]?
6. Are there currently efforts toward contextualization of liturgy, music, and church architecture/art in the member churches of the given region? What help is needed in those efforts?

Specific Issues for Inquiry

1. Eucharistic prayers
2. Church year calendar and liturgical colors
3. Hymn texts and music
4. Choral and instrumental music for worship
5. Church architecture, art, and furnishings[6]
6. Eucharistic vessels and vestments
7. Lectionary
8. Baptism
9. Healing rites
10. Linguistic style of liturgical texts
11. Participation of the congregation in worship, and the sharing of liturgical leadership through the use of lay ministers (lectors, intercessors, etc.)
12. Patterns of reverence and of hospitality/community
13. Preaching
14. Confession and absolution

4. Regarding cultural values and patterns, see Anscar Chupungco, "Liturgy and the Components of Culture," in *WCD*, pp. 153-65.

5. *WCD*, p. 133.

6. See Stauffer, "Contemporary Questions on Church Architecture and Culture," in *WCD*, pp. 167-81.

The regions were at liberty to explore these issues as it seemed most appropriate in the given place, as well as to consider other questions and issues. Regional and subregional research conferences were held in Africa, Canada, the Nordic region, eastern Europe, central Europe, Papua New Guinea, and the United States. In Brazil, graduate students of one study team member were trained in both anthropology and worship to conduct field research. Seminary students were also involved in the research in Papua New Guinea. Elsewhere in Asia, study team members conducted their research largely through individual interviews. The Spanish translation of the Cartigny Statement was the focus of an ecumenical conference in Latin America. The substance of the study has been used by the liturgical commission of the Evangelical Lutheran Church of the Central African Republic.

In 1996 the international study team met in Nairobi (1) to analyze and synthesize the findings of the regional research; (2) to consider methodologies for contextualizing the Eucharist; (3) to explore the countercultural nature of the Eucharist; and (4) to plan a variety of ways to implement the discoveries of the study thus far, as each region and LWF member church decides is helpful. The papers, report, and statement of the Nairobi consultation are contained in the present volume. As a way of making a connection between *Worship and Culture in Dialogue* and the present volume, it is possible to consider several basic statements related to some of the intersections between culture and Christian worship.

1. There is an ecumenical core of Christian worship.
Most briefly, the core consists of assembly around word, baptism, and Eucharist. People come together, assemble, gather around Jesus Christ, to hear the word proclaimed and to receive God's gracious sacramental gifts of baptism and Eucharist. Christian worship is a corporate event in the sense of the church being the body, or corpus, of Christ. Christianity is not a private, individualistic religion: that is, unlike in a religion such as Hinduism, Christian worship does not essentially consist of individual cultic acts. We assemble together for God's gifts of word and sacrament, and we offer our response of prayer and praise.

Lutherans usually describe this core in the phraseology of the Augsburg Confession, article 7: The church "is the assembly of all believers among whom the Gospel is preached in its purity and the holy sacraments are administered according to the Gospel."[7] However, this core is shared

---

7. English translation in *The Book of Concord: The Confessions of the Evangelical Lutheran Church,* trans. and ed. Theodore G. Tappert (Philadelphia: Fortress, 1959), p. 32.

across confessional and cultural lines, and it endures from one generation to the next. There is the witness of teaching that leads to baptism in water and in the triune name, and the assembly of the baptized around Christ present in proclaimed word and the shared thanksgiving meal. The ecumenical consensus on this core, these liturgical shapes or patterns, was made clear in the 1982 WCC Faith and Order Paper 111, "Baptism, Eucharist and Ministry,"[8] and more recently by the Ditchingham Report in Faith and Order Paper 171.[9] This core is further explored in the chapters by Gordon Lathrop in this book. Ironically, the regional research discovered that the liturgical core is simply ignored in some Lutheran churches around the world, either out of ignorance of it, or because of influence from charismatics, for example.

As the LWF Worship and Culture Study has progressed (and "in conversation" with recent WCC Faith and Order work in worship), it has become ever more clear that the subject has significant ecumenical trajectories. Further work in contextualization, particularly work done locally and regionally, should be ecumenical. There are particularly rich possibilities in many areas of the world for Anglican-Lutheran cooperation, and one hopes that Roman Catholic-Lutheran cooperation can grow. These are the two Christian world communions in the Western church in which the liturgical core is most deeply and most fully shared.[10]

2. Christian worship has always interacted with culture.

From apostolic times, Christians have examined and critiqued the cultures in which they lived, making decisions about which cultural elements can be adopted and adapted, transformed and reinterpreted, for their worship. It is and has always been a necessary task in evangelization — in New Testament times, in the patristic era, in the Reformation, and ever since. Worship is a human activity, and it is thus inevitably and inherently related to culture. Anscar Chupungco puts it this way: "The core of the liturgy is a supracultural reality which the Church received through apostolic preaching and preserves intact in every time and place. What inculturation means is that worship assimilates the people's language, ritual,

8. Geneva: WCC, 1982.

9. "Report of the Consultation," in Thomas F. Best and Dagmar Heller, eds., *So We Believe, So We Pray: Towards Koinonia in Worship* (Geneva: WCC Publications, 1995).

10. For detailed attention to the contextualization of baptism and Eucharist in history, see *WCD*, part 2.

and symbolic patterns. In this way the people are able to claim and own the liturgical core. . . ."[11]

Liturgical contextualization and Christian evangelization have always gone hand in hand, as they still do today. It is equally true that questions of the ways in which worship is countercultural (see #4 below) are also crucial to evangelization and to church renewal. Therefore, sometimes the interaction between worship and culture has been a conscious rejection by the church of an element of culture. In church architectural history, for example, it is significant that, during the third and fourth centuries, when special places for Christian worship began to be constructed, pagan temples were rejected as the model. There has always been an effort by the Christian church to contextualize its worship life, but also to avoid syncretism — that is, to avoid those cultural elements that would contradict or undermine the gospel, or would confuse the people regarding Christian identity.[12]

3. Cultures are to be respected but also critiqued.

It is all too common in attempts at liturgical contextualization for cultures to be dealt with in a shallow way, even (perhaps inadvertently) to be played with. It is not enough simply to take elements from a culture and insert them into Christian worship without understanding what those elements mean in their own cultural context. There is a need to explore a given culture in depth before elements from it are imported into worship. Christians need to understand, for example, the cultural meanings of an African tribal king's hut before they use it as the model for a Christian church, or the Buddhist meaning of a pagoda before they use it as a Christian baptismal font. Christians need to understand the dynamics of the entertainment culture before they use a theater or an opera house as the model for a worship space. One of the leading proponents of contextualization in Africa says that "syncretism occurs when enthusiastic missionaries conduct a superficial adaptation in ignorance of the true meaning of cultural symbols."

Superficial adaptation of cultural elements is no less a problem in today's "consumer and entertainment culture in North America" than it is in the developing world.[13] Sometimes it will be decided — after thorough anthropological and theological exploration — that some cultural elements are

---

11. Anscar Chupungco, "Baptism in the Early Church and its Cultural Settings," *WCD*, p. 40.

12. Aylwald Shorter, *Evangelization and Culture* (London: Geoffrey Chapman, 1994), p. 33. Note that I, like Shorter, use the word "syncretism" in the negative sense.

13. And perhaps, so far, still to a lesser extent in northern Europe. See *The Consumer*

appropriately adapted for liturgical use, sometimes not. If the verdict is positive, usually it calls for adaptation rather than mere adoption, for it is often the case that cultural elements need critique, transformation, and reorientation for such use. They must be able to serve the gospel, to be oriented toward Christ present in word and sacrament.

Chupungco has articulated this balance of respect and critique: "[W]hile we assume that not everything cultural can be assimilated by the liturgy and that what is assimilated must undergo a strict critical evaluation, we should keep in mind that culture is not something we play around with or, worse, impose upon in the name of liturgical inculturation." On the other hand, he adds, "Christian liturgy welcomes the values, cultural patterns . . . of peoples and races, so long as they can be vehicles of Christ's message."[14] In a sense he explores this balance further in this present volume as he considers criteria for contextualization methodologies.

The relationship between worship and culture is always a two-way interaction; both the liturgy and the culture are challenged, and both are changed. The 1994 Vatican instruction on inculturation of the Roman liturgy says it well: "The liturgy, like the Gospel, must respect cultures, but at the same time invite them to purify and sanctify themselves."[15] The paradigm for contextualization is not just the incarnation, but also the paschal mystery — the death and resurrection of Jesus Christ — and our transforming baptismal participation in it (Rom. 6:3-5). There is also a crucial pneumatological element: as Georg Kretschmar has pointed out, faith taking shape in various cultures is "the gift and work of the Holy Spirit."[16]

4. Christian worship relates to culture in at least three ways: worship is transcultural, contextual, and countercultural.

First, worship is transcultural. The resurrected Christ himself transcends cultural lines, of course, and our worship of Christ is thus inherently transcultural. The basic pattern of word and eucharistic meal, baptism in water

---

Society as an Ethical Challenge: Report for the Norwegian Bishops' Conference 1992 (Oslo: Church of Norway Information Service, 1992).

14. Anscar Chupungco, "Liturgy and the Components of Culture," in *WCD*, p. 154.

15. Congregation for Divine Worship and the Discipline of the Sacraments, *The Roman Liturgy and Inculturation: Fourth Instruction for the Right Application of the Conciliar Constitution on the Liturgy* (Nos. 37-40), sec. 19 (Vatican City, 1994.) The English text also appears in *Origins* 23, no. 43 (April 14, 1994).

16. Kretschmar, "The Early Church and Hellenistic Culture," *International Review of Mission* 84, nos. 332/333 (January/April 1995): 44.

in the triune name, and use of the ecumenical creeds and the Our Father — these all witness to the nature of the church as a worldwide communio.[17] The important Faith and Order document entitled "Baptism, Eucharist and Ministry" can be considered a consensus statement of transcultural as well as ecumenical commonalities. The Nairobi Statement, printed in this book, summarizes the transcultural nature of worship in section 2.

Second, worship is — or should be — contextual. The term inculturation has often been used for this, though there has been no agreement on its definition. I prefer the terms "contextualization" and "localization" because they are broader than the term "inculturation." In church architecture, for example, contextualization is concerned with topography, climate, and indigenous building materials — as well as culture. The meaning of contextualization is obvious: it is the use or echo of local cultural and natural elements in worship and in the space in which it occurs. It is making the bridge between worship and local context, so that worship can be meaningful to the people in their everyday lives. It is the process toward enabling a church building in China or central Africa to look like it has architectural roots in those places rather than in Europe or the United States. It is encouraging congregations in Latin America or South Africa to sing at least some hymns from their own cultures. It is the preparation and use of eucharistic prayers that rehearse salvation history not only with biblical images but also with local terms and images to which the people can relate. The Anglican Province of Kenya, for example, has made a start on this in the preface of the eucharistic prayer in their 1989 rite:

It is right and our delight to give you thanks and praise, great Father, living God, supreme over the world, Creator, Provider, Saviour and Giver. From a wandering nomad you created your family; for a burdened people you raised up a leader; for a confused nation you chose a king; for a rebellious crowd you sent your prophets. In these last days you have sent us your Son, your perfect image, bringing your kingdom, revealing your will, dy-

---

17. The introduction to "Confessing the One Faith," Faith and Order Paper No. 153 (Geneva: WCC, 1991) implicitly affirms the transcultural nature of the Nicene Creed: "[C]hurches which belong to different Christian traditions and live in diverse cultural, social, political, and religious contexts, need to reappropriate their common basis in the apostolic faith so that they may confess their faith together. In so doing, they will give common witness to the saving purposes of the Triune God for all humanity and all creation" (sec. 5). For more on creeds and culture, see Kretschmar, "The Early Church and Hellenistic Culture," pp. 33-46.

ing, rising, reigning, remaking your people for yourself. Through him you have poured out your Holy Spirit, filling us with light and life. Therefore with angels, archangels, faithful ancestors and all in heaven, we proclaim your great and glorious name, forever praising you and saying: "Holy, holy, holy. . . ."[18]

This text echoes both the Bible and the Kenyan situation. Using imagery that is locally comprehensible, it makes clear that the congregation is giving thanks for the mighty acts of God, and it is an appropriate liturgical adaptation and reinterpretation of African respect for their ancestors.[19] Both core and culture are taken seriously. Another example is the following section of a eucharistic prayer, giving thanks for Christ and for creation, from the Roman Catholic liturgy in Zaire, an early effort at contextualization:

Holy Father, we praise you through your Son Jesus, our mediator.
He is your Word, the Word that gives us life.
Through him you created the heaven and the earth;
Through him you created our great river, the Zaire;
Through him you created our forests, our rivers, our lakes;
Through him you created the animals who live in our forests and the
    fish who live in our rivers.
Through him you have created the things we can see, and also the things
    we do not see.[20]

The same is true of the Anglican Province of New Zealand, which includes the islands of Polynesia. In a eucharistic liturgy approved in 1989, a canticle of praise in the opening section contains this section of thanksgiving for creation, following a thanksgiving for Christ:

So now we offer our thanks
for the beauty of these islands;
for the wild places and the busy,
for the mountains, the coast and the sea.[21]

18. A Kenyan Service of Holy Communion (Nairobi: Uzima Press, 1989), pp. 27-28.
19. For commentary on linking to the ancestors in the context of African eucharistic prayers, see Elochuwu Uzukwu, "Inculturation and the Liturgy (Eucharist)," in Rosino Gibellini, ed., *Paths of African Theology* (London: SCM Press. 1994), esp. pp. 105-8.
20. "The Zaire Rite for the Mass," *African Ecclesial Review* 17, no. 4 (July 1975): 246.
21. *A New Zealand Prayer Book* (Auckland: William Collins), p. 477.

Proclamation of the Word — preaching — is also a vital area for relating to culture. What are the images, the customs, the stories in a culture that can help the Word come alive? For example, Aylward Shorter has described preaching in Africa in the form of a "choric story, with a refrain to be sung at different points by the congregation."[22] It might also be asked to what extent a lectionary should relate to a given cultural context, or, by contrast, to what extent a lectionary should be a more global element of worship. This, of course, is also an important ecumenical question.

Contextualization needs to occur with church music and church architecture as well. Regarding church music, Mark Bangert has described Balinese music accompanied by gamelans and a musical setting of the liturgy in east Africa that uses the typical African call-response pattern.[23] Hymnody, too, needs to reflect to some degree the local context, both musically and textually. A good early example of such hymnic contextualization is "'Twas in the Moon of Wintertime," the earliest Canadian carol in existence, written by a Jesuit missionary to the indigenous Huron people in the seventeenth century:[24]

> 'Twas in the moon of wintertime when all the birds had fled,
> That God, the Lord of all the earth, sent angel choirs instead.
> Before their light the stars grew dim,
> and wond'ring hunters heard the hymn:
> Jesus, your king is born![25]

In the southern hemisphere, where Christmas occurs in the summer, different imagery is needed. Consider this hymn text from New Zealand:

> Carol our Christmas, an upside down Christmas;
> snow is not falling and trees are not bare.
> Carol the summer, and welcome the Christ Child,

---

22. Aylward Shorter, *Evangelization and Culture* (London: Geoffrey Chapman, 1994), pp. 129-30. See also Shorter, "Form and Content in the African Sermon: An Experiment," *African Ecclesial Review* 11, no. 3 (1969): 263-79.

23. See Mark Bangert, "Dynamics of Liturgy and World Musics: A Methodology for Evaluation," in *WCD*, pp. 183-203.

24. Marilyn Kay Stulken, *Hymnal Companion to the Lutheran Book of Worship* (Philadelphia: Fortress, 1981), p. 175.

25. Hymn 42, stanza 1, *Lutheran Book of Worship* (Minneapolis and Philadelphia: Augsburg Publishing and LCA Board of Publication, 1978).

warm in our sunshine and sweetness of air.
Sing of the gold and the green and the sparkle,
water and river and lure of the beach.
Sing in the happiness of open spaces,
sing a Nativity summer can reach![26]

In church architecture, one could cite the exemplary St. Mary's Anglican Church, Causeway Bay, Hong Kong, which uses a number of traditional Chinese artistic motifs on both the exterior and interior; or the new Lutheran Theological Seminary in the New Territories, Hong Kong.[27] One can also cite the new baptismal font in an African-American parish in Chicago (St. Benedict the African Roman Catholic Church), which is in the form of a natural body of water, reflecting the traditional African respect for the earth. The font is a round pool, resembling a pond, approximately eight meters across and more than one meter deep.[28]

In all three areas of liturgy, music, and the visual environment for worship, however, one could also cite shallow and inappropriate examples of "contextualization." (If Bonhoeffer could write of "cheap grace," perhaps we could add the term "cheap contextualization.") There is a clear need for intensive work by all the churches, so that contextualization can be done in an ever deeper way, respecting both culture and Christian faith. Methodologies for contextualization, especially those of dynamic equivalence and creative assimilation, are explored by Anscar Chupungco in his chapter in this volume, and they are summarized in the Nairobi Statement, in sections 3.3 and 3.4 (criteria are suggested in 3.6).

Third, Christian worship is countercultural. Perhaps the traditional Lutheran phrase *simul justus et peccator* can describe cultures as well as people. Sometimes, from the critique of culture comes the conclusion that Christian worship must contradict the culture, must sometimes say "no" to it.[29] Some-

---

26. Hymn 143, stanzas 1-2, "Sound the Bamboo" (hymnal of the Christian Conference of Asia), text by Shirley Murphy (Manila: Christian Conference of Asia and the Asian Institute for Liturgy and Music, 1990).

27. See *WCD*, pp. 167-81. For an introduction to Asian church architecture, see Masao Takenaka, *The Place Where God Dwells* (Hong Kong: Christian Conference of Asia; Kyoto: Asian Christian Art Association, 1995). For photos, see *The Place Where God Dwells*, pp. 62-63, 64-65.

28. For photos, plan, and description, see S. Anita Stauffer, *On Baptismal Fonts* (Bramcote, Notts, UK: Grove Books, 1994), chap. 4.

29. Regarding the need to say both "yes" and "no" to culture, see Gordon W. Lathrop's

times the values, patterns, or root paradigms of a culture contradict the gospel to the extent that they cannot be reoriented and adapted for worship. In my own culture of North America, for example, the narcissism and overwhelming consumerism are contradictory to the fabric of Christian faith and worship. Worship is inherently both corporate and participatory; therefore, it cannot be planned primarily for consumption or entertainment.

Or in India, for a different kind of example, societal rejection of the Dalit people as untouchable is antithetical to the gospel and simply cannot be a part of Christian worship. The reported practice of some upper-caste people refusing to take communion if they cannot do so before Dalits do in their congregations is a scandal.[30] The Eucharist is countercultural, a paradigm for an alternative way of life in which there is food for all and for all alike. It is a meal in which there is neither Jew nor Greek, neither male nor female (Gal. 3:26-28) — and neither Dalit nor Brahmin. We are all baptized into the one Lord and one body (1 Cor. 10:16-17; 11:27-29). Gordon Lathrop explores the countercultural in his first chapter in this book, and a summary of the study team's conclusions are in the Nairobi Statement, section 4.

5. Work at the intersections of worship and culture can never end.
Even before the seven-year LWF Study on Worship and Culture was proposed and approved, it was clear that such a study could never be the final word. The issues are too complex and controverted, and the cultures of the world are always changing and evolving. Furthermore, the work necessary in churches around the world cannot be done quickly — especially not if it is to be deep and pastoral. Additional scholarship and education are necessary in liturgy/music/architecture and in cultural anthropology, as the basis then for local teaching and local contextualization. Such teaching and such change require much local study and nearly infinite pastoral patience as well as leadership. Also, the Christian faith must take root in every new generation, and thus contextualization is a never-ending task of evangelization and Christian formation.

While considerable regional research was accomplished in Phase 2 of this study, it is clear that additional research is necessary. The needs differ by region: in some regions further research regarding contextualization of

chapters in *WCD*, esp. "A Contemporary Lutheran Approach to Worship and Culture: Sorting Out the Critical Principles," pp. 137-51.

30. "Discriminations Against Dalit Christians in Tamil Nadu," published August 9, 1992, at the Institute of Development, Education, Action, and Studies Centre, Madurai, India (reported in SAR News, Sept. 19-25, 1992).

the liturgy per se is needed, while in other regions more work is necessary regarding church music and/or church architecture and art. The contextualization of preaching still must be addressed in all regions, especially for Lutherans, who value the proclamation of the word so highly. In many regions, the question of the relationship between nature's seasons and the church year, as well as liturgy itself, needs to be explored. This is particularly true in the Southern Hemisphere, but one might also raise the question in the Nordic churches, for example, concerning the impact on worship of the extreme seasonal differences between light and darkness.

Around the world, further attention is also needed regarding several basic questions, such as: What is beauty in a given cultural context, and how does it relate to a sense of the holy?[31] What are the cultural manifestations in a given place of gathering into a community, of offering hospitality to strangers, and of expressing reverence in the presence of the transcendent God? As with liturgical renewal itself, careful reflection and experimentation in contextualization are necessary, followed by evaluation and further revision.

Considerable work on the contextualization of the Eucharist was done at the Nairobi consultation, but some additional international work on this subject is also still necessary (on particular topics such as preaching, offertory, eucharistic prayer, spatial environment, and hymns and other music). Study of the localization of the church year, baptism, daily prayer, and occasional services (including the important topic of healing rites) and rites of passage has not yet even begun.[32] Not all of this can or will be accomplished by the LWF Worship and Culture Study, but we can hope that at least starting points could be established, and that the consciousness of the member churches — and perhaps even ecumenical partners — on these topics will be raised.

31. Unfortunately, this question is very rarely discussed in literature about contextualization. For three examinations by Western writers, see James A. Martin, Jr., *Beauty and Holiness: The Dialogue between Aesthetics and Religion* (Princeton, NJ: Princeton University Press, 1990); Richard Harries, *Art and the Beauty of God: A Christian Understanding* (London: Mowbray, 1993); and John D. Witvliet, "Toward a Liturgical Aesthetic: An Interdisciplinary Review of Aesthetic Theory," *Liturgy Digest* 3, no. 1 (1996): esp. 50-61. For an introductory Asian approach, see Takenaka, *The Place Where God Dwells*, pp. 17-20.

32. It should be noted, however, that study team member Mark Luttio has made a significant beginning with regard to the contextualization of funerals in Japan; see his case study in this volume. Also, the liturgical commission of the Evangelical Lutheran Church of the Central African Republic has done bold new work on contextualizing certain rites of passage; see the section on Africa in the Report on Regional Research in this volume.

Christians can neither ignore culture nor reject it. Since human culture can never be an absolute to which our highest allegiance is given, we see it in relative terms. Liturgical contextualization is not a luxury for the church; it must be done in and by local churches all over the world. However, the danger in it is not only syncretism but also cultural captivity. And cultural captivity of any kind is idolatry, because God alone is the holy one. This is what Kosuke Koyama meant when he wrote that the gospel cannot be completely adjusted, indigenized, contextualized, accommodated, adapted, resymbolized, acculturated, inculturated, or incarnated with regard to culture. "The gospel displays its authentic power in its refusal to be completely indigenized. . . . A perfect indigenization is an idolatry of culture."[33]

We must be intentional about liturgical contextualization or localization; however, we must simultaneously strive for balance between the particular and the universal and among the contextual, the countercultural, and the transcultural. "Behold, I am making all things new," says the Lord (Rev. 21:5; NEB). Christ transcends and transforms all things human, including ourselves and our cultures. Interaction between worship and culture influences both. In the final analysis, we are called not to conform to the world but to be transformed ourselves (Rom. 12:2), and, in turn, to help transform the world. All things in creation, including all earthly cultures, need this redemption, this transformation.

---

33. Kosuke Koyama, "The Tradition and Indigenisation" *Asia Journal of Theology* 7, no. 1 (April 1993): 7.

Christian Unity and Christian Diversity, Lessons from Liturgical Renewal: The Case of the Christian Church (Disciples of Christ)

Thomas F. Best

I could add to my title the words "within a populist sacramental church." The church in question is my own church, the Christian Church (Disciples of Christ), and the memorable description of our church as "populist sacramental" comes from the seminal liturgist we have produced, Keith Watkins.[1] I invite you to see what follows as a case study of how this particular church has come, through the liturgical renewal movement, to a new and more profound understanding of its own identity and mission.[2]

The Origin and Distinctive Quality of the Christian Church (Disciples of Christ): From the Early Nineteenth Century On

To understand this story, it is essential to know something of the distinctive history and beliefs of our church, but also its character and ethos. It began in the first two or three decades of the nineteenth century (1820-1830) on the "frontier" in the United States, the frontier then being western Virginia, Pennsylvania, Kentucky, and Ohio, from the coalescing of impulses for the

1. "Breaking the Bread of Life: The Eucharistic Piety of the Christian Church (Disciples of Christ)," *Mid-Stream* 36, no. 3/4 (1997): 293-307, esp. 296, citing Keith Watkins, *Celebrate with Thanksgiving: Patterns of Prayer at the Communion Table* (St. Louis: Chalice Press, 2001), esp. pp. 11ff.

2. The following discussion draws on my recent articles on Disciples' worship published in P. Bradshaw, ed., *The New SCM Dictionary of Liturgy and Worship* (London: SCM Press, 2002), pp. 44-45, 76-77, 110-12, 181-82, 349-50, 483-84.

"restoration" of the "clear picture," as was thought, of the church as found in the New Testament. Principal founders of the movement were father and son Thomas and Alexander Campbell, who were Presbyterians from Scotland but who had also lived in Ireland, plus another Presbyterian, Barton W. Stone. The movement was a remarkable combination of Enlightenment rationalism and evangelistic zeal. It was said that Alexander Campbell would arrive on horseback at frontier camp meetings and revivals with saddlebags full of books — Greek texts and the Bible in various translations, including one that he issued himself, on one side of the horse, and the writings of Isaac Newton and John Locke on the other side.[3]

These founders were driven by the desire to lead the divided churches (Presbyterian, Methodist, Baptist, and others) toward a unity rooted in the weekly celebration of the Lord's Supper. Four things in particular characterized this early unity movement: observance of the Lord's Supper (or communion or Eucharist) on each Lord's Day (or Sunday); baptism by submersion, or full immersion, of not only professing but penitent adult believers; a decidedly congregational polity, with elders providing leadership; and a hunger for the unity of Christians. I have been told, upon describing this constellation of core beliefs, that we are a "cafeteria church" that was formed by adopting the eucharistic frequency of the Anglicans, the baptismal practice of the Baptists, and the polity of the Congregationalists. But we would say that the reality is just the reverse: we have taken each one of those practices, as well as the imperative for unity, from a single source, the New Testament, while other churches have devolved from this coherent pattern, specializing in one aspect of the New Testament picture, sometimes to the extent — as with the Baptists — that the church has taken its very name from that one aspect of Christian faith and practice.

The early Disciples of Christ were also shaped and characterized by two negative factors. The first was a positive dislike, born of personal experience, of the divisions and rivalries among Christians. One of the Disciples' foundational myths relates how one of the Campbells, still in the old country, was excluded from the Lord's Supper in a Presbyterian church, not because he was not a Presbyterian (he was), but because he was the wrong *kind* of Presbyterian. The will to unity in this early period had a radical, almost

---

3. G. Campbell, J. MacKnight, and P. Doddrige *The Sacred Writings of the Apostles and Evangelists of Jesus Christ: Common Styled the New Testament. Translated from the original Greek, with Prefaces, Various Emendations, and an Appendix by Alexander Campbell* (Bethany, VA, 1833), compiled by Alexander Campbell.

visceral, side to it; the cause of unity was something — ecclesially speaking at least — to die for. In the "Last Will and Testament of the Springfield Presbytery," one of the more remarkable documents of church history, an ecclesial body publicly declared the following: "We will that this body die, be dissolved, and sink into union with the Body of Christ at large." It was not for nothing that the early leaders called Christian unity the Disciples' "polar star," for us the fixed point around which all else revolves.[4]

A second negative factor in these formational days was a healthy suspicion of creeds, not so much in themselves as positive statements of faith, but in their negative use. As Campbell said (and remember, he was thinking of divisions among Protestant bodies at least as much as between Protestants and Roman Catholics), wherever he saw divided churches, he saw their respective creeds justifying — and maintaining — them in their division. But the situation was nuanced: the Apostles' Creed was considered "catholic" (of value for *all* the churches) "because it is a recital of the facts of the gospel."[5] And I myself grew up in a Disciples of Christ church that recited the Apostles' Creed every week.

But let us now look in more detail at the worship practice of the churches in the early Disciples movement. Since no definitive, detailed rite is described, much less prescribed, in the New Testament, it was incumbent upon congregations, and particularly their elders, in the maturity of their faith and exercising reason, to order the community's worship (which, remember, included the Lord's Supper each Sunday). Typically, the service included prayers, hymns, Scripture readings, the celebration of the Supper itself, preaching (if, and only if, a person of suitable gifts was available!), and a concluding collection. Leadership was provided, at each point in the service, by those best suited according to the gifts they had received from the Lord.

A clear and colorful sense of these early days comes from Alexander Campbell's account, taken from his "memorandum-book," of Lord's Day worship in one church that he had visited:

> Not having any person whom they regarded as filling Paul's outlines of a bishop [meaning a local overseer or pastor], they had appointed two senior members, of a very grave deportment, to preside in their meetings.

4. The image continues to fascinate Disciples. See, for example, P. A. Crow Jr., "Three Dichotomies and a Polar Star," *Mid-Stream* 21, no. 1 (1982): 21-30.

5. W. J. Richardson, "Alexander Campbell as an Advocate of Christian Union," in *Lectures in Honor of the Alexander Campbell Bicentennial, 1788-1988* (Nashville: Disciples of Christ Historical Society, 1988), p. 104.

These persons were not competent to labor in the word and teaching; but they were qualified to rule well, and to preside with Christian dignity. One of them presided at each meeting.[6]

At a certain point in the service,

[the presiding officer] then called upon a brother, who was a very distinct and emphatic reader, to read a section of the evangelical history. He arose and read, in a very audible voice, the history of the crucifixion of the Messiah. (p. 291)

Later on, Campbell records with satisfaction, following one of the prayers "the whole congregation, brethren and sisters, pronounced aloud the final *Amen*"(p. 291).

Note particularly the early eucharistic practice of the Disciples of Christ, this being the most distinctive aspect, the heart of their identity as a church, and, as we shall see below, perhaps the area of their greatest interaction — and learning — from the liturgical movement. As Campbell's account continues, then, we have his description of the Lord's Supper as conducted in a Disciples congregation in a frontier town, perhaps in western Virginia and perhaps about 1830:

The president [usually a lay elder, duly appointed by the congregation] arose and said that our Lord had a table for his friends, and that he invited his disciples to sup with him. [Following a brief meditation, focusing on Christ's giving of himself for the world's salvation:] He [the president] took a small loaf from the table, and in one or two periods gave thanks for it. After thanksgiving he raised it in his hand, and significantly brake it, and handed it to the disciples on each side of him, who passed the broken loaf from one to another, until they all partook of it. There was no stiffness, no formality, no pageantry; all was easy, familiar, solemn, cheerful. He then took the cup in a similar manner, and returned thanks for it, and handed it to the disciple sitting next to him, who passed it round; each one waiting upon his brother, until all were served. The thanksgiving before the breaking of the loaf, and the distributing of the cup, were as brief

6. A. Campbell, *The Christian System*, 2nd ed. (Cincinnati: Standard Publishing Company, 1839), p. 290. Hereafter, page references to this work appear in parentheses within the text.

and pertinent to the occasion, as the thanks usually presented at a common table for the ordinary blessings of God's bounty. (pp. 291-92)

Significantly, the Supper was followed by prayers of supplication on behalf of the afflicted, the poor and the destitute, and on behalf of the conversion of the world (p. 292).

As the account of the service continues, no sermon is mentioned, and indeed the practice was to dispense with the sermon when no one considered suitable to preach was at hand. But Scripture readings and some sort of reaction to them were always included, and after the collection, a number of persons rose to read biblical passages and to propose, and inquire on, matters "tending to the edification of the body." Following several spiritual songs, "on the motion of a brother who signified that the hour of adjournment had arrived," the president pronounced the apostolic benediction (p. 292). Characteristically, Campbell offers this whole account, not as a fixed prescription for worship among the Disciples, but as an example that included the essential elements, conducted in a way that he found to be commendable in practice, of the Lord's Day service, that is, the Lord's Supper service.

If gathering at the Lord's Table was "the one essential act of Sunday worship," repeated again and again, then it was balanced by baptism as a decisive single moment in the believer's lifelong journey in faith. Disciples' baptismal theology and practice were, I think, less distinctive than their understanding and conduct of the Eucharist, and here we need only outline it briefly. Their baptismal position was, of course, explained with the usual vigor and clarity of thought. Again, the determining factor was what was understood to be New Testament practice, and so baptism for Disciples was characterized by the profession of faith offered by a penitent believer, the use of the Trinitarian formula, and full immersion in water. In excluding "indiscriminate" (including, but not limited to, infant) baptism, the Disciples founders also sought to distinguish the church from the surrounding culture and from the state, and to expunge the memory of baptismal practice in the established churches of the Old World. This was one area where the early Disciples leadership had significant differences of opinion among themselves, notably over whether immersion was the only valid "mode" of baptism. Barton Stone did not insist absolutely on it, but Alexander Campbell did: partly to make the point, in his own translation of the New Testament, he famously rendered every occurrence of *baptizein* as "immerse."

Let us conclude this initial exposition by looking more closely at the *sacramental* dimension of this frontier unity movement. Early Disciples found the term "sacrament" uncongenial (mainly, I think, for historic reasons) and preferred to speak of "ordinances," that is, practices "ordained" (or commanded) by Christ as a means of making God's saving action present and visible in the world. They understood the Lord's Supper and baptism to be the chief ordinances: each uses material substances (bread, the fruit of the vine, water), and each is a visible sign and seal of God's grace. Each ordinance, moreover, has its own particular grace, or special role in the plan of salvation: for baptism, it is the remission of sin unto newness of life in Christ; for the Supper, nourishing the faith and unity of believers. I have spoken elsewhere about the "starkly realistic nature" of early Disciples' sacramental thought and life, which was indeed rationalist (though never reductionist).[7] Thus for Alexander Campbell, "the Holy Spirit works on *the understanding and affections* of saints and sinners,"[8] so that Christians "must perceive, realize, appropriate, and feel the *blood* of Christ *applied* to our reason, our conscience, our will, and to our affections."[9]

The Table is Christ's; he is our host, and the whole church is invited to his Table. He is present; he enters into head and heart alike in a way that is tangible and has visible effects in our lives. If that's not "presence," and if it isn't "real," then I don't know what is.

Developments within the Christian Church (Disciples of Christ) — Through the Mid-Twentieth Century

Thus, by about 1840 or so, were the main outlines of this "populist sacramental" church established, its most distinctive feature being the observance each Lord's Day of the Lord's Supper, presided over by elders, who used extemporaneous prayers at the Lord's Table.[10] But my topic is finally the encounter of the Disciples with the movement for liturgical renewal, and the early nineteenth-century Disciples of Christ church that I have just described was not, of course, the same as the one that encountered the liturgical movement in the mid-twentieth century. To understand *that* church,

7. T. F. Best, "Disciples Identity and the Ecumenical Future," *Disciples Theological Digest* 8, no. 1 (1993): 5-20.

8. *Millennial Harbinger* (May 1855): 258 (italics added).

9. *Millennial Harbinger,* Extra, no. 8 (October 1935): 508; see *Millennial Harbinger* (December 1855): 662.

10. Watkins, "Breaking the Bread of Life," pp. 293-307.

and thus the significance of that encounter, we must see how the Disciples developed over the hundred years or so from about the 1840s to 1940 or 1950.

In some areas of the church's faith and life, there was growth and development; in other areas, there was simply growth. The "Restorationist" movement stemming from the Campbells, Barton Stone, Walter Scott, and others had brought together diverse persons and viewpoints; as these leaders died and the movement moved into its second and third generations, a fault line became apparent between more "progressive" and more "conservative" wings of the church body.

One fundamental problem was the interpretation of Scripture, particularly on the question of how to order the life of the church on matters not resolved by the first generation of leaders, and about which the New Testament was inconveniently silent. This came to a head on the question of how far musical instruments could be used in worship, since such use was not recorded in the New Testament. A second problem was the relationship of local congregations to church structures beyond the local level, with some refusing to join cooperative institutions — even for reasons of mission — which were seen as threatening local autonomy. A third problem was the relationship of the church to the state, with some pastors or congregations refusing to take actions that might be interpreted as seeking "recognition" by the state. By the early twentieth century, the most conservative forces had left, coalescing to form separate churches that carried a different (and from a Disciples of Christ perspective, more limited) form of the Campbell-Stone "Restoration" vision. Meanwhile, the Disciples of Christ, through a series of specific decisions (all tending in a progressive direction) about the issues named above, had defined itself as a recognizably "mainline" denomination.

But the pattern was different in different areas of the church's life, and we need to consider a number of factors in more detail, beginning, inevitably, with the Lord's Supper. The conviction remained that since the table was Christ's, the church had no authority to exclude anyone from the table who had been claimed by Christ, that is, who had been baptized. The practice of elders offering prayers — usually one elder praying over the bread and one over the wine — continued. I say "wine," but in fact (reflecting the founders' aversion to alcohol, based on their experience on the frontier) the use of unfermented grape juice continued as the norm.

What did change, and for the worse, was the relationship of the table to the word, that is, of the Last Supper to the sermon. Originally the sermon was dispensed with if no suitable elder or traveling evangelist was on hand.

In any case, the sermon was placed at the conclusion of the service, partly because there it could be more easily dispensed with if necessary. But with the gradual development of an ordained, professional, paid clergy, the sermon became the prerogative of the local pastor, and a fixed and necessary part of the Lord's Day service. It remained at the conclusion of the service, but increasingly for a different reason: as a divine rhetoric, an evangelistic message reinforcing or calling out belief, the sermon increasingly replaced the Supper as the climax of the service.

Furthermore, the ordained minister came to have a prominent role in the service of the table itself. It became the norm for elders and deacons to be joined at the table by the ordained minister, who would recite the words of institution from the Gospels or 1 Corinthians 11, and perhaps give a brief meditation, before the elders' prayers for the loaf and the cup. The deacons would then distribute the elements to the congregation, who remained seated and passed the elements to one another. At best, this sharing of leadership by laity and ordained clergy modeled the ministry of the whole people of God; and some elders' prayers reflected, in simple and beautiful language, a lifetime of growth into Christ. But often enough the elders' prayers showed neither theological understanding nor spiritual depth, thus only reinforcing the dominance of the sermon that followed. Meanwhile, the liberal theology of the first half of the twentieth century and a general resistance to representational thought diminished the sense of the sacred in worship and encouraged a commemorative understanding of the Supper as an event that evoked the lively memory — but not the actual presence (however understood) — of Christ.

In the case of baptism, there is a twofold story to be told. We noted earlier that Barton Stone and Alexander Campbell differed on the necessity for immersion, and in this case it was the stricter position of Campbell that prevailed generally in the church, at least until about 1900. This meant that persons joining a Disciples of Christ congregation who had been baptized, but in practices other than immersion, were normally expected to "complete their obedience to Christ" by undergoing full immersion. I hesitate to call this "re-baptism," since the language of "completing" obedience implied at least the partial efficacy of the baptism that had already been received elsewhere. It was striking that the logic of Disciples' eucharistic theology led to the practice of an open table, so that many congregations that required full-immersion baptism for membership would nevertheless receive at the Lord's Supper persons who had been baptized in other ways.

While full immersion remained — and indeed remains — the practice in Disciples churches for persons first entering the body of Christ, the attitude to a "re"- (or "completing") baptism began to change from about 1900, with some congregations beginning to accept the earlier baptism of persons transferring membership from "non-immersion" churches. I am not sure of the reasons for this, but I like to regard it as representing a rebirth or reawakening of the early Disciples' ecumenical conviction and zeal, which had faded somewhat as the Disciples consolidated their position as a denomination in the latter half of the nineteenth century. Perhaps this renewed sense of their vocation to unity came from the increasing ecumenical experience of Disciples as they engaged with others in associations for practical Christian work (such as the Sunday School movement around the turn of the century). Perhaps it came from the awareness of figures such as Peter Ainslie, who became a well-known proponent of the nascent Faith and Order movement worldwide. Perhaps it reflected the emergence of the Disciples as one of the principal actors in the formation of councils of churches at all levels, from local to national. It would be a mistake to say that the "mind" of the church had fully changed on this issue by 1950, but there was certainly a growing reluctance to call into question baptisms duly performed in other churches.

Other points in our profile can be noted more briefly. As mentioned before, this period saw the emergence of professional, salaried clergy who were understood as the — or a — leader of the local congregation. But that was precisely the question: Was it *the* or was it *a* leader? The role of the elder was so deeply ingrained in the Disciples ethos that there was no question of the professional ministry supplanting it. Yet the functions of the elders, who were ordained locally to oversee the life of a local congregation, including administering the Lord's Supper and baptism and, if suited for it, to preach as well, were precisely those for which the professional clergy was being trained. I should emphasize that the pattern described earlier, with both elders and the minister active at the Lord's Supper, was understood as an enrichment of the church's life, drawing on the gifts of both lay and clerical leadership. But the fundamental questions remained: What is the relationship of pastor and elders, and what is the role of lay leadership in an age of increasing specialization and professionalization — in the church as everywhere else?

A special word is in order about the Disciples' use of liturgical books and resources. They produced their first authorized liturgical book, for voluntary use, in 1953. That is, through the whole period that we are presently considering, there was no official, standard worship text. This was a result of the fact that local congregations had, from our earliest days, been entrusted with the responsibility of ordering their own worship, and from a reluctance to introduce anything other than the New Testament as authoritative in matters of faith and practice, including worship practice.

Yet there was, in fact, a discernible, distinctive "Disciples" worship practice that was based primarily on two factors. The first factor was, inevitably, the widely followed pattern of the Lord's Supper observance (with minister and elders, as described above). The second factor was the hymnals published by Disciples, which, through widespread use rather than official prescription, gave a considerable measure of common worship experience throughout the whole church. The tradition began with Alexander Campbell's own widely used hymnal.[11] Perhaps the most prominent later hymnal was *Hymns of the United Church* (1924), coedited by C. C. Morrison and Herbert L. Willett), whose title reflects the growing appeal of things ecumenical for many Disciples of that day.[12] In this — but not only in this — the hymnals were prophetic forces in the life of the church. The next widely used hymnal, *Christian Worship: A Hymnal* (1941), was published by the Disciples' denominational press together with the American Baptist Convention.[13]

I should make a final note; it is implicit in my description of the Lord's Day service as normative for Disciples but may have escaped the reader's notice. Simply put, Disciples, as they had developed through the mid-twentieth century and in contrast to the Reformed aspects of their heritage, had little idea of a service of the word in the classical Reformed sense, that is, a Sunday service including entrance, Scripture reading, proclamation of the gospel and response, statement of faith, and prayers of intercession — but stopping short of the sharing of Christ's body and blood at the Lord's Table.

There were, of course, frequent and fervent small-scale occasions for prayer and meditation on Scripture, such as personal devotions or the

---

11. For one form in use as early as 1834, see *Psalms, Hymns, and Spiritual Songs, Original and Selected* (Bethany, VA: printed by A. Campbell, 1834), and *Psalms, Hymns, and Spiritual Songs, Original and Selected: Adapted to the Christian Religion* (Carthage, OH: printed by W. Scott, 1835); later versions include *The Christian Hymn Book: A Compilation of Psalms, Hymns, and Spiritual Songs, Original and Selected, by A. Campbell and Others* (Cincinnati: H. Bosworth, 1968 [1865]).

12. C. C. Morrison and Herbert L. Willett, eds., *Hymns of the United Church* (Chicago: Christian Century Press, 1924).

13. *Christian Worship: A Hymnal* (St. Louis: Christian Board of Publication, Bethany Press, 1941).

prayers held by staff in church offices. These were understood to be sufficient unto themselves. But there were also occasions on which a more elaborate, but noneucharistic service was called for, especially in interchurch and special ministry contexts, for example, installation services for officers of councils of churches, services in institutional settings such as church camps or hospitals, or services in observance of special occasions in the life of the local community. Such services would normally include the reading of Scripture and some form of response to it, but other elements — and their overall order — followed no fixed or classical pattern. And I think it is fair to say that most Disciples, attending a noneucharistic service beyond the level of personal devotions or of any complexity, would have felt that "something was missing" when the service did not include the Lord's Supper.

This was, then, in broad outline, the personality of the Disciples of Christ in the United States around the middle of the twentieth century: centered on Scripture as the basis of faith and the life of the church; populist, that is, solidly middle class and with a preference for direct, simple symbols; sacramental, with the center of the church's life found, in every Lord's Day worship, at the Lord's Supper service led by elders and (often) the minister, but less sacramental, perhaps, than earlier in our history as the sermon tended to overshadow the Supper; firmly committed to the baptism of professing believers by submersion, but increasingly ready to respect the practice of other churches; recovering its original ecumenical vocation; searching for the right relationship between professional pastoral leadership and the witness of elders; evincing a fervent piety, especially in personal prayer and congregational hymn singing; with a firm sense of order in worship, maintained not through prescribed worship texts but through widely used hymnals and other worship resources. Worship had settled into nurturing, comfortable patterns and, I suppose, seemed likely to continue that way.

The Christian Church (Disciples of Christ) and Liturgical Renewal: Developments since 1950

Fifty years later, at the beginning of the twenty-first century, we find ourselves as Disciples in the midst of a transformation in our self-understanding as a church. My own understanding is that this has been caused by, and expressed through, our engagement in two of the central movements of the Holy Spirit within the whole church in our times. Through interaction with these movements, we have clarified our own identity as a church, have come to a new appreciation of our strengths, and have learned to see where, perhaps, our own history has left us lacking in some things we need in order to be church fully and faithfully today.

The first of these movements is the ecumenical movement. We came early to it — or, indeed, were born of it — as I have made clear above. However, particularly over the past fifty years, ecumenical engagement has become a central part of the life of our church. Here I will simply mention a few examples of this. There is our engagement, almost from its beginning, in the Consultation on Church Union (now Churches Uniting in Christ) in the United States (indeed, two of the general secretaries of that consultation have come from our church). There is our seconding, since the 1970s, of an executive staff position in the Faith and Order secretariat of the World Council of Churches. There is our serious engagement with the Faith and Order convergence text *Baptism, Eucharist and Ministry*.[14] There is our close partnership with the United Church of Christ in the U.S., to the extent that these two major denominations share the same common board for overseas mission. There is our international bilateral dialogue with the Roman Catholic Church, which has been of deep importance to our own self-understanding.[15] And there is the striking fact that we have encouraged Disciples-related churches around the world not to continue relating primarily to us as their missioning, or "parent," church but rather to enter church unions, so that Disciples in the Republic of Congo, Thailand, Japan, Jamaica, the United Kingdom, and elsewhere would now be found not as a separate church bodies but as part of a united church.

Perhaps it was this ecumenical contact with the larger church that made us more aware of the need for responsible ecclesial structures beyond the congregational level. In any case, one of the most profound developments in our life was a process of "Restructure" in the 1960s, which established much clearer patterns of oversight at regional and national levels. A robust sense of local responsibility and initiative remains, but we are much more aware now that local congregations belong to the whole of our church — and

---

14. For an early example of the liturgical context, see Keith Watkins, "The Lima Liturgy: When Theology Becomes Liturgy," *Mid-Stream* 23, no. 3 (1984): 285-89.

15. For the first series of discussions (1977-1982), see *Apostolicity and Catholicity* (Indianapolis: Council on Christian Unity, 1982); for the second (1983-1992), see "The Church as Communion in Christ," *Mid-Stream* 33, no. 2 (1994): 219-39; for the third (1993-2002), see "Receiving and Handing on the Faith: The Mission and Responsibility of the Church (1993-2002)," *Mid-Stream* 41, no. 4 (2002): 51-79; the reports from the first and second series are also printed in *Mid-Stream* 41, no. 4 (2002): 80-95 and 96-114, respectively.

to the whole of the whole church. Certainly, the encounter with ecumenical theology has had serious consequences for our understanding of both the Lord's Supper and baptism, as we shall see in a moment.

The second movement that is transforming our church is, of course, the movement for liturgical renewal. We should note at the beginning that our encounter with this movement was a very particular one, and perhaps quite different from that of other churches. To understand this, we need to recall the intention of the liturgical reform movement, as is well stated by Ellsworth Chandlee:

> [The liturgical movement] seeks a recovery of those norms of liturgical worship of the Bible and the early church which lie behind Reformation divisions and medieval distortions, and which are fundamental to Christian liturgy in every time and place. It aims, however, not at an attempt to resuscitate the liturgy of the early Church in the twentieth century, but at the restatement of the fundamentals in forms and expressions which can enable the liturgy to be the living prayer and work of the church today.[16]

Thus the liturgical movement presented Disciples with an understanding of the sources of Christian worship that was broader than that of our own tradition and ethos. In particular, it not only called us to an encounter with the worship of the earliest Christian communities as described in the New Testament; but it required us to engage seriously with the worship traditions of the early Christian centuries, and indeed beyond. Thus it called us to an engagement with liturgical scholarship in the strict sense of the development of liturgies historically, but also with research on the psychological, sociological, and cultural factors at play in the experience of worship.

Allow me to sketch the course of our encounter with the liturgical movement, indicating the main personalities involved and some results as reflected in worship materials produced in and for our church. Three persons have been central to the process. G. Edwin Osborn produced the church's first "semi-official" worship book in 1953. Osborn was a student of the psychology of worship and favored "relevant worship" focused on themes of direct concern to the community, but he emphasized the importance of a sound biblical and ecumenical basis for worship. William Robinson was in the forefront of our recovery of the centrality of the Lord's Supper, to which we will come in

---

16. J. C. Davis, ed., *A New Dictionary of Liturgy and Worship*, 2nd ed. (London: SCM Press, 1986), p. 314.

a moment. Both Osborn and Robinson died in the 1960s, and since then it has been Keith Watkins who has led both in recovering our own distinctive worship heritage and in our engagement with the liturgical movement.

Watkins's approach was through a series of liturgical studies aimed at renewing worship practice in the Disciples of Christ. The book *Thankful Praise: A Resource for Christian Worship* (1987) sought "to strengthen Christian public worship and especially the celebration of the Lord's Supper."[17] Its goals can serve as a summary of Disciples' aspirations for their worship today: to connect our worship with the great tradition of Christian worship through the ages; to reflect liturgically the results of ecumenical convergence; to be faithful to the crucial features of traditional Disciples' worship; to be sensitive to social injustice, especially in its anti-Jewish and sexist expressions; to enhance the beauty and diversity of worship through vivid, biblical, and felicitous language; and to encourage a healthy variety within our worship life.[18] In 1991, Watkins followed this book with *Baptism and Belonging: A Resource for Christian Worship,* which sought a parallel renewal in Disciples' understanding and practice of baptism.[19]

This liturgical process has proceeded alongside a theological one, namely, a study of our church's ecclesiological self-understanding that was begun by its Commission on Theology in 1978. Three of the texts from this study touch directly on worship: the one on ministry (1985), on baptism (1987), and on the Lord's Supper (1993). The overall report, issued in 1997, affirms that in worship the church makes "defining signs of its true identity" as it listens to Scripture, proclaims the word, confesses sin and receives God's forgiving grace, celebrates the sacramental acts of baptism and Holy Communion, and communicates in prayer with God.[20] This is unfamiliar language for some Disciples, who still expect divine worship to be described more subjectively and in terms of pious emotions warmly felt. Yet it *is* where Disciples find themselves today in their worship. Furthermore, we realize that the theology study could not have come to its conclusions without the study on worship that ran parallel to — and in interaction with — it. One of the

17. *Thankful Praise: A Resource for Christian Worship* (St. Louis: Christian Board of Publication, 1987).

18. See T. F. Best, "Christian Church (Disciples of Christ) Worship," in P. Bradshaw, ed., *The New SCM Dictionary,* p. 181.

19. Keith Watkins, *Baptism and Belonging: A Resource for Christian Worship* (St. Louis: Christian Board of Publication, 1991).

20. P. A. Crow Jr. and J. O. Duke, eds., *The Church for Disciples of Christ: Seeking to Be Truly Church Today* (St. Louis: Christian Board of Publication, 1998), p. 56.

true gifts of the Spirit to our church in this process is that we have not only visionary liturgists but also theologians, such as Paul Crow and James O. Duke, who understand that theologians need to listen to liturgists. Many of you will understand how precious that is.

Now allow me to illustrate our encounter with the liturgical renewal movement and the ecumenical movement by looking in more detail at a number of specific issues.

The Lord's Supper

We have experienced, I think, a dramatic renewal of eucharistic practice and theology of the Disciples in the past thirty years. Today we would understand the Eucharist as

> a public act in which the church, having heard the proclamation of the word, partakes of Christ's body and blood, thereby remembering God's reconciling initiative in Jesus Christ, celebrating the gift of the Spirit upon the Church, and anticipating the coming reign of God. The Lord's Supper is a sacrament, an expression of Christ's body and blood in the visible signs of bread and wine. The host is the Lord, and the whole church is invited to his table. The Supper has immediate social consequences; sharing at Christ's table compels the church to work in order that all may have "bread and enough" to eat. The Lord's Supper is central to the faith and piety of Disciples, who refer to themselves as "people of the chalice."[21]

The service suggested in *Thankful Praise* includes the classic dimensions of gathering, proclamation of the word, response to the word, coming together around the Lord's table, and sending forth. The Lord's Supper service includes an invitation extended "upon Christ's behalf for all baptized believers," an offering, the classic Disciples feature of elders' prayers over the loaf and cup, responsive prayers, the institution narrative from Scripture, the breaking of bread, the Lord's Prayer, an expression of peace, the sharing of the elements (normally by passing the loaf and cup through the congregation, who remain seated), and a final prayer.

We noted above the Disciples' drift, through the first half of the twen-

---

21. T. F. Best, "Eucharist: Christian Church," in P. Bradshaw, ed., *The New SCM Dictionary*, p. 181.

tieth century, toward a restricted "memorial" view of the Supper, in which Christ was more a memory than an actual presence at the table. Thus one of the central challenges posed to us by the liturgical and ecumenical movements was the recovery of the biblical notion of *anamnesis,* of an *active remembering* that brings into the present the power and effective action of a past event. But as we tackled this question, we remembered that we had resources from our own tradition. Our great early evangelist and theologian Walter Scott had spoken of baptism and the Lord's Supper as "the crucifixion, or death, burial and resurrection of Christ, repeating themselves in the life and profession of the disciples," plus, he might have said, of those who down the ages have followed.[22] The liturgical and ecumenical movements, then, helped us recover something that had been central to our own identity as a church, but that we had lost through a forgetting of our past and an accommodation to the surrounding culture. We have recovered the true meaning of the words traditionally carved on the face of the Lord's Table in most Disciples of Christ churches: "Do this in remembrance of me."

Another challenge posed to us was the recovery in the liturgical movement of the *social sense* and significance of worship, a recovery of the awareness that the liturgy led to, demanded, and was the source of the "liturgy after the liturgy," namely, our Christian service in the world. Recall from the ecumenical movement the famous statement in *Baptism, Eucharist and Ministry:*

The eucharist embraces all aspects of life. . . . The eucharistic celebration demands reconciliation and sharing among all those regarded as brothers and sisters in the one family of God and is a constant challenge in the search for appropriate relationships in social, economic and political life. . . . All kinds of injustice, racism, separation and lack of freedom are radically challenged when we share in the body and blood of Christ.[23]

Some claimed that if we took this liturgical and ecumenical insight too seriously, it would introduce "the world" into worship, threatening to divide congregations on social issues. But then we recalled words of Alexander Campbell himself, who wrote the following:

22. W. Scott, *The Messiahship; or Great Demonstration* (Cincinnati: H. S. Bosworth, 1859), p. 284.

23. *Baptism, Eucharist and Ministry,* "Eucharist," par. 20, Faith and Order Paper 111 (Geneva: WCC, 1982).

The Lord says to each disciple, when he receives the symbols into his hand. . . , "For *you* my body was wounded; for *you* my life was taken."

— and then he continued:

Each disciple in handing the symbols to his fellow-disciples, says in effect, "You, my brother, once an alien, are now a citizen of heaven: once a stranger, are now brought home to the family of God. You have owned my Lord as your Lord, my people as your people. Under Jesus the Messiah we are one. Mutually embraced in the Everlasting arms, I embrace you in mind: thy sorrows shall be my sorrows, and thy joys my joys." Joint debtors to the favor of God and the love of Jesus, we shall jointly suffer with him, that we may jointly reign with him. Let us, then, renew our strength, remember our King and hold fast our boasted hope unshaken to the end.[24]

Thus for Campbell, in contrast to the "rugged individualism" of his culture, the Supper was both profoundly personal and profoundly social. The Supper,

[i]n relating us each to God, links us to our brothers and sisters in Christ; through the Supper we are made one family and given that eschatological hope which sustains us in suffering, and which enables us mutually to sustain one another. The *koinonia* which we share and express at the Lord's Table compels — and empowers — our *diakonia* in all of life.[25]

Such texts have brought a new awareness within our church of the social dimension of the Lord's Supper and encouraged us to see our witness in the world as coherent with, and faithful to, the central role of the Supper in our worship and our self-understanding. Thus again, challenged through the liturgical movement, we rediscovered in our own heritage an aspect that had fallen fallow: the integration of the whole of life, both personal and social, in and through the meal offered by Christ at his table.

But we did not draw all the elements of our eucharistic renewal from

24. A. Campbell, *The Christian System*, p. 273.
25. I have treated this text also in T. F. Best, "Koinonia and Diakonia: The Ecumenical Implications of Two Biblical Perspectives on the Church," in D. Fiensy and W. D. Howden, eds., *Faith in Practice: Studies in the Book of Acts* (Atlanta: European Evangelistic Society, 1995), pp. 365-66.

our own tradition. Perhaps the most striking development has been in our understanding of the proper *structure* of the Lord's Day service. We noted above that by 1950 the norm was that the service concluded with a powerful sermon as its high point. But through the liturgical movement we gradually learned another pattern, and today it is the norm in our churches that the Supper comes at its conclusion and as its climax, with the sermon seen increasingly as a preparation for the Supper.

Through this shifting of the Supper within the structure of the Lord's Day service, we restored the coherence between our liturgical expression of the meal and the role that it plays in our life and thought. And in so doing we have aligned our liturgy with the great tradition of eucharistic worship through the ages. Some of our members, to be sure, would be very surprised to hear our change in practice described in these terms, but that is indeed what we have done. Along with this structural change, we find an increasing desire to symbolize the unity of the church in our liturgical practice. If, for instance, the communion is given in small, individual cups (as is still usual), then the congregation will hold these and then partake all together. On special, more intimate occasions, a common cup may be used. In all these areas the liturgical renewal movement has been our main inspiration and challenge.

Our understanding and practice of the Lord's Supper is still developing — and, I hope, deepening.[26] Some important issues remain to be resolved. While at the table the combination of ordained and lay leadership is the norm, in some congregations the line between lay *presence* and lay *presidency* is blurred.[27] In many congregations the prayers offered by elders at the table are an area where growth is needed, in both liturgical sensitivity and theological content. There is a cultural pressure for children to be admitted to the table before baptism, and a corresponding pressure for baptism to be performed at younger ages. We want to explore the meaning of Christ's presence at the meal more fully and are suggesting, with our Catholic colleagues,

---

26. See further "A Word to the Church on the Lord's Supper (1991), A Report of the Committee on Theology," in P. A. Crow Jr. and J. O. Duke, eds., *The Church for Disciples of Christ*, pp. 139-52; and "A Word to the Church on Ministry (1985)," in *The Church for Disciples of Christ*, pp. 109-20. See also J. O. Duke and R. Harrison Jr., *The Lord's Supper* (St. Louis: Council on Christian Unity by Christian Board of Publication, 1993).

27. On the historical background and present extent and significance of lay presidency in some Disciples congregations, see K. Watkins, "Worship as Understood and Practiced by the Christian Church (Disciples of Christ)," in T. F. Best and D. Heller, eds., *Worship Today: Understanding, Practice, Ecumenical Implications* (Geneva: WCC Publications, 2004).

that the next (fourth) round of the Disciples-Roman Catholic dialogue should focus on "the presence of Christ in the church, with special reference to the eucharist."[28] This is "important, given the emphasis that both Disciples and Roman Catholics put on the weekly celebration of the Lord's Supper and its link with the visible unity of Christians."[29]

Baptism

The past fifty years have seen significant developments in our appreciation of baptism as well. Our current understanding can be stated in this way, parallel to our grasp of the Lord's Supper:

> [B]aptism is a public act of the church in which a believer, responding by personal profession of faith to God's saving initiative in Jesus Christ, is immersed in water in the name of the Father, Son and Holy Spirit and thereby incorporated into the church and set on a path of lifelong growth into Christ. Baptism is a sacrament, an expression of God's grace in the visible sign of water. It has immediate social consequences, for the life entered into is one of love of neighbor and sacrificial service in the world.[30]

Our baptismal practice is a process that continues several characteristically Disciples traditions: the personal profession of faith often comes in response to a "hymn of invitation" that is sung at the end of a Sunday service; the candidate affirms Jesus as the Christ, the Son of the living God, and his or her own personal Lord and Savior; the period of instruction is meant to explore the depth of this profession and to set it within the faith of the church as a whole, as well as to prepare the candidate to embark on a lifetime journey with and toward Christ.[31] Baptism is normally performed within a Lord's Day service and in a baptistery visible to the whole congregation.

28. "Receiving and Handing on the Faith: The Mission and Responsibility of the Church (1993-2002)," par. 6.2.
29. "The Church as Communion in Christ," par. 53a, quoted in "Receiving and Handing on the Faith," par. 6.2.
30. T. F. Best, "Baptism: Christian Church," in P. Bradshaw, ed., *The New SCM Dictionary,* p. 44.
31. For a current example of Disciples of Christ baptismal practice and commentary thereon, see K. Watkins, "Christian Baptism: The Christian Church . . ." (pp. 124-28).

A number of developments in our practice of baptism are due to the influence and challenge of the liturgical movement and the ecumenical movement. Increasingly, Disciples agree that the rite itself should include the following elements: proclamation of Scripture; repentance and renunciation of evil; profession of faith in Jesus Christ; invocation of the Holy Spirit; full immersion; administration "in the name of the Trinity," normally following the formula in Matthew 28:19; and welcome into the life of the church. The study *Baptism, Eucharist and Ministry* has been influential, especially in its insistence on the social as well as personal dimensions of baptism, and in its emphasis on the fact that baptism, as a sacrament of unity, is unrepeatable. Since 1950, more and more congregations have refused the practice of "re"-baptism, and the Disciples' official response to *Baptism, Eucharist and Ministry* may be taken as having consolidated the church's official rejection of that practice. At the same time, we have increasingly emphasized the fact that baptism is into the *whole* church, not just "our" particular part of it.

Open questions remain, perhaps more with baptism than with the Lord's Supper. For example, what is the proper age for baptism, and what is its relationship to church membership? Should there be a blessing or dedication of children, anticipating their later personal commitment, or perhaps a dedication of parents, solemnizing their intention to raise the child in the faith? Thoughtful and honest questions have been raised about the masculine imagery of the traditional baptismal formula, but the traditional formula remains for us very much the norm, not least in view of our extensive ecumenical commitments. How can the service of baptism be enriched liturgically — perhaps by a blessing of the water — to emphasize God's initiative in the event? How can we renew the awareness of our own baptismal commitment, perhaps by incorporating a renewal of baptism vows into other worship events? How can we convey the broader dimensions of the baptismal commitment? Here, strikingly, the church's Theology Commission has proposed a new form of the profession of faith, emphasizing the ecclesial and social as well as the personal dimensions of baptism: "Do you, with Christians of every time and place, believe that 'Jesus is the Christ, the Son of the Living God' (Matt. 16:16)?"[32]

32. See "A Word to the Church on Baptism (1987), A Report of the Committee on Theology," in P. A. Crow Jr. and J. O. Duke, eds., *The Church for Disciples of Christ*, pp. 121-37, quote from p. 133. See also C. M. Williamson, *Baptism, Embodiment of the Gospel: Disciples Baptismal Theology, The Nature of the Church*, Study Series 4 (St. Louis: Council on Christian Unity by Christian Board of Publication, 1987).

The "Service of the Word"

Let us look briefly at another area of growth that has come largely due to the Disciples' encounter with the liturgical movement. This is the increased awareness of the service of the word as a liturgical event with its own proper structure and process, normally including the elements of entrance, Scripture reading, proclamation of the gospel, response, prayer and intercession, the Lord's Prayer, and dismissal/sending forth with a blessing. The discovery that this basic structure or pattern of worship, the notion of *ordo* (which has been central to current Faith and Order work on worship, and which Gordon Lathrop has taken up elsewhere in this series; see pp. 87-100) is one shared by Christians of many times and places has done much to increase the vitality of our own noneucharistic worship.[33] Here, too, we have learned from the liturgical renewal movement that we stand within the long tradition of the church, even as we bear witness to our distinctive worship traditions.

Worship Materials

None of these developments would have had an impact liturgically without worship materials to bring them into the lives of local congregations. And thus we need to conclude this review of developments in the second half the twentieth century with a brief look at Disciples' hymnals, worship books, and other materials. Already the *Hymnbook for Christian Worship,* published in 1970[34] (done jointly with the American Baptist Convention, as was *Christian Worship: A Hymnal* of 1941) included many modern hymns, including some from other continents and from the ecumenical movement, while discreetly "'retiring' hymns considered overly sentimental or theologically simplistic."[35]

---

33. See T. F. Best and D. Heller, eds., *So We Believe, So We Pray: Towards Koinonia in Worship,* Faith and Order Paper 171 (Geneva: WCC Publications, 1995); T. F. Best and D. Heller, eds., *Eucharistic Worship in Ecumenical Contexts: The Lima Liturgy — and Beyond* (Geneva: WCC Publications, 1988); T. F. Best and D. Heller, eds., *Becoming a Christian: The Ecumenical Implications of Our Common Baptism,* Faith and Order Paper 184 (Geneva: WCC Publications, 1999); "One Baptism: Towards Mutual Recognition of Christian Initiation," FO/2001:24, text under development, publication forthcoming.

34. *Hymnbook for Christian Worship* (St. Louis: Bethany Press, 1970). See also A. N. Wake, *Companion to Hymnbook for Christian Worship* (St. Louis: Bethany Press, 1970).

35. T. F. Best, "Books, Liturgical: Christian Church," in P. Bradshaw, ed., *The New SCM Dictionary,* p. 76.

The principal worship book at this point was still *Christian Worship: A Service Book* (1953), the work of G. Edwin Osborn.[36] Its emphasis on "relevant" worship on specific themes is not perhaps in accord with much of the liturgical movement, yet it was advanced for Disciples in including a lectionary, and it did encourage a more positive attitude toward practices in worship common to the whole of our church.

These materials are now superseded by fully modern resources, including both a strong hymnal and a service book produced in the 1990s. The *Chalice Hymnal* (1995) combines classic hymns from the long Christian tradition with a generous collection of songs from churches around the world and from the ecumenical movement, as well as from African-American and Hispanic contexts.[37] It is also sensitive to issues of language. Reflecting Disciples' piety and tradition, it "includes probably more communion hymns than any other currently available hymnal."[38] A partial psalter, a lectionary for years A, B, and C, quotations from a wide variety of sources — some ancient and some service materials — are also included. Happily, it has been warmly received within the church. A companion to the hymnal for worship leaders was published in 1998.[39]

The hymnal is beautifully complemented by *Chalice Worship* (1997), the service book edited by Colbert Cartwright and Cricket Harrison.[40] With this the church has, finally, a rich collection of services and material that honor both its own tradition and that of the wider church, and is thoroughly modern in its engagement with the liturgical and ecumenical movements, as well as its attention to contemporary worship needs. Thus, in addition to Lord's Day services (one including a clear *epiclesis* in the eucharistic prayer) and baptismal rites, there are services for the installation of elders, an Easter Vigil service, material for use during the Week of Prayer for Christian Unity, three examples of worship in ecumenical contexts (including one for use on Martin Luther King Jr. Day), a prayer service for healing, and prayers for special and difficult pastoral situations (e.g., for "one who has been molested" or for those "in a coma or unable to communicate"), as well as, of course, the more familiar special occasions of weddings and funerals. The worship book has

36. *Christian Worship: A Service Book* (St. Louis: Christian Board of Publication, 1953).

37. *Chalice Hymnal* (St. Louis: Chalice Press, 1995).

38. T. F. Best, "Books, Liturgical," p. 76.

39. S. L. Adams, C. S. Cartwright, and D. B. Merrick, eds., *Chalice Hymnal: A Worship Leader's Companion* (St. Louis: Chalice Press, 1998).

40. Colbert Cartwright and Cricket Harrison, *Chalice Worship* (St. Louis: Chalice Press, 1997).

a "message," namely, that worship is important and worth doing well. And that is a message of hope for our church as a whole.

Finally, I want to mention the wealth of worship materials being produced by individuals within the church. These are unofficial or semi-official, but they bear witness to important trends in our life as a church. Especially important is the first Disciples of Christ set of lectionary-based communion and postcommunion prayers, *Fed by God's Grace: Communion Prayers for Year A* (2001), *Year B* (1999), and *Year C* (2000).[41] These are broadening the appreciation for the lectionary within the church, as well as improving the quality, both theological and liturgical, of the elders' prayers offered during the service of the Supper.

A normative liturgy or body of hymns would be inimical to Disciples' ecclesiology and ethos alike, yet all these materials are clear evidence of our new liturgical vitality and our engagement with our tradition, the tradition of the whole church, and the modern world.

Lessons from Liturgical Renewal

And now let us return to my title for this chapter as amended: "Christian Unity and Christian Diversity, Lessons from Liturgical Renewal in a Populist Sacramental Church: The Case of the Disciples of Christ." For Disciples, the fundamental questions raised by the liturgical movement have been how to hold unity and diversity together within our own church and how we, as a church, fit within the diversity of churches that make up the church as a whole.

From this perspective, I see three central lessons that we have learned in the course of our engagement with the movement for liturgical reform. The *first* is that the liturgical and ecumenical movements are part of one larger movement of the Holy Spirit, within the whole church, for renewal and toward unity. The two movements together have pressed us to a closer coherence between what and how we pray and what we believe. The new material in our hymnal and worship book is the fruit of both movements, especially the liturgical, but informed by — and in some dialogue with — the ecumenical movement. If William Temple had spoken in 1980 rather than 1930, perhaps he would have spoken of "the ecumenical *and liturgical* movements" as "the great facts of our era."

41. M. E. Dixon and S. Dixon (St. Louis: Chalice Press, 1999-2001).

A *second* thing we have learned is that the liturgical renewal movement has been a force both for unity and diversity. After our first century and more, from 1820 to about 1950, we Disciples found ourselves internally very united, reflecting cultural and social factors, to be sure, but due principally to our common practice of the Lord's Supper on each Lord's Day, with the active participation of elders as well as the pastor at the table. Looking outside ourselves, it was precisely this frequent eucharistic practice that distinguished us from our immediate ecclesiological neighbors, the churches stemming from the Calvinist/Reformed tradition, as well as from the churches of the Baptist tradition, to whom we were linked by our baptismal understanding and practice. In this sense we were a sign of diversity in the broader Reformed tradition; but, looking more broadly still, we were a sign of unity to Anglicans and even Roman Catholics, as a church stemming from the Reformation that had preserved the weekly celebration of the Lord's Supper as the heart of the life of the church.

What the liturgical reform movement has done over the past fifty years is to make us much more *diverse* internally, by bringing new worship materials and by encouraging the development of specific, focused worship forms for particular occasions of noneucharistic worship. But at the same time, it has strengthened our witness to *unity* and our sense of being part of the whole church by emphasizing the basic patterns or structures of worship shared by many churches. And liturgical reform has strengthened our unity as a church internally by making it a unity that embraces greater diversity — first of all, of course, in our worship life, but also throughout the life of the church as a whole. And this we have experienced as the action of the Holy Spirit.

This brings me to our *third,* and final, learning point: liturgical renewal has taught us much about the meaning and process of renewal in the life of the church as a whole. My conviction is that most churches — and in some sense the church itself — have begun as movements for reform. And at any point in the life of a church, even when it has settled down into comfortable patterns of life and worship, as ours had, the Holy Spirit appeals to the church, calling it to new life.

To the extent that a church carries the memory of its origin as a renewal movement, that church has within itself the seeds of reform and renewal. The Spirit calls that church to a rediscovery of its own roots, as we discovered, encouraged by the liturgical reform movement and in the writings and witness of our founders, Alexander Campbell and Walter Scott; the vision of the Lord's Supper as a moment of Christ's actual presence, not just of his memory; and as we discovered that the Lord's Supper is profoundly social as well as personal. Here the Spirit has taken us more deeply into ourselves, enabling us to rediscover who we are.

But that is not the whole story, for the resources for renewal in a particular area of a church's life are not always available within that church itself. And then the Spirit calls that church to look beyond itself and its own resources, to look to other churches, to the whole church and its long tradition. And in doing that, encouraged by the liturgical renewal movement, our own church was inspired to reorder and renew our observance of the Lord's Supper, moving its position within the structure of the Lord's Day service so that the Supper was its culmination and climax, thus restoring the Supper to the center of our church's worship and life, where we had longed for it to be all along. Here the Spirit has taken us beyond ourselves, enabling us to see who we are called to become.

In taking us more deeply into ourselves, and in calling us *beyond* ourselves, the liturgical movement has been a blessing for our "populist sacramental" church, and for this we give thanks to God, the Father, Son, and Holy Spirit.

Worship with a Brazilian Face: Dialogue between Culture and Worship as a Way of Caring for and Transforming Life

Julio Cézar Adam

Introduction

The studies on worship and culture conducted by the Lutheran World Federation (LWF), especially the reports and essays in the first two volumes in the Spanish-language version, had a significant impact on the Evangelical Church of the Lutheran Confession in Brazil (Igreja Evangélica de Confissão Luterana no Brasil, or IECLB).[1] The texts had a particularly strong influence on the IECLB's main institution of theological formation, the Escola Superior de Teologia (EST) in São Leopoldo, in the state of Rio Grande do Sul, for example, the articles by Gordon Lathrop and Anscar J. Chupungco about baptism and the Eucharist as cultural milestones in the New Testament and in the early church, were part of the basic readings in the courses and exams at EST.[2] In the graduate program and the extension courses, Chupungco's two inculturation methods were applied to shape the liturgies in the community.

The broad research study directed by Professor Nelson Kirst as part of the LWF project, Culto e Cultura no Vale da Pitanga ("Worship and Culture

---

1. The IECLB originated in the German immigration to Brazil, which began in 1824. For many decades it remained a church gathered around German ethnicity and culture. From 1970 onward, it decided to become increasingly integrated into the local culture and take on Brazil's reality. This process is ongoing.

2. Gordon Lathrop, "The Shape of the Liturgy," in S. Anita Stauffer, ed., *Christian Worship: Unity in Cultural Diversity* (Geneva: LWF, 1996), pp. 67-75; Anscar J. Chupungco, "Two Methods of Liturgical Inculturation," in Stauffer, *Christian Worship*, pp. 77-94 (in the Spanish version).

in the Valley of Pitanga"), was also very important.[3] As part of the overall "case studies" of the project, our study meticulously investigated a small but typical congregation of the IECLB as a way of understanding its culture and its worship. We discovered many things via this research project. The main insights were these: (1) people attend worship services in order to experience God as they interact with others in the assembly, and thus better manage their own lives outside, beyond the liturgy; (2) people do not go to church primarily to understand God, but to experience God; (3) in worship, what matters most is what people do as they participate in the gathering (e.g., pray), and not so much what is said by the preacher (e.g., in the sermon).

At the same time — and more restricted to the IECLB and to EST — through the motivation provided by liberation theology, there was a broad discussion about culture itself and its political role in a Brazilian context. There was a sense of a negative impact of the "culture of the other," more specifically of the culture of the American North, as a standard culture, and its power of domination over the continent's autochthonous, indigenous, African, and popular cultures in general. This discussion also had a strong impact on our discourse concerning the relationship between worship and culture, especially within the Roman Catholic Church. For those embracing premises born out of the mix of liberation theology and the questions raised by the LWF project, it was not enough simply to seek to inculturate; it was necessary to ask how to inculturate, what to inculturate, and for whom to inculturate.

A text by Marcelo Barros, entitled *Celebrar o Deus da vida: tradição litúrgica e inculturação,* was and is especially important for local attempts at liturgical inculturation. In this volume Barros challenges the view of the church's "culturally imported" liturgy as a closed, shut off, absolute culture to which other cultures must submit. The liturgical *ordo* is the result of an inculturation process: God's incarnation occurs in a concrete time and place.

We often talk about inculturating the revelation of God, or inculturating the Eucharist, as though the revelation existed in itself, externally, and then, in a second act, it became inculturated. But this is unreal. The revelation of our God has already taken place as a human Word in a particular culture and in a way conditioned to that time and place.[4]

---

3. See Marcus P. B. Felde, "Report of Regional Research," in Stauffer, *Christian Worship,* pp. 38-41.

4. Marcelo Barros, *Celebrar o Deus da vida: tradição litúrgica e inculturação* (São Paulo: Loyola, 1992), p. 113.

Barros thus proposes a liturgy that is not only inculturated, but a liturgy that has an Afro-indigenous-Latin-popular face. Considering Barros's proposal, it is essential to establish a dialogue with the inculturation paradigms present in the LWF's material, particularly the transcultural, contextual, countercultural, and cross-cultural (in Brazil often translated as "intercultural") dimensions of liturgy.

What is at stake here — adapting a foreign rite to a culture or allowing the gospel to really become incarnate in the culture? Barros says: "In Brazil, either the liturgy becomes incarnate in the Brazilian culture, or it is not really evangelical."[5]

My intention in this essay is precisely to take up this matter again. Based on the shape of liturgy, the *ordo* (as, e.g., in Lathrop) and the criteria for inculturation — the transcultural, countercultural, contextual, cross-cultural, or intercultural nature of faithful liturgy (as, e.g., in Stauffer) — I wish to reflect on what would be worship with a Brazilian face, a worship that would look like the people and that, at the same time, would help this people to see itself as part of the incarnation of the gospel. In other words, I want to think about a worship in which the people, in their different Brazilian cultural matrices, can recognize the transcultural, contextual, and countercultural elements of Christian worship and thus can free themselves from all manner of structures of social, cultural, and economic domination — either local or imposed from the outside. Even today, we can and should ask about the cultural elements that are to be taken into account in a reality where we still experience transplanted worship elements, which are only adapted to the local culture on the basis of a foreign standard. But we must also offer a clear critique of cultural elements that are self-serving politically or socially, and are incongruous with the nature of the gospel of Jesus Christ.

In this movement, embraced and proposed by various Brazilian theologians, there is not a mere inversion of ethnic and cultural elements, but rather an inculturation that makes sense to the people themselves, yet

---

5. Barros, *Celebrar o Deus da vida,* p. 72. Inspired by this movement, I dealt with this question in my doctoral dissertation at the University of Hamburg, Germany (2004): To what extent does the liturgy liberate or dominate its people? I focused precisely on the function of the liturgy and worship service in a liturgy with a popular face, the "Romaria da Terra" (Pilgrimage of the Land). Here it became clear that the dialogue between worship and culture has political implications, as the LWF studies so well suggest. See Júlio Cézar Adam, *Romaria da Terra: Brasiliens Landkämpfer auf der Suche nach Lebensräumen* (Stuttgart: Kohlhammer, 2005).

manifests the gospel and the unity of the church everywhere. Certainly, Brazilian corporeity, movement and agitation, beauty and lightness (Jaci Maraschin); the indigenous, African, and popular cultural-religious matrices (Marcelo Souza Barros, Ione Buyst); the popular festivals and traditions such as Carnival, soccer, pilgrimages (Roberto DaMatta); syncretism and the crossing of religious borders (Carlos Rodrigues Brandão, Oneide Bobsin) — all these elements should be present but viewed through a critical lens, as we speak both in an affirmative and an admonitory way. "Affirmation and admonition" are elements about which Gordon Lathrop speaks a great deal in his writings, including his texts in the LWF conferences, which are often used in ecumenical dialogue. It is also very important to take seriously the sociopolitical dimensions involved in the culture (Buyst, Barros, Adam) and the environmental issues that are related, for instance, to baptism (Buyst). I will take the concrete case of the IECLB as an example.

This chapter is organized into four parts. (1) theoretical contributions to the reflection on inculturation; (2) aspects of Brazilian culture to be taken into account; (3) the reality of worship in context; (4) clues to an inculturated worship, a worship with a "Brazilian face" that at the same time transcends a Brazilian locality. Local yet global; global yet local.

Theoretical Contribution to a Critical Reflection on Culture, Inculturation, and Worship in Brazil

Inculturation is a process by which the church's liturgy relates and interacts with the local culture, allowing the gospel to become incarnate in a specific culture, the life and the history of the liturgical community in a particular time and place. This is the immediate objective of inculturation: to allow the congregation to celebrate a worship service that will reflect its culture and thus help its members hear and experience the gospel appropriately. What is inculturated, obviously, is the gospel of Jesus Christ. Lutherans believe that this gospel comes to the church through concrete elements: the word of God and the sacraments in the worship service. These elements, inherited from a broad and long process of contextualization, become a "form" or "order" *(ordo)* — word, baptism, and Eucharist — an ecumenically embraced shape for the liturgy. Even if the *ordo* is the result of an incarnational process, a process of inculturation, it is the *ordo* itself that repeatedly becomes inculturated. In other words, inculturation starts from this already

established *ordo*.[6] The Sunday worship service of the congregation is organized around this grounding or framing *ordo*, that is, the act of congregating
on the basis of baptism, hearing the word, sharing Communion around the
table, and then leaving to worship in the world in acts of justice, peacemaking, and liberation from the oppression of poverty, exclusion, and all
other social ills.

As proposed by the Nairobi Statement, every inculturation process of
this liturgical *ordo* takes four aspects into account. Inculturation considers
that worship to be *transcultural, contextual, and countercultural,* or *intercultural.* The *transcultural* aspect points to the risen Christ, who transcends
cultural constructs. The event of Christ — his life, passion, death, and resurrection — is above culture and the cultures. It is something universal. On
the other hand, the *contextual* aspect allows the *ordo* — word, baptism, and
Eucharist — to dialogue with the cultural and natural elements of the context
where the worship service is held. However, not everything can be contextualized: everything begging for gospel critique, for Christian worship, is
also *countercultural,* challenging and opposing elements of the local cultures
in the light of the gospel. Finally, worship is also the result of a *cross-cultural*
(or *intercultural)* process in which elements of different cultures are received
and shared in worship services in various contexts, such as, for example,
hymns and liturgical art.[7]

Another important point we need to take into account with respect to
the LWF studies on worship and culture is the method — that is, how liturgical inculturation can be performed. Anscar Chupungco proposes two inculturation methods: *creative assimilation* and *dynamic equivalence*. Elements of the local culture, such as rites, symbols, and institutions, are
reinterpreted and resignified via creative assimilation into the contents, elements, and forms of a locally held worship, thus allowing the liturgical *ordo*
to be better understood and experienced by the celebrating community.
Dynamic equivalence makes the opposite movement: it begins with what
exists in Christian liturgy to see how the culture could develop its *ordo*. The
equivalence is a kind of translation, replacing elements of the liturgical *ordo*
with something that has the same meaning or equal value in a people's
culture.[8]

---

6. Lathrop, "The Shape of the Liturgy," p. 67.
7. S. Anita Stauffer, "Worship: Ecumenical Core and Cultural Context," in Stauffer,
ed., *Christian Worship*, pp. 14-19.
8. Chupungco, "Two Methods of Liturgical Inculturation," pp. 77-94.

JULIO CÉZAR ADAM

Aspects of Brazilian Culture

Let us, then, look at aspects of Brazilian culture that are significant for this essay. It is impossible to describe a culture in a few paragraphs. To describe the Brazilian culture, considering the vastness of the country's territory, as well as its ethnic, historical, and cultural diversity, renders this task even more unfeasible. The ideal way to explore the matter would be to focus on a local culture. Therefore, my intention here is to think only about general aspects of the broad Brazilian culture, elements that characterize it and are found north to south and east to west, especially its social contradictions and complexities, and, based on them, to point to clues for a dialogue between worship and culture in the general context of Brazilian worship.

Anthropologist Roberto DaMatta describes Brazil and its culture not in a linear way (which would have a beginning, middle, and end) but rather as a complex, paradoxical drama in which roles are confounding and often contradictory at best.[9] According to DaMatta, in this drama there are at least two Brazils.

> To understand Brazil, it is necessary to establish a radical distinction between a "brazil" written in lower case letters, the name of a type of timber or of a farm building, a sickly and condemned ensemble of races that, mixing under the influence of an exuberant nature and a tropical climate, are fated to degeneration and death; and a Brazil with a capital B — an internationally acknowledged country, culture, geographical place and territory — and also home, a piece of land paved with the warmth of our bodies, a Brazil that is also home, the memory and consciousness of a place with which one has a special, unique, often sacred connection.[10]

Understanding Brazil's culture at least minimally — its institutions, values, and standards — implies looking at it in this complexity and drama, in the clash and encounter between the different cultures, histories, and dilemmas that dwell in the same territory:

> To discuss the peculiarities of our society means to study also these zones of encounter and mediation, these squares and yards given by the carni-

9. Roberto DaMatta, *Carnavais, malandros e heróis: para um sociologia do dilema brasileiro*, 6th ed. (Rio de Janeiro: Rocco, 1997), p. 15.
10. Roberto DaMatta, *O que é o Brasil?* (Rio de Janeiro: Rocco, 2004), p. 7.

vals, the processions and the rogueries, zones where time is suspended and a new routine must be repeated or innovated, where the problems are forgotten or faced; because here — suspended between the automatic routine and the feast that reconstructs the world — we touch the kingdom of liberty and of the essentially human. It is in these regions that the power of the system is reborn, but it is also here that one can forge the hope of seeing the world topsy-turvy.[11]

All possible social clashes of this sui generis culture, and all syncretism and crossings of religious and liturgical borders are implicated in this Brazilian drama.[12] We are a hybrid culture in all senses of the word. José Honório Rodrigues defines us as follows: "We are an ethnically and culturally hybrid republic. We are neither Europeans nor Latin Americans. We are indigenized, africanized, orientalized and westernized. The synthesis of so many antitheses is the unique and original product which is Brazil today."[13] We are a conglomerate of various worlds, various times, ethnicities, and languages, which is part of the dilemma. That is perhaps why Carnival is the best way of showing our diversity and our roguery, as well as our subversion and "Brazilian way of doing things [*geitinho*]." Soccer may be the best way of expressing our aspiration to organization and our hope of winning — after ninety minutes of drama. Our rural and urban violence is possibly our way of showing our protest against the social conditioning that has always been imposed on the majorities. Our religious syncretism may be a way of saying that we are hybrids in body and soul. Speaking of worship and culture in Brazil means taking all of this into account. As Jaci Maraschin points out, "Culture depends on impulses, desires, will, emotion and intelligence":

In my country I can detect the existence of two impulses that are important to understand culture. The first is what one could call Apollonian. It depends mainly on reason, order, measure, correction and, almost always, symmetry. In this sense, culture is what we learn in schools, in the family, in the churches, through study, research and experimenting transformed into a body of knowledge and of doctrines. . . . But there is another very

11. DaMatta, *Carnavais, malandros e heróis,* p. 18.

12. Oneide Bobsin, *Correntes religiosas e globalização* (São Leopoldo: CEBI/PPL/ IEPG, 2002), pp. 13ff., 30ff.

13. José H. Rodriges, quoted by Leonardo Boff, *Depois de 500 anos que Brasil queremos?* 2nd ed. (Petrópolis: Vozes, 2000), p. 19.

strong cultural impulse in Brazil. That is the Dionysian impulse. This level of culture is expressed mainly in the popular classes and is much more closely related to the emotions than to the intellect. It is visible in popular festivals such as carnival, religious processions, soccer games, Pentecostal and charismatic worship services, and worship places of Afro-Brazilian religions. These events emphasize imagination, dance, fantasy and music.[14]

The Reality of Worship in Brazil: An Imported, Transplanted Worship

To speak of the relationship between worship and culture in the Brazilian context necessarily implies thinking about it based on the contradictions and social drama pointed out by DaMatta and Maraschin because, historically, worship and culture have always been harnessed to some form of institutional power distant from the practices and experiences that authentically belong to the people.

> It is impossible to deny the historical evidence of a worship that has so often been ideologized as an integral or homologating part of the national status quo, thus making the faithful leave the concrete paths of their liberation, suppressing the freedom of the children of God, instead of expressing it. . . . Many feel that the liturgical world limits, alienates, isolates and paralyzes, and that for this very reason the church, through the performance of rites, for centuries has kept successive generations under its control, turning the suffering populations into docile "customers" of its sacraments and promises of a later, eternally happy life.[15]

In this context we may say that Brazilians do not have a systematic formulation about what drives Christian worship. The primary interest of liberation theology, which was developed on the continent beginning in the 1960s, was not worship and liturgy, and the liturgical proposals that resulted from it were not accompanied by a consistent *liturgical-theological* reflection. There was no reflection about liturgical inculturation, which could have in-

---

14. Jaci Maraschin, *Da leveza e de beleza: liturgia na pós-modernidade* (São Paulo: ASTE, 2010), pp. 20-21.
15. Aldo Vannucchi, *Liturgia e libertação* (São Paulo: Loyola, 1982), pp. 9-10, 77.

spired people to think about worship with a Brazilian and Latin face, as Buyst points out.

> There is not sufficient following up of the emerging liturgical practices, nor critical analysis and a search for the causes of stagnation of liturgical renewal. While in the field of dogmatic theology, of church history and exegesis, the Latin American church produced a new and genuine thinking with Liberation Theology and exegesis and history from the perspective of the poor, Liturgical Science appears very timidly, without an autochthonous Latin American face. . . . We [i.e., liturgical scientists, compared to other fields of theology] are at least twenty years behind. This absence of the liturgical dimension may cause an imbalance in theological reflection and in the life of the church in Latin America.[16]

In Brazilian society, the institutional church historically took the side of power, for centuries strongly defending a neutral, standardized worship, distant from the diverse and contradictory culture experienced by the people. The intended neutrality was actually nothing but the integration of worship into the system of power. Hence, in the context of the Latin American theology of liberation, liberation of human beings and liberation of worship itself are a primary part and/or result of faithful worship. Liturgical inculturation in Brazil necessarily implies a revision of the excluding and class-defined culture itself, particularly if encountered in the Sunday gathering. Before the contextual aspects come into play, the transcultural aspect — the gospel of justice — and the countercultural aspect of worship are essential to any process of evangelical inculturation. Otherwise, inculturation risks becoming an exotic, extravagant, socially bent makeup, ultimately counter-gospel, which does not entice, instill, provoke, and enable changes in people's consciences, in the spirituality and culture of the community itself. Buyst says:

> The struggle for power, which in the Bible always appears as a "battle of gods," is therefore reflected, even today, in a battle for celebratory expressions. Thus, no celebration is politically neutral. . . . Liturgy as a social event is inserted in a socio-political-economic-cultural system and has political weight. It can both serve to reinforce the status quo of oppres-

---

16. Ione Buyst, *Como estudar liturgia: princípios de ciência litúrgica,* 2nd ed. (São Paulo: Paulinas, 1990), p. 1.

sion, or to feed the hopes and struggles for a social change that will favor the oppressed.[17]

Regarding the specifically Protestant context in which the IECLB is inserted, reflection on worship and liturgy has not, for a long time, been seen as an important matter; nor was it a priority in the interest of new congregations. For these congregations, the greatest challenges were the adaptations and the concrete survival in the new world. Save for a few cases, Protestant liturgies — be they of the immigration churches or of the missionary churches — were always imported from the context from which they came (Europe and North America) and adapted to the new reality. Often the adaptation simply means the translation of liturgical handbooks and hymns, when the original language was not maintained. The institutional church tends to see these liturgies, hymns, and traditions as being theologically more true and more "sacred."

Maraschin, speaking of the liturgies of the historic churches, says that "our liturgies are generally Apollonian insofar as they are still based on the logocentric form of communication, and are governed by rules, codes, and ideas." It appears, to her, that we are caught in our liturgy books, hymnals, and traditions: our liturgies are strongly clerical; our preaching is moralistic and tends toward fundamentalism; and our liturgies are still male-oriented.[18]

The research study *Culto e cultura no Vale da Pitanga,* conducted in the context of studies on worship and culture of the LWF, points out this gap between institutional worship and the way a congregation perceives and experiences worship.[19] The study was done in a congregation in the south of Brazil, under the fictitious name *Vale da Pitanga* (Berry Valley), aiming to observe the culture of the people and how the local congregation understands the Sunday worship service, and, based on the analysis of the information, to provide contributions and help for liturgical work with other congregations.

---

17. Egídio Balbinot, *Liturgia e política: a dimensão política da liturgia nas romarias da terra de Santa Catarina* (Chapecó: Grifos, 1998), p. 168. The article by Lathrop supports this position. He proposes the juxtaposition of culture and Jesus Christ as a criterion (Gordon W. Lathrop, "Enfoque luterano contemporáneo sobre culto y cultura: discernimiento de principios críticos," in S. Anita Stauffer, ed., *Diálogo entre culto y cultura* [Genebra: FLM, 1994], pp. 37-152).

18. Maraschin, *Da leveza e de beleza,* p. 25, 28.

19. *Culto e cultura em Vale da Pitanga,* ed. Nelson Kirst (São Leopoldo: IEPG, 1995).

In the multiplicity of data and information collected, special attention was sparked by the fact that much of the liturgy is spoken and led by the pastor and is, in many respects, different from what the congregation thinks about the gatherings. At the base of the congregation's life and understanding of worship, there is no great dogmatic principle, but rather the *effort and involvement* — for life — of the individual and of the other, not only sociologically but also theologically, both during times of difficulties and of joy.[20]

Liturgical inculturation in Brazil and Latin America is still urgently in need of evaluation and study, considering that the main function of inculturation is to enable locally transparent worship. This is worship through which people can recognize their precise context, life, history, culture, time, and place, all grounded in the mercy of the triune God at the center of the meeting. It is culture and context in which the gospel becomes incarnate and is expressed through worship.

Worship with a Brazilian Face: Inculturation as a Liberating Incarnation of the Gospel

In seeking clues to think about worship with a Brazilian face, we will look at elements of the liturgical *ordo* (especially Eucharist and baptism), liturgical space and place, time and memory, and, finally, the feast.

The Liturgical Ordo: *Culture and Brazil's Sociopolitical Issues*

One of the bases of the Christian liturgical *ordo* is "the gathering of the congregation in the context of a meal, the Eucharist. Its original *Sitz im Leben* is Jesus' table fellowship." In accordance with the example of Jesus, "at the Lord's Supper the unequals continued to be united, it was a place of integration, of the fellowship of the body of Christ that abolished the natural, social, and historical-salvific boundaries." "The liturgy of the early church was differentiated and diversified regionally and locally . . . and the church was almost a world in itself."[21] It constituted the rise of a new model of relating to

20. Felde, "Report of Regional Research," pp. 38-41.
21. Peter Cornehl, "Öffentlicher Gottesdienst zum Strukturwandel der Liturgie," in *Gottesdienst und Öffentlichkeit: zur Theorie und Didaktik neuer Kommunikation,* ed. Peter Cornehl and Hans-Eckehard Bahr (Hamburg: Furche Verlag, 1970), pp. 123, 125, 127, 129. See also Lathrop's remarks "On keeping the meal," in "The Shape of the Liturgy," p. 75.

people. *Liturgia* and *diaconia* formed a unity. Something became new daily, and a new view of life together was founded. A new politics was born from liturgy.[22] And this left universal footprints in the history of the church. It is essential to think about the inculturation of worship in Brazil from the perspective of this eucharistic foundation.

Church music, or liturgical music, is probably the most inculturated element in Brazilian worship, both in terms of contents, rhythms, styles, and the inclusion of musical instruments. Thus one of the eucharistic songs by Jaci C. Maraschin serves as a good example of contextualization of this sociopolitical aspect of worship. Here the gospel opposes an unfair and excluding culture:

> O Lord, we give you thanks because around this table
> You renew our strength to fight against poverty.
> Transform our gluttony our thirst for plenteousness
> into a new feeling of justice and of hope.
> O Lord, may our dishes in a divided earth
> one day be divided in a reunited earth.
> Forgive us now at this unjust meal
> until the whole earth be fed from your bread.[23]

Based on this eucharistic social construct in Brazil, "worship cannot be non-political" (P. Watzlawick).[24] More than assimilating local cultures around local food and eating practices, what is necessary is an exercise of equivalence of the eucharistic justice: a call for all to have food, home, health, education, security, a worthy life for all, those at the table/altar and those in

---

22. "The condition of a Eucharist acceptable to God is that the poor should materially eat. . . . It is the banquet which requires that all who share it have satisfied their material hunger through historical justice. The Eucharist is a reminder of justice, it celebrates justice and foreshadows the justice of the Kingdom (by justice we mean also salvation and liberation" (Enrique Dussel, "Christliche Kunst des Unterdrückten in Lateinamerika," *Concilium* 16 [1980]: 106). See also Rafael P. Avila, *Implicaciones socio-politicas de la eucaristia* (Bogotá: Policrom, 1977); Elisabeth Schüssler Fiorenza, "Participação à mesma mesa e celebração da eucaristia," *Concilium* 172 (1982): 125-38; Leonardo Boff, "Como celebrar a eucaristia num mundo de injustiças?" in Boff, ed., *Do lugar do pobre* (Petrópolis: Vozes, 1984), pp. 103-17; Romeu Ruben Martini, *Eucaristia e conflitos sociais* (São Leopoldo: IEPG, 1997).

23. PPL, *O povo canta* (Palmitos: PPL, 1996), p. 246.

24. Jürgen Ziemer, "Gottesdienst und Politik: Zur Liturgie der Friedensgebete," in Reinhold Morath and Wolfgang Ratzmann, eds., *Herausforderung Gottesdienst: Beiträge zur Liturgie und Spiritualität, vol. 1* (Leipzig: Evangelische Verlagsanstalt, 1997), p. 182.

the world beyond it. It is urgent that this culture, one that emerges from the liturgical *ordo,* be inculturated in Brazilian worship. The political-theological element of worship, then, is no longer understood as something external, based on its consequences in the context, but as belonging to the essence of liturgy itself. From Jesus Christ's Eucharist, another culture emerges — and, significantly, leads us to conclude that

> God's mercy for human beings, as embodied in Jesus of Nazareth, should be made the criterion of one's own acting. In the worship service human beings respond with praise and gratitude to what they have received and receive from God. Being able to understand the reality of one's own life as a gracious gift is a challenge to live in accordance with it.[25]

Just as the Eucharist has driven reflection on the relationship between gospel and politics, baptism has aroused the need to relate theology, ecology, and sustainability. Buyst suggests including this ecological dimension, which is expressed in the water prayer:

> The looks and attention of all turn to the baptismal font. What we see is common water, a gift from the God of creation, a reason for gratitude. It is the water we find in nature: in rainfall, in seas and rivers, in creeks and bayous, in quiet lakes and roaring cascades and waterfalls. It is the water we receive in our taps and enables us to bathe, to clean up dirt, to water our crops, to make food, to give people and animals drink. . . . It is over this water that the ritual words will be proclaimed which make them become "baptismal water" for us, into which we are immersed as a symbolic-sacramental sign of our new life in Christ, of our immersion into his death and resurrection. Salvation presupposes nature. The sacramental signs are based on the sacredness of the cosmos, and they support and expand it. And in this way they give us a further theological reason to take care of all waters and keep them clean, alive, and beneficial.[26]

In other words, "the water of our baptism inserts us into the history of salvation of the cosmos and of humankind, into co-responsibility for the life of

---

25. Benedikt Kranemann, "Feier des Glaubens und soziales Handeln: Überlegungen zu einer vernachlässigten Dimension christlicher Liturgie," *Liturgisches Jahrbuch* 48 (1998): 213.

26. See Ione Buyst, *Símbolos na liturgia,* 4th ed. (São Paulo: Paulinas, 2004), pp. 9-18.

the planet." Considering the abundance of water and, at the same time, the abuse and misuse of water in Brazil, we have here ahead of us a long path of inculturation. According to Buyst, one of the possible baptismal questions in the rite of profession of faith and the renunciation of evil, before the baptismal bath, should be this:

> Do you renounce the accumulation of goods and the consumerism that make it impossible to sustain the economy of the country and the world? Do you promise to do everything within your reach to protect life and prevent its destruction? Do you promise to take the protection of the environment into account in practicing your profession? Do you promise to take care of the water of the planet by not wasting or polluting it?[27]

Inculturation, Space, and Place

Speaking of liturgical inculturation involves thinking about spaces and places for worship. The worship service does not occur only in a place. Liturgy and worship take place in specific sanctuaries and/or places. The LWF studies on worship and culture discuss in detail the importance of the culture and of each particular place for the church's worship.[28] The three liturgical centers — word, baptism, and Eucharist — around which the assembly gathers establish a dialogue with the local culture and nature.[29] This is an extremely important aspect to be considered in the process of inculturation in our context. Very often Brazilian places of worship are replicas of European architecture, particularly of Roman Catholic, Anglican, and Lutheran churches. There is no concern for environmental and locally based designs. In the relationship with space, inculturation may take us beyond it, to the

27. Ione Buyst, "Batismo cristão e compromisso ecológico," *Tear: Liturgia em Revista* 31 (2010): 3-4. On the cosmic dimension of water, see also Gordon Lathrop, *Holy Ground: A Liturgical Cosmology* (Minneapolis: Fortress, 2003), pp. 104ff.

28. S. Anita Stauffer, "Marcos culturales de la arquitectura bautismal en la Iglesia Primitiva," in Stauffer, *Relación entre culto y cultura* (Genebra: FLM, 2000), pp. 57-66; see also "Problemática contemporánea sobre arquitectura eclesial y la cultura," in Stauffer, *Relación entre culto y cultura,* pp. 167-80.

29. The African religious matrix, which has a very strong influence on Brazilian culture, in its rituals values elements of nature, open space, open air, contact with the ground — and values the earth as a form of access to the holy. This cultural wealth should be assimilated in our Christian liturgical spaces. See also Marcelo Barros, *Celebrar o Deus da vida,* pp. 75-90.

deprivation of places. For people who were expelled from their places, such as thousands of the impoverished who migrate to the low-income neighborhoods of Brazilian cities, or to other parts of the country, or the constant moving displacement of indigenous peoples and those of African descent in Brazil, the specificity of a visual, local cultural-liturgical space and a form of life connected to it are important elements in the discussions surrounding inculturation. For displaced people, the search for and valuing of places enables access to life itself, access to the God of life in fullness.

> The place where a group lives is not the same as a blackboard on which one writes numbers and figures that are then wiped out. . . . Each aspect, each detail of this place has itself a meaning that can be perceived only by the members of the group, because all spatial areas in which they lived correspond to a particular number of various aspects of the structure and life of their society — at least to what was most durable in it.[30]

Displacement is a fact that does not only have to do with Third World poverty. Displacement and the loss of the foundation of identity today are possibly part of every culture in the world. A study by the Lutheran World Federation made a theological theme of this: "The theological significance of the question of land or territory can be framed precisely in the conjunction between the place that provides for the sustenance of life and the animated space in which the spiritual dimensions of existence, the space of the sacred, the space of feast, can flourish."[31]

The places, not just the church rooms, characterize people's faith, and faith also finds its expression through places.[32] Hence we can understand why people ascribe such importance to their venues of worship. Members of the IECLB, for instance, cross most of the city of Porto Alegre — and they need an hour or more for that travel — to attend worship services in *their* churches, because that is where their faith life is visibly inscribed. Others express the wish that when they die they will be buried near their place of

---

30. Maurice Halbwachs, *Das kollektive Gedächtnis* (Frankfurt am Main: Fischer Taschenbuch Verlag, 1985), p. 130.

31. Vítor Westhelle, "Re(li)gion: The Lord of History and the Illusory Space," in Viggo Mortensen, ed., *Region and Religion: Land, Territory and Nation from a Theological Perspective* (Geneva: LWF, 1994), p. 85.

32. Klemens Richter, "Der liturgische Raum prägt den Glauben: Zu einem wenig beachteten Aspekt liturgischer Erneuerung," in Anselm Bilgri and Bernhard Kirchgessner, eds., *Liturgia semper reformanda* (Freiburg: Herder, 1997), pp. 243-50.

birth, often in the countryside where they grew up, even if this sometimes means high costs and hours of travel.[33]

In other words, the symbolic valuing of sanctuaries (in Portuguese referred to as "templos") dignifies people because those sanctuaries give people their location in the world. Worship spaces play this important role, and they may help us rediscover places as generating life, dignity, and dreams. Pedro Casaldáliga says: "This is our task: to discern the signs of places in which we do not yet belong but in which we will belong — 'no places' that will become concrete utopias."[34]

Therefore, worship should more clearly and visibly portray the face of its place as God's place, until the day when we will celebrate the eschatological liturgy with God in the new Jerusalem, in the new place inhabited by justice in its fullness.

Inculturation, Time, and Memory

With respect to liturgical time, those of us in the Southern Hemisphere experience a form of imposition. "The Christian liturgical calendar was transported from the Northern Hemisphere into this reality, without any attempt to adapt it to the different climatic conditions which indeed varied so much among themselves," as Hoornaert points out.

> With the European invasion, the American and Caribbean peoples did not lose their living space alone; they also lost the other elementary coordinates of human life — their own, authentic, feeling for time. Because Latin America and the Caribbean lie principally in tropical and subtrop-

33. The foundation of this belonging to a place was ancient and vital in colonial times: "On Sundays, church, the worship service, the pastor's house are the mandatory meeting places. No matter how small a congregation, it insists on having a church choir. The church hymns and popular songs are always sung in German. Feasts and events are inconceivable without a choir. In the parish hall, next to the church, topics of common interest are discussed. There too are celebrated balls, weddings, baptisms, barbecues and popular festivals. On Sunday afternoon, men play bowls or card games in the community hall. . . women meet once a week to chat, do handwork or play cards. Tea and coffee with cakes and pies complement their fun" (Ricardo Teles, *Saga: retrato das colônias no Brasil* [São Paulo: Terra Virgem Editora, 1997], pp. 108ff.).

34. Vítor Westhelle, "Creation Motifs in the Search for a Vital Space: A Latin American Perspective," in Susan B. Thistlethwaite and Mary P. Engel, eds., *Lift Every Voice: Constructing Christian Theologies from the Underside* (New York: Orbis, 1998), p. 148.

ical climate areas, the imposition of the Catholic calendar meant that their inhabitants forfeited the rhythm whereby time corresponded to nature. We know how important are time and space for the location of human beings in the world and in society. People who lose the correct sense of time and space gradually lose their identity.[35]

Even so, a brief study that I conducted shows that people create their own adaptation of meaning. Rather than thinking about a calendar for the Southern Hemisphere, it is necessary to rediscover people's view of the liturgical times. According to this study, people ascribe to Easter (in autumn) and Christmas (in summer) a theological meaning that is appropriate to the Southern Hemisphere.

> According to a theology student, Easter is a time of reflection, a time of changes. Just as the trees renew their foliage, so also we understand Easter as a time in which someone changes our life and gives us a new garment. A church member observed that Easter is renewal; it is death and resurrection. Leaves fall from the trees in the autumn so that new leaves may appear and renew the life of the tree. The wind sweeps the fragile away. A new life is shown in nature. So also Jesus purifies our hearts by forgiving our sins and bringing new life. Christmas is light and divine love which spreads human warmth among people by the birth of our King Jesus Christ, just as in the summer the earth is warmed and illuminated by the sun, the king of the stars.[36]

In connection with time, inculturation leads us to also think about the issue of memory. Where people were displaced and had their calendars and natural cycles supplanted, the recovery and exercise of memory is a must. The people of Israel in exile experienced this reality and worship acted as an agency of survival through memory:

> The Jerusalem Temple lay in ruins (6th century), and the nationalized worship centered there had come to an abrupt halt. There was no way to pick up elsewhere the temple cult of sacrifice, which by that time had

---

35. Eduardo Hoornaert, *História do cristianismo na América Latina e no Caribe* (São Paulo: Paulus, 1994), p. 304.

36. Júlio Cézar Adam, "The Church Year in the Southern Hemisphere: A Case Study from Brazil," *Studia Liturgica* 40 (2010): 173.

become identified exclusively with Jerusalem. A new beginning had to be made to enable Israel to survive. The synagogue apparently originated as a survival agency. . . . Israel kept its identity by remembering. It remembered what God had done for God's chosen people whose history made them unique. . . . Israel could survive through worship when countless other kingdoms were obliterated by the sword. And the power to remember, reinforced generation after generation by worship, was too powerful even for the tyranny of Babylon.[37]

Memory is not created. It already exists among people and their culture. People appeal precisely to this reserve of memory to call the group into existence. That is why it is, at the same time, a source of identity and of resistance, dangerous to the powerful but liberating for the simple people.[38] For the excluded, memory has a countercultural function: "It starts from experiences of deficiencies in the present and asks in memory for a past that usually has the contours of a heroic time."[39] Christian memory, therefore, is related to the articulation, by means of liturgical tradition, of the *memoria passionis Christi*, which Johann B. Metz calls "memory of suffering":

> [Memory] claims history not only as a scenario for the projection of current interests. It mobilizes tradition as a dangerous tradition and, in this way, as a liberating power over against the one-dimensionality and the security of those whose "time is always here" (John 7:6). . . . The memory of suffering, in the Christian sense, does not flee into the nebulousness of social and political arbitrariness, but it sharpens the social and political awareness for the sake of the suffering of others. It avoids privatizing and internationalizing suffering and leveling its social dimension. In this memory of suffering, history of suffering and history of social oppression are not simply identical, but they are also not concretely separable.[40]

37. James White, *Introduction to Christian Worship* (Nashville: Abingdon Press, 1990), pp. 142-43.
    38. "Under the conditions of oppression, memory may become a form of resistance" (Jan Assmann, *Das kulturelle Gedächtnis: Schrift, Erinnerung und politische Identität in frühen Hochkulturen*, 3rd ed. [München: Beck, 2000], pp. 73, 78ff.).
    39. Ellen Fensterseifer Woortmann, "Deutsch-Brasilianische Memoiren," in Sibylle Benninghoff-Lühl and Annette Leibing, eds., *Brasilien — Land ohne Gedächtnis?* (Hamburg: Uni Hamburg, 2001), pp. 194-95.
    40. Johann Baptist Metz, *Glaube in Geschichte und Gesellschaft: Studien zu einer praktischen Fundamentaltheologie*, 5th ed. (Mainz: Mathias-Grünewald, 1992), pp. 95, 116.

All these things invite liturgical theologians to consider the deepest meanings of anamnesis: What is it that we are asked to remember? What is the occasion in which we hear the words "in remembrance of me" in our liturgical settings? At the same time, when we hear, taste, and see the present grace of God for all our hungers — and the challenge it brings — then we, too, remember the poor, the oppressed, the forgotten ones, whose memories still hold them as victims. In Brazil these many victims are not abstract subjects. They are the blacks, the indigenous people, women, street children, children in general, people from the slums, landless and homeless, people who suffer from substance dependence, illiterates, homosexuals — and so many others who are generally absent from our liturgies. The sufferers and the victims continuously rewrite and write history, what Metz calls an "antihistory" — a memory that was forgotten. Thus is memory no mere exercise in thinking. Memory of suffering provokes a change in culture: "It obliges us to look at the public *theatrum mundi* not only from the perspective of those who managed to get through and arrive, but also from that of the defeated and the victims."[41] This is very promising in a context such as that of Brazil.

Worship is the privileged place of this memory. The exhortation "do this in remembrance of me" (1 Cor. 11:24f; Luke 22:19) was given to us as a criterion. The church is founded on this memory, which is greater than all our memories.

> Now, if the Christian congregation keeps in its worship the memory of its crucified, resurrected Lord, who is in the process of consummation, it not only realizes over and over again his death, that sealed a new alliance, but then this Lord is with the congregation, with all that he did for it and will still do. So the congregation is present in the exodus to freedom and in the institution of the Lord's Supper, and then it experiences again the fellowship with the resurrected one in a marvelous way, and then over it lies the shine and foreshadowing of an indescribable glory.[42]

The memory of the cross of Christ as an announcement of death and proclamation of resurrection, as a redemption-already-and-not-yet, corrects our

---

41. Johann Baptist Metz, "Zukunft aus dem Gedächtnis des Leidens: Eine gegenwärtige Gestalt der Verantwortung des Glaubens," *Concilium* 8 (1972): 401, 402.

42. Hans-Christoph Schmidt-Lauber, *Die Zukunft des Gottesdienstes: Von der Notwendigkeit lebendiger Liturgie* (Stuttgart: Calwer, 1990), p. 71.

past and frees us from the absolutizing of our partial memory. The dimension of anamnesis of worship thus helps us to say who we were, who we are, and who we shall be. It helps us experience this constant incarnation in everyday life, in different places, also amid a culture that excludes difference.

> In a worship service that presents itself as a fellowship of memory and narrative, there is space for the experiences of life and faith of those who existed before us. They are heard when the Bible texts are read and interpreted. They are heard when we sing their hymns, when we appropriate their prayers and join them in praising God. They are present — they are "commemorated" — when we celebrate the Eucharist. The history of salvation that we tell by remembering and remember by telling, includes them. . . .[43]

Inculturation and the *Festa*

Even if it is sometimes difficult to imagine Brazilian evangelical worship as a *Festa* (feast), that is precisely what it is. The whole church year informs the festive character of worship and its importance in people's lives. Worship at its best is a feast in its playful, quasi-purposeless dimension. But in contrast to the popular festivals in Brazil, Protestant worship lacks laughter, dancing, gestures, and expressions of joy, colors, and sounds. Instead, the worship service in our churches often resembles a somber, circumspect, and sad meeting of the congregation, as though Jesus were still in his tomb — like a yearlong Good Friday. Only the subversive memory of the resurrection brings the feast into the church, into the congregation gathered for worship amidst its sufferings in the world.

Although the feast, in its playful nature, must not be made into an instrument, must not be triumphal in nature, and must even include lamentation for the way things are — for the sins of the world, of the church, and of those in the assembly — it is still a feast, a true *Festa*. But it cannot be prepared without a relationship with the context — everyday life. Worship is the place in the Christian world where people do not go in order to undertake something. "Feast," therefore, does not mean only exodus from every-

---

43. Karl-Heinrich Bieritz, "Heimat Gottesdienst?" in Christoph Bizer, Jochen Cornelius-Bundschuh, and Hans-Martin Gutmann, eds., *Theologisches geschenkt: Festschrift für M. Josuttis* (Bovenden: Foedus, 1996), pp. 265-66.

day life, nor only continuity with everyday life, nor forgetfulness of the pains all members of the congregation encounter in life. It is not a compensatory valve for everyday life either.[44] The Sunday Christian feast and everyday life have a complementary relationship: in a Christian sense, this is made possible through word and table, the presence of Christ among us and the nearness of the reign of God in bath, word, the prayers, the table, and the sending — in Brazilian terms, but still the gospel beyond culture or cultures.

This is nothing less than a new quality of life before God, since there is a new time and a new place with and in Jesus Christ, and with that comes a new human being, a new God, a new world. The dualism of feast and non-feast was overcome, as well as the dualism between cult-related and profane, pure and impure. Hence, according to Paul, service in the everyday life of the world becomes worship (Rom. 12). This does not mean that joy and freedom in the worship service were forbidden or lost, that they capitulated when facing everyday poverty, but that they must permeate everyday life like yeast, moving from lovelessness to the quiet corners of a supposedly healthy world, and a lovely and loving God.[45]

In the concrete case of the worship service in the IECLB, the graciousness of a real *Festa* must gain force. We need to say farewell to an excessively rational worship service that places great accent on a sense of remembering Christ's suffering and death only. In faithful worship we enact new life, new hope of resurrection, with the local gifts of more "Brazilianness," in which the dimension of the holy will be perceived, welcomed, and celebrated in word, gestures, processions, dance and music, and all arts — those things manifesting a Brazilian face. It must be a worship service of the whole congregation: *returned* to the hands of the laypeople and preserved at the altar as a genuine development of the priesthood of all believers.[46]

This writer dearly hopes that worship in his native land can increasingly take on the shape and content of a feast in the Brazilian culture, without losing sight of the cross at our center, or the Lutheran sobriety of our history. Nor should we unduly set aside the ecumenically shared central elements of the liturgy. In all these matters, not one or the other, but "both/and."

44. Martin, *Fest und Alltag: Bausteine zu einer Theorie des Festes* (Stuttgart/Berlin/Köln/Mainz: Kohlhammer, 1973), pp. 36-41.

45. Martin, p. 48.

46. Wolfgang Grünberg, "Freiheit ins Spiel bringen: Ernst Langes Vision vom Gottesdienst," in Klaus Hoffmann, ed., *Spielraum des Lebens, Spielraum des Glaubens: Entdeckungen zur Spielkultur bei Ernst Lange und Spiel und Theater in der Kirche heute* (Hamburg: EB-Verlag, 2001), pp. 102-3.

The source of hope of the feast emerges from the nearness of God. Divine nearness can already be perceived in the core of our culture, for example, in our laughing and our solidarity, in our *mate* (a special tea very common in the south of Brazil, shared as a common cup), and in our greetings' physical demonstrations of care (Brazilians, male and female, kiss each other twice — once on each side of the face — and in some parts of Brazil, three times). It is also seen in the country's stubborn sense of joie de vivre, often boisterous, colorful, always hoping for the best, for liberation from poverty and oppression. But even Brazil's popular music often brings with it a great sense of pathos: when you hear bossa nova music, you can hear suffering, patience, love, hope, and despair. Hear the folk music of northern Brazil, where poverty is the greatest, and ponder the modal quality of pain in lingering, yet also playful hope. A well-known and widely sung hymn found in many hymnals in the United States and beyond is *Cantai ao Senhor um Cantico Novo* ("Sing to the LORD a New Song," Psalm 96). In North America churches often sing this as a dance, fast-paced with much handclapping. But sing this very hymn in Brazil, and it is soulful singing, slow, gentle, and somewhat sad, a true example of Brazilian hymnody that is faithful to its cultural context: poverty abounds, even where many churches' altars are covered in gold; yet hope and faith abounds more. Sing the faith and the hope, but frame these things in local cultural contexts. And more, pray for the people behind it as you sing the hymn. Worship with a "Brazilian face": Shouldn't worship in Brazil include just such cultural expressions? Grünberg puts it this way:

> The worship service on Sundays is *ekklesia,* therefore the gathering of those who no longer blindly believe in the claims of the facts that mark everyday life, not in order to have a separate world in a distant niche, but to experience a foretaste of freedom in the alternative culture of the worship gathering, which encourages, creates freedom and provides incentives to take a position against the demands of power made by the facts.[47]

The LWF and "Worship with a Brazilian Face": Concluding Thoughts

The LWF studies were and still are an invitation for a dialogue between the gospel assembly and life naked and raw — as it is. The reports and essays in

47. Grünberg, "Freiheit ins Spiel bringen," p. 107.

those studies reveal the fact that these juxtapositions are indispensable dimensions, and are required for faithful liturgy in any context: both *Kyrie eleison* and *Gloria in excelsis;* lament and *festa;* denouncement and announcement; judgment and mercy. These things together, not one without the other, make possible liturgy that in fact concretizes, actualizes, contextualizes, and thus proclaims the gospel for the assembly's daily life, wherever and whenever that assembly gathers — North, South, East or West.

The parity and the connections between the Nairobi Statement's paradigms cannot be far from liturgical discourse and worship life, in Brazil or elsewhere: faithful worship is contextual (needs to be inculturated in its locality); it is cross-cultural, for it borrows from cultures everywhere; it is transcultural, for its central things are visible and audible in any assembly. But these things together must take into account — indeed, be framed by — an embrace of the challenging dimension of the countercultural nature of the gospel, and thus also of the liturgy. Therefore, to imagine worship with a Brazilian face means tending to these dialogical tensions: faithfulness to the historical *ordo,* on the one hand, and the cultural gifts and realities of everyday Brazilian colors, sounds, movements, and injustices of the context, on the other. The questions could be summarized this way:

> Does the entire service show forth Jesus Christ, crucified and risen, for the life of the world?[48]

and

> How is the grace of Jesus Christ, the love of God, and the companionship of the Holy Spirit made present *here,* at this hour, on this day, with this people, in this place?

May the triune God, whom alone we worship and serve, enable our questions on liturgical inculturation to prod and enliven the church in all places and times in the world in such a way that all encounter not only a face in its cultural context but the very face of Jesus Christ in every person, in every place, in every assembly, and in the world outside the assembly, until he comes in glory.

---

48. For contextualization, see Gordon Lathrop, "The Shape of the Liturgy," pp. 74, 75.

Methods of Liturgical Inculturation

Anscar J. Chupungco, OSB

Introduction

The inculturation of Christian worship is a subject that requires a sound working definition of both culture and liturgy as well as the parameters of relationship that should exist between them. But in order to make that definition work concretely, we need to have methods. This paper proposes three methods (which obviously can work in combination with each other): creative assimilation, dynamic equivalence, and organic progression.

Before we engage in an analysis of these methods, it may be useful to briefly review the definition of liturgical inculturation.[1] It is a process

---

1. See Congregation for Divine Worship, *The Roman Liturgy and Inculturation,* 4th Instruction for the Right Application of the Conciliar Constitution on the Liturgy (Rome, 1994). For a fuller explanation of "inculturation" and related terms, see A. Chupungco, *Liturgical Inculturation: Sacramentals, Religiosity, and Catechesis* (Collegeville, MN: Liturgical Press, 1992), pp. 13-36; see also Mark Francis: "Liturgical Adaptation," in Peter E. Fink, ed., *The New Dictionary of Sacramental Worship* (Collegeville, MN: Liturgical Press, 1990), pp. 14-23; Peter Schineller, "Inculturation of the Liturgy," in *The New Dictionary of Sacramental Worship,* pp. 598-601; Peter Schineller, *A Handbook on Inculturation* (New York: Paulist Press, 1990).

This essay is a revised version of "Two Methods of Liturgical Incorporation," which the author originally published in *Christian Worship: Unity in Cultural Diversity,* vol. 2 of the LWF study series on worship (Geneva: LWF, Department for Theology and Studies, 1996), pp. 77-94.

whereby pertinent elements of a local culture are integrated into the worship of a local church. Integration means that culture influences the composition and proclamation of prayer formularies, the performance of ritual actions, and the expression of liturgical message in art forms. Integration can also mean that local rites, symbols, and festivals, after due critique and Christian reinterpretation, are assimilated into the liturgical worship of a local church.

One result of inculturation is that the liturgical texts, symbols, gestures, and feasts evoke something from the people's history, traditions, cultural patterns, and artistic genius. We might say that the power of the liturgy to evoke local culture is one sign that inculturation has taken place.

The immediate aim of inculturation is to create a form of worship that is culturally suited to the local people — so that they can claim it as their own. Its ultimate aim, on the other hand, is active, intelligent, and devout participation that springs from the people's conviction of faith. Incultura-tion, properly understood and rightly executed, should lead the assembly to a more profound appreciation of Christ's mystery that is made present in the celebration by the dynamic mediation of cultural signs and symbols. Incul-turation, in other words, should aim to deepen the spiritual life of the assem-bly through a fuller experience of Christ, who reveals himself in the people's language, rites, arts, and symbols. If inculturation does not do this, it remains a futile exercise.

Historical models of inculturation are not lacking, and they are always useful references, especially in the area of baptism, Eucharist, architecture, and music.[2] But it is necessary to know how to handle them. One aspect of this question is learning to identify the cultural components that are present in Christian worship and to explain how and when they got there. The his-tory of the liturgy teaches us that Christian worship, whose origin dates from the time of Christ and the apostles, has in the course of centuries integrated the culture of the Greeks and the Romans, the Franco-Germanics, and the people of the late middle ages in Europe. With such models, history chal-lenges us, as it were, to imitate the good things that our ancestors in the faith accomplished, while avoiding the errors that seem to inevitably mark any human enterprise.

This brings us to the next step. How do we go about inculturating Chris-tian worship? The question is one of methodology. Correct method is the key to correct inculturation. An examination of historical and contemporary

2. See the articles on these topics by G. Lathrop, A. Chupungco, and A. Stauffer in Stauffer, ed., *Worship and Culture in Dialogue* (Geneva: LWF Studies, 1994).

models of inculturation shows that there are at least three methods that we can possibly use.

It is important to premise the work of inculturation by stating several factors that affect the application of the above-mentioned methods: the theological accent in a given period in answer to doctrinal controversies; the evolving cultural expressions of peoples, especially in the missions; and the pastoral needs of a particular worshiping community.

The Method of Creative Assimilation

During the age of patristic creativity, especially in the time of church fathers such as Tertullian, Hippolytus, and Ambrose, inculturation often came about through the integration of pertinent rites, symbols, and linguistic expressions — religious or otherwise — into the liturgy. Examples are anointing at baptism, the giving of the cup of milk and honey, and the foot-washing of neophytes. We should include the kinds of ritual language Christian writers had introduced into the liturgy.[3]

The Greeks and the Romans had commonly practiced these rites during the first four centuries. Some of them belonged to household rites, others to religious acts such as the mystery rites. But by the method of creative assimilation they became part of Christian worship. They elaborated the core of the liturgical rite, and they developed the shape of the liturgy. For example, the rite of baptism developed from the apostolic "washing in water with the word" (Eph. 5:26) to a full liturgical celebration that included, after the fourth century, a prebaptismal anointing, an act of renunciation toward the west and profession of faith while facing the east, the blessing of the baptismal water, and the postbaptismal rites such as foot-washing, anointing with chrism, clothing in white robes, and the proffering of a lighted candle.

It is useful to mention here that those who applied the method of creative assimilation often had recourse to biblical typology. This means that cultural elements, such as the people's rites, symbols, and institutions, are reinterpreted in the context of biblical personages and events. We can recall the ancient Roman practice of feeding a newborn infant with milk and honey, which could have been the origin of a similar rite for initiates into some mystery religions. The author of the third-century *Apostolic Tradition* reinterprets

---

3. See A. Chupungco, "Baptism in the Early Church and Its Cultural Settings," in Stauffer, ed., *Worship and Culture in Dialogue,* pp. 39-56.

this practice in the light of God's promise that he would lead the chosen people into a land flowing with milk and honey. When creatively assimilated into the rite of communion, the cup of milk and honey assured the church's newborn sons and daughters, or neophytes, that when they passed through the waters of baptism they crossed over to the new land of promise.

This method offers a wide range of possibilities and hence a wild range as well. One can easily abuse the method. With little effort, one can discover similarities between the liturgical rites and those of one's own culture, between liturgical symbolism and the local system of symbols, and between liturgical language and the ritual language of a people. Encouraged by similarities, one might even unjustifiably utilize biblical types in an attempt to integrate incompatible cultural elements with the history of salvation.

But certain questions need to be asked. First, supposing the newly added cultural elements possess what one can call "co-naturalness" with the Christian liturgy, have they duly undergone the process of doctrinal purification? Similarity is not a gauge of orthodoxy and orthopraxis. Second, are the biblical types that are utilized appropriate? It is possible to do violence to the biblical text in order to accommodate culture. Third, do the local elements enhance the theological understanding of the Christian rite? It can happen that they divert attention from the Christian rite by being overly evocative of their cultural provenance or, worse, sending a wholly different message. Fourth, do they harmonize with the other elements of the rite, and are they sufficiently integrated with them? Perhaps they are no more than useless decorative appendages or cultural tokens with little or no role to play in the unfolding of the rite. And fifth, we need to ask a question too easily forgotten by people who undertake projects of inculturation: Do people accept them as authentic contributions of their culture to the enrichment of Christian worship?

The method of creative assimilation can be a useful reference when one intends to develop or expand the shape of a given ritual for use in a local church. Certain parts of the *eucharistic* celebration, such as the rite of gathering and the preaching of the word, can be developed by appropriate rites borrowed from the local culture after due process of purification. Suitable rites of initiation that are found in people's traditions can also enrich the rite of *baptism*.[4] The rite of *marriage* is another instance where ritual and linguistic elaboration can be made on the basis of local marriage rites.[5]

4. A. Chupungco, *Liturgies of the Future: The Process and Methods of Inculturation* (New York: Paulist Press, 1989), pp. 56-101, 125-39.

5. R. Serrano, *Towards a Cultural Adaptation of the Rite of Marriage* (Rome, 1987).

The institution in a local church of new liturgical feasts inspired by contemporary sociocultural or civil festivities is another area where the method of creative assimilation can be useful.[6] Through this form of inculturation, the liturgical year is grafted on the seasons of the year, the traditional feasts of peoples, the cycle of human work, and political systems of nations. The church should not isolate itself from what goes on in the world. Its liturgy should interplay with the academic year, the business year, the political year, the cause-oriented years, the years of struggles and hopes, and the years of war and peace — in order to imbue them with the mystery of Christ.

The method of creative assimilation can be considered in those instances where the liturgical rite is too austere or sober, if not altogether impoverished. In the liturgy, people need to see, feel, touch, and taste. Sometimes it is in their culture to want to be impressed by the solemnity of a rite, to experience a dramatic effect that they can relish for a long period of time. Creative assimilation can bring these things about by enriching the liturgical rite with people's own rites. In other instances, however, where there is a fully developed liturgical rite, this method carries the danger of overloading the rite with secondary and peripheral elements or of courting repetitiousness. In such cases the method of dynamic equivalence is the right option. But there can also be instances when both methods can fruitfully be used hand in hand.

During the patristic period, words like *eiuratio* (for baptismal renunciation), *fidei testatio* (for profession of faith), *mystagogia,* and *initiatio* were admitted into the liturgical vocabulary.[7]

The Method of Dynamic Equivalence

Another method of inculturation is dynamic equivalence, as opposed to formal correspondence or literal translation. As a method, dynamic equivalence applies to both the rites and the texts. While creative assimilation starts with what culture can offer and hence what can be added to Christian liturgy, dynamic equivalence starts with what exists in the Christian liturgy and how culture can further develop its *ordo,* or shape. In other words, dynamic

---

6. A. Adam, *The Liturgical Year* (New York: Pueblo, 1981).

7. P.-M. Gy, "The Inculturation of the Christian Liturgy in the West," *Studia Liturgica* 20, no. 1 (1990): 8-18. Gy gives other linguistic examples, such as *confessio, absolutio,* and *paenitentia.*

equivalence is a type of translation. It reexpresses the liturgical *ordo* in the living language, rites, and symbols of a local community. Concretely, dynamic equivalence consists of replacing elements of the liturgical *ordo* with something that has an equal meaning or value in the culture of the people and hence can suitably transmit the message intended by the *ordo*. Because dynamic equivalence draws its elements from people's culture and traditions, the liturgy is able to evoke life experiences and paint vivid images rooted in the people's history, traditions, and values.

"If I translate word by word, it sounds absurd; if I am forced to change something in the word order or style, I seem to have stopped being a translator."[8] With these words Saint Jerome articulated the experience of every conscientious translator. Word-by-word translation often does not make sense, but a change in the meaning of the word betrays the message.

German Reformer and Bible translator Martin Luther admitted having encountered the same difficulty with literal translation:

> We do not have to ask about the literal Latin or how we are to speak German. Rather we must ask the mother in the home, the children on the street, the common person in the market about this. We must be guided by their tongue, the manner of their speech, and do our translating accordingly. Then they will understand it and recognize that we are speaking German to them. . . . The literal Latin is a great barrier to speaking proper German.[9]

When the Second Vatican Council approved the use of the vernacular in the Roman liturgy, it was implied that the Latin liturgical books would have to be translated into the local languages. This was the underpinning for Article 36 of the Liturgy Constitution, whose formulation drew much debate in the council hall. The final text reaffirmed that "the use of the Latin language is to be preserved in the Latin rite," though the use of the vernacular was to be extended.

In his address to the translators of liturgical texts in 1965, Pope Paul VI summed up the conciliar and postconciliar thinking on translation. The address covered the basic principles of liturgical translations, which were faith-

8. Jerome, *Eusebii Interpretata Praefatio, Einleitung des Hieronymus,* Eusebius *Werke* VII, 1, *GSC* 47, ed. R. Helm (1954), 2: "Si ad verbum interpretor, absurde resonat: si ob necessitatem aliquid in ordine, in sermone mutavero, ab interpretis videbor officio recessisse."

9. Martin Luther, *An Open Letter on Translating,* September 15, 1530.

fully echoed by the 1969 Instruction *Comme le prévoit* on Liturgical Translations. Pope Paul VI's reminder is timely:

> The vernacular now taking place in the liturgy ought to be within the grasp of all, even children and the uneducated. But, as you well know, the language should always be worthy of the noble realities it signifies, set apart from the everyday speech of the street and market place, so that it will affect the spirit and enkindle the heart with love of God.[10]

The Instruction *Comme le prévoit* guided the difficult work of translation in the Roman Church for thirty-two years. According to it, the purpose of liturgical translation is to "faithfully communicate to a given people, and in their own language, that which the Church by means of this given text originally intended to communicate to another people in another time" (no. 6). What does the Instruction mean by faithful translation? "A faithful translation cannot be judged on the basis of individual words: the total context of this specific act of communication must be kept in mind, as well as the literary form proper to the respective language."

This method of translation, which is generally favored by the Instruction, is called "dynamic equivalence," or sense translation into the current speech. It communicates the *meaning* of a text more than merely translating into the receptor language the individual words and phrases of the source language. It was promoted by biblical scholar Eugene Nida and is recommended by experts of cultural anthropology and linguistic sciences.[11]

The Instruction establishes that "the prayer of the Church is always the prayer of some actual community, assembled here and now. It is not sufficient that a formula handed down from some other time or region be translated verbatim, even if accurately, for liturgical use. The formula translated must become the genuine prayer of the congregation, and in it each of its members should be able to find and express himself or herself" (no. 20). Hence, "in the case of liturgical communication, it is necessary to take into account not only the message to be conveyed, but also the speaker, the audience, and the style" (no. 7). In short, we are dealing here with the method of dynamic equivalence.

---

10. Pope Paul VI, "Address to Latinists," in *Documents on the Liturgy* (Collegeville, MN: Liturgical Press, 1982), pp. 272-74.

11. Eugene Nida, *Towards a Science of Translating, with Special Reference to Principles and Procedures Involved in Bible Translating* (Leiden: Brill, 1964).

C. Kraft points out the following traits of dynamic equivalence: (1) each language — and the same can be said of the other components of culture — has its own genius and special character; (2) to communicate effectively in another language, one must respect this uniqueness and work in terms of it (he notes that attempts to "remake" languages to conform to other languages have been monumentally unsuccessful); (3) in order to preserve the content of the message, the translator must change the form. Different languages express quite similar concepts in very different ways, and no concepts are expressed in exactly the same ways. Kraft concludes that "the faithful translator, in attempting to convey an equivalent message in terms of the genius of the receptor language, must alter the form in which the message was expressed in the original language."

The opposite of dynamic equivalence is formal correspondence. It is called "formal" because it remains on the level of form or shape or external appearance. It does not take into consideration the cultural pattern, history, and life experience of the local church. In the area of language, formal correspondence tends to be no more than a literal, word-for-word or phrase-by-phrase translation to the point of ignoring the linguistic traits of the audience. Thus, while it may appear "faithful" to the original, it fails to communicate the message effectively. According to Kraft, formal equivalence "aims to be faithful to the original documents. But this 'faithfulness' centers almost exclusively on the surface-level forms of the linguistic encoding in the source language and their literal transference into corresponding linguistic forms in the receptor language."[12] According to the proponents of formal correspondence, no word, even if it is merely a rhetorical device peculiar to the Latin oration, such as the word *quaesumus,* may be dropped in the receptor language.

Some literal translations are no more than mere transliterations, such as, for example, "mystery" for *mysterion* and "sacrament" for *sacramentum.* Such transliterations, though doctrinally safe, do not enrich the assembly's understanding of what the liturgy is talking about. Others are literal equivalents that do not take into account the sociocultural or religious context of the receptor languages. For example, "in memory of" as a translation of *anamnesis* does not take into account the receptor's use of the phrase "in memory of" in connection with tombstones. Thus, speaking of the Eucharist as an *ordo* "in memory" of Jesus can create in some cultural contexts the image of the dead more than of the risen Savior.

---

12. C. Kraft, *Christianity in Culture: A Study in Dynamic Biblical Theologizing in Cross-cultural Perspective* (New York: Orbis, 1994), p. 265; see esp. chaps. 13-15, pp. 261-312, 265.

Language and Dynamic Equivalence

Examples of formal equivalence in the liturgy are those translations that try to account for every word found in the original Latin texts. Thus, the congregation's reply to the greeting *Dominus vobiscum* is a literal translation of *et cum spiritu tuo* ("and with your spirit") regardless of the cultural and linguistic connotations of "spirit" in local congregations. The concept of dynamic equivalence will become clearer with examples of how to translate technical terms. The two basic terms in liturgy, namely *anamnesis* and *epiklesis,* are probably also the basic problems of liturgical inculturation. Anamnesis is commonly defined as the ritual memorial of Christ's paschal mystery; by virtue of this ritual memorial, the paschal mystery becomes present to the worshiping assembly. In the Roman liturgy, in order to express anamnesis, the Latin eucharistic prayers use *memores* (Eucharistic Prayers 1, 2, and 3) or *memoriale celebrantes* (Eucharistic Prayer 4).

An attempt to use dynamic equivalence for anamnesis was made in the Philippines in 1975 with the proposed *Misa ng Bayang Pilipino,* which was submitted to Rome the following year.[13] The narration of the Last Supper begins with the Tagalog phrase *Tandang-tanda pa namin* (literally, "how clearly we remember"). It is the phrase used to start the narration of a historical event. By using it, the narrator claims to have been present when the event happened and to have witnessed it in person; that is why the narrator can recount it vividly and to the last detail. Is this not perhaps what the church wishes to say at the narration of the Last Supper? The church was there, remembers what took place as Jesus sat with his disciples, and now passes on the experience from one generation to the next.

The other concept is *epiklesis,* which may be defined as the prayer invoking God to send the Holy Spirit on sacramental elements and on people, who then receive the sacraments in order to be sanctified or consecrated to God. The *Misa ng Bayang Pilipino* uses a graphic expression for epiklesis: *lukuban ng Espiritu Santo.* The verb *lukuban* means "to protect," to gather under the wings, to brood. Used with epiklesis, it calls to mind the action of the bird brooding on her eggs; thereby it conveys the idea of the vivifying and transforming action of the Holy Spirit on the bread and the wine — and on the assembly.

Idiomatic expressions, which often defy translation, are some of the best material for dynamic equivalence. For example, the Latin word *dignitas* is

13. Text in A. Chupungco, *Towards a Filipino Liturgy* (Quezon City, 1976), pp. 96-118.

normally translated as "dignity," and people have a notion of what the word means. But we are dealing here with inculturation. An attempt to use an idiomatic expression for *dignitas* is made by a proposed translation of the Christmas collect *Deus, qui humanae substantiae dignitatem* of Pope Leo the Great. Although Igbo, the language of Nigeria, has the equivalent word for "dignity," the proposed Igbo translation prefers the idiomatic expression "to wear an eagle's feather." The eagle's feather stuck in one's hair shows the dignity and the position a person holds in society. The proposed Igbo prayer praises God, who gives the eagle's feather to every man and woman he creates.[14]

Dynamic equivalence in the Roman liturgy took a heavy blow on March 28, 2001, when the Congregation for Divine Worship published the Instruction *Liturgiam authenticam.* The Instruction sets forth the principle that "the translation of the liturgical texts of the Roman liturgy is not so much a work of creative innovation as it is of rendering the original texts faithfully and accurately into the vernacular language" (no. 20). The Instruction firmly declares that "the original text, insofar as possible, must be translated integrally and in the most exact manner, without omissions or additions in terms of their content, and without paraphrases or glosses. Any adaptation to the characteristics or the nature of various vernacular languages is to be sober and discreet." This method of translation is known as "formal correspondence," or the word-for-word rendering of a text into the vernacular.

The Instruction *Liturgiam authenticam* is as hard as nails in its rejection of dynamic equivalence. Its norms, which replaced *Comme le prévoit,* have been applied to the new English Missal. Whether or not the assembly will understand more fully the message of the liturgical texts and derive spiritual benefit from them, as envisioned by Vatican II's Constitution on the Liturgy, is a question that only time can answer.[15]

Rites and Dynamic Equivalence

The method of dynamic equivalence works also through ritual elaboration. The emphasis here is on the word "dynamic." For example, in the Philippines

---

14. A. Echiegu, *Translating the Collects of the "Sollemnitates Domini" of the "Missale Romanum" of Paul VI in the Language of the African,* (Münster, 1984), p. 313.

15. E. Foley, ed., *A Commentary on the Order of Mass of the Roman Missal* (Collegeville, MN: Liturgical Press, 2011).

ANSCAR J. CHUPUNGCO, OSB

the Tagalog rite of marriage *(Pagdiriwang ng Pag-iisang Dibdib),* approved
by Rome in 1983, expands on the exchange of consent: "Before God and his
church I enter into a covenant with you to be my wife/husband. You alone
shall I love and cherish as the extension of my life now and forever." The key
words and the phrase that expand on the exchange of consent are "covenant"
(tipan) and "extension of life" *(karugtong ng buhay):* the first refers to the
covenant between Christ and his church and to the eucharistic new and
everlasting covenant, while the second is an idiomatic expression for the
biblical concept of one body in marriage. The formula for the giving of rings,
which expands the original text, is a solemn promise of fidelity: "I shall never
betray your love! Wear this ring and prize it, for it is the pledge of my love
and faithfulness." The Tagalog word *pagtaksilan* (to "betray") refers to marital infidelity, while *sangla* ("pledge") signifies the sacrifice or deprivation
espouses must endure in exchange for love. What is pledged must be redeemed with something that is at least of equal value.[16]

Other examples of ritual elaboration are given by the twelve points approved by the *Consilium ad exsequendam* in 1970 for India. The entrance rite
incorporates the presentation of gifts, the Indian rite of welcome, the ceremony of lighting the lamps, and the rite of peace. At the conclusion of the
eucharistic prayer, the assembly performs the *panchanga pranam* (kneeling
and touching the floor with the forehead) as a sign of adoration. These ritual
elaborations are meant to illustrate in a cultural way the meaning of the
various parts of the eucharistic celebration.[17]

Regarding ritual elements, a fine example is the Zairean sign of peace at
Mass. In the Zairean Order of Mass the sign of peace takes place after the
penitential rite, which concludes the liturgy of the word. The sign may consist of washing hands in the same bowl of water which is passed around in
the congregation. In the culture of the people, the gesture is a way of saying,
"I wash away anything I have against you."[18]

16. *Pagdiriwang ng Pag-iisang Dibdib* (Manila, 1983), pp. 20, 23; see R. Serrano, *Towards a Cultural Adaptation.*

17. *New Orders of the Mass for India* (Bangalore 1974); see D. S. Amalorpavadass, *Towards Indigenisation in the Liturgy* (Bangalore 1971).

18. Text in "Conférence épiscopale du Zaïre," in *Rite zaïrois de la célébration eucharistique* (Kinshasa, 1985). The decree of approval by the Holy See, "Zairensium Dioecesium," is in *Notitiae* 264 (1988): 457.

The Method of Organic Progression

The method of organic progression may be described as the work of supplementing and completing, when necessary, the shape of the liturgy established in the official edition, or *editio typical,* of liturgical books. In the case of the Roman liturgy, the method of organic progression consists of rereading the official edition, with the purpose of supplying what they lack or bringing to completion what they only partially and imperfectly state. It is progressive because it operates through two dynamics that develop the shape of the liturgy: (1) supplementation, whereby new elements are inserted into the liturgy; and (2) continuance, because it is a sequel to the work begun by the council and the Holy See. The method is organic because it results in a new shape that is coherent with the basic intention of the liturgical documents and, more broadly, with the nature and tradition of Christian worship.[19]

Article 23 of the Constitution of the Liturgy contains the concept of organic progression: "Care must be taken that any new forms adopted should in some way grow organically from forms already existing." The key words in this statement are "new forms" *(novae formae),* "grow" *(crescere),* "organically" *(organice),* and "existing forms" *(formae iam exstantes).* The conciliar commission explains that the text, "using the words, innovations and new forms, suggests that new rites can be produced; it closes no doors, but instills the need to preserve continuity in the process of evolution and puts us on guard against impertinent innovations."[20]

When we compare the present state of the official liturgy in the Roman Catholic Church with the provisions of the council, we realize that there are lacunae in the conciliar reform. Nowhere in Chapter 2 of the Constitution is inculturation of the Order of Mass by the local churches addressed. Article 50 confines itself to the principles and criteria of revision on the part of the Vatican. There are also lacunae in the *editio typica* of the postconciliar liturgical books. Article 77, recognizing the textual and ritual poverty of the current rite of marriage, has ordained that it "be revised and enriched *(ditior fiat)* in such a way that it more clearly signifies the grace of the sacrament and imparts a knowledge of the obligations of spouses." The rite was revised,

19. A. Reid strongly opposes this method in his article "Sacrosanctum Concilium and the Organic Development of the Liturgy," in *The Genius of the Roman Rite* (Chicago, 2010).

20. *Schema Constitutionis de Sacra Liturgia,* Caput I, Emendationes 4 (Vatican City, 1967), p. 8.

but there is a consciousness that certain lacunae still remain. Thus the introduction to the new rite allows that the formularies "be adapted, or as the case may be, supplemented (including the questions before the consent and the actual words of consent)." Furthermore, "when the Roman ritual has several optional formularies, local rituals may add others of the same type."[21]

It is useful to note at this point that organic progression does not consist of emending or modifying what has been established by superior authority. The text of the liturgical provision must remain intact. In the Roman Catholic Church, the Holy See does not rewrite the Constitution on the Liturgy, and the conferences of bishops do not reedit the *editio typica* of liturgical books. But the former can supplement or complete what is lacking in the conciliar document, and the latter what is lacking in the *editio typica*.

No one should take the Holy See under Pope Paul VI to task for having revised all the liturgical books after the council. On the contrary, Pope Paul VI deserves gratitude and praise. But neither should anyone be disturbed if, in some particular instances, the work of postconciliar revision went beyond the limits set by the text of the constitution. The use of the vernacular in all liturgical celebrations, the incorporation into the *editio typica* of new elements such as general absolution, the introduction of new eucharistic prayers, the ability to repeat the sacrament of anointing in the course of the same illness, and the permission to use another kind of plant oil in the sacrament of the sick are a few instances where the process of organic progression was clearly at work. The process of organic progression should continue on the level of local churches. For them, the process of organic progression may be laid out in several steps.

The first step calls for a close examination of the *editio typica*. Besides the necessary historical, theological, and linguistic study of the document, there should be an examination of the various options of inculturation offered in the text. The second step deals with singling out the cultural and pastoral needs of the local church as a worshiping community and the areas that require the process of organic progression but were not addressed by the *editio typica*. The third step is an inquiry into whether the new form to be introduced responds to a legitimate need of the local church. Article 23 of the Constitution on the Liturgy cautions: "There must be no innovations unless the good of the Church genuinely and certainly requires them." Fur-

---

21. *Ordo Celebrandi Matrimonium,* Editio typica altera, no. 40 (Vatican City, 1991), p. 9. See R. Serrano, *Towards a Cultural Adaptation,* pp. 4-112; see also *Marriage Rites for the Philippines* (Manila, 2009).

thermore, it should be ascertained whether the new form is not alien to the authentic spirit of the liturgy, whether it is coherent with the general program of renewal initiated by the council for the Roman Catholic Church, and whether it harmonizes with the rest of the rite.

Conclusion

This chapter has discussed three methods of liturgical inculturation, namely, creative assimilation, dynamic equivalence, and organic progression. They can be useful, depending upon the local situation. Creative assimilation starts from what exists in culture, while dynamic equivalence starts from what there is in liturgy. Organic progression completes an unfinished agenda of liturgical reform. Creative assimilation tends to introduce new elements, while dynamic equivalence, which is a type of translation, confines itself to transmitting the content of a liturgical rite in a new cultural pattern. One thing to remember is that these three methods can overlap and need one another for fuller effect.

This exposition has many loose ends. The method of dynamic equivalence, when taken seriously, can be quite complicated and requires much effort. For some churches, the basic questions still revolve around the concept of a liturgical *ordo,* which is in a fluid state because of the lack of a typical edition. For others, the problem is how to define their own cultural patterns. For still others, the challenge is to be more flexible with liturgical norms in the face of a local culture that is distinct from the cultural background of the official *ordo.* We can hope that by engaging in the work of inculturation, local churches will uncover the riches of a common liturgical tradition and effectively and faithfully transmit such riches to every generation.

Inculturation of Worship:
Forty Years of Progress and Tradition

Anscar J. Chupungco, OSB

Introduction

For four years last century I had the rare privilege of taking part in a series of liturgical consultations organized by the Lutheran World Federation. I say "rare" because it is not often that a Roman Catholic becomes a member of an international study group of Lutherans and, to my gratification, declared by the group an honorary Lutheran! By coincidence or perhaps providence, Martin Luther and I were born on the same day. During those memorable years I made lasting friendships with Lutheran scholars like Gordon Lathrop and S. Anita Stauffer. Friendship meant dialogue, and dialogue with them richly endowed me with liturgical knowledge. Thanks to my Lutheran connection, the World Council of Churches paired Lathrop and me in a number of conferences on Christian worship.

A Lutheran Experience

Two volumes resulted from the consultations held in Switzerland (1993), Hong Kong (1994), Nairobi (1995), and Chicago (1996). The titles of these volumes convey the common concern that brought Lutheran theologians, liturgists, musicians, and pastors together. The first is *Worship and Culture in Dialogue* (LWF Studies, 1994) and the second is *Christian Worship: Unity in Cultural Diversity* (LWF Studies, 1996).[1] It is evident from these titles that

1. Editor's note: A third volume, *Baptism, Rites of Passage, and Culture,* was published

the participants wanted to study the influence worship and culture have on each other and to set the conditions or parameters for the inculturation of Christian worship.

To answer these questions, the participants followed a well-defined methodology, which is worth developing here. Since the chief components of Christian worship are baptism and Eucharist, the discussions focused on them, even though questions concerning other church ceremonies, such as marriage and funerals, were also addressed.

The methodology consisted of several steps. The first step was to expound the biblical teaching and Lutheran tradition on the essential elements of baptism and Eucharist. This defined the basic premise of the entire consultation. What is essential is nonnegotiable, though it can be reexpressed in ways that are more congenial to the people of today, without prejudice to the doctrine of Scripture. To reexpress what is essential requires the participation of culture. This was the second step. Historical researches on baptism and Eucharist have uncovered the fascinating influence of different cultures on the ritual development of these sacraments. In the case of the Western liturgy, one should indeed speak of the Jewish, Greco-Roman, and Franco-Germanic cultural strata. The third step concluded the process by proposing — or at least envisioning — possible cultural reexpressions of the rites of baptism and Eucharist. This final step had to take into account the experiences of local communities, the unity in faith and baptism of the Christian churches, and the dos and don'ts of liturgical inculturation.

My principal role in the Lutheran consultations rested with the definition of inculturation. I described it as a process whereby pertinent elements of a local culture are integrated into the worship of a local church. Integration means that human values, cultural patterns, and institutions form with Christian worship a unified whole, so that they are able to influence the way prayer formularies are composed and proclaimed, ritual actions are performed, and the message expressed in art forms. Integration also means that local festivals, after due critique and Christian reinterpretation, become part of the liturgical worship of the local assembly.

The immediate aim of inculturation is to create a form of worship that is culturally suited to the local assembly, which should be able to claim it as its very own. The ultimate aim of inculturation, on the other hand, is active

---

in 1998. "Rites of Passage" here applies to healing rites, burial, and marriage. The volume also includes a series of case studies and analyses and reports on rites in various nations and churches (Geneva: LWF Studies, 1998).

and intelligent participation of all in the congregation. Inculturation properly understood and rightly executed will lead the assembly to a profound appreciation of Christ's mystery made present in the liturgy through the dynamism of cultural signs and symbols. Inculturation, in other words, aims to deepen the spiritual life of the assembly through a fuller experience of Christ, who is revealed in the people's language, rites, arts, and symbols.

To achieve inculturation, one needs to work within a given method. I proposed to the Lutheran participants the method of dynamic equivalence, as opposed to formal correspondence. Dynamic equivalence starts with the liturgical *ordo,* which I will briefly define below. Dynamic equivalence is a type of translation. It reexpresses the *ordo* in the living language, rites, and symbols of the local community. Concretely, dynamic equivalence consists of replacing elements of the *ordo* with something that has equal meaning or value in the culture of the people, and hence can suitably transmit the message intended by the *ordo.* Because dynamic equivalence draws its elements from people's culture and traditions, the liturgy is able to evoke life experiences and paint vivid images rooted in the people's history, traditions, and values.

At some point during the consultations a question of terminology was amply discussed. Is it contextualization, or is it inculturation? In the 1970s the World Council of Churches adopted the word "contextualization" to signify the process of updating church structures so that they would keep pace with the changes in the modern world. The context in which the Christian community lives should be a chief player in the modernization of church structures. Context includes socioeconomic, political, cultural, religious, and geographical factors. In a way, it is more encompassing than inculturation, but unlike inculturation, it does not focus specifically on culture. Let me note that the Roman Catholic Church later adopted the word "contextualization," but with a distinctly political meaning. It became synonymous with the liberation movement, especially in Latin America and some countries in Asia that were under dictatorial and abusive political leadership.

"Inculturation," on the other hand, was a word that cultural anthropologists preferred, because it expresses the creative and dynamic relationship between two cultures. In 1981, Pope John Paul II said that inculturation, though a neologism, "expresses one of the elements of the great mystery of the incarnation." In 1985 the Extraordinary Synod of Roman Catholic Bishops defined it as "an interior transformation of authentic cultural values through their integration into Christianity and the rooting of Christianity in various cultures."

I must admit that during the Lutheran consultations I advanced the adoption of the term "inculturation." Both Lathrop and Stauffer were understandably hesitant to abandon the term "contextualization," which was in the active vocabulary of Reformed Churches. I am now delighted to see that my Lutheran sisters and brothers are starting to take interest in the word "inculturation."

The Lutheran consultations were an experience of the process of inculturation. Many questions were raised and several left unanswered. I reproduce two salient questions. The first question was where to set the boundaries to the incursion of culture in Christian worship. Failure to do this could lead to a situation where violence is done to biblical doctrine in order to accommodate culture. It could also happen that the cultural elements that are integrated in worship overly evoke their cultural provenance and thus divert attention from the Christian rite or, worse, send an altogether different message to the assembly.

Another scenario would be the mere incorporation of cultural elements into Christian worship without the benefit of integrating them. They could be attractive, perhaps even entertaining, but if they are not integrated with the Christian rite they are no more than decorative appendices or cultural tokens with a small role to play in the unfolding of the rite.

In the course of the consultations a few put across a rather negative view of culture. They raised the warning that culture is inherently evil because of human sin: it needs to be redeemed. As someone who is engaged in inculturation — and with all due respect — I could not disagree more. I reasoned that, while some elements of culture are sinful and erroneous, not all fall under that category. The incarnation of the Son of God proves that after the Fall, human nature had kept redeemable traits. The work of inculturation is precisely to integrate what is liturgically suitable in order to redeem and transform it interiorly into a vehicle of Christ's grace.

Thus the challenge was, on the one hand, how to protect the doctrinal integrity of Christian worship and, on the other, how best to utilize whatever is good, noble, and beautiful in culture. The second question dealt with the liturgical *ordo* of Lutheran communities. By *ordo* we understand a standard liturgical rite that contains the essential elements of Christian worship as handed down by tradition and accepted as such by the church. The standard *ordo* for baptism, for example, would include the following components: proclamation of the word of God; blessing of water; renunciation of Satan; profession of faith; immersion or infusion while reciting the baptismal formula; and possibly anointing with chrism and the vesting of the neophyte in a white garment. The *ordo,* however, is not a mere arrangement of the various components of the liturgical rite; rather, it is the proclamation of what the church believes about the sacrament. This belief is expressed by the choice of the biblical reading and the formulation of the liturgical texts. These are the articulation of the ancient adage *lex orandi, lex credendi* ("the rule of prayer is the rule of belief"). Centralized churches such as the Roman Catholic and several in the Orthodox Communion use a standard *ordo* for baptism and Eucharist. Is the same true of the Lutheran churches? The absence of a fixed *ordo* has a disadvantage: since the *ordo* should generally be the starting point of liturgical inculturation, where does one begin in its absence?

I devoted a significant portion of my paper to the Lutheran experience of liturgical inculturation in order to get across the message that an international group of Lutheran theologians, liturgists, musicians, and pastors had already begun the work. This is what they have initiated and done so far; their effort and dedication are truly remarkable and worthy of emulation. The question now is: Where do Lutherans go from here?

The Roman Catholic Experience

Forty years ago, on December 4, 1963, 2,152 Council Fathers gathered in the Vatican to vote on the Constitution on the Liturgy. The result was a solid 2,147 votes in favor. Of this document, Pope Paul VI, in his address at the conclusion of the second session of the council, said: "The arduous and intricate discussions have certainly borne fruit, for one of the topics, the schema on the sacred liturgy — the first to be discussed and, in a certain sense, the first in order of intrinsic excellence and importance for the life of the Church — has been brought to a happy conclusion." The Liturgy Constitution of Vatican II has a particular significance for me and for us gathered here, because it enshrines the Magna Carta of liturgical inculturation.

Forty years have elapsed and much water has passed under the bridge, but it is surely not out of place to recall here how the Liturgy Constitution was shaped and to review what it says about the relationship between Christian worship and culture. For the Roman Catholic Church the Constitution is the official instruction on how to update and reform worship. Alas, after forty years, several of its directives have yet to be brought to "a happy conclusion," if I may use the words of Pope Paul VI. This is the case with those Roman Catholics who spurn changes in worship, firmly believing that progress in worship ended with the Council of Trent. For other Christian churches, Vatican II's Liturgy Constitution is an invitation to take a closer look at their worship services, especially where there is question of culture. I guess it is not presumptuous to say that the Liturgy Constitution somehow influenced the Lutheran consultations that I discussed earlier.

After Pope John XXIII announced Vatican Council II, a preparatory commission on the liturgy was established on June 6, 1960. The composition of the preparatory commission was indicative of the kind of reform that the Liturgy Constitution would eventually espouse. Most of the members and consultants were scholars who knew their liturgical history. They admired the noble simplicity and sobriety of the original Roman liturgy before it had merged in the eighth century with Franco-Germanic rites. Ironically, the inculturation of the Roman liturgy by the Franco-Germanic churches induced the disappearance of its classical shape. It took twelve centuries for the Roman Catholic Church to recover the noble simplicity of its worship. It would not have taken that long had Rome, in the sixteenth-century, heeded Martin Luther's call for liturgical reform.

In the thinking of the preparatory commission, history is not static. The dynamism of history led it to regard the recovery of the classical shape as a prerequisite to the "adaptation" or inculturation of the Roman liturgy. There is a need to retrieve the original simplicity of the Roman liturgy before it can be effectively inculturated. The preparatory commission set the Franco-Germanic churches, which inculturated the classical form of the Roman liturgy, as a model for the churches today.

With this background in mind, we can easily understand why, in the Liturgy Constitution, there is constant shift from the classical shape of the Roman liturgy to various measures that would ensure that the reformed liturgy was truly contemporary — contextual, if you wish. Such salient reforms as active participation, use of the vernacular, and the frequent references to sociocultural situations are indeed part of a bigger agenda to inculturate the Roman liturgy. Articles 37-40 of the Liturgy Constitution (SC 37-40), for which we are forever indebted to the American Benedictine Godfrey Diekmann, are the articulation of what implicitly runs through the pages of the constitution, namely, the inculturation of the liturgy. Pastoral liturgy should be addressed in the light of human values, patterns, and institutions, or, in short, local culture. The Latin word *aptatio,* which is translated as "adaptation," refers to Pope John XXIII's catchword for the council: *aggiornamento.* Without inculturation this word would be empty.

Throughout the Liturgy Constitution there is interplay between tradition and progress. Article 23 is a significant statement: "That sound tradition may be retained and yet the way remain open to legitimate progress, a careful investigation is always to be made into each part of the liturgy to be revised." The investigation should be theological and historical — in order to determine liturgical tradition — and should be pastoral in order to open the door to inculturation. The phrase "sound tradition and legitimate progress" adequately describes the thrust of the Liturgy Constitution. The phrase also lays down the foundations of liturgical inculturation. In fact, inculturation does not create new liturgical rites apart from the Roman rite. What inculturation aims to achieve is to dynamically translate the Roman liturgy into the culture of local churches. The sound tradition of the Roman liturgy is the basis of legitimate progress that inculturation seeks to achieve.

Firmly rooted in the premises of the liturgical movement, the Liturgy Constitution sets forth active participation as the principle and criterion of the conciliar reform of the liturgy. Article 14 declares: "In the reform and promotion of the liturgy, this full and active participation by all the people is the aim to be considered before all else." The theology on which the constitution bases itself is the doctrine of what would later be called "common priesthood" by the Dogmatic Constitution on the Church, *Lumen Gentium.* According to the Liturgy Constitution, active participation is "called for by the very nature of the liturgy" and that such participation by Christian people "is their right and duty by reason of their baptism" (Art. 14). I am certain that Martin Luther would have smiled in triumph were he to read those lines. Let me note that the ultimate aim of liturgical inculturation is to foster active participation in consonance with the cultural patterns or traits of the local community.

The Liturgy Constitution regards the use of the vernacular as an effective means to promote active participation. Article 36 is a classic case of a via media, or conciliar compromise, on the use of the vernacular. The shadow of Martin Luther still caused uneasiness among the Vatican II fathers. Nonetheless, the Liturgy Constitution embraced the principle that active participation requires understanding, and understanding requires the use of the vernacular. For this reason — and within the spirit of compromise — Article 36 prioritizes those parts of the liturgy where the vernacular may be used to great advantage, namely, the readings and instructions and some prayers and chants. Thus the Constitution allows the use of the vernacular for the purpose of implementing its fundamental principle of active participation. At the same time, the vernacular language is one of the most significant elements of culture. The adoption of the vernacular is a basic work of liturgical inculturation. Lutherans might flatter Roman Catholics for their current progress in this area; the reality, however, is that the Lutherans in the sixteenth century already engaged in the work of inculturation when they used the vernacular in worship.

The Liturgy Constitution uses the word "adaptation," but it should be read as "inculturation," a word that the Roman Catholic Church adopted in the 1970s, thanks to Pope John Paul II. The Constitution devotes four articles to inculturation, and thus a brief description of the articles might be useful.

Article 37 advances the principle of liturgical pluralism among local churches. Pluralism includes respect for the culture and traditions of local communities and the integration of suitable cultural elements found among them, provided they are not indissolubly bound up with superstition and error.

Articles 38-39 deal with "legitimate variations" in the Roman rite. "Legitimate variations" means that the changes introduced by local bishops for the churches they are responsible for are those suggested or recommended in the liturgical books published by Rome. Article 38 cautions that "the substantial unity of the Roman rite" should be preserved in the process. The expression "substantial unity" is somewhat difficult to define. Article 40 addresses the question of radical adaptations in the Roman rite. "Radical" means that the changes local bishops make in their local churches are not envisioned by the official books. The bishops are given the task to "carefully and prudently weigh" what elements from the people's culture may suitably be introduced into the Roman rite. I should add that all intended changes on the local level need the approval of the Vatican.

I realize that the above description of the provisions of the Liturgy Constitution on inculturation has little or no relevance to Lutherans, who need not grapple with a centralized system and hierarchical prerogatives. However, underneath such provisions we can detect a certain valid concern that might interest Lutherans. The concern is the unity of churches through the confession and celebration of the same faith. In light of this, the second volume of the Lutheran consultations was entitled *Christian Worship: Unity in Cultural Diversity*. The problem that besets the Roman Catholics is that some want unity to embrace not only belief but also its cultural expressions.

A Roman Catholic Attempt at Inculturation

At this point, allow me to offer an example of liturgical inculturation that attempted to implement the provisions of Vatican II's Liturgy Constitution.

The example comes from my home country, the Philippines, where the Roman Catholic Church has produced two major attempts to inculturate the Roman liturgy. The first is the *Misa ng Bayang Pilipino,* or Mass of the Filipino People. Unfortunately, Rome has not yet approved this Mass, which was submitted to it in 1976! Rome, it is said, is eternal. The second is the rite of marriage. Fortunately, this second attempt has received the Roman *placet.* In view of time and space constraints, I will concentrate on the first.

Several criteria guided the shaping of the *Misa.* First, the prayers, which were composed in the Tagalog language, must clearly express the church's doctrine on holy Mass as both Christ's sacrifice on the cross and a sacred meal. Second, they should incorporate genuine Filipino values — idiomatic expressions, proverbs, and images drawn from the experiences of people. Third, without forgetting the needs of the universal church, the texts should include such contemporary concerns of the church in the Philippines as social justice, peace and development, and lay leadership. Fourth, when proclaimed, the texts of the prayers should be clear, dignified, and prayerful. Fifth, enough occasions should be provided for active and prayerful participation through bodily posture, songs, and responses. And last, an atmosphere of prayer and reverence should be encouraged amidst the Filipino pattern of festive, or fiestalike, celebration.

At the introductory and concluding rites, people are blessed with a large cross, which is afterwards venerated with a song of praise. The veneration of the cross stems from the Filipino Catholics' great devotion to the cross. They venerate crucifixes at home, and they carry them around. Indeed, they make the sign of the cross at every significant moment of the day. Basketball players sign themselves before coming on to the court. People make the sign of the cross when they pass a church or a cemetery. Beginning and concluding the Mass with the cross is the Filipino way of underscoring the doctrine that the Mass is the memorial celebration of Christ's death on the cross.

Before the readings, the gospel book is venerated with a song in praise of God, whose word reveals his will and teaching, and who guides us on the path of life. The readers make the *mano po* to the priest and receive his blessing. The gesture is done by placing the right hand of the elder person on one's forehead. It is part of Filipino religious culture to ask for the elder's blessing before performing a special task. At the general intercessions that follow the homily, the people kneel rather than stand, which is the Roman posture. But Filipinos associate kneeling, rather than standing, with urgent petitions.

The *Misa* has other characteristics that every Filipino Catholic would easily associate with solemn prayer. For example, at the beginning of the eucharistic prayer, which highlights the words of consecration, the candles on the altar are lighted, the church bells are rung, and the priest and people make the sign of the cross. At home people light candles and sign themselves before they kneel to pray.

A Filipino cultural tradition has found a worthy place in the *Misa*. Just as the head of the family or the host eats last, the priest receives communion after he has distributed it to the assembly. It is the Filipino way of expressing the values of leadership, hospitality, and parental concern. Incorporated into the Mass, this practice alludes to the saying of Christ that the first should be the last and the servant of all (Matt. 20:26-28).

Language plays an essential role in the liturgy, which is made up of two basic elements, namely, proclaimed texts and gestures. Regarding the language of the *Misa,* much effort was made, including several consultations with experts in the Tagalog language, to ensure that the texts, when proclaimed or sung, are clear, dignified, and prayerful. The language is also slightly poetic, often observing terminal as well as internal rhyme. Filipinos have a predilection for sentences that rhyme and place value on rhythmic cadence in solemn speech. Because of the cultural value of idioms, the *Misa* is attentive to idiomatic speech. Finally, the *Misa* pays special attention to words and phrases that express genuine Filipino values. At the penitential rite, the typical Filipino value that combines humility, unworthiness, and embarrassment stands out. At collection time the priest reminds the assembly of a popular saying: "God blesses those who give with open hands" — that is, generously. At Communion the value of meal shared among members of the family and friends underscores the meaning of the Mass as a celebration of God's family.

Conclusion

Forty years ago, Vatican II's Constitution on the Liturgy formalized what was in reality an existing practice in the church: liturgical inculturation. The constitution did not introduce something new; it merely codified what had always been there. Inculturation is as old as the church of Jesus Christ.

Two phrases sum up the thrust of the Liturgy Constitution. The first is "tradition and progress." Inculturation is a form of progress, and the local churches are invited to embark on it. However, the constitution desires that progress should be rooted in genuine tradition. Inculturation must give the assurance that the local church can trace its origin to the apostolic teaching and practice. The question that arises in the minds of theologians and pastors is how to define the meaning of legitimate progress and genuine tradition. The second phrase is "unity in cultural diversity." Local churches form a communion of belief, but between them certain diversity exists. Such diversity springs from the cultural differences obtaining in local churches. People do not believe and pray in a cultural vacuum. Inculturation means that the same universal belief is celebrated in different cultural patterns proper to the local community. The question that needs to be addressed by liturgists is the role culture plays in the liturgical unfolding of Christ's mystery.

The task of liturgical inculturation extends beyond confessional diversity. Lutherans and Roman Catholics are called to renew the worship in their local liturgical assemblies in the context of their culture and traditions. Forty years have passed, but it is never too late to start.

A Response and a Tribute to Anscar Chupungco

Gordon W. Lathrop

In Memoriam: Anscar Chupungco, OSB
November 10, 1939–January 9, 2013

The idea for the volume you hold in your hands was born in a conversation whose participants were Gláucia Vasconcelos Wilkey (this book's editor), Fr. Anscar Chupungco, and I, immediately following Fr. Chupungco's address to the Sydney Congress of Societas Liturgica in Australia in August 2009. Then, as work was proceeding on this volume, those who have known of the LWF Worship and Culture Study and all those who have cared about Christian liturgical reform in our time were saddened to learn of Fr. Chupungco's death.

Anscar Chupungco was a learned and gracious Roman Catholic priest and Benedictine monk, long a teacher in Rome, long an inspiring Christian leader in Asia, and long an important voice for all the churches. He was also a beloved participant in and scholarly resource for the LWF study from its very beginning. He died unexpectedly in the Philippines on January 9, 2013. The preceding essay, "Inculturation of Worship: Forty Years of Progress and Tradition," was first intended as a lecture for the 2003 Valparaiso Institute of Liturgical Studies. As it turned out, Fr. Chupungco was unable to attend that meeting, though the paper was publicly read in his absence. As far as we know, however, the paper was never published, and shortly before his death he submitted it for inclusion in this volume — ten years after he wrote it. It is an honor for me to speak about this little, important, and yet otherwise unknown essay by writing a few notes about him and his text.

When pastor Anita Stauffer was first organizing the Worship and Culture Study of the LWF, she had the brilliant idea of inviting the participation of the person who was most known in the world as a scholar of Christian liturgical inculturation, even though this person was not a Lutheran. Already deeply aware of his important books, Pastor Stauffer traveled to Rome to talk Anscar Chupungco into joining the study. To her surprise, she succeeded.

Ultimately, there were to be several other fine ecumenical participants who took part in the study, but Chupungco's agreement to serve as resource person from the beginning ensured that, while the study would be anchored in Lutheran theology, it would also be concerned profoundly with the wider Christian conversation, with a broader and deeper unity in cultural diversity. The study would also, with Fr. Chupungco as resource, be making use of the thought of the contemporary scholar who was most known for his engagement with the issues of liturgical inculturation. It would be thinking with the very best.

Chupungco himself, in this essay — as also in his book *What Then Is Liturgy? Musings and Memoir* — recalls his participation in the meetings of the study.[1] But he does not represent, at least not nearly fully enough, how beloved he was to the other participants, how important his reflections and lectures were, how much he influenced both the Nairobi Statement and the Chicago Statement, and with what joy the participants acclaimed him an "honorary Lutheran." His repeated chuckling over sharing a birthday — November 10 — with Martin Luther was an endearing pleasure to everyone. He became important to all of those involved with the study, and I am sure I speak for all of them in saying that we give thanks for his life and mourn his death, commending him in confidence to God.

Alongside Fr. Chupungco, I was the other regular resource person for the LWF study. It's true that our shared work on this study did lead to an invitation to Fr. Chupungco and me to work together on the Faith and Order studies on worship and Christian unity sponsored by the World Council of Churches (WCC), especially in the conference that produced the Ditchingham Statement of those studies.[2] It also led to our common work in a remarkable gathering called together by the Council of Churches of Sweden, held in Sigtuna, Sweden, in October 1995, which focused on the wonderfully honest Swedish question, "Why celebrate worship services?" But that report of our teamwork and cooperation in various events also does not begin to

1. Anscar Chupungco, OSB, *What Then Is Liturgy? Musings and Memoir* (Collegeville, MN: Liturgical Press, 2010), p. 165.
2. See Thomas F. Best and Dagmar Heller, *So We Believe, So We Pray* (Geneva: WCC Publications, 1995), esp. Best's contribution to this volume.

represent how deep the friendship between us had become and how serious our dialogue. Besides being a world-class scholar, Anscar Chupungco was for me a dear friend, and I shall not forget him.

That does not mean I always agreed with him. While what he says in this essay about Luther's liturgical reforms — especially about liturgy in the vernacular and the participation of the whole priestly people — is wonderfully insightful, he did not always get Lutherans right. With his own commitment to the Roman *editio typica* as a basis for inculturation, he did not understand that Lutherans also have an *ordo,* already implied in the Lutheran confessions as well as in Lutheran liturgical conservatism. And what he wrote about Luther on eucharistic rites — that Luther "purged them of any reference to the sacrifice of the cross, and practically reduced the Mass to a community meal" — is simply wrong.[3] Furthermore, I was among those participants in the LWF study, as he says disapprovingly in this essay, "who put across a rather negative view of culture," though I do not think that view was ever about the "inherently evil" character of human cultural life.

Indeed, it always struck me with a kind of amusement that our dialogue was frequently marked by what seemed the charisms of both Roman Catholic and Protestant positions: the commonly Catholic optimistic estimation of culture and the classically Protestant suspicion of human self-deception. But then, we expected Anscar to be Roman Catholic! And I am indeed a classical Protestant. Both were needed. In the end, however, as Anscar himself makes clear, a kind of balanced view prevailed. The Nairobi Statement talks in a way rare for reflections on liturgy and culture not just about transcultural, contextual, and cross-cultural characteristics, but also about the necessary countercultural themes. Both Anscar and I agreed with that statement.

But where I did most deeply agree with Anscar Chupungco, with all my heart, and where all of us participants in the study learned from him repeatedly was in his steady insistence that liturgical inculturation belongs to the essence of Christianity and has been part of its character from the beginning. As he would say, there is nothing more traditional to Christian communities than inculturation of the liturgical practice of the gospel. Christianity is a translation religion. The belief in the incarnation requires this. And "translation" is not only a matter of language — though it certainly is that — but also a matter of gestures and symbols and festivals and ritual practices, that is, of culture and context. Chupungco's devotion to "dynamic equivalence"

3. Chupungco, *What Then Is Liturgy?* p. 164.

and "creative assimilation," ideas that both came to expression in the statements of the study, mattered to us immensely. What we did not realize at the time was that subsequent leadership in the Roman Catholic Church, with its authoritarian accent on literal and Latinist translation, would make the LWF study one of the few places where Chupungco's expression of these ideas could be free and effective. And, as he says in this essay, Luther's work in the sixteenth century was already bringing these very principles to bear.

Therefore, the book you are reading represents a continuation of these themes and an explicit disagreement with the anti-inculturation stance of such documents as the recent Roman Catholic *Liturgiam Authenticam*. Here is one place where the work of Anscar Chupungco and his many friends and students continues.

May the work go on. It is indeed, as he says, not too late to start. As we seek to continue to reform our liturgical communities — in all of the churches, and not simply among Lutherans and Roman Catholics — so that the gospel of Christ stands forth in clarity in every culture and context and language, calling us all to active participation in Christ's mystery, we will miss his voice. Still, in his several books and once again in this volume, we continue to have that voice. It is the voice of a beloved, gracious, honest, gently humorous, faithfully Roman Catholic, honorably Lutheran, fully ecumenical man.

May he, in the mercy of God, rest in peace.

PART III

BAPTISM, RITES OF PASSAGE, AND CULTURE

The Chicago Statement on Worship and Culture

Lutheran World Federation, 1998

This statement is from the fourth international consultation of the LWF's Study Team on Worship and Culture, held in Chicago in May 1998. The members of the study team represented five continents of the world and had worked together for five years. The first consultation, in Cartigny, Switzerland, in 1993, focused on the biblical and historical foundations of the relationships between Christian worship and culture; it produced the "Cartigny Statement on Worship and Culture: Biblical and Historical Foundations." The second consultation, in Hong Kong in 1994, explored contemporary issues and questions concerning the relationships between the world's cultures and Christian liturgy, church music, and church architecture/art. The papers of these first two consultations were published as *Worship and Culture in Dialogue*.[1] The third international consultation, held in Nairobi in 1996, focused on the Eucharist in its relationships to culture, and issued the "Nairobi Statement on Worship and Culture: Contemporary Challenges and Opportunities."

The papers and statement from the Nairobi consultation were published

---

1. S. Anita Stauffer, ed., *Worship and Culture in Dialogue* (Geneva: LWF, 1994; also published in French, German, and Spanish).

Ipsissimis verbis S. Anita Stauffer, ed., *Baptism, Rites of Passage, and Culture* (Geneva: LWF, Department for Theology and Studies: Reports of International Consultations in Cartigny, Switzerland, 1993; Hong Kong, 1994).

as *Christian Worship: Unity in Cultural Diversity.*[2] The 1998 Chicago consultation examined the dynamics by which world cultures relate to holy baptism and certain rites of human passage (healing rites, burial rites, marriage rites). This Chicago Statement built on the prior Cartigny and Nairobi statements, applying their insights to the topics considered at the Chicago consultation.

1. Introduction

1.1. The foundational event in the life of any Christian community is the "one Baptism" (Eph. 4:5), which constitutes the church as a "royal priesthood," proclaiming the mighty acts of the life-giving God for all the world (1 Pet. 2:9). Baptism is the burial of Christians together with Christ in order that they may be raised with him to newness of life (Rom. 6:4) as signs of God's new creation. It is the "washing of water by the Word" (Eph. 5:26) that proclaims and offers the forgiveness of sins and, at the same time, identifies the Christian community with Jesus Christ, who identifies himself with outsiders and sinners and all the needy in the world.

It is the outpouring of the Holy Spirit that draws the baptized into communion with the triune God and with each other. As such, baptism always introduces the newly baptized into life in a local community of Christians, but in communion with all the churches of God. And baptism has a lifelong significance, giving Christians the dignity and responsibility of their vocation in Christ. All other changes and transitions in the life of a Christian must be seen to reflect this basic transition and this basic dignity: "Once you were not a people, but now you are God's people" (1 Pet. 2:10). Baptism thus informs and shapes rites related to the life cycle.

1.2. Rites of passage are those communal symbolic processes and acts connected with important or critical transitions in the lives of individuals and communities. In almost all cultures, giving birth, coming to adulthood, marrying, reconciling, leave-taking, passage into and sometimes through sickness, and dying and grieving, among several other transitions, are marked by diverse communal rites that express the process of separation, liminality (the transitional or "in between" stage), and incorporation. To accompany people in many of these moments of transition, the Christian

2. S. Anita Stauffer, ed., *Christian Worship: Unity in Cultural Diversity* (Geneva: LWF, 1996; also published in German).

community celebrates rites of passage. These are rites whereby the church invokes God's care and providence for people in transition/liminality to find their efficacy in the power of the Word. Foremost among these rites observed by the church are those associated with sickness, funerals, and marriage. For Christians, however, these are rites that extend or renew or conclude their original and essential rite of passage through the waters of baptism. Therefore, it is good that baptism should be often remembered and affirmed in these diverse life-cycle rites. And, for Christians, these ways of marking life's transitions are appropriately celebrated in the community of the baptized.

1.3. All Christian worship, whether the sacraments or rites of passage, relates dynamically to culture in at least four ways. First, worship is transcultural: it is the same substance for everyone everywhere, beyond culture. Second, worship is contextual: it varies according to the local natural and cultural contexts. Third, worship is countercultural: it challenges what is contrary to the gospel in each given culture. Fourth, worship is cross-cultural: it makes sharing possible between different local cultures.[3]

1.4. Among the various methods of contextualization, those of dynamic equivalence and creative assimilation are particularly useful.[4] Dynamic equivalence is the reexpression of components of Christian worship with elements from a local culture that have an equal meaning, value, and function. Creative assimilation is the addition of elements from local culture to the liturgical *ordo* to enrich its original core.

1.5. The design of worship space, the selection of music, and other elements of all rites should never be dismissed as matters of indifference or of personal choice. Rather, they stand under the imperative to do everything in accordance with the gospel of Jesus Christ, in ways that make clear the baptismal values in the rites.

2. Baptism

2.1. The transcultural nature of baptism arises from God's gift of this "visible Word," this tangible proclamation of the gospel, to all the church in all the

---

3. For further explanation and examples of this fourfold dynamic, see the Nairobi Statement, *Christian Worship*, pp. 24-27.

4. For methodology and criteria, see the Nairobi Statement, 3.2–3.6, in *Christian Worship*, pp. 25-26.

world. Water, the tangible earthly element of the sacrament, is everywhere available where human life exists. But the pattern, or *ordo,* of baptism is also a universal ecumenical inheritance.[5] Baptism involves: (a) formation in the one faith (traditionally known as the catechumenate); (b) the water-bath; and (c) the incorporation of the baptized into the whole Christian community and its mission.[6] This latter incorporation is expressed by the newly baptized being led to the table of the Lord's Supper, the very table where their baptismal identity will also be strengthened and reaffirmed throughout their life. The events around the water-bath itself have also come to be practiced in a widely used pattern that is very nearly transcultural. In a gathering of the Christian assembly in which the Word is proclaimed, the following events usually occur: God is praised and thanked over the water; together with the church, the candidates and their sponsors renounce the forces of evil and confess the universal church's faith in the triune God; water is used generously in the triune name of God; prayer is made for the Holy Spirit's gifts; and several "explanatory symbols" (e.g., anointing, hand-laying, signing with the cross, and often also clothing and illuminating) may accompany this prayer, disclosing and teaching something of the powerful act that God does in baptism. Any contextualization of baptism or of the rites of passage will depend on the churches' allowing these transcultural characteristics of baptism to be continually renewed in their midst. "We should do justice to the meaning of baptism and make of our practice a true and complete sign of the thing Baptism signifies."[7]

2.2. But this transcultural gift needs to be contextualized in each local place. The local community will have its own ways of teaching and passing on the faith to baptismal candidates and their families, forming them in heart and life as well as mind. These ways may best be developed in connection with other local Christians, in witness to the baptismal unity of the whole church. The assembly of Christians will have its own ways of gathering. The space for baptism may be locally designed, as long as this design recalls the need for the baptismal event to take place in the presence of the worshiping

5. Parallel to the LWF Worship and Culture Study has been work by the WCC Commission on Faith and Order, a part of whose work has focused on baptism. Regarding the *ordo* for baptism, see the statement "Becoming a Christian: The Ecumenical Implications of Our Common Baptism" (1997).

6. Prebaptismal catechumenal formation is not merely education; rather, it involves the whole person being formed by the Holy Spirit in the word, prayer, worship, Christian community, and service in the world.

7. Martin Luther, "The Holy and Blessed Sacrament of Baptism," p. 1.

assembly, with the generous use of water. In many places this may mean that communities will recover the use of fonts or pools that enable baptism by immersion (as Luther so strongly advocated[8]). The traditional "explanatory symbols" of baptism may need to be replaced by the means of dynamic equivalence, or reinforced by the means of creative assimilation, so that the power of the water-bath may be more clearly perceived in local context. Each local church will need to ask: What local symbols may express the gift of the Spirit, the adoption of a new identity, baptismal dignity, and vocation, death, and resurrection, and the unity of the community, and do so without obscuring the central importance of the water and the Word? The "explanatory symbols" should never overshadow the water-bath itself.

2.3. Baptismal unity will never be that of an "insider" group. Baptism, which constitutes the church, also calls Christians to identify in solidarity with all people. Its celebration will therefore have certain countercultural elements as well. The poor will be baptized with at least as great a dignity as the rich. Women and men, children and adults, and people from all ethnic/class/caste backgrounds will stand here on equal footing, equally in need of God's mercy, equally gifted with the outpoured Spirit. Baptism, which creates members of the local community, also simultaneously creates these people as members of the one universal body of Christ. Baptism calls us to unity, not to division.[9]

2.4. As the churches once again find this gift of God renewed in their midst, they may also be assisted by cross-cultural gifts between the churches that share the one baptism. The hymns and music of one church may helpfully illuminate the practice of baptism in another church in a different culture. One local church's use of baptismal space (fonts/pools and the surrounding area) may suggest possibilities to other churches elsewhere. And new "explanatory symbols" that are discovered or developed by local churches in one area may be used by Christians in other places, who may thereby discover a depth of meaning in baptism that they had not previously imagined.

8. Martin Luther, "Large Catechism," p. 4; "The Holy and Blessed Sacrament of Baptism," p. 1; "The Blessed Sacrament of the Holy and True Body of Christ," p. 3; and "The Babylonian Captivity of the Church," *Luther's Works,* vol. 36, pp. 67-68.

9. See the papers of the Strasbourg Institute/LWF consultation on this subject, in Michael Root and Risto Saarinen, eds., *Baptism and the Unity of the Church* (Geneva: WCC Publications; Grand Rapids: Eerdmans, 1998).

3. Healing Rites

3.1. When we call on Jesus as the Christ for healing, we appeal to what is close to his heart, that is, concern for those who suffer because of physical illness and other afflictions of the human spirit. Through rites of healing, the church, represented by its pastors and the local community, invokes the comforting presence of Christ and the Spirit, especially in serious illness that can cause anxiety, break the human spirit, weaken faith, or isolate the person from society and even from the church community. Churches that have no such healing rites may wish to consider developing them, thereby ministering to and expressing solidarity with those who suffer (1 Cor. 12:22-26).

3.2. Anointing, hand-laying, and the prayer of faith, whenever possible in the presence of the community, are the core elements of Christian rites of healing. They are handed down to us by apostolic tradition (Mark 6:13; 16:17-18; James 5:14-15). They are transcultural in the sense that they have been preserved, though possibly reexpressed ritually in the course of contextualization. The Eucharist itself is a primary transcultural expression of the church's concern for the sick. The congregation's care of the sick includes the eucharistic celebration by the pastor (together with representatives of the congregation) in the home or hospital (or other) room of the sick person, or the ministry of sharing the Word and bringing the Holy Communion from the Sunday assembly to those who, because of illness or disability, are unable to be present in that assembly. All the rites of healing and all the extensions of eucharistic ministry are intended to surround people who are isolated or excluded with God's gift of the baptismal community.

3.3. To enrich and make Christian rites of healing understandable to the people (the task of contextualization), it is necessary to identify elements of local rites of healing that can suitably, after critical evaluation, be substituted for elements of the traditional Christian rites through dynamic equivalence, or as will more often be the case, illustrate the original core of the rite through creative assimilation. Elements of local rites of healing include pertinent gestures, symbols, and material elements that can be integrated into Christian use.

3.4. In situations where certain kinds of illness are regarded as the result of sorcery or witchcraft, Christian catechesis and health education should be instituted. In no way should elements of healing related to sorcery or witchcraft be integrated into Christian rites. The countercultural aspect of Christian healing should also challenge practices based on those superstitions that sometimes lead to injustice and cruelty toward persons suspected of witchcraft, as well as health practices that are based on wealth or egocentrism, or such modern institutions that demean the dignity of the sick.

3.5. The biblical readings and prayers should emphasize that the church's rites of healing embody Christ's concern for the sick, that they express faith in the power of Christ's death and resurrection, and that they are intended primarily to heal (make whole) the entire person, as well as to enable the community to pray for the curing of an illness (whether physical or mental). Rites of healing should include varying provisions for situations of acute, chronic, and terminal illnesses.

4. Funeral Rites

4.1. Christian funeral rites conclude the passage from this world to God (John 13:1) that began at baptism. They celebrate the baptized's *transitus,* or exodus, and mark the day of her or his *dies natalis* (birthday) into eternal life. At the same time, they accompany the bereaved in the time of loss by the comforting words of Scripture and the support of the Christian community and its singing.

4.2. The funeral practices of Christians have traditionally included the following elements, arranged as a pattern: (a) washing, anointing, and dressing the body — rites reminiscent of baptism; (b) a communal vigil (wake) and then a service of the word or the Eucharist rites expressing the baptismal community; and (c) a final commendation and a procession to the place of entombment while hymns are sung or paschal psalms are recited — rites alluding to the Exodus.

4.3. In some places outside the Christian tradition, a number of the aforementioned rites already exist, such as the washing and clothing of the body and the funeral procession. In such cases, the work of contextualization is to infuse these rites with baptismal and paschal dimensions through reading and singing from the word of God and through prayers.

4.4. It is clear that texts, gestures, dirges, and symbols that contradict the foundational Christian faith in the resurrection cannot be integrated into the rite; this is a countercultural task in developing funeral rites. Another countercultural task necessary in some contexts is the avoidance of practices (e.g., expensive coffins, elaborate meals) that impose a severe financial burden on the family of the deceased. On the other hand, Christian funeral rites might include provision for funeral processions as the final stage of the paschal journey in which the community accompanies the dead and the bereaved.

4.5. When cremation is practiced, Christian rites should provide Bible readings and prayers that affirm the faith in the resurrection and norms for the appropriate disposition of the ashes.

4.6. The tradition of chanting or singing psalms during funerals should be encouraged, as should the use of the local and worldwide treasury of hymnody. In all cases, the texts and music should appropriately express the Christian faith.

4.7. Christians have always shown care and respect for cemeteries and other places where the faithful who "sleep in Christ" await the day of his coming. Efforts should be made to express the Christian character of the diverse burial places used by our churches. Further, church buildings where the Eucharist is celebrated in the presence of the body should have interior design appropriate for such occasions.

5. Marriage Rites

5.1. The process of transition in which a couple moves from being unmarried to being socially recognized as married may be regarded as itself transcultural in its shape and general character. Still, for Christians, the truly transcultural gift is (a) the proclamation of the word of God in connection with such a transition, and (b) the prayer for God's blessing on the couple and their household. The word of God and the nuptial blessing are the universal Christian additions to the human process of marriage.

5.2. But these additions are made within a ritual that will have deep cultural connections, and here is the task of contextualization. The way the process of marrying is unfolded, the way the couple is betrothed, the way their assent is expressed, and the way the society gathers around them — all these may be richly different from culture to culture. The kind of music used in the celebration may borrow from the local musical tradition, provided that both music and text are appropriate to the communal intention to proclaim the word of God and pray for blessing. In addition, the marriage rite may take place in the church or in the home or in another assembly place. However, when a civil marriage has taken place and the couple comes to the Christian community asking for the nuptial blessing, the consent and marriage vows need not be repeated in the church.

5.3. There are countercultural aspects of weddings. It is important that the rite maintain and express the baptismal dignity of the parties to the marriage. Thus the couple must both freely assent to the wedding, and neither bride nor groom should be dealt with as if he or she were "property." Furthermore, the status of being married must be seen as neither better nor worse than the status of anyone else in the assembly — these all are the baptized. Baptism is their basic dignity and vocation, and a particular marriage will be seen as one wonderful unfolding of that vocation for the sake of the life of the world. It may be that such baptismal dignity will come to expression by the wedding being held within the context of the Eucharist of the assembly. Or it may be that the nuptial blessing will express the vocation of baptized Christians who are married. In any case, the church may do well to resist the spread of consumerist or dowry-system patterns of marriage that are often inappropriately expensive without expressing authentic Christian values.

5.4. Among the cross-cultural gifts that the churches may share with each other may be new ways in which the baptismal vocation of the married is brought to expression — in signs, songs, or gestures — in a local dialogue with the community's cultural traditions of marriage.

6. Call to the Churches

6.1. We who have served on the study team offer our work during 1993-1998 to the glory of God and for the renewal of the church. We call on the Lutheran World Federation and its member churches to receive this work in ways that will renew their life and mission. Such reception involves the translation of the LWF Worship and Culture statements and books into local languages, and their wide distribution; local, regional, and/or subregional workshops and meetings of various kinds; pastors' retreats; courses in seminaries and theological institutions; regional newsletters on worship and culture for networking and communication; articles in ecclesial and academic periodicals; consultations with parishes; consultations with architects, artists, and musicians — and so on. Reception also involves sharing with ecumenical partner churches, seminaries, and journals, and other ecumenical efforts.

6.2. We continue to call on all member churches of the LWF to undertake further intentional study and efforts related to the transcultural, contextual, and countercultural natures of Christian worship, and its cross-cultural sharing. We call on all member churches to recover the centrality of baptism for their life and worship, and as the foundation of rites of human passage, and to do so whenever possible in ecumenical partnerships with wide participation. The challenge is to develop and use forms of worship that are both authentic to the gospel and relevant to local cultural contexts.

A Faith and Order Saga: Towards
One Baptism: Towards Mutual Recognition

Thomas F. Best

We belong to Christ: we are his and no other's. This fact is the foundation of our identity as persons, and our unity as Christians, experienced and expressed first in our baptism in Christ and into Christ's body, the Church. In our baptism Christ has claimed each of us for his own, and thus made all of us one in him. The unity we share in Christ is greater than all the differences — historical, theological, cultural — that divided Christians and the churches today: unity is our birthright, shown forth brightly in our common baptism.[1]

These are the convictions that have driven Faith and Order's work on baptism since that organization's very beginnings. In the context of the present volume — celebrating as it does the Lutheran World Federation's long and storied work on worship — it is a pleasure to note that these same convictions are as strongly expressed in the three main statements from that LWF work: (1) the Cartigny Statement on Worship and Culture, with its biblical, theological and historical foundations;[2] leading to (2) the Nairobi Statement

---

1. Thomas F. Best, "Introduction," in Thomas F. Best, ed., *Baptism Today: Understanding, Practice, Ecumenical Implications* (Collegeville, MN, and Geneva: Pueblo-Liturgical Press and WCC Publications, 1989), p. vii.
2. "Cartigny Statement on Worship and Culture: Biblical and Historical Foundations," in S. Anita Stauffer, ed., *Worship and Culture in Dialogue, Reports of International Consultations,* (Cartigny, Switzerland, 1993; Hong Kong, 1994 (Geneva: LWF, Department for Theology and Studies, 1994), pp. 129-35.

on Worship and Culture,[3] and culminating in (3) the Chicago Statement on Worship and Culture.[4] In particular, the third volume in the LWF series, *Baptism, Rites of Passage and Culture,* establishes and explores the deep connections between LWF and WCC Faith and Order work on baptism, and its foundational role for the ecumenical movement today.[5]

But let's return to Faith and Order's commitment to the unity of the body of Christ, particularly as embodied in its work on baptism. With the publication in 2011 of the study text *One Baptism: Towards Mutual Recognition,* Faith and Order has capped a long journey indeed, one that began most immediately at the time of its world conference at Santiago de Compostela in 1993; but that ultimately harks back to its origins at the beginning of the twentieth century.[6] To understand the text and its significance, we must first look at the role of worship in the long history of Faith and Order's life and work, and then at Faith and Order's more recent focus on the role of baptism in the search for Christian unity. Any account of such a process must be both personal and selective. I hope that the following survey will encourage both churches and individual Christians to study and respond to the text of *One Baptism: Towards Mutual Recognition.* I hope, too, that it will suggest something of the ecumenical commitment and passion — and sometimes personal cost — involved in producing such a text.

Worship: A Continuing Passion for Faith and Order

Already in 1913, the nascent Faith and Order movement recognized the centrality of worship. The pamphlet *Prayer and Unity. By a Layman* emphasized

---

3. "Nairobi Statement on Worship and Culture: Contemporary Challenges and Opportunities," in S. Anita Stauffer, ed., *Christian Worship: Unity in Cultural Diversity* (Geneva: LWF, Department for Theology and Studies, 1996), pp. 23-28.

4. "Chicago Statement on Worship and Culture: Baptism and Rites of Life Passage," in S. Anita Stauffer, ed., *Baptism, Rites of Passage, and Culture* (Geneva: LWF Department for Theology and Studies, 1998), pp. 13-24.

5. See, e.g., the following comment by the LWF series editor S. Anita Stauffer: "Parallel to the LWF Worship and Culture Study has been work by the WCC Commission on Faith and Order. A part of that work has focused on "Baptism; regarding the *ordo* for Baptism." See the statement "Becoming a Christian: The Ecumenical Implications of Our Common Baptism" (1997), in *Baptism, Rites of Passage, and Culture,* p. 16, n. 5.

6. Thomas F. Best and Günther Gassmann, eds., *On the Way to Fuller Koinonia: Official Report of the Fifth World Conference on Faith and Order, Santiago de Compostela 1993,* Faith and Order Paper 166 (Geneva: WCC Publications, 1994).

the importance of prayer in eradicating self-interest in the search for unity, in providing realism about our own faith, and in granting charity to see the good in others' thoughts and lives: "Such prayers will burn out of us the conceit that we can, of ourselves, do things which shall bring unity to pass" (pp. 7-8).[7] The centrality of worship has long been enshrined in Faith and Order's Aim and Functions, expressed as the imperative

> to proclaim the oneness of the church of Jesus Christ and to call the churches to the goal of visible unity in one faith and *one Eucharistic fellowship,* expressed *in worship* and in common life in Christ, in order that the world may believe. . . . The functions of the standing commission and plenary commission are: (a) to study such questions of faith, order *and worship* as they bear on this aim and to examine such social, cultural, political, racial and other factors as affect the unity of the church. . . .[8]

Faith and Order has repeatedly reaffirmed its commitment to this aspect of the search for the unity of the church, for example, insisting at its commission meeting in Louvain in 1971 that all Faith and Order studies include the dimension of worship: "In all Faith and Order studies the importance of considering the subject in close relation to its expression in worship should continually be remembered. Indeed sometimes such expression may form basic material without which the study cannot yield fruitful results."[9]

7. *Prayer and Unity. By a Layman,* Faith and Order Paper 15, Series I (New York: Joint Commission Appointed to Arrange for a World Conference on Faith and Order, January 6, 1913), pp. 7-8, 12-14, passim. Quoting a letter from prominent church leaders in England to the editor of *The Times,* calling for prayer for unity on Whitsunday 1907, the pamphlet concludes by urging prayer for Christian unity on Whitsunday 1913 (p. 23). Significantly, the pamphlet was reprinted twice in 1913, then again in 1914, 1917, and 1920. Dame Mary Tanner noted that the text was by "most probably the honorary secretary and jurist Robert H. Gardiner." See Mary Tanner and Günther Gassmann, "Preface," in Thomas F. Best and Dagmar Heller, eds., *So We Believe, So We Pray: Towards Koinonia in Worship,* Faith and Order Paper 171 (Geneva: WCC Publications, 1995), p. vii.

8. Commission on Faith and Order, WCC, "By-laws of Faith and Order," in John Gibaut, ed., *Called to Be the One Church: Faith and Order at Crete; Report of the 2009 Meeting of the Plenary Commission,* Faith and Order Paper 212 (Geneva: WCC Publications, 2012), app. 3, pp. 236-41; quotation from p. 236 (italics added).

9. See "Worship Today," in *Faith and Order: Louvain 1971,* Faith and Order Paper 59 (Geneva: WCC Publications, 1971), pp. 102-16; see also *Studia Liturgica* 7, no. 4 (1970): 23-40. See also the plenary discussion at the Faith and Order Plenary Commission meeting in Moshi, Tanzania (1996), in Alan Falconer, ed., *Faith and Order in Moshi: The 1996 Commission Meeting,* Faith and Order Paper 177 (Geneva: WCC Publications, 1996). Speakers

Faith and Order has put that commitment into practice: apart from its surveys of church union negotiations, the longest-running Faith and Order program is its work on *The Week of Prayer for Christian Unity*, prepared and published jointly with the Pontifical Council for Promoting Christian Unity of the Roman Catholic Church.[10] Given this commitment, it is surely no accident that *Baptism, Eucharist and Ministry* — up to now, the best-known and most influential of all Faith and Order studies — focused on the two liturgical actions central to the life of the church, baptism and the Eucharist, and on the ministry, the persons and office designated by the church to perform these actions.[11]

The unprecedented interest that *Baptism, Eucharist and Ministry (BEM)* aroused within the churches was surely due to the fact that it treated topics of concrete, existential concern, not only to church leaders but to laypeople alike: Should we have our children baptized at birth, or should we wait until they can confirm their own readiness for incorporation into Christ? At what age should we present our children for participation in the Eucharist? Why do certain churches find it necessary to exclude me, as a duly baptized member of Christ's body, from Christ's table? And my own pastor — who brings the gospel faithfully to me in worship each week — why is his or her ordination not understood by all churches as being fully legitimate? Faced with these questions, one may dare to ask: "Rabbi, who sinned, this man or his parents . . . ?" (John 9:2).

By all accounts, the section on baptism was the most broadly accepted aspect of *BEM*. Upwards of two hundred official church responses and one thousand "unofficial" responses from seminaries, pastors' groups, and

---

at the plenary discussion appealed for a recovery "of the earlier awareness of the fundamental importance of worship in all aspects of the search for unity" (p. 154).

10. Among many other resources, see "100 Years of the Week of Prayer for Christian Unity," special issue of *The Ecumenical Review* 59, no. 4 (October 2007), and Catherine Clifford, ed., *A Century of Prayer for Christian Unity* (Grand Rapids: Eerdmans, 2009). For recent Week of Prayer texts, and for further information, see: http://www.oikoumene.org/en/resources/week-of-prayer.

11. *Baptism, Eucharist and Ministry*, Faith and Order Paper 111 (Geneva: WCC, 1982-2007; 25th anniversary printing with additional introduction, 2007). On *BEM*, see Max Thurian, "Baptism, Eucharist and Ministry," in Nicholas Lossky, José Miguez Bonino, John Pobee, Tom F. Stransky, Geoffrey Wainwright, and Pauline Webb, eds., *Dictionary of the Ecumenical Movement*, 2nd ed. (Geneva: WCC Publications, 2002), pp. 90-93; see also the recent critical review by Lukas Vischer, "The Convergence Texts on Baptism, Eucharist and Ministry: How Did They Take Shape? What Have They Achieved?" *The Ecumenical Review* 54, no. 4 (October 2002): 431-54.

theologians reflected a growing consensus that baptism was fundamental to the churches' acceptance of one another as members together of the one body of Christ.[12] *BEM* declared unequivocally that baptism "is an unrepeatable act," and emphasized its ethical implications, both personal and social.[13] Noting forthrightly that baptism "upon personal profession of faith" is "the most clearly attested pattern in the New Testament documents," it nonetheless sought rapprochement between proponents of "adult" and "infant" baptism; and it sought to identify the elements necessary for a valid baptismal service.[14] All these affirmations have significantly influenced the work of Faith and Order, and the broader ecumenical discussion on baptism since *BEM*.

Yet it was also clear from the responses to *BEM* that issues remained in liturgical and pastoral practice, as well as in theological understanding: the continuing practice in some churches of a "repeated" baptism for those baptized before an "age of consent," however defined; the increasing pastoral practice in some churches of admitting persons to the table even before baptism; the question of what elements — the use of water, the threefold form ("in the name of the Father, the Son, and the Spirit?") — were essential to authentic baptismal practice.[15] And for some of us, for all the involvement of some liturgists in the preparation of *BEM*,[16] the suspicion remained that, despite its paragraphs on baptismal and eucharistic liturgical practice ("baptism," §20, and "Eucharist," §27), *BEM* was essentially a theological rather than a liturgical document, reflecting the church's thought rather than its

12. The broader focus on baptism as the basis of common Christian identity owed much to the Roman Catholic Church's affirmation that "all those justified by faith through baptism are incorporated into Christ . . ." and the fact that the recognition of baptism became the "pivot point" for that church's engagement with the ecumenical movement. See "Unitatis Redintegratio," in Walter M. Abbott, SJ, ed., *The Documents of Vatican II* (New York: Guild Press, 1966), §3, 345.

13. "Baptism," in *Baptism, Eucharist and Ministry*, §13, 4, and §10, 4.

14. "Baptism," §11-13, 4, and §20, 6.

15. See *Churches Respond to BEM: Official Responses to the "Baptism, Eucharist and Ministry" Text*, vols. 1-6, Faith and Order Papers 129, 132, 135, 137, 143, 144, ed. Max Thurian (Geneva, WCC Publications, 1986-1988), passim. See above the "response to the responses" from the Faith and Order Commission: *Baptism, Eucharist and Ministry 1982-1990: Report on the Process and Responses*, Faith and Order Paper 149 (Geneva: WCC Publications, 1990), esp. pp. 107-12.

16. Particularly Geoffrey Wainwright. There is much to be learned from his *Doxology: The Praise of God in Worship, Doctrine, and Life; A Systematic Theology* (New York: Oxford University Press, 1980).

worship life. And for all that *BEM* had achieved, further progress toward unity would require informing theological reflection with liturgical *practice and reflection.*

This was confirmed, unexpectedly, by the extraordinary interest aroused by the "Lima Liturgy," a eucharistic service prepared as the closing worship for the meeting in Lima, Peru, in 1982, where the Faith and Order Plenary Commission agreed to send *BEM* to the churches for study and official response. Not itself an official text, it intended to embody something of the richness of the whole church's eucharistic experience and practice. As such, it gathered steam and was used among Protestant churches in an astonishingly wide range of ecumenical gatherings. It came to be seen as an alternative to another ecumenical practice, that of celebrating the Eucharist according to a single specific tradition (Anglican, Lutheran, Disciples of Christ, etc.). In both cases, as Faith and Order was careful to insist, the ecclesial "identity" of the Eucharist stemmed from the tradition of the presider, with worshipers from other traditions able to participate so far as their own church discipline — and individual conscience — allowed.[17] Yet the Lima Liturgy, combining as it did the eucharistic practice of various traditions, responded to the widespread hunger for a broader, more "ecumenical" alternative to traditional practice.

The Witness of the World Conference: The Role of Baptism at Santiago de Compostela, 1993, and Beyond

The Fifth Faith and Order World Conference, held in Santiago de Compostela in 1993, the first such meeting since the historic Toronto gathering forty years earlier, held worship at the very center of its life and work, from the opening service, with its use of the *bottafumeiro,* the legendary quarter-ton

---

17. On the Eucharist in *BEM,* see Geoffrey Wainwright, "The Eucharistic Dynamic of BEM," in Thomas F. Best and Tamara Grdzelidze, eds., *BEM at 25: Critical Insights into a Continuing Legacy,* Faith and Order Paper 205 (Geneva: WCC Publications, 2007), pp. 45-86. For the Lima Liturgy, see, e.g., the workshop held at Bossey, Thomas F. Best and Dagmar Heller, eds., *Eucharistic Worship in Ecumenical Contexts: The Lima Liturgy — and Beyond* (Geneva: WCC Publications, 1998), esp. "Celebrations of the Eucharist in Ecumenical Contexts: A Proposal," pp. 29-35 (English); pp. 36-43 (German); pp. 44-50 (Spanish). The latter text sought especially to offer a basic detailed *ordo* for eucharistic worship, something that *BEM* had hesitated to do. See "Eucharist," in *BEM,* para. 27, pp. 15-16. Significantly, the workshop enjoyed a strong participation by liturgists of the first order.

censer swung from the cathedral ceiling eighty feet above,[18] to a daily service of the word based on a fixed, traditional *ordo*, enriched by prayers and hymns from churches all around the world, to the evening vespers that were led by sisters from the Communauté de Grandchamp in Switzerland.[19] But the core of the worship experience in Santiago de Compostela was a moment of silence — and one related to baptism. Baptism was the focus of the service of the word on the fourth day of the conference. In the chapel, worshipers shared this prayer of confession:

> In baptism you make us members of the body of Christ and call us into communion. We confess that we are hesitant to recognize each other's expressions of baptism; we are often reluctant to practice the measure of agreement we have already achieved; we remain satisfied to live in division. Therefore we cry to you, our God.

After that they left the chapel and processed to the cloister, forming a large circle around its central flowing fountain. After affirming their common faith in the words of the Creed, some 400 worshipers fell silent. Inspired by the sussuration of the water flowing from the fountain, they remembered their own baptism, or the community in which they had been baptized. No one touched the water, lest there be any suggestion of "(re)baptism"; but they allowed the water to speak powerfully to them of their common incorporation into the *one body of Christ*. Then, in obedience to their common belonging to Christ, they dared to say together:

> We affirm and celebrate together, through the gift of Jesus Christ, that we and our churches are in a real though still imperfect communion. We affirm and celebrate the increasing mutual recognition of one another's baptism as the one baptism into Christ. We will dare to explore all the ways, known and unknown, to become one in Christ Jesus. We will not

---

18. See the remarkable nineteenth-century account — by a Protestant in Spain! — of the cathedral and *bottafumeiro* in Santiago de Compostela: George Borrow, *The Bible in Spain, or The Journeys, Adventures, and Imprisonments of an Englishman, In an Attempt to Circulate the Scriptures in the Peninsula*, The World's Classics, vol. 75, The Works of George Borrow, vol. 3 (London: Humphrey Milford, Oxford University Press, 1925), pp. 284-295, esp. p. 285.

19. For a listing of worship events at the Fifth World Conference on Faith and Order, see "Summary of Worship and Bible Study Elements," in Thomas F. Best and Günther Gassmann, eds., *On the Way to Fuller Koinonia*, app. 3, p. 306.

give up even in the face of difficulties. As baptized Christians clothed with Christ, let us claim each other as sisters and brothers in Christ, joint heirs of the promise.

[We exchange the peace while the choir sings.[20]]

Inspired and challenged by the experience of worship at Santiago de Compostela, Faith and Order redoubled its commitment to worship as a fundamental aspect of the search for Christian unity,[21] not least at its historic meeting with liturgists in Ditchingham, near Norwich, England.[22]

Meanwhile, the liturgical experience around the fountain in Santiago de Compostela — if truth be told, far more than the formal statements on baptism in the world conference preparatory documents and reports — energized a renewed Faith and Order commitment to work on baptism.[23] With the recognition of the fundamental significance of baptism for the churches' mutual recognition, an initial meeting was held in Faverges, France, in 1997 on the theme "Becoming a Christian: The Ecumenical Implications of our Common Baptism." This emphasized the importance of a common *ordo* of baptism, explored issues of inculturation with respect to baptism, and noted the ethical implications stemming from our common baptism into the one body of Christ.[24]

20. "Morning Worship, Day 4," in *Worship Book: Fifth World Conference on Faith and Order, Santiago de Compostela, 1993*, pp. 10-12. During the passing of the peace, the choir sang the hymn "As Many of You as Were Baptized into Christ" to a traditional Serbian melody, arranged by Milos Vesin.

21. See Janet Crawford, "Faith and Order Work on Worship: An Historical Survey," in Commission on Faith and Order, *Minutes of the Meeting of the Faith and Order Standing Commission, 4-11 January 1994, Crêt-Bérard, Switzerland* (Geneva: WCC Commission on Faith and Order, 1994), pp. 45-52; see also Crawford, "Worship at Previous Faith and Order World Conferences," in Commission on Faith and Order, *Minutes of the Meeting of the Faith and Order Standing Commission, 4-11 January 1994, Crêt-Bérard, Switzerland* (Geneva: WCC Commission on Faith and Order, 1994), pp. 53-59; see also Crawford and Thomas F. Best, "Praise the Lord with the Lyre . . . and the Gamelan? Towards Koinonia in Worship," *The Ecumenical Review* 46, no. 1 (January 1994): 78-96; and see Crawford, "The Role of Worship in the Search for Christian Unity," in Alan Falconer, ed., *Faith and Order in Moshi: The 1996 Commission Meeting*, Faith and Order Paper 177 (Geneva: WCC Publications, 1996), pp. 141-42.

22. See Thomas F. Best and Dagmar Heller, *So We Believe, So We Pray*.

23. See Best and Heller, *On the Way to Fuller Koinonia*, "Discussion Paper, 3:2, Sacramental Life," §67, p. 283; "Report of Section III, Baptism," §§11-15, pp. 247-48.

24. Thomas F. Best and Dagmar Heller, eds., *Becoming a Christian: The Ecumenical*

The Faith and Order Text *One Baptism: Toward Mutual Recognition*

Following the seminal Faverges gathering in 1997, Faith and Order's work on baptism pressed forward through a series of consultations and drafting group meetings. The developing text was sent at various points to a wide range of liturgists and theologians, and was revised in light of comments received. The details of this process need not concern us here; they can be traced through the successive meetings of the Faith and Order Standing and Plenary Commissions.[25] What is important is the guiding principle behind the process: that the text should reflect not only theological and doctrinal considerations but also Faith and Order's traditional concern for the actual liturgical *experience and reflection* of both the churches and believers. Therefore, besides decisive input from Faith and Order commissioners and consultants, the process was nourished from two other sources. The first source was increasing collaboration with liturgists, particularly from the leadership

---

Implications of Our Common Baptism, Faith and Order Paper 184 (Geneva: WCC Publications, 1999). See the "Report of the Consultation," pp. 74-97, and, for the topics cited, see esp. the chapters by Gordon Lathrop, "The Water that Speaks: The *Ordo* of Baptism and Its Ecumenical Implications"; Anscar J. Chupungco, "Criteria for the Inculturation of Baptism," pp. 54-64; and Vigen Guroian, "On Baptism and the Spirit: The Ethical Significance of the Marks of the Church," pp. 65-73.

25. These details — at least as far as the official record is concerned — can be traced through the theme of "Worship in Relation to the Unity of the Church," in, e.g., *Minutes of the Meeting of the Faith and Order Board, 15-24 June 1999, Toronto, Canada,* Faith and Order Paper 185 (Geneva: WCC Faith and Order, 1999), pp. 84, 100-107; *Minutes of the Meeting of the Faith and Order Standing Commission, 30 September–7 October 2000, Matanzas, Cuba,* Faith and Order Paper 188 (Geneva: WCC Faith and Order, 2000), pp. 65-66; *Minutes of the Meeting of the Faith and Order Standing Commission, 9-16 January 2002, Gazzada, Italy,* Faith and Order Paper 191 (Geneva: WCC Faith and Order, 2002), pp. 45-64; *Minutes of the Meeting of the Faith and Order Standing Commission, 3-10 July 2003, Strasbourg, France,* Faith and Order Paper 193 (Geneva: WCC Faith and Order, 2004), pp. 18-24, esp. p. 23; Thomas F. Best, ed., *Faith and Order at the Crossroads: Kuala Lumpur 2004, The Plenary Commission Meeting,* Faith and Order Paper 196 (Geneva: WCC Publications, 2005), pp. 111-58; *Minutes of the Standing Commission on Faith and Order: Aghios Nikolaos, Crete, 2005,* Faith and Order Paper 200 (Geneva: WCC Faith and Order, 2005), pp. 24-26; *Minutes of the Standing Commission on Faith and Order: Faverges, Haute-Savoie, France,* Faith and Order Paper No. 202 (Geneva: WCC Faith and Order, 2006), pp. 42-45, 74-75, 88, 111-115; *The Standing Commission on Faith and Order Meeting in Crans-Montana, Switzerland, 2007,* Faith and Order Paper 206 (Geneva: WCC Faith and Order, 2007), pp. 24, 45-46; and *The Standing Commission on Faith and Order Meeting in Cairo, Arab Republic of Egypt, 2008,* Faith and Order Paper 208 (Geneva: WCC Faith and Order, 2009), pp. 28-31, and (giving the penultimate version of the text), pp. 72-101.

of Societas Liturgica, the leading grouping of Protestant, Anglican, Roman Catholic, and Orthodox liturgists worldwide.[26]

The second source was the continuing inspiration from the LWF's work on worship, as noted above.[27] This helped place Faith and Order's concern for baptism firmly within the broader church and ecumenical framework by insisting that the "ecumenical core of Christian Worship . . . consists of assembly around Word, Baptism, and Eucharist," and by noting further that "[a]s the LWF Worship and Culture Study has progressed (and 'in conversation' with recent WCC Faith and Order work in worship) it has become ever more clear that the subject has significant ecumenical trajectories. Further work, particularly that done locally and regionally, in contextualization, should be ecumenical. . . ."[28] Not the least of this LWF work's contributions was a reminder of both the universal and the local dimensions of the church and its worship:

> [The universal church] is always *local* . . . always a local gathering of people with their leaders, around the Scriptures and the sacraments, knowing Christ risen and *here*. . . . [But] it is not only a reflection of local attitudes and local realities. The communion of this local assembly with the other assemblies around Christ in other places is enabled by certain "instruments" of communion in Christ . . . that do affect our worship: the central presence of the Gospel of Jesus Christ, crucified and risen; the use of the scriptures of Old and New Testaments; Baptism and the formation of all baptized in the faith of the triune God; the Holy Eucharist of Christ's gift; and a recognized ministry serving the assembly around these central things. Each of these things, while done locally, active locally, expresses at the same time a linkage between this assembly and the other worshiping assemblies in time and space. Indeed, these very things are always at the center of the "catholic [universal] Church dwelling in this place."[29]

Even as *One Baptism: Towards Mutual Recognition* was being developed, the text exercised an important influence on the wider ecumenical movement.

26. For one fruit of this collaboration, see Thomas F. Best, "Memory and Meaning: Liturgy as Transformation; To Heal a Broken World; The Ecumenical Dimension," *Studia Liturgica* 36, no. 1 (January 2006): 60-73.

27. See footnotes 3, 4, 5, and 6 above.

28. S. Anita Stauffer, "Worship: Ecumenical Core and Cultural Context," in Stauffer, ed., *Christian Worship*, pp. 10, 11.

29. Gordon W. Lathrop, "Worship: Local Yet Universal," in Stauffer, *Christian Worship*, pp. 48-49.

A notable example is the strong affirmation of baptism — and its crucial role in the churches' wider search for unity — in "Called to be the One Church," the statement on ecclesiology prepared by Faith and Order and adopted unanimously by the WCC's member churches at the WCC's Ninth Assembly in Porto Alegre, Brazil, in 2006. The text affirms that "[b]aptism bestows upon the churches both the freedom and the responsibility to journey toward common proclamation of the Word, confession of the one faith, celebration of one eucharist, and full sharing in one ministry."[30] The sense that baptism "drives" the churches' wider search for unity in all aspects of their faith and practice came directly from *One Baptism: Towards Mutual Recognition.* And as we shall see below, this was prophetic of the later Faith and Order convergence text *The Church: Towards a Common Vision.*[31] *One Baptism* also influenced work done by the Joint Working Group between the WCC and the Roman Catholic Church, as well as other significant surveys of baptismal thought and practice within and among the churches today.[32] In addition to these international efforts, valuable work on baptism was also being pursued in national ecumenical contexts. Here the most notable example is the Catholic/Reformed Dialogue in the United States (2003-2007), which produced the remarkable text "These Living Waters: Common Agreement on Mutual Recognition of Baptism."[33]

From 2008 until 2010, the text *One Baptism: Towards Mutual Recognition* benefited from a time of lying fallow. Then, following creative and courageous revisions by Faith and Order staff and commissioners, as well as liturgical consultants, it was "accepted as a study text of the Commission on Faith and Order" at its standing commission meeting at Holy Etchmiadzin

---

30. For Porto Alegre, see "Called to be the One Church: An Invitation to the Churches to Renew Their Commitment to the Search for Unity and to Deepen their Dialogue," in Luis N. Rivera-Pagán, ed., *God, in Your Grace . . . : Official Report of the Ninth Assembly of the WCC;* (quotation is from §8, 258); see, more broadly, §§8-9, p. 258, and §14, Question C, p. 260. The Porto Alegre text is cited in *One Baptism,* §109, p. 20.

31. *The Church: Towards a Common Vision,* Faith and Order Paper 214 (Geneva: WCC, 2012).

32. See "Ecclesiological and Ecumenical Implications of a Common Baptism," in *Joint Working Group between the Roman Catholic Church and the World Council of Churches, Eighth Report 1999-2005* (Geneva: WCC Publications, 2005), pp. 45-72, and the review of (and commentary on) actual baptismal practice in a wide range of churches in Thomas F. Best, ed., *Baptism Today.* See also the recent valuable survey of the current ecumenical "scene" with respect to baptism: Dagmar Heller, *Baptized into Christ: A Guide to the Ecumenical Discussion on Baptism* (Geneva: WCC Publications, 2012).

33. The text is available at: http://www.pcusa.org/resource/these-living-waters/.

in 2010, and it was finally published in 2011.[34] Capping almost twenty years of work, that study text reflected Faith and Order's renewed commitment to the role of worship (and particularly the role of baptism) in the search for Christian unity. *One Baptism: Towards Mutual Recognition* tells a story of success: the growing mutual recognition of baptism within the ecumenical movement. It fulfils one crucial role of ecumenical texts: to record and consolidate agreements reached among the churches. Yet it also faithfully records persistent problems that continue to dog efforts by Faith and Order and the churches toward a mutual recognition of baptism. Reviewing the most important of these issues will take us, I believe, into the heart of the ecumenical discussion on baptism today.[35]

A first concern is the relationship between the rite of baptism as a *specific event* at one moment in time and baptism as an *ongoing process,* as the believer's lifelong growth into Christ. From the beginning, *One Baptism* was illuminated and inspired by the comment in *BEM* that "baptism is related not only to momentary experience, but to life-long growth into Christ."[36] As *One Baptism* notes, "the churches have discerned three elements which encompass the believer's full incorporation into Christ: (1) formation in faith, (2) baptism and Christian initiation . . . and (3) participation in the life of the Christian community, fostering life-long growth into Christ."[37] The strategy of the text was to "relativize" (and there is a good sense of that term) differences between "infant" baptism and "adult" baptism, noting that in both cases persons — at whatever age they have undergone the water rite — continue to grow in Christian faith within a Christian community. Therefore, personal affirmation of faith is essential; but in all Christian contexts, that faith is tested and developed over one's lifetime — and within a broader community of faith.

---

34. See *One Baptism: Towards Mutual Recognition, A Study Text,* p. 1, n. 6. For the formal approval of the text, see *Minutes of the Faith and Order Standing Commission meeting at Holy Etchmiadzin, Republic of Armenia, 21-25 June, 2010,* Faith and Order Paper 211 (Geneva: WCC Faith and Order Commission, 2011), pp. 6, and esp. pp. 11-12. The brilliant guidance of the current Faith and Order director, Canon John Gibaut, was essential in this process, especially in shepherding the text to its final approval by the Faith and Order Standing Commission.

35. To a remarkable degree, these issues have persisted through the long history of ecumenical work toward the churches' mutual recognition of baptism — and of one another as churches in the fullest sense. See, among many examples, the issues noted at the Faith and Order Standing Commission meeting in Gazzada, Italy, in 2002 (see n. 26 above).

36. "Baptism," in *Baptism, Eucharist and Ministry,* §9, p. 4.

37. "Baptism and Life-long Growth into Christ," in *One Baptism,* §§41-55, pp. 9-11.

A second concern is the *ordo*, or basic structure or pattern, of the baptismal rite. What elements are necessary, and sufficient, for baptism performed in one church to be considered as valid by other churches? The discussion of "The Liturgy of Baptism" in *One Baptism* consolidated and enriched the affirmation already made at the meeting in Faverges in 1997.[38] Recognizing that every act of baptism is inculturated, the Faverges text affirms "the fundamental *ordo* of baptism as it was developed in the tradition. . . . No form of inculturated baptism can dispense with the basic elements of the baptismal *ordo*: formation in faith, washing in water and participation in the life of the community."[39] Again, the hope is "that churches might arrive at a greater mutual recognition of baptism through recognizing and affirming the similarity of wider patterns of initiation and formation in Christ" (§83, p. 15).

A third concern is the role of the Holy Spirit, both at the moment of the baptismal rite and throughout the believer's lifelong growth into Christ within the Christian community. Here the text seeks to respond to the growing interest in the Spirit within many churches today, and to foster ecumenical contacts with Pentecostal and other "Spirit-oriented" churches. Thus *One Baptism* notes:

> Some biblical texts stress the pneumatological and Trinitarian aspect of baptism: for example, the gift of the Spirit and the presence of the Father, Son, and Spirit at the waters of the Jordan. . . . Where candidates offer a personal testimony at the time of their baptism this is seen as a powerful sign of the working of the Holy Spirit in their lives, thus recalling God's power to convert and to save. . . . The individual and communal confession of faith at baptism expresses the faith of the church, inspired by the Spirit, into which this candidate is now baptized . . . the unique event of baptism reflects and recapitulates the catechumenate, and the processes of nurture and growth guided by the Holy Spirit, that lead to and follow it. . . . Throughout the whole of their lives Christians are empowered by the Holy Spirit to seek faith, hope and love. . . (§19, p. 6; §39, p. 9; §41, p. 9; and §50, p. 10).

---

38. See esp. *One Baptism*, "The liturgy of baptism," §§32-40, pp. 8-9; and "Baptism and Life-long Growth into Christ," §§41-55, pp. 9-11. Hereafter, references to *One Baptism* appear in parentheses within the text.

39. Thomas F. Best and Dagmar Heller, eds., *Becoming a Christian: The Ecumenical Implications of Our Common Baptism*, Faith and Order Paper No. 184 (Geneva: WCC Publications, 1999), "Report of the Consultation," §39, p. 86.

A fourth concern is the relationship of baptism with the Eucharist, particularly why some churches recognize baptisms performed in other churches but do not admit persons so baptized to their eucharistic rites. This is an issue that causes much pain and confusion for Christians who have been duly baptized in their own churches but find themselves excluded from the Lord's Table in some other churches. As is well known, for some churches the ordination of the presiding minister at a eucharistic service is central to determining the "validity" of that Eucharist. Does not the same issue apply to the presiding minister at a baptismal service — and the "validity" of that baptism? Yet, in fact, churches show greater mutual acceptance of one another's baptisms than of one another's eucharistic practice. Ecumenical texts, including *One Baptism,* cannot solve issues that the churches themselves have not resolved. The role of ecumenical texts, then, is to clarify the issues that divide the churches and perhaps point the way toward further work on them.

Therefore, *One Baptism* recognizes the "intimate and intrinsic link between baptism and Holy Communion," and notes (1) that some churches "recognize one another as full expressions of the one church of Jesus Christ," thus allowing "both mutual recognition of baptism and Eucharistic fellowship"; (2) that when "churches do not recognize one [an]other as full expressions of the church of Jesus Christ," "mutual recognition of baptism may be possible if a church discerns apostolicity in another's understanding and practice of baptism; but a common eucharist would still not be possible if apostolicity is not discerned in the understanding and exercise of ordained ministry"; and (3) "in some cases where mutual recognition of baptism does not exist, a common eucharist is still possible." For example, churches that do not recognize infant baptism may offer communion to persons baptized as infants in another church. They do so in recognition of Christ's welcome to "'all baptized Christians' to partake at his table" (§61, p. 12, (a), (b), and (c) respectively).

This is closely related to a fifth — and even more complicated — concern. This is the relationship between the churches' recognition of each other's baptisms, validly performed, and the churches' recognition of each other as churches: Does the one recognition imply the other? In most cases, churches recognize each other as churches, and thus they recognize each other's baptisms. In some cases, however, churches do not recognize each other, and thus they do not recognize each other's baptisms. But a third case exists, in which churches recognize persons baptized in another church as baptized Christians, members of the body of Christ, yet do not recognize the full ecclesiastical status of the church in which that baptism was performed.

On a primal level, this reflects the churches' recognition of the *primacy of Christ* and should be celebrated. To put it colloquially, in such baptisms Christ "has gotten there first"; Christ has already claimed that person for his own, and has incorporated that person into his body. Therefore, to deny Christ's baptism would be not only to "unchurch" the person so baptized, but to "un-Christ" that person. And that is impossible, for Christ holds us firm. On the liturgical and ecclesiological level, of course, questions remain: What practices are necessary for a "valid" baptism? And how can churches recognize apostolicity in each other, thus enabling mutual recognition of each other as full expressions of the one body of Christ? Again, the text of *One Baptism* cannot solve problems that the churches themselves have not resolved; instead, it seeks to clarify the issues that divide the churches, and perhaps to suggest a way forward. After lengthy reflection, the Faith and Order Standing Commission agreed on the following formulation to cover this specific situation, with the word "some" proving to be crucial:

> On certain conditions some churches recognize a person as a baptized Christian without, however, recognizing either the baptism as it is exercised in that church, or the ecclesial character of that church itself. Some have asked whether this is possible ecclesiologically. With this in mind, they pose the following question: How far does recognition of a person as a baptized Christian imply some recognition of the baptism [that person] received, and of the church in which it was performed?[40]

This well describes the situation facing some churches today, but it also poses difficult questions: if "some" — "partial" — recognition exists, what is lacking for "full" recognition? If something is lacking, how can this "deficit" be overcome? Such questions put *One Baptism,* and Faith and Order's work on baptism in general, within the broader context of work on issues of liturgy, ecclesiology, and mutual recognition. It also raises the issue of *mutual accountability,* pressing beyond the churches' formal recognition of one another to the question of how to express that recognition in the daily lives of churches and believers alike.[41]

---

40. In *One Baptism,* see the sections on "Mutual recognition and discernment," §§10-15, pp. 3-5; "Common baptismal practice and mutual discernment," §§83-84, pp. 15-16; and "Baptism, the churches and the church," §§85-86, p. 16. The quotations are from §86, p. 16.

41. On mutual accountability, see Thomas F. Best, "A Tale of Two Edinburghs: Mission, Unity, and Mutual Accountability," *Journal of Ecumenical Studies* 46, no. 3 (Summer 2011): 311-28, esp. 326-28; and John A. Radano, "Mutual Accountability: Building Together on the

Looking Ahead

This review of Faith and Order's long and passionate engagement with issues of worship in general, and baptism in particular, can only suggest the richness of the work culminating in *One Baptism: Towards Mutual Recognition.* Yet it makes clear one central achievement of the modern ecumenical movement: the fact that, despite the remaining challenges in the churches' practice, understanding, and recognition of baptism, we are moving toward greater agreement on this fundamental aspect of Christian faith and practice.

The study document not only consolidates much ecumenical work on baptism, but also points ahead. Not least, it has informed *The Church: Towards a Common Vision,* Faith and Order's seminal 2012 convergence text on ecclesiology — only the second convergence text, following *BEM,* in Faith and Order's long history.[42] Whereas the study document on baptism sought to increase the churches' mutual recognition of each other's baptisms, and of each other as churches, the convergence text places baptismal recognition within the broader framework of the churches' growing ecclesiological convergence:

> Just as the convergence on baptism in the responses to *Baptism, Eucharist and Ministry* gave rise to a fresh impetus toward mutual recognition of baptism, similar ecclesial convergence on ecclesiology will play a vital role in the mutual recognition between the churches as they call one another to visible unity in one faith and in one eucharistic fellowship.[43]

Strikingly, the text aims to foster not just "theological agreement on the Church" *but also renewal* within the churches and the ecumenical movement.[44] As such it has already stirred keen interest within and among the churches, and played a prominent role at the WCC's Tenth Assembly at Busan, South Korea, in 2013. In the manner of *BEM,* it should generate hun-

---

Achievements of the Ecumenical Movement," *Journal of Ecumenical Studies* 47, no. 3 (Summer 2012): 333-54.

42. For links between *The Church: Towards a Common Vision* and *One Baptism: Towards Mutual Recognition,* see *The Church: Towards a Common Vision,* p. viii; p. 24, n. 7; p. 25, n. 12; p. 46, n. 30.

43. *The Church: Towards a Common Vision,* p. viii.

44. An ecumenical document that aims at *renewal!* See *The Church: Towards a Common Vision,* p. viii.

dreds of official church responses, as well as responses from councils of churches, seminaries, pastors, laypersons, and others.[45] Again, it is a pleasure to note the essential congruence between Faith and Order's long work and the LWF study on worship and culture:

> [T]ogether they proclaim the saving grace that declares all the baptized as part of the one Body of Christ; together they attest to the Gospel of Jesus Christ beyond cultural contexts. . . . Whereas each denominational body, each part of the Body of Christ the Church, celebrates and suggests the Gospel's deeper meanings in images, metaphors of the place and time they abide, and even modes of the "water that speaks" . . . all are part of the One Baptism, of the One Gospel, of the One Christ, beyond time, place, and space, all seen through the lenses of the counter-cultural nature of the Gospel and of Christian Unity itself — though these elements are to be strongly expressed in local language and colors, as both the WCC and the LWF documents so clearly envision.[46]

This forms a beautiful complement to reflections in *The Church: Towards a Common Vision* on the crucial issue of unity and diversity within the one body of Christ:

> Unity must not be surrendered. Through shared faith in Christ, expressed in the proclamation of the Word, the celebration of the sacraments and lives of service and witness, each local church is in communion with the local churches of all places and all times. . . . Christians are called not only to work untiringly to overcome divisions and heresies but also to preserve and treasure their legitimate differences of liturgy, custom and law and to foster legitimate diversities of spirituality, theology and method, and formulation in such a way that they contribute to the unity and catholicity of the Church as a whole.[47]

---

45. Responses to *The Church: Towards a Common Vision* may be sent from churches, groups, and individuals to the Faith and Order Secretariat, World Council of Churches, 150 Rte. De Ferney, 1211 Geneva, Switzerland.

46. Gláucia Vasconcelos Wilkey, personal communication, May 2013. As she notes, "the water that speaks" is a phrase of Gordon Lathrop's; see, e.g., his "The Water that Speaks: The *Ordo* of Baptism and its Ecumenical Implications," in *Becoming a Christian: The Ecumenical Implications of Our Common Baptism*, pp. 13-29 (see n. 5 above).

47. *The Church: Towards a Common Vision*, §29, p. 16; §30, p. 17.

A Continuing Legacy

But even as we await responses to *The Church: Towards a Common Vision,* we may celebrate Faith and Order's work on baptism over many years. The text of *One Baptism: Towards Mutual Recognition* has taken forward the prophetic hopes shared by those gathered around the fountain at the Fifth World Conference on Faith and Order in Santiago de Compostela in 1993. As they did then, we continue to listen to "the water that speaks" to us of our incorporation into Christ, and of our belonging together to Christ's one body, the church. And as they did then, we continue to say together: "We affirm and celebrate the increasing mutual recognition of one another's baptism as the one baptism into Christ. We will dare to explore all the ways, known and unknown, to become one in Christ Jesus. We will not give up even in the face of difficulties."[48] But we also look beyond baptism to the full unity of the church in eucharistic fellowship. And thus we insist, with the concluding words of *One Baptism:*

> Baptism looks beyond itself. As the basis of our common identity in the one body of Christ, it yearns to be completed through the full eucharistic fellowship of all the members of Christ's body. We should be one at the one table of our one Lord. . . . The churches are thus called to renewed efforts towards full ecclesial communion, in order that the unity which is theirs in Christ through the waters of baptism may find its fulfilment at his one table.[49]

48. See n. 21 above.
49. *One Baptism: Towards Mutual Recognition,* §111, p. 21.

Of Frogs, Eels, Women, and Pelicans: The Myth of Tiddalik and the Importance of Ambiguity in Baptismal Identity for the Contemporary Christian Church

Anita Monro

Introduction

The "Chicago Statement on Worship and Culture: Baptism and Rites of Life Passages"[1] attempts to hold the tensions of baptismal flood and drought in the important space of ambiguity/alterity between faith and culture, all and some, insider and outsider: "Baptism, which constitutes the Church, also calls Christians to identify in solidarity with all people."[2] One significant strategy for holding these tensions is the invocation of the *ordo* of baptism as a three-stage process: formation, ritual act, and incorporation into community.[3] The holding of tensions in the Chicago Statement mirrors discussion on baptismal identity and faith in and around *Baptism, Eucharist, and Ministry:*[4] "Baptism is both God's gift and our human response to that gift."[5]

In its response to *BEM*, the Uniting Church in Australia, a union of Congregationalist, Methodist, and Presbyterian traditions, acknowledged some of the issues that ambiguous baptismal identity raised for it:[6] (1) "the

---

1. S. Anita Stauffer, ed., *Baptism, Rites of Passage, and Culture,* LWF Studies (Geneva: LWF, 1999), pp. 13-24 (hereafter referred to as the "Chicago Statement").
2. Chicago Statement, §2.3.
3. Chicago Statement, §2.1.
4. *Baptism, Eucharist and Ministry,* Faith and Order Paper No. 111 (Geneva: WCC, 1982) (hereafter referred to as *BEM).*
5. *BEM,* "Baptism," §8.
6. "Response to *BEM* by the Uniting Church in Australia (1985)," in Robert Bos and Geoff Thompson, eds., *Theology for Pilgrims: Selected Theological Documents of the Uniting*

practice of indiscriminate Baptism"; (2) "willingness of some to comply with a request for rebaptism"; (3) "confusion of Baptism with naming ceremonies"; (4) "nurture in faith of those baptised"; (5) the focused celebration of baptism at festivals such as Easter and Pentecost; and (6) providing opportunities for the reaffirmation of baptism at such festivals and the baptism of others.[7] The practical means of negotiating this reconciliation/integration relationship between the opposites embodied in baptismal identity remains a significant question for the Christian church, and for the Uniting Church of Australia as a particular denomination within the one, holy, catholic, and apostolic church.

The Australian aboriginal myth generally known as the story of Tiddalik the frog provides a metaphorical counterpart to the issue of baptismal identity for Christians in an Australian context, and, by virtue of the transcultural nature of liturgical *ordo,* a narrative model for ensuring the maintenance of the inherently ambiguous nature of baptismal identity as Christic identity.[8] The most popular form of the myth of Tiddalik is a truncated version that omits important aspects of the story.[9] The omission of the pelican who rescues the animals from the flood on contemporary retellings of the myth parallels the widespread practice of "indiscriminate baptism" in certain mainline churches in Australia by emphasizing the importance of releasing the water from the overindulgent Tiddalik. The popular form of the story does not mention the consequences of the flood. Indiscriminate baptismal practices that omit the important elements of Christian formation, preparation for baptism, and incorporation into the community of the body of Christ present the aim of the process as the flood — the releasing of waters of life. Who can argue against the imagery of the overflowing, abundant grace of God?

And yet there are consequences to this flood. Where many children are baptized without due preparation, and whether or not the family is formally linked to a faith community, the practice of baptism becomes connected to the celebration of the birth of a child, an act of creation, not of re-creation. Baptism is thus removed in communal imagination from its primary theo-

---

Church in Australia (Sydney: Uniting Church Press, 2008), pp. 210-29 (hereafter referred to as "UCA Response to *BEM*").

7. "UCA Response to *BEM,*" p. 215.

8. I use the adjective "Christic" to denote the specific (and ambiguous) identity of the person of Christ, and to seek to assist the reclamation of the defining of the adjective "Christian" in a Christ-centered way.

9. Robert Roennfeldt, *Tiddalick: The Frog Who Caused a Flood* (Melbourne: Penguin, 1981).

logical role as the celebration of the entry of a person into Christ; it becomes a very different rite, though perceived as equally — and perhaps even more — valid by the general civic communal interpretive process. In part, this practice (and its hermeneutical result) may be a legacy of Christendom and the expectation that all who reside in a particular area are Christian, that is, have the same allegiances. In part, it may be a result of the strong emphasis in contemporary Christianity on openness and inclusiveness, coupled with the theological linkage between baptism and receiving salvation. How dare we turn any of our "own ones" or the "little ones" away?

The truncated story of Tiddalik the frog offers a contextual morality tale that reinforces the ethics of openness in its account of the need to release the water that Tiddalik has hoarded, producing drought throughout the land. However, drought is not the only peril that faces those who live in a land of "droughts and flooding rains."[10] The release of Tiddalik's hoarded water produces a flood, from which other animals must be rescued, and the pelican enters the longer and older versions of the story. John Morton observes the importance of attending to the older, longer versions of the myth of Tiddalik as a recognition of the role that relationships between opposites plays in Australian aboriginal cosmology and sociology.[11] Similarly, Gordon Lathrop reminds us of the importance of juxtapositions within liturgical cosmology — the markers of "healthy Christian liturgy."[12] Within the framework of my theological methodology's "subjecting ambiguity," based on the philosophy of Julia Kristeva, healthy subjective identity is clearly understood to be ambiguous, as is Christian theological identity founded on the ambiguous identity of the two-natured Christ.[13] The truncation of the story of Tiddalik in the popular Australian imagination is a salutary lesson about the dualistic temptation inherent in any process of identity formation, and it is a warning about the loss or avoidance of difficult juxtapositions. The two additional

10. This phrase comes from the poem "My Country" by Dorothea Mackellar (© 2011 the estate of Dorothea Mackellar; all rights reserved): http://dorotheamackellar.com.au/index.html. The poem was first published as "Core of My Heart" in the *London Spectator Magazine* in 1908; it was learned and recited by hundreds of thousands of Australian schoolchildren since that time.

11. John Morton, "Tiddalik's Travels: The Making and Remaking of an Aboriginal Flood Myth," in Aldo Poiani, ed., *Floods: Environmental, Social and Historical Perspectives*, Advances in Ecological Research, vol. 39 (New York: Elsevier, 2006), pp. 139-58.

12. Gordon Lathrop, *Holy Ground: A Liturgical Cosmology* (Minneapolis: Fortress, 2003), p. 65.

13. Anita Monro, *Resurrecting Erotic Transgression: Subjecting Ambiguity in Theology*, Gender, Theology and Spirituality series (London: Equinox, 2006).

major characters in the story of Tiddalik are the eel and the woman whom the pelican wishes to marry. Their function is to ensure that the ambiguity of identity is held throughout the story. The eel represents lament when water/life is withheld; and the woman represents protest when there is no rescue from the flood. They offer the opportunity to explore those aspects of faith and culture that may help to promote the ambiguous tension of healthy identity in Christ.

In this chapter I explore the difficult and conflicting juxtapositions in the rite of Christian initiation in an Australian context. I specifically refer to the struggle of the Uniting Church in Australia to reinstitute a baptismal preparation and incorporation process through its "Becoming Disciples" campaign, which was designed by Robert Bos, then national director of theology and discipleship within the Uniting Church, in conjunction with the national working groups on worship and theology. Daniel Benedict, general board of discipleship of the United Methodist Church in the United States, consulted on the project. "Becoming Disciples" was developed over the period 2002-03, and accepted by the Tenth Assembly of the Uniting Church in mid-2003. Development of resources and encouragement for congregations to take up the process continues.[14]

Issues of Theological Hermeneutics

When the baptismal *ordo* is reduced to the ritual action that occurs on a particular occasion at a particular time, ordinary church members find it difficult to distinguish between:

(1) baptism as God's gift, and the indiscriminate baptizing of infants immediately upon request and presentation;
(2) the gift of faith and the request for baptism; and
(3) baptism as the sign of forgiveness of sins, and the failure to baptize infants on request and presentation as a withholding of salvation and all its benefits.

When infants are presented for baptism, baptized upon request without due preparation of families, and those families fail to participate in the com-

14. See the website of the National Assembly of The Uniting Church in Australia for further details: http://assembly.uca.org.au/resources/disciples

munity of faith at any point after that, ordinary church members acknowledge a sense of dissonance between that practice and the understanding of baptism as incorporation into Christ and the body of Christ, the church, and between their lived experience and baptism as a foretaste of God's reign and commissioning for Christian vocation.

Local Context

When I arrived to be the minister of a Uniting Church congregation in a small regional city in rural Australia, I discovered a situation that is fortunately not as prevalent in Australian cities now as it was in my childhood. Its recent mitigation, though, is probably due more to the disconnect of the Christian church from Australian society than to any major changes in ecclesial practice.

The congregation celebrated a number of infant baptisms annually. However, there was almost no contact with the children baptized and their families before or after the event. It was still a prevalent civic community expectation that all babies would be "christened." However, this event was quite disconnected from participation in the life of a community of faith. Baptism, for the wider civic community, was largely about celebrating a child's birth. Previous ministers and elders had been reluctant to "refuse" baptism upon any request. Little interaction with parents presenting children for baptism meant that there was minimal attempt to raise matters of Christian formation (e.g., explaining what the church understands about baptism, and inviting parents and children to be part of the formational activities of the congregation in worship, witness, and service). The sense of demoralization imbued in the congregation's participation in their response within the ritual act of baptism was palpable. How could they "promise to maintain a life of worship and teaching, witness and service so that [the child] may grow to maturity in Christ" if they were very sure they would never see the family again despite repeated attempts by their elder(s) to keep in contact with them?[15]

When we began asking families to take some time to explore what baptism was all about, and to participate in the practices of the community of faith to find out about the Christian faith, the responses of families requesting "christening" tended to treat baptism as some kind of consumer right: We ask and you supply. The idea of any preparation for baptism was treated like an adverse character judgment. Parents presenting their children were very open about having no intention of having anything to do with the community of faith either before or after the event. They would often tend to argue the case strongly by appealing to the possibility that their child might be prevented from attending their chosen school (an unlikely event in Australia) if we did not acquiesce. We always offered an alternative in the form of a service of thanksgiving for and blessing of the child, but it was seldom taken up. If we could not supply what they requested, they would not ask us to supply anything at all.

The elders were somewhat anxious. They had been uncomfortable with the flood, but the threat of drought was no more palatable. In my four years in that community of faith, we celebrated about a half dozen baptisms and had many opportunities for reaffirming our baptism into Christ. The newly baptized were participants in the congregation who had never been baptized and were discovering its significance; or they recognized that this next step was the right one for them after having returned to or entered the community of faith; or they were actually bringing new children into the community of faith in which they were already well immersed themselves. No one who requested baptism on demand without prior contact with the community of faith took up the offer to be engaged in its meaning or participating in the congregation. The place of ambiguity was uncomfortable, though we perhaps understood our identity as the baptized ones a little better.

Tiddalik the Frog

In brief, the story of Tiddalik the frog goes like this. A horrific drought prompts a council of creatures to be called. Overcoming their differences, they gather to explore the problem. Investigation reveals that a gigantic frog, Tiddalik, has drunk all the water in the land. The solution is to make the frog laugh, thereby releasing all the water. Various creatures put their talents to work to achieve that outcome: Kookaburra laughs; Frill-Necked Lizard parades in full display, and Brolga dances — all to no avail. The creatures begin to argue among themselves. Then Eel begins to writhe, and Tiddalik laughs. All the water is released and a great flood ensues. Pelican, who was then black, rescues survivors from the highest peaks in a canoe. At one site, he rescues everyone but one woman; he wants her to be his wife (and he may be entitled to her as his reciprocal right for the rescue). The reluctant woman deceives Pelican and escapes. Pelican seeks revenge. He paints himself white and goes to kill the woman's male relatives. The first man that Pelican meets is so shocked by Pelican's appearance that he strikes Pelican dead with a club. From that time, pelicans become both black and white. The flood eventually subsides. The land is renewed. A new morning breaks with a flood of sunlight.

This story, probably originally from the Gippsland region in the state of Victoria in southeastern Australia, has been recorded and retold in many permutations by storytellers and anthropologists, children's book authors and researchers. It is perhaps the most well-known story from the Australian Aboriginal Dreaming, the mythological truth/wisdom world of the indigenous people of the continent. It has inspired nonindigenous imagination as much as indigenous. Yet its most popular versions are generally truncated versions, that is, they end when Tiddalik laughs. Perhaps the most famous repetition of this shortened version is found in Roberts and Mountford's illustrated coffee-table text.[16]

John Morton examines the story of Tiddalik in the context of its function within both "classic" (preinvasion) and "post-classic" (postinvasion) aboriginal society, and as a contributing symbol to the development of an appropriate environmental consciousness in contemporary multicultural Australian society. When the whole story is taken into account, Morton says, it "is not just a lesson about people sharing," the moral of the truncated children's version of the tale, but "a lesson about institutional balance," and it is an account of the "need to arrange our institutions . . . in a responsible and collectively appropriate manner so that human life can be sustained." Morton explores the role of the myth of Tiddalik in the context of aboriginal dreaming (mythological cosmology).[17] Quoting Debra Bird Rose, he identifies the role of dreaming stories in establishing both the autonomy of aspects of the cosmos and the interrelationship of those aspects: "The goal of the system as a whole is to reproduce itself as a living system, while the goals of each part are: (1) to reproduce itself as a part; and (2) to maintain the relationship between itself and other parts."[18]

16. Ainslie Roberts and Charles P. Mountford, *The Dreamtime Book* (Adelaide: Rigby, 1973), pp. 24-25.

17. Morton, "Tiddalik's Travels," pp. 154, 145. Hereafter, page references to this essay appear in parentheses within the text.

18. Debra Bird Rose, "Consciousness and Responsibility in an Australian Aboriginal

Morton observes that this ecological balance, often confused in nonindigenous thinking as "a blueprint for an unchanging Eden or perfect harmony," is actually an account of the struggles and goals of a cosmos that is "in some sense imperfect and prone to become out of kilter" (p. 145). That is, it is an account of a continuing process of balancing, unbalancing, rebalancing, not of a certain destination of rigid symmetry. Each character in a story is "an autonomous agent needing to respond to the agency of others in a world where human beings seek to establish symmetry and balance through appropriate response" (p. 146). The stories themselves are not necessarily stories of symmetry and balance, but stories of the way in which the cosmos (and its various parts) seeks symmetry and balance as autonomous agents pull and push it out of balance. Attempts to redress excessive loss of water result in excessive release of water. Excessive release of water requires its own redress.

The characters of Eel, Pelican, and Woman in the longer versions of the story push back against both excesses of loss and release of water. The Eel engages in "a dance of death, writhing, and contorting in the way that eels are prone to do when caught or stranded (as in a drought)" (p. 148). Woman protests against the reciprocity of rights necessitated by the flood and the need for salvation. Pelican is the foil in the story: he acts like Tiddalik, moving from one extreme to another — from black to white — with the result that he is killed and becomes the archetype of balance, black *and* white. Morton, again referencing Rose, notes that within Australian aboriginal cosmology, "the fundamental unit is not singular; it is *plural* — not 'one' but 'two'" — as demonstrated by the kinship arrangements within classical aboriginal societies, where groups are divided into two halves, or *moieties* (p. 149). Each person is assigned to one particular moiety through patri- or matrilineage, but must marry or have children with someone of the opposite moiety. "These basic rules . . . generate complex sets of relationships governed through a moral economy of demands and obligations — 'sharing' " (p. 149). "In each case, the basic symbolism is that of 'same but different,' thus giving autonomy and relatedness equal weight in the definition of sociality" (p. 150). The story of Tiddalik is a story of the management of the balance between autonomous but interrelated agents, and of the process of seeking balance within an ambiguous identity — an identity that is always essentially not one but two.

Religion," in W. H. Edwards, ed., *Traditional Aboriginal Society,* 2nd ed. (Melbourne: Macmillan Education, 1998), pp. 239-51, esp. p. 242.

Order and Balance in Baptismal *Ordo*

The Chicago Statement affirms the transcultural aspect of baptism as located in the pattern of the *ordo* as "formation in the one faith," "the water-bath," and "the incorporation of the baptized into the whole Christian community and its mission."[19] In this affirmation, it sets out the parameters that undergird the "institutional balance" (the order) of the sacrament of baptism.

In an essay in the book *Baptism, Rites of Passage, and Culture,* Gordon Lathrop affirms that "the *ordo* gives the churches a transcultural connection, a basis for contextualization, support for counter-cultural resistance, and a framework for cross-cultural exchange of gifts."[20] Lathrop identifies the *ordo* of baptism (formation, washing, and participation) as the foundational process for seeking balance within the ambiguity of baptismal identity. This foundational process, together with the tension of individual and community (autonomy and interrelatedness) embodied within it, leads to "participation in Jesus Christ, to death and resurrection, hence to what was regarded as 'unclean,' to the meal of Christ's body and blood, to engagement with the poor and the outsiders, not to the pure life, cut off from others" (p. 24). By its very nature, the process and the identity engendered by it actively work against an unbalanced rigid identity that either separates the individual from the created order by means of an alternative salvific order or excludes those not baptized from that same presupposed order of salvation, that is, baptismal identity is an identity founded in both re-creation and creation, and neither of these theological themes in its singularity. Quoting the Faverges Report,[21] Lathrop affirms that, "[b]y means of God's continuing grace and presence Baptism is *process* and once-for-all eschatological *event* and *pattern* for all of life" (p. 40). The dismemberment of the process is a dismemberment of the balancing act that is baptismal identity — an identity founded in and governed by Christ: "hero-that-failed, hero-that-succeeded, both, neither" (pp. 110-11), the paradigmatic ambivalent identity (fully human, fully divine).

19. Chicago Statement, §2.1.

20. Gordon Lathrop, "Baptismal *Ordo* and Rites of Passage in the Church," in S. Anita Stauffer, ed., *Baptism, Rites of Passage, and Culture* (Geneva: LWF, 1999), pp. 27-46, esp. p. 27. Hereafter, page references to this essay appear in parentheses in the text.

21. Thomas F. Best and Dagmar Heller, eds., *Becoming a Christian: The Ecumenical Implications of Our Common Baptism,* Faith and Order Paper 184 (Geneva: WCC Publications, 1999), § 22.

Becoming Disciples and the Uniting Church

Since its union in 1977, the Uniting Church has struggled with a dismembered baptismal identity. "Understanding the Church's Teaching on Baptism (1988)" attempted to mediate between indiscriminate baptism of infants and "believer" baptism positions.[22] Both positions suffered from a lack of grounding in the theological and liturgical traditions of the Christian church and the overt expectations of a society that still proclaimed its "Christian" nature. Both positions, in different ways, wanted to uphold the significance of God's grace in the life of the baptized. Both positions were seeking to respond to a society where the church was not the center of the society's life and the identity of "Christian" was being questioned, challenged, and changed.

In 2003, the Uniting Church's national assembly sought to instigate a process by which the ritual act of baptism was placed in its broader *ordo*. "Becoming Disciples" placed the ritual act of baptism in a fourfold process of discipleship: "Touching the Edges"; "Discovering the Riches"; "Exploring the Depths"; and "Living the Life".[23] The ritual water act was intended to occur between "Exploring the Depths" and "Living the Life," with candidates for baptism or their parents having been given the opportunity to explore the Christian faith and participate in the life of the Christian community in order to recognize, accept, and respond to God's gift. It is unclear how many congregations have really taken up the challenge of "Becoming Disciples." It was the Becoming Disciples process that governed the renewed baptismal practice that we developed for my congregation mentioned above.

Yet the separating out of the ritual act of baptism from the process of the *ordo* of baptism remains an issue for the Uniting Church today. More recently, it has been raised in the context of questions about church membership and the questioning of the necessity for baptism to participate in the life of the one holy, catholic, and apostolic church as that church is embodied in the local congregation.[24] Again, the question shows a limited understanding of the Uniting Church's theology, but it also indicates a protest or lament against a practice that does not quite capture the sense of Christian identity that the church currently seeks.

22. "Understanding the Church's Teaching on Baptism (1988)," in Robert Bos and Geoff Thompson, eds., *Theology for Pilgrims: Selected Theological Documents of the Uniting Church in Australia* (Sydney: Uniting Church Press, 2008), pp. 509-57.

23. http://assembly.uca.org.au/resources/disciples/item/279-introduction

24. See the definition of "congregation" in the Uniting Church's "Basis of Union," §15(a) (1971), in Bos and Thompson, eds., *Theology for Pilgrims*, pp. 191-205.

Ambiguous Identity

The story of Tiddalik is not really Tiddalik's story in its oldest and longest versions. It is the story of a community (a cosmos) seeking order through imbalance and struggle. The eel and the woman successfully lament and protest against the excesses exhibited in the imbalance, and the pelican bears the mark of what is necessary to bring about balance once more. The coincidence of the black and white pelican — and the use of the pelican in early Christian imagery for Christic identity — is fortuitous for its attempt at cross-cultural analogy.[25]

In *Resurrecting Erotic Transgression,* I affirm the ambiguous Christic identity as the paradigm par excellence for the deconstruction/reconstruction of ineffective identity formed in a dualistic environment.[26] The Chalcedonian Definition sets out the fundamental principle on which the personhood of Christ is understood in a Christian theological context. The principle seeks to hold the two "natures" of humanity and divinity together in the one personhood:

[A]cknowledged in two natures which undergo no confusion, no change, no division, no separation; at no point was the difference between the natures taken away through the union, but rather the property of both natures is preserved and comes together into a single person and a single subsistent being; he is not parted or divided into two persons.[27]

This principle undergirds recognized Christology, which undergirds Christian theology generally and establishes the nature of Christic — and thus Christian — identity as ambiguous, that is, as of two natures "unconfusedly, unchangeably, indivisibly, inseparably; the distinction of the natures being in no way denied because of the unity."[28] Ambiguous identity is inherently unstable; the pull of the polarities is strong. Yet it is also inherently healthy, dominated by neither side of any particular duality and yet attentive to the neediness of both ends.

---

25. Asher Ovadiah, "Symbolism in Jewish and Christian Works of Art in Late Antiquity," *Deltion of the Christian Archaeological Society* 38 (199): 62.

26. Monro, *Resurrecting Erotic Transgression,* pp. 17-18.

27. Norman P. Tanner, SJ, ed., "Chalcedon," in *Decrees of the Ecumenical Councils,* vol. 1, *Nicaea I to Lateran V* (London: Sheed and Ward, 1990), p. 86.

28. Stephen W. Need, *Human Language and Knowledge in the Light of Chalcedon* (New York: Peter Lang, 1996), p. 47.

The theological method "poetic reading," which I outline in *Resurrecting Erotic Transgression,* offers a three-stage process for destabilizing identities that have solidified at either end of a polarity in order that new *jouissant* identities might emerge.[29] The three-stage process involves:

1. "identification of dualities";
2. "attention to the subversion of the dualities and the symbolic order which they advance"; and
3. "re-presentation of the focal discourse, highlighting its ambiguous nature and the alterity which underlies it."

A series of strategies within the second subversive stage is also explored. They are:

1. "privileging of the lesser term of the duality";
2. "treatment of the lesser term as the precondition for the dominant one";
3. "introduction of a third term outside and precedent to the dualities";
4. "highlighting of spaces or gaps . . . which undermine dominant and unitary interpretations";
5. "playing with slippages of terms both contained within the discourse itself, and infused from the contexts in which the discourse is played";
6. "paying attention to the intertextuality of the discourse"; and
7. "placing alongside each other . . . different readings of the textual dualities."[30]

Poetic reading offers a methodology for the continuing process of maintaining ambiguous identity, that is, of recognizing that the baptismal story is not "a blueprint for an unchanging Eden or perfect harmony," but an account of the struggles and goals of a cosmos that is "in some sense imperfect and prone to become out of kilter" — a mythology of continual becoming rather than a narrative of static being.[31]

---

29. *Jouissance* is the "joying in the truth of self-division," a "balancing act between the two brinks of language and subjectivity," and "an ambivalent and risky recognition of both the subject's complicity in the use of the tools of meaning construction, and the limitations of such tools in exploring the complexity of an identity which defies them" (Monro, *Resurrecting Erotic Transgression,* p. 114). See also Julia Kristeva, *Powers of Horror: An Essay on Abjection,* trans. Leon S. Roudiez (New York: Columbia University Press, 1982), p. 89.

30. Monro, *Resurrecting Erotic Transgression,* p. 137.

31. Morton, "Tiddalik's Travels," p. 145.

Ambiguous Baptismal Identity

In *Holy Ground,* Lathrop draws out the inherent ambiguity of baptismal iden-tity by describing the "fullness" of the *ordo* of baptism, with its "cosmological resonance," as being both "locative" and "liberative."[32] The "locative" role of ritual maps "echo and reinforce the lines that organize both the cosmos and the society, celebrating the important — even central — location of the partic-ular place within that structure and giving yet greater weight to the importance of each of us 'keeping our place.'" The "liberative" function of the ritual map speaks "of a place beyond the oppressive structures and will enact and assist a journey" (p. 100). The dangers of the locative function concern the overenthu-siastic drawing of the boundaries between inside and outside, where the " 'cos-mic order' may simply be the order around us" (p. 107). Conversely, the dan-gers of the liberative function concern the overlooking of the locational reality, "the goodness or the real struggles of the place where we are" (p. 110). These polarities of the ritual map of baptism reinforce the significance of a baptismal *ordo* that resists solidification at one end or the other. Here Lathrop identifies a primary structural duality within the baptismal identity and the baptismal *ordo,* which demands ambiguity for the sake of the integrity of the rite and the formational subjectivity it seeks to promote and evoke.

Thus, when Lathrop offers a series of suggestions for baptismal practice in light of the need to balance the locative and liberative functions of the ritual map of baptism, he is providing a series of strategies for maintaining ambivalent baptismal identity. Building the strength of the bath as ritual symbol empha-sizes an event where process seems to be an impediment to the receiving of the gracious gift of God. Ensuring that catechetical and mystagogical formation are part of the baptismal *ordo* subverts the focus on the event as a magical act and emphasizes the journey of Christian discipleship before, during, and after the baptismal event. Connecting baptismal identity with both the one holy, catholic, and apostolic church and with participation in one of its local embod-iments destabilizes the local-universal duality. Exploring the theological nar-ratives of creation and re-creation, and the twin motifs of the waters of creation and the waters of salvation, broadens the ritual baptismal map. Baptism is not simply connected with the celebration of human birth or with the separation of the newly second-birthed, but with the complex drama of the human-divine relationship in creation and salvation (re-creation).

---

32. Lathrop, *Holy Ground,* p. 106. Hereafter, page references to this work appear in parentheses in the text.

Furthermore, that drama is not simply between the human and the divine, but between the created order (not just humanity) and the Creator. Liturgical formation that highlights lamenting and beseeching as well as thanksgiving reinforces the complexity of that drama. Placing salvation in a cosmic context prevents the narrow focus on the salvation of the baptized individual, and it links baptism with the practices of compassion for and solidarity with the whole creation. Opening up the vision of a God who "is a flowing, communal reality, holding all things in mercy, under the hole in the heavens, not a patriarchal monarchy with the authority inherited along a masculine line of succession" upsets notions of any hierarchical social status being conferred by baptism. Ensuring that baptism is linked with the eucharistic table — as meal for the baptized and foretaste of the fullness of God's re-creation — connects the baptized not just with the others baptized but with the world for which baptism is wrought as a salvific act. When baptism is about process as well as event, the polarities are challenged, and the possibility of upholding a healthy ambiguous baptismal identity is extended (pp. 112-14).

It is just such a balancing act that the Uniting Church has sought to promote through its "Becoming Disciples" process, and that my regional rural congregation sought in our attempt to establish a more complex baptismal identity through our local practice. No map is completely accurate. No practice is perfect.

The joyful ritual map of baptism is capable of containing within itself the failure and sadness of maps. Neither the locative nor the liberative map alone suffices to tell the truth about the cosmos as it is held in the mercy of the triune God. Baptism should not be used to support the status quo; neither should it present a world-denying way of getting out of here. This place where we stand is, indeed, a small place, dwarfed and marginalized and threatened in the vast chaos of things. Yet this place is beloved, dear — even central. This place where we stand thus matters immensely, yet it is connected to all places (p. 111). Baptism as "a once-for-all event . . . takes a whole lifetime to unfold" (p. 115).

The Last Word from the Story of Tiddalik

The eel, the black pelican, and the woman function in the story of Tiddalik to challenge solidity at either end of the drought-flood polarity. The eel laments the drought; the black pelican rescues creatures from the flood, seeking to benefit from his efforts; and the woman protests against the necessity of the rescue and the reciprocal rights it entails. These characters, along with Tiddalik, represent a cosmos that is not static but in process. The narrative is a story with a plot. While the plot has resolution in the transformed pelican, it does not resolve the dilemma of the seesawing floods and droughts. The cosmic identity is ambiguous and thus cannot be solidified, though its ambiguity can be embodied in the marks of the process (the black and white pelican).

Likewise, baptismal identity cannot be solidified. Its ambiguity demands our constant attention to the dualities within it and their destabilization. Just as a baptismal flood does not uphold the ambiguous nature of Christic — and thus Christian — identity, neither does a baptismal drought. There is no moment of solidified baptismal identity, only its powerful embodiment in the body that bears the marks of the process — the local-global, contextual-universal, singular-multiple, one holy, catholic, and apostolic church — and the continuing process of becoming the people of God inherent within it. In these marks of the continuing balancing process — the marks of deconstruction and reconstruction, of death and resurrection — the ambiguous Christic baptismal identity is upheld as both constituting the church and sealing it in solidarity with the whole creation, both by the gracious gift of God and through the limited, grasping, searching human response to that undeserved gift.

A Thanksgiving over the Font, a Thanksgiving at the Table

Gail Ramshaw

A Thanksgiving over the Font

In our century, many Christian assemblies that gather to baptize assume that water will always be available, clean and free. They turn on the tap, and out flows life for all. Other Christian assemblies that gather to baptize rely on women who daily trudge to a distant well where they may perhaps find enough. The women are relieved when, despite the heavy task before them, there is indeed water for them to lug home. Both assemblies are united in baptism, yet diverse in their access to and appreciation of water. My grandmother, who knew drought in the North American farm country, chastised my urban behavior when I would let the faucet run. Water is precious, she said. Human history can be narrated from one well to the next, one river to its rival. From sea to sea we have sought ready water, being constituted by it, forming our identity around it — killing for it, if need be.

It is time for all Christians to thank God for water. Western Christians can learn from the East to gather annually and bless, not only the water dedicated for use in worship, but also all the lakes and streams and oceans of the earth, as if Christ stepping into the Jordan River made all waters as precious as that in our fonts.

Here, for your interest — and perhaps your use — is a text for a thanksgiving over the font. Along with many prayers of blessing, it is transcultural in that it flows from biblical wells. The stories of Noah, the Red Sea, and the Jordan remind us of millennia of God's mercy to the people. As Christians we remember also the waters that fill the stories of Jesus: his baptism, his calming the sea, his drinking from the well, his washing our feet — though on the cross he was thirsty, thirsty. All Christians tell these stories, no matter their time or culture.

The prayer also means to be inculturated, for the second line of the thanksgiving must be contextualized. We praise you, O God, for the Wissahickon Creek, the Delaware River, the Atlantic Ocean. The prayer also means to be countercultural. We are not, after all, a nature religion, finding in the chemical ingredients of water alone all the life we seek. Rather, we acknowledge that water is a gift from God, not somehow ours by right. So we pray for yet more of the Spirit's breath on a world marked by sin and violence and suffering.

The thanksgiving also is transcultural in that it borrows images from the human imagination, from Jung's collective unconscious, perhaps even from Hinduism. God, whom we name Father, Son, and Spirit, is ocean and river and stream. The hope is that these metaphors assist our prayer as we drench our baptismal candidates in Christ and as we draw a watery cross on each other's forehead. One night prayer that I prayed with my preschool daughters was, "Thank you, God, for being our Father. Thank you, God, for being our mother. Thank you, God, for being our friend. Thank you, God, for being our castle." One daughter always concluded the prayer by saying, "God is not a castle. God is God." True, God is not the ocean, nor a river, nor a stream. But like a ship, the images may help sail us into the Trinity.

This prayer is provided for your use. You may find a need to alter a line here or there, but I do ask that, if you print out the text for distribution, please reproduce it as is. Or use it as inspiration for a prayer of your own, one that stands within the tradition, allows for local reference, acknowledges that human life is not enough, and reaches toward an always greater mystery.

The text of this thanksgiving has been crafted so that a printed text is not necessary for worship. A cantor may lead the acclamations using a simple tone. The alternate fourth paragraph is to be used at an affirmation of baptism without a baptism. The assembly responds as indicated.

Thanksgiving over the Font

Water! Water! We praise you, O God, for water —
the *local bodies of water,*

the rain that nourishes animals and plants,
the water for drinking and bathing.
We praise you, O God, for water. **We praise you, O God, for water!**

We praise you, O God, for our water stories —
a flood that cleansed the earth,
the sea that drowned the enemy,
a river that can heal leprosy.
We praise you, O God, for water. **We praise you, O God, for water!**

We remember the waters of Jesus —
baptized in the Jordan River,
calming the Sea of Galilee,
drinking from Jacob's well,
washing the disciples' feet,
on the cross thirsting for us.

We praise you, O God, for this font.
Breathe into this water,
wash away our sin,
and birth _____ [name/s] anew into your peace and joy.
We praise you, O God, for water. **We praise you, O God, for water!**

or

We praise you, O God, for this font,
for your breathing into this water
to wash away sin
and birth us anew into your peace and joy.
We praise you, O God, for water. **We praise you, O God, for water!**

O God, you are the ocean, the source of all life.
O God, you are the river, saving us from death.
O God, you are the stream, restoring our community's strength.
We praise you, O God, Father, Son, and Holy Spirit,
today, tomorrow, forever.
Amen, and Amen! **Amen, and Amen!**

A Thanksgiving at the Table

Some of the sisters and brothers united with us in baptism choose not to pray a thanksgiving over the bread and wine. But I would ask: Praising God for the earth, for the history of salvation, for Jesus Christ, and for the outpouring of the Spirit — how bad can that be? Yet those of us who do make that prayer will raise our arms as we gather around the table, will compose and authorize prayers that are different from each other. The order of topics in my church's prayer, for example, is not the same as that of the Christians across the street. Yet we hope that our historical diversity expresses a mystical unity, the whole people of God joining the women in *orans* in those third-century catacomb paintings. Together we thank God for simple food that becomes an extraordinary meal, for we all believe that by eating Christ at the table, we become Christ in the world.

Here for your interest, and perhaps also your collaboration and use, is a thanksgiving at the table. In its Trinitarian outline, it unites us with the ancient churches of West Syria; yet in its open third lines, this variable eucharistic prayer requires expressions of our local diversity. The prayer is transcultural in its evocation of biblical stories, from creation through Scripture, from the life of Christ through the many manifestations of the Spirit.

This thanksgiving is also intentionally inculturated. Were a minimal prayer sought, for example, in a situation of pastoral care, the presider would use only the first of each set of three lines. (Try it.) Were a more substantial thanksgiving sought, the first two lines of each set would be used. (Try it.) But for festivals and at times of expansive worship, a third line is to be added to each set. Keeping to three stresses per line, each assembly is to add local natural sites, local communal centers, favorite biblical figures and beloved saints, prized manifestation of the Spirit, the community's choice of divine metaphors. The first two lines of each set will bind you to assemblies around the world, while the third contextual line will ground your assembly in its place.

The thanksgiving also means to be countercultural, acknowledging the many ways that Christians beg God to save and remake the world. Even during the joy of our communal meal we remain aware of the world's injustices and the magnitude of human suffering. The thanksgiving also means to be cross-cultural, thanking God for fields and wild animals and schools. Perhaps you can fill in some of these open third lines with imagery from Christians on the other side of the globe, thus making your prayer open to the experience of vastly different Christian communities.

Here are several other notes of interest: The opening praise, calling God maker, lover, and keeper, is a quote from Julian of Norwich, who would probably be astounded that six hundred years after her tightly contained life, thousands of Christians are praying with her words. When we praise God for the created universe, we acknowledge that creation was not only a divine act some three billion years ago, but that it continues today — in seas and forests, homes and cities. The readings appointed for the day's liturgy will probably suggest other biblical characters whom we honor, another aspect of Christ's ministry, and other gifts of the Spirit. The opening address and the final doxology, inspired by an Eastern practice of the Eucharist, address not only the first person of the Trinity but the fullness of God — Father, Son, and Spirit. Perhaps the three more images of the divine will derive from the season, the readings, the community, or even the day's international news.

This thanksgiving is provided for your use. You may find a need to alter lines one or two of each set, but I do ask that if you print out the text for distribution, please reproduce it as is. Or use it to inspire one such prayer of your own, one that praises God for the gifts of the earth, honors the salvation that your local believers receive, acknowledges our need for God's food and the Spirit's blessings, and reaches toward language always more expressive of mercy.

A Variable Eucharistic Prayer

For a concise eucharistic prayer, use the first line of each unit; for an ordinary Sunday, use the first and second line of each unit; for festivals, add an appropriate third line, keeping three stresses to each line.

Thanksgiving at the Table

We praise you, all-holy God,
     our maker, our lover, our keeper,
          [here may be added three more descriptors of God]

for the universe beyond our knowing,
     for seas and forests and fields,
          [here may be added three more phenomena of nature]

339

for creatures seen and unseen,
> for animals both wild and tame,
>> *[here may be added three more living things]*

and for the places we humans call home,
> for cities and churches and schools;
>> *[here may be added three more locales]*

We praise you for your covenant people,
> for Moses and Miriam and Aaron,
>> *[here may be added three more Old Testament figures]*

and for centuries of faithful Christians,
> for Mary Magdalene, Peter, and Paul,
>> *[here may be added three more saints]*

We praise you, O God, for Jesus Christ,
> who saves us from sin and from evil,
>> *[here may be added another aspect of Jesus' ministry]*

who on the night before he died . . . .

And so we remember your Word,
> his life, his death and his glorious resurrection,
>> *[here may be added another reference to Christ]*

and we proclaim the mystery of our faith:
> **Christ has died, Christ is risen, Christ will come again.**

We pray, O God, for your Spirit,
> your breath, your fire, your wisdom,
>> *[here may be added three more gifts of the Spirit]*

Bless this meal and all who share it;
> inspire your people for service;
>> *[here may be added another action of the Spirit]*

and renew the world with your mercy,
> with your healing, your justice and your peace,
>> *[here may be added more signs of grace]*

We praise you, all-holy God,
  the Father, the Son, the Holy Spirit,
    [here may be added other Trinitarian language]

today, tomorrow, and forever.
Amen!

Life Passages, Occasional Services, and Cultural Patterns: Necessary Tensions

Melinda A. Quivik

This essay will examine the church's liturgical relationship with marriage, healing, and funeral in accordance with the *Chicago Statement on Worship and Culture,* which examined each through various essays and summarized the baptismal center at times of life passage. These occasional services are found today as rites in several denominational church orders and exemplify the creative dynamism between the church's witness and cultural expectations.[1] The categories articulated by the Nairobi and Chicago statements defined worship as related to culture by being transcultural, contextual, countercultural, and cross-cultural. These four themes will serve as a means by which to name the tensions that exist in shaping and conducting occasional services.

The overriding issue in any occasional service is the question of its purpose, because the intentions of the liturgy and the intentions of culture may either undermine the goals of both or nourish each other (creating something greater than either could have engendered on its own). In North America, for example, the rise of the wedding industry (e.g., the dress, the consultants, florists, caterers, and more) has introduced market demands that can either subvert the purposes of the wedding as worship or enlarge it. Liturgies of healing have come into greater prominence just as the sector of our culture that defines itself as "spiritual but not religious" has gained in numbers and

1. See, as examples, *Evangelical Lutheran Worship* (Minneapolis: Augsburg Fortress, 2006), pp. 273-91; the Presbyterian *Book of Common Worship* (Louisville: Westminster John Knox Press, 1993), pp. 841-1030; the Episcopal *Book of Common Prayer* (New York: Oxford University Press, 2007), pp. 420-38, 447-507; and *United Methodist Hymnal* (Nashville: United Methodist Publishing House, 1989), pp. 864-75.

voice. Technological advances in embalming and cremation — and concomitant discomfort with death — have made it possible in many parts of the world for liturgical practice to give way to work and travel schedules, putting social convenience ahead of accommodation to the finality of death.

Tension between sometimes conflicting purposes is not only inevitable but necessary and healthy. The church benefits from cultural practices and values because, through them, God's incarnate world is given shape and import. In the same way, religious commitments offer to the secular world transcultural truths that underlie Christian witness even as they challenge the culture with gospel wisdom.

The goodness, questions, and problems that each of these occasional services presents to the church are endemic to each. In order to bring specificity to the interactions between liturgical/theological and cultural matters, I will in this chapter explore some of the issues that call on the church to engage in balancing the tensions between worship and its transcultural, contextual, countercultural, and cross-cultural meanings.

Marriage

Over the centuries and in diverse cultures, the history of marriage has acquired its shape by circling around a slim body of biblical references (creation, the wedding at Cana, Paul's admonitions) and a short list of ritual acts (consent or vows, giving of rings, and blessings) in both domestic settings and in churches. Today church and society are pressed to juggle numerous changes that force questions about sacramentality, divorce, equality of the partners, the meaning of vows, and the definition of "marriage" to include same-sex relationships. These issues have long roots and engender huge additional questions about the relationship between the couple and the church. In societies that are decreasingly Christian, we may ask whether there can be a baptismal core to an occasional service that is not focused solely on the baptized. How can the church assert baptismal values in a marriage between persons of different religions — or none? Is such a goal appropriate?

LWF Essays

The essays included in the 1999 Lutheran World Federation (LWF) publication roamed over marriage rites from Sweden, Latin America, and

China.[2] Each essay offered a window into the issues facing the church at that time. Transculturally, the notion of the marriage covenant extends to both the Chinese society's notion of marriage and to the Christian, but other than that broad commonality, the differences can be stark. For example, language like "till death do us part" has no place in the Chinese conception of eternal bonds in marriage.[3] Contextually, red is the color of joy and should be worn rather than white. Counterculturally, the church's witness to faith as a source of marital strength goes against the matching of wedding partners according to birth dates.[4] Cross-culturally, Wu mentions musical choices that may or may not reflect Christian witness.

Marriage rites in Latin America assume that a civil service had first taken place except, as in Colombia, where the Roman Catholic Church held the religious service first. Taken together, the marriage rites in several Latin American countries are considered to include blessings and toasts, essentially double blessings from the church and from family and friends. Finding commonality between these double blessings, the authors of the LWF study proposed a marriage rite for Latin Americans that would include toasts interspersed with prayers, a speech about the couple's responsibility toward children, vows, the giving of rings, and a pastoral blessing. It was unclear whether this was to replace or repeat parts of the civil service.

Recounting Scandinavian practice in medieval and post-Reformation times, Nilsson notes that elements of the rite included the consent and vows on the steps outside the church door, mass including nuptial blessing, and then blessing the bed in the home. In the thirteenth century, the consent and vows involved a transfer of the bride from the priest to the groom, as if the woman needed to be handed over from male to male.[5] This pattern of "giving away the bride," although discouraged today, is not unknown.

In his summation of their content, Marcus Felde notes the diversity of issues in these essays and posits the need for greater clarity and focus on the transcultural aspects of the marriage rite, suggesting that the rite is about blessing.[6] God's action within a marriage, the very heart of blessing — which

2. S. Anita Stauffer, ed., *Baptism, Rites of Passage, and Culture* (Geneva: LWF, 1998).

3. Mabel Wu, "Marriage Rites in the Chinese Cultural Context," in Stauffer, ed., *Baptism, Rites of Passage, and Culture*, p. 222.

4. Wu, "Marriage Rites," p. 224.

5. Nils-Henrik Nilsson, "Marriage Rites in the Swedish Cultural Context," in Stauffer, ed., *Baptism, Rites of Passage, and Culture*, p. 198.

6. Marcus Felde, "Summary on Marriage Rites," in Stauffer, ed., *Baptism, Rites of Passage, and Culture*, p. 242.

Felde claims to be creative, redemptive, and sanctifying — inevitably leads, he writes, to an emphasis on the link between marriage and the sacraments of baptism and Eucharist.

We continue to ask what the blessing actually means and how its link to sacraments is possible unless both of the persons in the marriage are Christians. These are theological issues that must be seen in the context of the times.

Practices Today

Market forces, in addition to theological matters, also impinge on the rite, affecting the shape of the rite and its meaning. In North America in the early twenty-first century, the average cost of a wedding is almost $27,000, which includes $5,000 for the engagement ring and $12,000 for the reception.[7] An illustration of the financial burden surfaced when one bride, who paid $2,700 for her dress, discovered that the fabric was worth $500, and the labor, $200.[8] Believing that she had found a bargain, she concluded that her purchase resulted from her inexperience: she had succumbed to the marketing notion that the dress "signals" to future generations significant information about the bride. The wedding dress, in fact, may be seen as a symbol of much that governs weddings today, because the dress may serve to crystallize the issues of market influence.

A study of brides as they entered the liminal stage of preparing for the wedding ceremony showed that the transition from single to married woman began, for most women, in the search for the dress.[9] "People use objects to form or re-formulate their self-concept, thus to integrate self and object."[10]

7. http://usatoday30.usatoday.com/money/perfi/basics/story/2012-08-09/wedding-costs/56921020/1 Other average costs: Reception band $3,122; photographer and videographer $3,785; ceremony site $1,600; gown $1,121; florist $1,894; wedding planner $1,753; rehearsal dinner $1,078; reception $930; transportation $670; musicians $536; cake $535; invitations $330; favors $217; catering $61. The survey included 18,000 weddings; these averages are available at: http://www.ewednewz.com/2012/06/average-price-of-a-wedding-dress-holds-steady/

8. http://www.slate.com/articles/video/slate_v/2012/04/why_are_wedding_dresses_so_expensive_.html. The study's author is an economic reporter on National Public Radio's "Planet Money."

9. Susanne Friese, "A Consumer Good in the Ritual Process: The Case of the Wedding Dress," *Journal of Ritual Studies* 11:2 (Winter 1997).

10. Friese, "A Consumer Good," p. 50.

The brides-to-be believed that, as a result of their search, the right dress would "reveal itself," thus giving it the stature of a sacred object. The dress became "a producer of meanings," a path to new identity, and a source of bonding between women.[11]

The wedding dress was not always the center of this transitional movement. It was also not always white, and it did not become white simply on the basis of what is often thought to be a concern for purity. Many colors were worn in eighteenth-century Europe, and black was preferred in the nineteenth century. When thinner, more expensive — and thus more desirable — fabrics (muslin, organdy, gauze, linen) took on greater status over the heavy brocades and silks that were previously popular, the white dress came into vogue because the thin textiles were only produced in white.[12] It is common today, for liturgical considerations, to take account of the wedding dress, often taking attention away from the wedding as worship. Clergy know this: they have watched a shift toward holding weddings at "destinations," often outside of churches, and on Saturdays instead of connecting the marriage to Sunday worship.

A study of shifting wedding practices in North American Mennonite communities (1960s-1990s) noted that when dress, food, and invitations were available for purchase and no longer had to be homemade, wedding preparation came to be less a project of the whole community of women and more that of the bride and her mother. A further change occurred as the wedding as a worship event was overshadowed by focus on the couple — and especially on the bride. "A cyclical relationship developed between religious leaders condemning increases in 'materialism' and women embracing ready-made and labor-saving clothing."[13] In 1953, a Mennonite minister found fault with "low-cut wedding gowns, veils, bridal attendants, nail-polish, nontraditional music and ceremonies in which the bride and groom did not 'take the time' to sit down."[14] The image of the couple today determined to have

11. Friese, "A Consumer Good," pp. 54-55. The importance of a transitional object is more common for women than for men, because the status of a woman is more greatly altered by marriage than that of a man. This matter may be much different with same-sex couples.

12. Friese, "A Consumer Good," p. 52. The relationship between market forces and liturgical considerations would benefit from a fuller exploration than is possible here. I hope that raising the issue may spur further thinking about it.

13. Pamela E. Klassen, "Practicing Conflict: Weddings as Sites of Contest and Compromise," *The Mennonite Quarterly Review* 72, no. 2 (April 1998): 228.

14. Klassen, "Practicing Conflict," p. 231.

a unique "destination wedding" where travel expense prohibits the presence of a faith community is a vastly different understanding of marriage than the wedding couple individually "crowned" by God on the wedding day in the midst of God's people (an Eastern rite practice).

Challenges Remaining

Without clarity about the meaning of blessing and the relationship between church and society, the power of a couple's baptismal identity remains a matter pertinent only on the basis of the couple's own understanding. No theology of marriage exists that can embrace the significance of marriage. Where the theological understanding of marriage remains caught in the web of procreation as a goal, and where the state uses clergy for its own task of determining who is and who is not married (for tax and other purposes), the marriage rite is in need of graceful answers that will benefit all people.

Felde lists myriad questions that could be summarized to demonstrate the tight connection between what is *contextual* and *countercultural*. What emerges, however, is how difficult it is to pinpoint what is *transcultural*. Furthermore, the particularity of the marriage rite — its intense *contextuality* — may mute the *cross-cultural* elements that a liturgical event of the church might desire. Here, then, are some of the questions still facing the church:

(1) What is the church's fundamental view of marriage? Those who contend that marriage is a sacrament ordained by God, evidence of God's creation and of God's intention that a man and a woman produce offspring, and essential as society's foundation, usually admit only heterosexuals to receive the church's blessing. Those who recognize, in contrast, that God intends joy, love, stability, and fruitfulness in all committed relationships will hold to a more complex understanding of human development and orientation and will define marriage as appropriate for two persons who wish to make vows of fidelity aside from sexual orientation.

(2) What language best expresses the church's witness regarding marriage? Much marriage rite language points to procreation. The Scripture texts chosen can slant the understanding of marriage (see #3 below). Yet other words present problems as well. "Nuptial" has been used for centuries referring to the vows, the ceremony itself, and the priest's blessing. The origins of "nuptial" may be in *nymphe* (bride), also in the characteristics of breeding, and the word is related to "nubile," a reference to a sexually mature

female.[15] It may unnecessarily emphasize sexuality over building a faithful life together. Restricting the image of marriage to the procreative potential in the relationship (even subconsciously) inevitably invites pernicious prejudice, as is clear in the fact that the Roman Catholic Church makes so complete an association between sex and procreation that they prohibit contraception. Obviously, lifelong commitments blessed by the church may be made between persons who cannot or do not desire to create children. The Chinese cultural context describes a similar concern for lineage (offspring), but adds that while marriage is an occasion of joy for the extended family, the announcement is made "also to heaven and earth."[16] The ritual events show forth the merging of families, the exchange of evidence that the couple's future is propitious, and the importance of the feast.

Ritual has also emphasized procreation. The canopy in Swedish Lutheran and Roman Catholic churches (perhaps echoing Jewish wedding practice) was used from medieval times until the mid-twentieth century as a sign of honor, much as a canopy would be held over communion elements or royalty in processions. Nils-Henrik Nilsson says that the canopy was a "sign of honor for the bride as she was transferring from her virginal state into that fellowship with the man for which . . . she had been created. The very purpose of a woman's life was to be married in order to become a helpmate. . . ." The canopy was not to be used for "elderly brides," thus signaling honor only for those who could reproduce.[17] At least in the mind of our ancestors, offspring were paramount in a marriage. It is no wonder that we have difficulty today imagining marriage without a procreative focus.

(3) What is the church's view of woman? The use of the Genesis 2 story of woman's creation from Adam's rib, rather than the story of mutual creation in Genesis 1, has perpetuated a diminished valuing of woman.

(4) What is the relationship of the couple to the church? What is the meaning of wanting a "church wedding"? Why engage a minister or a church space that is not one's own? Whether marriage in the church is appropriate for a couple that has no relationship with the church is not a question our churches have been able to address. All of the questions around the purpose of a church wedding come into play when this issue is raised.

(5) What is the relationship of the state to the church? the minister? the

---

15. *Third New International Merriam-Webster Dictionary* (Springfield, MA: Merriam-Webster, 1986).

16. Wu, "Marriage Rites," p. 217.

17. Nilsson, "Marriage Rites in the Swedish Cultural Context," p. 215.

couple? Lutherans in Scandinavia understood marriage to be a social contract blessed by the priest.

(6) How might the conflict between "literal" and "liberal/biblical" interpretation surrounding divorce be honored in the wedding rite? A theological conundrum exists about language that is disingenuous in a culture that accepts divorce while retaining its denial in the language of the marriage rite, for example, "till death parts us. . . ." How does or might the liturgical language engage this disjunction by accepting or opposing cultural norms?

(7) Is marriage, like baptism, marriage into the catholic church, such that the site of the rite is irrelevant to the larger relationship being enacted? This issue concerns a couple's status geographically, because in the United States some states acknowledge same-sex marriages while others do not.

(8) How are wedding practices affected by economic and consumer-oriented forces? We have discussed the influence of the dress. In recent decades, a "unity candle" has come to be very popular. Although of unknown origin, it is presumed to be a twentieth-century invention. The couple uses two candles already in flame to light a single, larger candle. This practice either has no basis in Scripture, or it is based on Matthew 5:16 ("let your light so shine") in which case it might become part of the liturgy to emphasize the couple's community-building relationships or offer a Quaker-like reference to the light within each individual.[18] The Roman Catholic bishops suggest that its use could only be relevant to the Christian wedding if the individual candles are lit from the paschal candle, and the unity candle does not rest on the altar table, perhaps offering a way to address a contextual matter in order to embed a theological promise in it.

There is much room in these questions for the church to find a broad vision of its purpose. Might Christ Jesus, given for the sake of the life of the world, "baptize" even a wedding dress so elaborate that the bride cannot be seated while wearing it? Klassen writes: "Memories of God and prayer are absent from the accounts of most women . . . I have interviewed. But they *did* gather meaning from the things of this earth: dresses, music and flowers created the environment in which to make the passage from girl to woman."[19]

When we ask what it means for a couple to gather with family and friends in the church building for the wedding in thrall to cultural attach-

---

18. Jeffrey A. Truscott, "What Are the Essentials of the Christian Marriage Service?" *Currents in Theology and Mission* 31, no. 5 (October 2004): 366.

19. Klassen, "Practicing Conflict," p. 233.

ments that seem to pull the focus away from worship, it may be possible to imagine that in their desire for the church's blessing (or even simply its architecture), the couple is collapsing the distinction and opposition between worship and culture by bringing the cultural trappings into the church. Could the church see in a couple's request to be wed in the church an articulation of the import of their relationship even when there is no discernible connection between the ceremony and the gospel proclamation?

In Western culture, where so little attention is paid to passage from one life stage to another, the church might challenge itself to find in the wedding (not a universal ritual, but available to most and practiced by many) an avenue toward the proclamation of God's real love for creation: that earth itself with its flowers, fabrics, and instruments of wood and string, skin and metal, is honored and adored when two people declare their promises surrounded by special ritual attention. Perhaps the crown has taken on shapes available in silk, lace, and candle flames.

Because "ritual is truly a *site* of conflict," it is capable of helping participants negotiate power relationships, thereby transforming lives.[20] By holding tension without resolving it, ritual practice gives people space in which to "enact their complex relationships and feel conflicting emotions."[21] This is the gift of liturgy: to gather the people together in order that all might hear from a wisdom beyond ourselves and be nurtured in it. Perhaps the church's task is to see in the wedding's offering up of culture a gift from the culture to the church.

Healing

The LWF essays offer a snapshot of diverse and changing experiences of healing. One essay demonstrates the evolution of the healing rite, from a focus on healing as an intellectual aid to help the sick person understand illness and learn to bear it (primarily acute illness) to healing as a pastoral rite within the Sunday assembly.[22] The change emphasizes Christ's presence with the ill person in the community of the faithful.[23]

This development, however, does not address the pervasive connection

20. Klassen, "Practicing Conflict," p. 238.
21. Klassen, "Practicing Conflict," p. 239.
22. Paul Nelson, "Healing Rites for Serious Chronic Illness in the North American Context," in Stauffer, ed., *Baptism, Rites of Passage, and Culture*, pp. 98-99.
23. Nelson, "Healing Rites," p. 102 — referring to "Service of the Word for Healing" and

made in North American culture between a person's condition and his or her worth. Noting the all-too-common assertion that circumstances are "all part of God's plan," Paul Nelson urges that healing rites contend with what are either "culturally conditioned or distorted popular religious" assertions about illness.[24] The focus of a healing rite should reorient those in need so that, despite the illness and inability to function in the way of healthy persons, those who are ill understand that they have value.

Other essays, raising issues endemic to healing, underscore how closely the shape of the rite is influenced by its intended purposes and the theological underpinnings of its hopes. Healing rites in Argentina, Central Africa, and Madagascar reveal the importance of an illness's origins for tailoring the "cure" to remedy the underlying cosmic cause of disease.[25] For many cultures — and for the church — healing is tied to relationships. Being whole requires belonging to community. According to some, if a healing rite intends a "cure," it may be a one-time event. If it intends to "heal," it may be considered part of a process, perhaps even taking a long time.[26] Clearly, the purpose of a healing rite invites multiple measurements of success. The church's response to Jesus' command to "heal the sick" depends on the church's understanding of the rite's real goal.[27]

Anscar Chupungco's essay separates the healing needs from remedies by limiting healing rites to concern for physical sickness (including psychological needs) rather than spiritual needs (or social, economic, or political needs). The latter, he wrote, call for "pastoral guidance and perhaps the rite of reconciliation," but not necessarily a healing rite.[28] This view is helped by Frederick Gaiser's reading of the ten lepers — all of whom are cured, while only one is also healed. For that one, it is not the temple priests, "who define social status, but Jesus" to whom he returns.[29] Similarly, in his summary,

---

"Laying on of Hands and Anointing the Sick," in *Occasional Services: A Companion to Lutheran Book of Worship* (Minneapolis: Augsburg, 1982), pp. 89-102.

24. Nelson, "Healing Rites," p. 96.

25. Péri Rasolondraibe, "Healing Ministry in Madagascar," in Stauffer, ed., *Baptism, Rites of Passage, and Culture*, p. 134. Writing from a Malagasy perspective, Rasolondraibe refers to the understanding that sickness is caused by a rupture "in the fabric of life."

26. Rasolondraibe, "Healing Ministry in Madagascar," p. 137.

27. Healing may be integration of the parts of the self toward reconciliation to God's will. Frederick J. Gaiser, *Healing in the Bible: Theological Insight for Christian Ministry* (Grand Rapids: Baker Academic, 2010), pp. 179, 243.

28. Anscar Chupungco, OSB, "Baptism, Marriage, Healing, and Funerals: Principles and Criteria for Inculturation," in Stauffer, ed., *Baptism, Rites of Passage, and Culture*, p. 63.

29. Gaiser, *Healing in the Bible*, p. 181-83.

Marcus Felde defines healing as overcoming "the separateness that often accompanies being sick by a renewal of the ties that bind us together in Christ."[30] These are all themes that persist today, particularly asking: When is healing prayer not reconciliation? When is reconciliation not healing? How should the church navigate the difference between healing and curing?

In recent years the church has seen a proliferation of healing rites for myriad disorders that call for pastoral responses.[31] Recognizing the many ways people are malformed by life circumstances and choices (addictions, sexual and other abuse, miscarriage, regretted decisions, grieving, and traumas of all kinds), the church has developed healing rites to address an increasing number of particular concerns. While this can be a welcome way for the church to open its doors, acknowledge the pain of a broken world, address injustices, and embrace those who are in need, the theological challenge of focus on the individual may invite renewed attention to the corporate nature of healing — the role of reorientation and the radical move away from isolation toward belonging. Questions about rites for healing persist.

Historically

However delicate the matter, God has called the church to engage in rites of passage regarding healing. Jesus himself healed many in his travels (Matt. 4:23-24) and was sought after by the sick and by those with "unclean spirits" (Mark 3:7-11), who recognized in him a power greater than themselves (Luke 6:17-18). Jesus commanded the disciples to "cure the sick, raise the dead, cleanse the leper, cast out demons . . ." (Matt. 10:8; Luke 10:9). A mark of the sheep (i.e., as distinct from the goats) is, among other things, care for the sick (Matt. 25:31-46).

How was the church to do that caring? Jesus' used physical presence, laying on of hands, spittle, and direct address to demons. The church, it may be said, translated Jesus' practices into its own. As early as the second century, the *Apostolic Tradition (AT)* sanctioned laying on of hands and blessing for bishops, presbyters, deacons, certain confessors, persons being exorcized, catechu-

---

30. Marcus Felde, "Summary on Healing Rites," in Stauffer, ed., *Baptism, Rites of Passage, and Culture*, p. 147.
31. See Janet S. Peterman, *Speaking to Silence: New Rites for Christian Worship and Healing* (Louisville: Westminster John Knox, 2007).

mens, and the bread and wine at the holy meal.[32] Hand-laying conferred a blessing. In a section of the *AT* concerning spiritual gifts and the church's appropriate response, we learn who may be blessed to pray over and anoint the sick: "If someone says, 'I have received the gift of healing in a revelation,' the hand is not imposed upon that person. The facts themselves will show whether such a person has spoken the truth."[33] This seems to indicate that no special blessing — and certainly no ordination — was conferred on persons who self-selected as healers. The designation was to come from the church.

Although the index to *Worship in the Early Church* does not contain a section called "healing," we do find mention of ritual actions relevant to what today are common healing practices: prayer, laying on of hands, use of anointing oil, and a gathering of at least two persons.[34] An exception to the notion that someone other than the sufferer "performs" the healing rite is found in Augustine's *City of God*, where he writes of a woman who "was freed from a devil" by anointing herself with oil while a presbyter prayed on her behalf.[35] (It might be argued that the intercessor is the presider in this case.) Regarding healing as reconciliation, a letter written in 601 by Pope Gregory I describes the rite appropriate to those whose heresies had been of varying degrees and required different rituals, either laying on of hands, anointing with oil, or profession of faith.[36] Despite our inability to know exactly how any given rite was enacted, we can see in the continued use of prayer, hands, anointing oil, and at least two persons gathered together, marks of a treasured heritage that comes to us from Scripture, ancient church documents, papal correspondence, and other writings.

Challenges Remaining

To pray over people who are ill, to bless anointing oil for the purpose of healing, and to go to the church for healing — all these entail stepping out

---

32. Lawrence J. Johnson, ed., *Worship in the Early Church: An Anthology of Historical Sources,* vol. 1 (Collegeville, MN: Liturgical Press, 2009), pp. 617-26.

33. Johnson, *Worship in the Early Church,* 1:640.

34. The index does contain "burial" and "marriage/wedding," and though "viaticum" appears, it is only for those who are dying.

35. Johnson, *Worship in the Early Church,* 3:2583; Augustine, *City of God, XXII.8* (Penguin Books, 1972), p. 1040.

36. Johnson, *Worship in the Early Church,* 4:4262, from Book IX, Letter 31, "To all the Bishops in Sicily."

in faith. Healing rites do not always result in physical health. Medical and technological advances have brought healing to many people who otherwise would not have relief. Yet we cannot explain every healing, nor can we address the question of why some are healed while others are not. Inherent in the church's practice of healing, therefore, is an inescapable tension between the command to heal and its failure.

Jesus healed many people, but not everyone. One response of the church has been to distinguish between "healing" and "curing." Orthodox and Roman Catholic theologians, especially, have articulated the goal of healing as renewal of the ill person's relationship with the body of Christ, a purpose that does not expect a "cure" but addresses the ultimate needs of the sufferer without dismissing the very real pain. This is a transcultural response. Where the church understands that God's work can be effected through human vocation, healing rites do not intend to subsume or replace reasoned, scientific, medical help for the sick. Changes in mission work in the last century speak to the church's embrace of rational modes of healing that do not stand in opposition to prayer. Indeed, the church can use human tools that actualize physical healing. Further complicating the characterization of the healing rite is the fact that, because healing "is not a specifically Christian topic or issue in and of itself," the church is called "to work toward an unbiased theological attitude toward healing," one that is appropriately integrated into the church's ministries.[37] However, where cultural assumptions assign the cause of an illness to the victim or the victim's family, the church is called to oppose unsupportable blame in order that the gospel can be proclaimed. This is a countercultural responsibility. The church's witness in those places articulates (1) God's desire for health and wholeness; (2) God's care for all people and all creation; (3) God's approval of human reasoning; and (4) God's call for justice. Because of the complex of issues at stake, healing rites need to be done carefully: both those in need and those addressing the need are in jeopardy if the expected outcome is frustrated. As it enacts healing rites, the church is also in perpetual need of its own healing — an ever-deepening theological embrace of the meaning of healing — in order to live within the contradictions that exist between accomplishment (or so may a change in health be deemed) and failure (as it is perceived). This position of

37. Christoffer H. Grundmann, "Healing — A Challenge to Church and Theology," *International Review of Mission* 40:356-357 (Jan.-Apr. 2001): 39; "He Sent Them Out to Heal! Reflections on the Healing Ministry of the Church," *Currents in Theology and Mission* 33, no. 5 (October 2006): 372-78.

life lived in ambiguity is much helped by the construction of the pastor's spirituality described by Gordon Lathrop as intensely wedded to liturgical practice.[38] Lathrop locates the pastor's spirituality in the tensions created by the central symbols of Christian liturgical practice. Just so might we understand the church's relationship with healing ministries as they are tied to the central symbols and borne out in their midst. Because the true power resident in the incarnate world — capable of healing the world's many ills — is in Christ Jesus' life, death, resurrection, and ascension, the church is always in danger of losing sight of its own healing strength. Situated in cultures that look to human agency for validation of God's approval, the church stands in need of perpetual humility in the face of mystery.[39]

Responding to liturgical issues of the twentieth century (still resonant in the twenty-first), Alexander Schmemann addresses the need for the church to regain a sense of the intrinsic healing power of the sacraments and a eucharistic life and mission.

> Here is a man suffering on his bed of pain and the Church comes to him to perform the sacrament of healing. . . . The Church does not come to restore *health* in this man. . . . The Church comes to take this man into the Love, the Light and the Life of Christ. It comes not merely to "comfort" him in his sufferings, not to "help" him, but to make him a *martyr*, a *witness* to Christ in his very sufferings. A martyr is one who beholds "the heavens opened, and the Son of Man standing on the right hand of God" (Acts 7:56). A martyr is one for whom God is not another — and the last — chance to stop the awful pain; God is his very life, and thus everything in his life comes to God, and ascends to the fullness of Love.[40]

Schmemann makes a bold statement here about the expectations regarding healing rites: that actual, physical health is not the goal; rather, it is the presence of Christ. In this understanding, healing is a reorientation, a reminder of the sufferer's true identity in and through suffering as a witness.[41]

38. Gordon Lathrop, *The Pastor: A Spirituality* (Minneapolis: Fortress Press, 2006), pp. 13, 15, 132-33.

39. Christoffer H. Grundmann, "Healing, Faith, and Liturgy: A Theological Reflection upon the Church's Ministry of Healing in the Context of Worship," lecture given at the Institute of Liturgical Studies, Valparaiso University, Valparaiso, IN, 2007.

40. Alexander Schmemann, *For the Life of the World* (Crestwood, NY: St. Vladimir's Seminary Press, 1988), p. 103.

41. See also Nelson, "Healing Rites," pp. 93-94.

MELINDA A. QUIVIK

This may not be the theological statement about healing acceptable to all communions, but it is a faithful starting point for this exploration.

Similarly, Lizette Larson-Miller's exploration of the use of anointing oil in care of the sick — especially following the liturgical changes in the healing rite resulting from Vatican II — begins by asking whether healing is a sacrament or a prayer practice. She concludes with the need for the anointing to be done in the context of sustained and prayerful attention to the sick.[42] The late-twentieth-century changes in the use of anointing oil made it available beyond those who are dying. Larson-Miller calls for continued reflection on "how the experience of sickness gives rise to new understandings of our participation in Christ" and how best the church might enact its ministry in those circumstances.[43]

The reflection called for may well embrace what an Orthodox theologian calls "the sacramentality of sickness itself . . . which is revealed in the sick person who lives through this experience . . . [and] who through this experience discovers God in a particular way and reveals this to the community."[44] Just as the holy meal of bread and wine manifests the mystery of the incarnation and the unity of the church through Christ, the act of anointing prayer relieves the hell of loneliness, pain, and fear by lifting up the presence of the ultimate healer.[45] "The purpose of holy unction is . . . to communicate spiritual power for the integration of body, soul, and spirit so that the trials of sickness — whether spiritual or physical — may be borne with courage, hope, and fortitude."[46] The power of healing prayer, along with that of bread and wine — through touch in anointing with oil, laying on of hands, nourishment in food and drink — bring "liberation from everything that fragments and damages the human person and separates us from the Author of life."[47] It is in this sense that we need to consider healing rites as a renewal of baptismal identity.

42. Lizette Larson-Miller, *The Sacrament of Anointing of the Sick* (Collegeville, MN: Liturgical Press, 2005), p. 134.

43. Larson-Miller, *The Sacrament of Anointing*, p. 136.

44. Alkiviadis C. Calivas, "Healing of Communities and Persons through the Sacraments," *Greek Orthodox Theological Review* 51, nos. 1-4 (Winter 2006): 137, quoting David N. Power, *Worship: Culture and Theology* (Washington, DC: Pastoral Press, 1990), p. 249.

45. "Holy communion . . . unites us to Christ but also to one another. We are made to realize sacramentally the eschatological mystery of unity in diversity." Calivas, "Healing of Communities," p. 143.

46. Calivas, "Healing of Communities," p. 137.

47. Calivas, "Healing of Communities," p. 139.

Baptismal Identity

At a 1972 conference on the liturgy of Christian illness and death, Thomas Talley said: "The meaning of every illness is dying, and every healing is resurrection."[48] Having discussed the scriptural bases for healing rites — the question of whether the ordained or lay Christian can rightly offer them, the change from the Tridentine focus on healing at the deathbed to the Second Vatican Council's emphasis on healing as address to the separateness felt by the ill, and the idea that healing is a sacrament — Talley summarizes healing in baptismal terms. Baptismal identity is implicit in his assertion that illness is dying and healing is resurrection. Recovery of health is, in very real ways, rebirth — new life.

At a yet deeper level, Talley reminds us that the goal of a healing rite is tied to the passion of Christ. Talley writes that, just as penance addresses the reconciliation of one who is separated,

> the object of the rite of anointing can be understood as renewal of the baptismal anointing by which each of us is *christos* so that the suffering and separation of sickness become identified as participation in the *pascha Christi*. By such anointing, *anamnesis* is made of the passage of Christ through death to life and of the patient's consecration to that mystery.[49]

The goal, in other words, is a deepened understanding of life in Christ. Such a conception of healing opens the rite to many forms of inculturation, brings to the sickbed the power and promise of the read and preached word of God and the visible word of the holy meal, and shows forth the liminality of the baptismal life as an image of the life of one in need.

The Chicago Statement on Worship and Culture places healing rites solidly in the context of baptism.[50] The focus on baptism suggests that churches might best be served by placing baptismal promises at the foundation as we consider a rite's transcultural, contextual, cross-cultural, and countercultural expressions. "Baptism always introduces the newly baptized into life in a local community of Christians, but in communion with *all* the churches of God."[51] By reason of the fact that baptismal identity is both tran-

48. Thomas Talley, "Healing: Sacrament or Charism?" *Worship* 46, no. 9 (November 1972): 525, a paper given at the University of Notre Dame.

49. Talley, "Healing: Sacrament or Charism?" p. 525.

50. Stauffer, ed., *Baptism, Rites of Passage, and Culture*, pp. 19-20.

51. Stauffer, ed., *Baptism, Rites of Passage, and Culture*, p. 14; see also Gaiser, *Healing in the Bible*, p. 244.

scendent of culture (and cultures) and is necessarily particular to place, it is in the power and promise of baptism that healing acquires its appropriate role in the life of the church. Rites of passage, especially during sickness, are meant to envelope the one in need in the embrace of the body of Christ.

Funeral

At some point, sickness may turn into death. And for everyone, because death is inevitable, the funeral rite is powerful and personal. We will all bury loved ones and tend to those who are bereaved. Christians do this in numerous ways on the basis of what is most expedient, what is normal practice in our various contexts, and what the Christian community has to say at the time of death. There are no fixed burial rites in the way of a liturgy celebrating the sacraments of baptism and holy communion, though many of our denominations have set forth an order of worship for funerals. However, the increasing secularization of our families has brought many people to the funeral home rather than the church. Yet even there, in a space dedicated to religious and nonreligious observance alike, the witness of Christians is often asserted. The questions that arise about funerals bring together fragile needs that either comfort or confound because the theological matters that lie behind what is said or omitted in a funeral are so very important.

Looking at the Rite Historically

How we have understood death has influenced how we mourn and what the funeral asserts. The diverse ways Scripture depicts death show us that, at base, our ancestors honored the deceased by taking care to bury the body. Precisely what was done is unknown. Metaphorically, Scripture images death as the enemy, as injustice, as punishment for sin, as the gate to eternal life, and as a hard reality defeated by God in the resurrection of Christ Jesus.[52] The various ways in which people have imagined the realm beyond death have overtly and covertly affected our views of death and the language we use to speak of it.

In the Middle East, Europe, and North America, the earliest practice

52. Melinda A. Quivik, *A Christian Funeral: Witness to the Resurrection* (Minneapolis: Augsburg Fortress, 2005).

was to wash the body at home or the place of death, carry the body in procession to the gravesite, and bury the body, accompanied by psalms and Scripture readings. By the fifth century, on the way to the gravesite, the body was taken first to the church for a service of prayer, psalms, chants, responses, and Scripture readings from Job. The history of funeral orders after that period primarily amended this basic structure with additional readings, hymns, prayers, and gestures. According to the Chicago Statement, worldwide Christian practice has included washing, holding vigil with word and Eucharist, commendation, and procession to the grave with psalms and singing.[53]

The earliest funeral orders image the mourners accompanying the deceased on the journey from earthly life to life eternal. The prayers asked God for release of the person's spirit, for safety from evil spirits who would otherwise thwart the journey, and for the help of the saints. Death as passage assumed God's promise of resurrection and meant that the mourners rejoiced at their loved one's entrance into final Christian life while also trembling before the promised judgment. In some ways this was a full picture of the two realities — life and death — at war with each other in lives of faith.

During the medieval era, with the ascendance of a view of death as punishment, sorrow and mourning overtook the sense of joy in the resurrection. Lost was the tension expressed in the earlier funeral by holding honesty about failures together with hope for forgiveness. Prayers focused on asking God to deliver the dead from hell, emphasizing penitence and fear of death. Commensurate with that concern, communion liturgies came to be held *in behalf of* the dead, leading to the sixteenth-century Reformers' revision of burial rites.

Reformation changes to the funeral sought to return the liturgy to caring for the bereaved rather than focusing on the fate of the deceased. Martin Luther and others urged an end to wailing and dirges, turning instead to comfort, forgiveness, and words of hope for the resurrection of the dead through Christ Jesus. While the Reformation churches took various paths in distancing themselves from medieval foci, they continued to read a common body of biblical texts at funerals, asserting the transformation promised in Christ, who "makes all things new," the power of baptism, and the promise of life eternal with all the saints.[54]

Mid-twentieth-century changes that were spurred by the Second Vati-

---

53. Stauffer, ed., *Baptism, Rites of Passage, and Culture*, p. 21.
54. Through the centuries, among the most beloved and common Scripture readings

can Council helped to solidify these shifts. In 1965 the Church of England Liturgical Commission laid out five purposes of the funeral:

- to bury with reverence;
- to be honest about the death and judgment of all;
- to proclaim the resurrection of our risen life in Christ here and hereafter;
- to commend the deceased into the care of the Lord; and
- to make real the communion of saints as the eternal unity of Christian people, living and dead.[55]

Taken together, these purposes assert the church's response to death as it has been expressed since the beginning. They have shaped the funeral. These purposes can serve as a plumbline for noticing the vast differences that exist with funeral issues in all cultures, for they are the transcultural bedrock of Christian witness.

LWF Essays

The summary essay for the LWF papers on funerals point to problems with burial of the dead that come primarily from the increased secularization of funerals. Felde mentions funerals that have no references to Christianity, the decreasing use of Christian worship spaces for funerals, and the difficulty of incorporating people who have no religious background.

Today we witness the loss of funeral rites in favor of life celebrations that may have no need of the church.[56] If a funeral is planned so that its intent is primarily or solely to rejoice over someone's life, it may fail to honestly depict the truth about death: that while we mourn, we also give thanks for the

---

at funerals are Job 19:25-27, Ps. 23, John 11:25-26; 12:23-26, Rom. 6:3-5, 9; 14:27, 1 Cor. 15:51-57, Col. 3:1-4, and Rev. 21:1-4, 7.

55. Church of England Liturgical Commission, *Alternative Services: Second Series* (1965).

56. Thomas G. Long, *Accompany Them with Singing: The Christian Funeral* (Louisville: Westminster John Knox, 2009). See also Hans H. Krech, "Funeral Rites in the German Cultural Context," in *LWF Studies: Baptism, Rites of Passage, and Culture* (Geneva: LWF, 1998), p. 169. In 1999, Krech noted that "the isolation of individuals in the urban society continues not only in life but also in death. The number of anonymous burials or sea-burials is constantly increasing."

deceased. What is a Christian funeral in the context of these forces? Felde answers that it is to attend to "the connections between the funeral situation and the rites of Baptism and Eucharist," since all are rites of passage.[57] He sees, in specific funeral practices mentioned in the LWF essays, images of Christian symbols related to life passages. Baptism, for example, is echoed both in the three shovels of dirt thrown on the coffin in Sweden and in the general practice of washing the body; in Germany and North America, the meal has become more common as part of the funeral.[58]

Questions remain, however, over whether such assertions can accomplish the goal of the funeral for those who are not part of the church. It is one thing for Felde to say that the funeral "is a time for us to be true in our witness to the hope that is in us."[59] It is another thing to make sure that witness is intelligible in a way that can give comfort to those who are estranged from the church's proclamation.

Challenges Remaining

The conflicting values of worship and culture acquire little resolution at funerals. While it is entirely possible to bury the body with reverence whether the funeral is held in a church sanctuary or in a funeral home with few religious symbols, the concern to tell the truth about life and death and to comfort the bereaved with words of hope cannot be accomplished in the same ways. The church uses imagery that may not be amenable to non-Christians. Proclaiming hope in the resurrection requires immersion in the world of the narratives and symbols that embody it.

This is problematic for Christians because the increasingly secularized funeral expectations — use of the funeral home, inclusion or omission of the body, and the actual burial (due to distances and time), divorce from the church, and others — impinge on what the church can offer at the time of death and burial. It is often difficult, for example, to sing hymns that may comfort some when others will not know the song and not be accustomed to singing.

Even for the church's own witness, thorny issues persist. As an occasional service, the funeral is unique. Hans Krech reminds us, "A funeral is a

---

57. Felde, "Summary on Healing Rites," p. 189.
58. Felde, "Summary on Healing Rites," p. 190.
59. Felde, "Summary on Healing Rites," p. 189.

very *special,* very *personal* worship. Present is the whole life of this one human being who died, and as well the unique and singular situation of the mourners."[60] The Christian funeral, then, is common to all, borne by the church, ripe with hope resident in eschatological imagery, yet personal. This cluster of factors is rich with tensions that are delicate to navigate. Krech pointed to the role of the funeral business taking care of burial and the use of newspaper death notices as the new place of burial.[61] In the twenty-first century we have seen the use of internet tributes to the dead. Is this yet a new place of (virtual) burial? Funerals have multiple purposes between such disparate goals as those outlined above in the Anglican study (to comfort, proclaim the gospel, and commend) and those of a South African funeral described by Biyela (to comfort, to "liberate people from the fear of sorcery," and to "teach people to accept death as part of life").[62] For cultures in which, as is said in southern Africa, "the human is a human through other humans," the funeral is a time when the pain of loss is felt by everyone in the village. One purpose in such a situation is for expression of that pain, sharing it, and releasing it. For cultures in which blame for a death is needed — whether the people blame witchcraft or blame God by saying God wills all things — the funeral's purpose is called to address unhelpful, even unfaithful, ideas (pp. 156-57). Where the church's and the culture's goals for a ritual event differ dramatically, the result may serve only to disappoint everyone.

What is the role of the church with respect to the funeral business, and vice versa? Given the increasing use of funeral homes, the rotation of pastors covering funerals, the costs, and the varying receptiveness of funeral directors to church practices, the church needs to discern how and where to work alongside these important partners.

How does the church proclaim the resurrection to people who cannot fathom it, or don't like it? If Felde is right to call for greater sacramental focus, how is this reconciled with offering comfort when the table is not open to everyone? Funerals are attended by a great mixture of people of faith, diverse religious traditions, and few, if any, traditions held in common.

In how the liturgy identifies and engages the communion of saints, what is being said about the body of Christ, living and dead? If prayers in the funeral speak of the deceased in a way that asks God's blessing and welcome,

60. Krech, "Funeral Rites," p. 166.

61. Krech, "Funeral Rites," p. 170.

62. Musawenkosi D. Biyela, "Funeral Rites in the South African Cultural Context," in Stauffer, ed., *Baptism, Rites of Passage, and Culture,* p. 154. Hereafter, page references to this essay appear in parentheses within the text.

is that expressed relationship between the living and the dead an acceptable or unacceptable depiction? What, in the end, is prayer if it includes or excludes the saints who are gone from earthly life? What does the burial of non-Christians mean in a Christian liturgy? Should a commendation be said at the funeral of a unbaptized person?

How is death imaged liturgically and culturally? What is the mourner's relationship with death? Is death a part of life, or opposed to life, or both? How do these perspectives affect the funeral liturgy? What is God's role in death? In South Africa, people may ask, "Did an angry ancestor take the life of the child? Or is it the work of a witch?" (p. 154). Regarding superstitions — religious and secular — that persist, how does the church either work with them or deny them?

If the meal will be held, what does this sacrament mean for those who are not baptized (the deceased and the mourners)? What possibilities exist liturgically to encourage a fuller understanding of the meal? According to Biyela, ritual cleansing after the burial usurps the place of Christian symbols, and for that reason the African church needs "to connect the Means of Grace with both life and death" (p. 163). This challenge might well be leveled at all churches. To make what this question is getting at more clear, some cultural and religious funeral practices focus on purification rituals, seeming to ignore the sacraments. Biyela argues that the funeral needs to express more clearly and completely the sacramental cleansing so that cultural practices can be understood to have been subsumed by Christian proclamation. "The African funeral liturgy must offer a Christology that will make purification rituals redundant" (p. 164). Is it the faith of the deceased or the faith of the church that is at stake?

The "green funeral" movement challenges Christians today to avoid chemicals (such as those used in embalming) and to encase the body in readily degradable containers (cardboard, shrouds, wood) rather than metal caskets and vaults. In some parts of southern Africa the bereaved plant a forest on the grave and see to it that no animal is killed or fruit eaten there except by other animals and birds. This practice is a powerful witness of honor to the earth and a challenge to the rest of us (p. 159).

In addition, the church may be called to articulate the ritual meaning of (1) cultural practices like leaving food and other objects in the coffin, (2) holding the funeral without the body and without ashes, (3) setting out a closed or open coffin, and (4) introducing nonreligious objects into the funeral (balloons, picture displays, gestures that connect the bereaved with the assembly). In additional, the culture's acceptance or rejection of cremation influences the church's funeral rite. Where ashes are used, the need for burial space easily points to the creation of columbaria beside or within church buildings — another way to image the communion of saints.

Baptismal Identity

With regard to the funeral's purposes that have ecumenical import, only one of those purposes is available to both church and secular society: to bury the body with reverence. Honesty about death and judgment will be differently handled by church and secular forces. Only the church can proclaim the resurrection. Only the church can commend the deceased to God. And only in the church can the communion of saints become for the mourners an image of hope and sustained community.[63]

The greater emphasis placed on baptismal identity in the funeral rite in recent decades is evidence of a steadily growing understanding that baptism's claim of belonging to Christ is the most profound source of comfort in times of greatest sorrow.[64] "When the church gathers to mark the end of life, Christ-crucified and risen is the witness of worship, the strength of mutual consolation, and the hope of healing."[65] Where the funeral is allowed to comfort with its most treasured vision resting in the crucified and risen one, the needs of the cultures in which the church finds itself might be most helpful as contextual additions to the service lest they convey the import that should only be accorded to foundational structures. Where the cultures' expectations obscure the proclamation of Christian hope, the funeral becomes less able to comfort.

The questions put to the church by its encounter with nonbelievers may be the spur Christians need for finding a language best able to speak at the time of death. "Our liturgy must . . . let Jesus Christ dialogue with people where they are and confirm what is right while also correcting what is wrong" (Biyela, p. 154). In keeping with the necessity for tension to exist in order for truth to be revealed, the hardest tensions to hold together may be those that approach the edge of the abyss. The funeral is rightly, then, a most propitious moment for evangelism, for speaking the good news of Christ

---

63. Quivik, *A Christian Funeral*, pp. 43-57.

64. See esp. *Evangelical Lutheran Worship*, pp. 279-85 and *Book of Common Worship*, pp. 911-27. Both of these rites begin with Romans 6 and include other references to baptism throughout.

65. *Evangelical Lutheran Worship*, p. 279.

Jesus, for articulating what baptism calls us to, and for welcoming the stranger into the communion of saints.

BIBLIOGRAPHY

Calivas, Alkiviadis C. "Healing of Communities and Persons through the Sacraments: A Theological Reflection." *Greek Orthodox Theological Review* 51, nos. 1-4 (Winter 2006): 119-53.
Church of England Liturgical Commission. *Alternative Services.* Second Series. 1965.
Evangelical Lutheran Church in America. *Evangelical Lutheran Worship.* Minneapolis: Augsburg Fortress, 2005.
Friese, Susanne. "A Consumer Good in the Ritual Process: The Case of the Wedding Dress." *Journal of Ritual Studies* 11, no. 2 (Winter 1997): 47-58.
Gaiser, Frederick J. *Healing in the Bible: Theological Insight for Christian Ministry.* Grand Rapids: Baker Academic, 2010.
Grundmann, Christoffer H. "Healing — A Challenge to Church and Theology." *International Review of Mission* 40, nos. 356-57 (Jan.-Apr. 2001): 26-40.
———. "He Sent Them Out to Heal! Reflections on the Healing Ministry of the Church." *Currents in Theology and Mission* 33, no. 5 (Oct. 2006): 372-78.
Johnson, Lawrence J., ed. *Worship in the Early Church: An Anthology of Historical Sources,* vol. 1. Collegeville, MN: Liturgical Press, 2009.
Klassen, Pamela E. "Practicing Conflict: Weddings as Sites of Contest and Compromise." *The Mennonite Quarterly Review* 72, no. 2 (Apr. 1998): 225-41.
Larson-Miller, Lizette. "Healing: Sacrament or Prayer?" *Anglican Theological Review* 88, no. 3 (Summer 2006): 361-74.
———. *The Sacrament of Anointing of the Sick.* Collegeville, MN: Liturgical Press, 2005.
Lathrop, Gordon W. *The Pastor: A Spirituality.* Minneapolis: Fortress Press, 2006.
Long, Thomas G. *Accompany Them with Singing: The Christian Funeral.* Louisville: Westminster John Knox, 2009.
Peterman, Janet S. *Speaking to Silence: New Rites for Christian Worship and Healing.* Louisville: Westminster John Knox Press, 2007.
Presbyterian Church U.S.A. *Book of Common Worship.* Louisville: Westminster John Knox, 1993.
Prothero, Stephen R. *Purified by Fire: A History of Cremation in America.* Berkeley: University of California Press, 2001.
Quivik, Melinda A. *A Christian Funeral: Witness to the Resurrection.* Minneapolis: Augsburg Fortress, 2005.
Schmemann, Alexander. *For the Life of the World: Sacraments and Orthodoxy.* Crestwood, NY: St. Vladimir's Seminary Press, 1988.

Stauffer, S. Anita, ed. *Baptism, Rites of Passage, and Culture*. Geneva: Lutheran World Federation, 1999.

————. *Christian Worship: Unity in Cultural Diversity*. Geneva: Lutheran World Federation, 1996.

Stevenson, Kenneth. "Marriage Liturgy: Lessons from History." *Anglican Theological Review* 68, no. 3 (July 1986): 225-40.

————. *Nuptial Blessing: A Study of Christian Marriage Rites*. New York: Oxford University Press, 1983.

————. *To Join Together: The Rite of Marriage*. New York: Pueblo, 1987.

Talley, Thomas. "Healing: Sacrament or Charism?" *Worship* 46, no. 9 (Nov. 1972).

Truscott, Jeffrey A. "What Are the Essentials of the Christian Marriage Service?" *Currents in Theology and Mission* 31, no. 5 (October 2004).

van Tongeren, Louis. "Individualizing Ritual: The Personal Dimension in Funeral Liturgy." *Worship* 78, no. 2 (March 2004): 117-38.

Williams, Ritva H. "The Mother of Jesus at Cana: A Social-Science Interpretation of John 2:1-12." *The Catholic Biblical Quarterly* 59, no. 4 (Oct. 1997): 679-92.

These Living Waters: Common Agreement on Mutual Recognition of Baptism by the Roman Catholic and Reformed Churches in Dialogue

COMMON AGREEMENT ON MUTUAL RECOGNITION OF BAPTISM

Roman Catholic–Reformed Church Dialogue (U.S.), contained in *These Living Waters,* and adopted by each of the member communions of the dialogue: the Christian Reformed Church of North America, the Reformed Church in America, the Presbyterian Church (USA), the United Church of Christ, and the U.S. Conference of Catholic Bishops:

1. Together we affirm that, by the sacrament of Baptism, a person is truly incorporated into the body of Christ (1 Cor. 12:13, 27; Eph. 1:22-23), the church. Baptism establishes the bond of unity existing among all who are part of Christ's body and is therefore the sacramental basis for our efforts to move towards visible unity.

2. Together we affirm that Baptism is the sacramental gateway into the Christian life, directed toward the fullness of faith and discipleship in Christ.

3. Together we affirm that incorporation into the universal church by baptism is brought about by celebrating the sacrament within a particular Christian community.

4. Together we affirm that Baptism is to be conferred only once, because those who are baptized are decisively incorporated into the Body of Christ.

5. Together we affirm that baptism is a sacrament of the church, enacted in obedience to the mission confided to it by Christ's own word. For our baptisms to be mutually recognized, water and the scriptural Trinitarian

formula "Father, Son, and Holy Spirit" (Matt. 28:19-20) must be used in the baptismal rite.

6. Together we affirm that the validity of Baptism depends on its celebration according to the apostolic witness by the church and its authorized ministers.

7. Together we affirm, as a sign of our unity and as a witness to ecumenical commitment, the practice of inviting the presence and, where appropriate, the participation of members of our respective communions in the celebration of Baptism. At the same time, we affirm our responsibility to respect the integrity of the distinct baptismal practices of the communions in which the rite of Baptism is administered.

8. Given our mutual recognition of Baptism, we encourage using baptismal registers in the local church community and, when requested by another church for a pastoral need in the life of an individual, providing written attestations of Baptism, including the liturgical formula used. Such cooperation and mutual accountability honors the dignity of the sacrament of Baptism.

The One Wounded, Baptized Body: A Memoir of Participation in the U.S. Reformed–Roman Catholic Dialogue (2003-2010)

Martha Moore-Keish

When I was first invited to represent the Presbyterian Church (USA) in this ecumenical dialogue, I accepted immediately and with delight. I came to the first meeting in Louisville eagerly anticipating an opportunity to work together to advance ecumenical unity — even a tiny step. Seven years later, I had learned that such unity is not something we achieve but something we glimpse — usually at odd, unanticipated moments. And it never comes pure. But when we see the body of Christ united, even for a moment, it is right to give our thanks and praise.

At the first gathering in Louisville, members of the dialogue shared stories about our own ecumenical journeys, revealing just how much we had personally traversed the boundaries between our communions, and how much even those of us who had lived our lives within a single denomination had grown from interaction with the other. Some Roman Catholic participants had grown up Reformed; some Reformed had been deeply affected by Roman Catholic piety. All yearned for our churches to have a deeper understanding of the other. All yearned for our ecclesial bodies to embody greater respect for and connection to the other. All yearned for our churches to witness more clearly to the unity of the body of Christ.

At this first gathering, however, we also confronted the depth of our separation one from another, particularly when it came to the Lord's Supper. In a memorable conversation, one of the Catholic participants clearly affirmed that to say "Amen" when receiving the Eucharist at Mass was to say "Amen" not only to the presence of Christ in the host but also to the priest serving, and to the system of apostolic succession. Ultimately, he explained, to say "Amen" at the Eucharist was to say "Amen" to the authority of the pope. Those of us representing Reformed churches realized at that moment that this ecumenical dialogue was not going to be any easy affirmation of what we have in common, but an excavation of the sharp edges of the divide.

Through the long middle of our dialogue, sharp edges of disagreement emerged not only between our two communions, but also among members of a single communion. At times, for instance, participants with a more systematic theological approach challenged those with a more liturgical approach, asking, "Does this baptismal rite adopted by our tradition actually represent what we believe? Does the apparent convergence of Reformed and Roman Catholic liturgical rites represent genuine progress in agreement, or are we evading significant theological and ecclesiological commitments on which we disagree?" These questions sometimes brought to the surface painful differences of interpretation and approach within communions as we argued over theological sources and hermeneutics in order to articulate our respective views on the sacraments.

The unity of the body of Christ was often hidden in our work, as we struggled to understand one another both within and between our churches. Together with moments of friction, however, there also emerged moments of illumination. One of my own discoveries arose in the process of researching Reformed baptismal rites from the sixteenth century to the present, trying to trace patterns of continuity and change over the centuries. Through this process, amid widely varying sacramental practices, I observed four consistent themes in Reformed baptismal practice: focus on the word of God read and proclaimed at baptism; the centrality of water; emphasis on the ecclesial dimension of baptism; and a strong connection of baptism with nurture. Though these emphases are not unique to Reformed Christians, they have clearly shaped baptismal rites of this communion through the centuries, sometimes in contrast to a perceived lack of such emphasis in other Christian traditions (for instance, the consistent insistence on baptisms being done in the church rather than privately). Seeing these patterns emerge in my own tradition helped to clarify baptismal values from this Christian family that really do persist over time, and which the Reformed might gladly offer as a contribution to the wider ecumenical world.

Another discovery, more difficult to demonstrate conclusively, emerged as we looked at convergences in baptismal and eucharistic practice over the past several decades. Those of us who served as "liturgists" in that dialogue compiled comparative charts of contemporary sacramental practices from the four Reformed churches and the Roman Catholic Church, showing a large degree of convergence in ritual structure — as well as biblical and patristic source material — used in contemporary baptismal and eucharistic rites of all five communions. This fact of ritual convergence was not surprising to those of us who have been engaged in liturgical renewal. The delight emerged for me, however, as we discussed our understandings of the five major themes in eucharistic theology that structured our report "This Bread of Life" (*epiclesis,* anamnesis, presence, sacrifice, and discipleship). It became clear in these conversations that our convergence in practice has truly both reflected and contributed to closer shared faith. Because our prayers more nearly resemble one another, remembering God's mercies and calling on the Spirit, as well as acknowledging Christ's presence and giving thanks for his sacrifice, and because our rites more clearly send us from the table to feed a hungry world, we confess a more common faith in what we do at font and table. Shared practices are helping us understand each other more deeply. Shared understanding, in turn, manifests itself in our common theological statements that go far beyond the sixteenth-century articulations that divided our churches.

A high point of our dialogue arrived in 2010, almost entirely unexpected. Our team had worked mightily on the baptismal report "These Living Waters," including a common agreement on mutual recognition of baptism, and had concluded that work in 2008. As we worked, we hoped that all our churches could receive this modest but important affirmation: that we do indeed recognize one another's baptisms as valid. For two years after the completion of this document, however, and in spite of the careful work of the Catholic members of our team, the reception process languished. It appeared that our work could not be officially recognized by the U.S. Conference of Catholic Bishops. Many of us lamented that so much time and effort had gone into work that would not be received. But we moved on, with some discouragement, to the Eucharist phase of our discussions.

Two years later, however, through a process mysterious to all of us on the dialogue team, the USCCB took a historic action: they passed the Common Agreement on Baptism by a vote of 95 percent. Astonished, we realized that this was the first time this body of American bishops had ever adopted an ecumenical statement on its own. With that action, they declared, with their Reformed sisters and brothers, that "baptism establishes the bond of unity existing among all who are part of Christ's body and is therefore the sacramental basis for our efforts to move towards visible unity." In that moment I realized that the unity of the church is not — and never can be — something we simply achieve through our own careful and steady efforts. The efforts were important, but the glimpse of the one body of Christ was simply a gift.

Through conflict and celebration, our dialogue also brought deeper awareness of our struggles, both personal and ecclesial. Each time we gathered, we shared news: of personal struggles, of illness and death, of diminished trust in our churches and fear for the future of our institutions. We shared this pain in prayers with and for one another. As we sat at tables together wrestling with draft documents, perfecting language and despairing of whether our efforts would ever make a difference, we were — despite ourselves — building a community of trust.

At our last meeting we joined together in a service of reaffirmation of baptism, a service that stands in my memory as the culmination of our work together. Not for the public, not for publication, this simple gathering around water, prayer, and the word marked our common identity and our common faith. Without ignoring our divides, and in painful awareness of those who had died during the years of our dialogue, as well as those who had left our company for other reasons, we stood around a glass bowl in the reflected autumn light and gave thanks:

> As those who have been baptized by water and Spirit,
> and united in the love of Christ, we offer our prayers.
> Eternal God,
> creator of all that is and yet will be,
> in the fullness of time you sent your Son to redeem the world,
> and daily you send the Holy Spirit to bring new life and peace.
> Faithful to the exhortation of Jesus,
> we ask you to send your Holy Spirit in abundance
> upon all those who have been part of this dialogue.
> We give thanks . . . .

At this point we named the people gathered around the water, looking one another in the eyes, with memories of the arguments and the prayers. We also named those who had died, whose words had shaped our work, and whose commitment to ecumenical unity inspired our own efforts. We named those who had left our company through the years, whose presence we had come to cherish, and whose absence was palpable. We recited the names, and then continued:

As we end our years of dialogue together, we commit our work into
    your hands.
Bless and prosper it according to your will,
that these efforts might nurture the unity of your church in the world.
Pour out your Spirit also upon the people in each of our churches,
that through Word and Sacrament,
we may continue to grow in deeper communion with your Son
and with each other,
until that day when we can share in full communion around your table.
We ask this in the name of Jesus Christ, our risen Savior,
who with the Spirit dwells with you, one God, now and forever. Amen.

Around that water, in that prayer, I glimpsed the one body of Christ,
wounded and whole. Here, perhaps, was a kind of unity that I did not know
to anticipate at our first meeting: not a triumphant step forward in ecumenical progress, but a living, breathing community gathered at the font, together giving thanks and praise. This simple, unadorned act embodied what
all our years and pages of work had sought to nurture: true, honest, and
mutual recognition of baptism.

An Eyewitness to the Seventh Round of the Roman Catholic–Reformed Churches' National Ecumenical Dialogue on Baptism and Eucharist

Joyce Ann Zimmerman, CPPS

Among the many opening comments and introductions during the first meeting of the national ecumenical dialogue between the Roman Catholic Church and the Reformed Churches, one stands out in my mind that I still think about today, several years after we have completed our work. The comment was that, no matter the disagreements and difficulties, the differences and tensions, the agreements and convergences, we would emerge from this dialogue as friends. I thought the comment odd: this would hardly be an outcome I would expect in such a formal, professional event. Indeed, though, it did happen. At a very deep level, that marked the trust and affirmation of this dialogue. My personal reflection on our almost eight years together, the processes and interchanges, attempts to flesh out this "friend" outcome through three motifs: understandings, surprises, and consensus.

Understandings

Three initial understandings about ourselves and time together clearly shaped the scope of the work and the two documents we produced: "These Living Waters" (on baptism) and "The Bread of Life" (on the Eucharist/ Lord's Supper). The first understanding was that we agreed to disagree, and we chose to focus on what we can affirm in order to move forward the dialogue. In no way did this sweep under the carpet our differences, which were often extended; occasionally heated discussions ensued concerning thorny theological points. From the outset we simply acknowledged the issues on which we knew we would not come to agreement, for example, the issues of predestination and original sin for baptism and the nature of the presence of Christ for the Eucharist. It was heartening for us that the acknowledgment of stumbling blocks was not a cause for deeper separation, but instead opened the space for developing greater trust, mutual respect, and humble recognition that all of us in the history of Christianity had acted on unfortunate judgments that we now desired to address openly and honestly. I think this insight drew us closer together as members of the one body of Christ.

A second understanding was a consequence of the unique makeup of the dialogue partners. A liturgical theologian from each of the five communions was intentionally invited to participate in this seventh round of ecumenical discussion. Sometimes, then, the lines of struggle were not drawn between the Roman Catholic and Reformed churches but between systematic and liturgical theologians. What emerged from this was the shared realization that our worship texts and rituals already had a great degree of convergence, and these would be rich resources for our dialogue. We found that our prayer (as prescribed in denominational services as well as the actual praying we embraced together as dialogue partners) acted to ease tensions, to place us all as servants before our redeeming God, and to constantly remind us that love and God's gracious grace in the end are more critical for salvation than whatever words we craft. Furthermore, we often raised the issue that we were no longer sixteenth-century churches fighting sixteenth-century issues. All of us throughout our history had grown and changed — theologically and liturgically. By acknowledging that we are squarely twenty-first-century churches, we could look at the earlier issues with fresh eyes and discuss them with renewed hearts. We could interpret our differences, then, in a twenty-first-century context that brought different language and perspective to the dialogue.

Surprises

Given these initial understandings (there were no doubt more, but these became particularly important for me), some surprises emerged. From my point of view, the knowledge that the Reformed Churches delegates had of the Second Vatican Council documents — and especially of *Sacrosanctum Concilium* (the Constitution on the Sacred Liturgy of December 4, 1963) — already suggested a solid foundation for beneficial discussion. All of us were concerned that our agreed-on statements concerning baptism and Eucharist/Lord's Supper be relevant to contemporary Christianity, offering something new theologically and ecumenically, and inviting our churches to come to a deeper spiritual appreciation for how these sacraments are ongoing in our daily living. Along with this, we regularly articulated ethical/ moral concerns: we cannot be living members of the one body of Christ and not care for our sisters and brothers who are lacking in basic human need, for our war-torn and violent world, and for the ravaging of our natural resources and planet.

A second surprise to me was the amount of time we spent on our formal statement of agreement on baptism: almost five years. We initially expected agreement on this sacrament to go rather quickly, assuming that we already had much about which we agreed, for example, that water and the Trinitarian names were essential (see the Great Commission in Matt. 28:19). The length of time spent on this document eventually indicated how fundamental this initial sacrament is to our shared identity and mission. What we learned in the process of producing our agreed-on statement about baptism facilitated our work on the Eucharist/Lord's Supper. Another surprise came during our times of denominational caucuses. We Roman Catholics were not always on the same page, of course; and among the Reformed Churches delegates there was sometimes much difficulty coming to agreement among their four communions represented at the dialogue table: Christian Reformed Church in North America (CRC); the Presbyterian Church, USA (PCUSA); the Reformed Church in America (RCA); and the United Church of Christ (UCC). In a sense, then, we were not simply two Christian traditions having a bilateral dialogue, but sometimes we were five. An important thing we learned was that sometimes misunderstanding occurred because different terms had different meanings for different participants. We spent a good deal of time defining terms and found this to be a time-consuming and difficult task; but in the end, pursuing a common understanding about terms facilitated our work together.

Consensus

Over the many years and countless hundreds of hours of research, reflection, presentations, prayer, and discussions, some issues of consensus emerged that were not included in the final documents, but they subtly shaped the documents we signed off on. Notable for me was our great awareness that we mutually accept each other's baptism. Beyond our denominational differences, there is the one body of Christ of which we are all members. This shared identity is the source of our mutual respect, our shared dignity, and our courage to place contentious points in the larger context of our belonging to Christ.

Second, we came to realize that, in many cases, we share similar pastoral challenges in our contemporary world. All of us struggle with diminishing numbers of congregants. Over and over we emphasized the importance of education in religious and liturgical matters, yet acknowledging how woefully lacking is our denomination members' understanding of the gospel, its demands, and the meaning and centrality of worship. We realized that our ecumenical efforts could not simply remain the esoteric work of scholars, but that it had to include concern for the membership. We agreed that our target audience for these documents had to be broader than the theological and pastoral "professionals." This affected the language and style of the final documents — for the better, in my estimation. Christianity is not a "book" religion but instead a "people" relationship with God and each other.

Third, we came back over and over again to the lived reality of these two sacraments. While there are surely differences among our denominations in belief, theology, and the worship practice of these two sacraments, we agreed that gospel values determined our way of everyday living, not denominational lines as such. Thus, the living out of these sacraments already witnesses to the unity we seek. This conviction even affected how we were in relationship together during our meeting times. Often our informal discussions and social times moved toward practice rather than theology. I found delight in discovering common values for everyday living, a commitment to improving our worship, and a shared dedication to caring for those less fortunate than ourselves. Deep faith is lived, not simply grasped as doctrine.

I conclude this brief reflection by going back to my statement about becoming friends that I made in opening these remarks. Friendships developed out of a deep sense of respect we gained for each other, not only as dedicated scholars, but also as committed Christians who seek unity. Our sense of being one in the body of Christ, no matter the denomination, underlay our prayer, discussions, and informal social times together. We share a common identity, something that is exceedingly precious to each of us. Our fidelity to our denominational histories, documents, and practices was laudable. At the same time, we were quite aware that something deeper even than that united us in the one body of Christ. One cannot engage in this depth of dialogue for so many years about something so personal as one's understanding of baptism and Eucharist/Lord's Supper without being changed. Strangers became individuals about whom we became personally concerned. We were concerned about illnesses of dialogue partners, and we grieved together about deaths that occurred. We lamented the inevitable changes in the membership of the dialogue partners over the years.

But perhaps the most important change in me personally was the new-found vision I have in what the eventual unity of Christians might look like. It will be characterized not by sameness, but by diversity. Diversity can be celebrated, and it can lead to greater insight into the gospel. Diversity can lead to a deeper, living faith. Diversity assures the unity of the body of Christ.

Reenvisioning "The Shape of the Liturgy: A Framework for Contextualization"

Gordon W. Lathrop

One paper given in the course of the LWF Study on Worship and Culture included these words:

> Liturgy is an event with a shape. It is more than a text. It is the flow of a communal action which expresses its meanings in gestures and concrete signs as well as in words. Indeed, the meanings of the liturgy come to expression by the continual juxtapositions of words and sign-actions.[1]

And, the paper continued, the basic traits of this shape can be found in the practice of many Christian communities, across denominational boundaries, regardless of their cultural setting.

The idea that there is a basic transcultural "shape" to the liturgy of Christians — "pattern" or *ordo* are alternative words used for the same idea — recurs at several places throughout the records of the LWF study, in all three of its published volumes. "Shape" is especially found in the statements from the study, statements that are reprinted in this book. Already the Cartigny Statement 3.7 expressed the idea. Then, for the Eucharist, the Nairobi Statement 2.1 strengthened the assertion:

1. Lathrop, "The Shape of the Liturgy," in Stauffer, *Christian Worship*, p. 68.

This chapter reworks material that was first published as "The Shape of the Liturgy: A Framework for Contextualization," in S. Anita Stauffer, ed., *Christian Worship: Unity in Cultural Diversity* (Geneva: LWF, 1996), pp. 67-75.

The fundamental shape of the principal Sunday act of Christian worship, the Eucharist or Holy Communion, is shared across cultures: the people gather, the Word of God is proclaimed, the people intercede for the needs of the Church and the world, the eucharistic meal is shared, and the people are sent out into the world for mission. . . . The ways in which the shapes of the Sunday Eucharist and the church year are expressed vary by culture, but their meanings and fundamental structure are shared around the globe.

And concerning baptism, the Chicago Statement 2.1 spoke similarly:

[T]he pattern or ordo of Baptism is also a universal ecumenical inheritance. Baptism involves: (a) formation in the one faith (traditionally known as the catechumenate), (b) the water bath, and (c) the incorporation of the baptized into the whole Christian community and its mission. This latter incorporation is expressed by the newly baptized being led to the table of the Lord's Supper, the very table where their baptismal identity will also be strengthened and re-affirmed throughout their life.

But these statements do not restrict themselves simply to asserting that such an ecumenical and transcultural shape can be found in Christian liturgical practice. They also invite congregations from all of the churches — not just Lutheran churches — to make use of this shape in their own work for renewal and in their own processes of localization or contextualization. The Nairobi Statement 2.3 says:

The use of this shared core liturgical structure and these shared liturgical elements in local congregational worship — as well as the shared act of people assembling together, and the shared provision of diverse leadership in that assembly (although the space for the assembly and the manner of the leadership vary) — are expressions of Christian unity across time, space, culture, and confession. The recovery in each congregation of the clear centrality of these transcultural and ecumenical elements renews the sense of this Christian unity and gives all churches a solid basis for contextualization.

Similarly, the Chicago Statement 2.1 on baptism continues:

Any contextualization of Baptism . . . will depend upon the churches allowing these transcultural characteristics of Baptism to be continually renewed in their midst.

Then the statement quotes an early treatise of Luther on liturgical renewal:

> We should do justice to the meaning of Baptism and make of our practice a true and complete sign of the thing Baptism signifies.[2]

Making our liturgical practices true and complete signs of the gospel that they signify, giving central place in our assemblies to the gifts of God that unite us with other Christians, and thereby finding together a "solid basis" for the interaction of our liturgies with the local cultures among which they are celebrated — the statements envision these as challenges that come to all of the churches. The LWF statements here speak clearly of an ecumenical undertaking.

This book has sought to be one small but concrete evidence of that ecumenical reality. Here Christian liturgical scholars from many churches and many cultures have reflected on the interactions of worship and culture. Their reflections have been occasioned by the hope to continue to rethink the LWF study and have been organized around the LWF statements. But they have not been limited by that study or those statements. Still, woven through these ecumenical contributions — and also behind many of the reflections here — has been the idea of the "shape of the liturgy" as a tool for contextualization and as a sign of unity.

The idea of a "shape" in liturgical practice came into the current conversation from the mid-twentieth-century studies of the Anglican scholar and monk Gregory Dix.[3] But linked with the reflections of the Russian Orthodox liturgist Alexander Schmemann about the *ordo* of the liturgy,[4] as also with further thought about the patterns found, for example, in the Emmaus story of Luke 24, in the liturgical descriptions of the First Apology of Justin Martyr, and in medieval *typica* and *ordines,* the idea also became an ecumenical treasure.[5] It began to appear not only in the works of liturgical scholars and theologians,[6]

2. See *Luther's Works,* 35: 29.
3. See esp. Gregory Dix, *The Shape of the Liturgy* (Westminster, UK: Dacre, 1945).
4. Alexander Schmemann, *Introduction to Liturgical Theology* (New York: St. Vladimir's Seminary Press, 1975), pp. 20, 32.
5. For a discussion of these and many further sources, see Gordon W. Lathrop, *Holy Things: A Liturgical Theology* (Minneapolis: Fortress, 1993), pp. 33-35, passim.
6. See the essays from the 15th Congress of Societas Liturgica meeting concerned the theme "The Future Shape of the Liturgy," *Studia Liturgica* 26, no. 1 (1996), and the essays in Dirk G. Lange and Dwight W. Vogel, eds., *Ordo: Bath, Word, Prayer, Table* (Akron, OH: OSL, 2005).

but also in the service books of the churches[7] and in ecumenical statements related to the World Council of Churches (WCC).[8]

There have certainly been objections to the idea, at least to the assertion that such a shape is universally found among Christians.[9] Such objections can indeed help us avoid turning the idea of basic liturgical patterns into a law we mostly apply as a weapon against other communities. Universal laws are hard to find and dangerous to identify in our times. And others should be allowed to speak for themselves. Perhaps we can best see "gathering, word, meal, sending" — to use one widely discussed summary of the shape of Sunday assembly, and "formation, bath, incorporation," as the Chicago Statement outlines the baptismal process — as gifts in our own communities, as ways that make the central matters of the New Testament present here to us, and as tools for us to inquire about the fidelity of our own practice. In any case, such a modest and disciplined reading of the *ordo* can recall for us what the "shape" is really about: Not any law, but the gift of Jesus Christ and his gospel set out amidst and continually transfiguring our gatherings, our reading of the ancient Scripture, our prayers, our meals, and the great bath that adds people to our number.

Still, the goal of talk about shape remains the same: the clarity and fidelity of our contextualizing work, our dialogues with our own diverse and hybrid cultures. Also with those who wish not to identify an ecumenically shared pattern, or *ordo*, in their liturgical practice we can carry on the mutual conversation — the mutual affirmation and admonition of Christians with each other — about how we together allow the gospel of Jesus Christ and the sacramental gifts of God to be at the center of our worshiping assemblies, how we both affirm and critically witness to our cultures, and how we avoid putting our own uncriticized selves at the center of our meetings.

For those, however, who do recognize the gift of an ecumenical shape as their own heritage, we can still say:

---

7. E.g., the *Book of Common Worship* (Louisville: Westminster John Knox, 1993), pp. 33-47; *Evangelical Lutheran Worship* (Minneapolis: Augsburg Fortress, 2006), pp. 91-93, 225-26.

8. E.g., "Celebrations of the Eucharist in Ecumenical Contexts: A Proposal," in Thomas F. Best and Dagmar Heller, eds., *Eucharistic Worship in Ecumenical Contexts* (Geneva: WCC, 1998), pp. 29-35; and "The Ordo of Baptism," Part 2 of "Report of the Consultation," in Thomas F. Best and Dagmar Heller, eds., *Becoming a Christian: The Ecumenical Implications of Our Common Baptism* (Geneva: WCC, 1999), pp. 76-83.

9. One survey of such objections, together with an initial response, is found in Gordon W. Lathrop, "Bath, Word, Prayer, Table: Reflections on Doing the Liturgical Ordo in a Postmodern Time," in Lange and Vogel, eds., *Ordo: Bath, Word, Prayer, Table,* pp. 216-28.

[We] have received the great history of Christian worship as [our] own, rejoicing in the recent evidence of an ecumenical consensus about the most basic patterns of Christian worship, and recognizing that this history and these patterns have already been influenced by many cultures.

And though we now know more clearly and gladly how diverse that history has been, and though we may now recognize how that consensus is not necessarily universal, we ourselves can still say:

We need this shape as a framework for our own contextualizing work. Without such a framework, we might be "contextualizing" only ourselves and our own ideas — swallowing our own tail, as it were. However, with such a shape, diverse, contextualized local churches can find a rich connection with each other. It is this shape which helps us think about local equivalents, local meanings, local transformations, and, sometimes, resistance to local cultural wrongs.[10]

Here, at the end of this book, by way of summary and as one way to speak concretely about ongoing liturgical renewal in all of our assemblies, we might once again experiment with using the shape of the Sunday assembly as a contextualizing tool. Similar use might be made of the shape of the baptismal process or of daily prayer. Here, however, as one example, we might again ask ourselves a series of questions that were already published in the LWF Study:[11]

1. On gathering and being sent:

How does our congregation gather in the grace, love and koinonia of the Triune God (2 Cor. 13:13)? Is Baptism remembered? How? Are strangers welcome? Is the space of our gathering hospitable and yet also reverently focused on the central matters of the gathering, the places of word and sacrament? Does our architecture reflect the land, the local place and the cultures in which the celebration takes place? Yet are the themes of those cultures transformed, in our architecture and in our gathering, by the values of the gospel of Christ? What roles do confession and forgiveness, processions, singing, the traditional *Kyrie* and *Gloria in Excelsis,* and the collect or prayer of entrance have in the gathering? How do these express

---

10. "The Shape of the Liturgy," p. 67.
11. "The Shape of the Liturgy," pp. 73-75.

the entire community gathering around God's word and sacraments? Then, what roles do postcommunion prayer, singing, blessing, words of dismissal, the sending of communion to the absent or food to the hungry have in the sending? How do these express the mission of the entire community? Furthermore, has the local cultural manner of assembling and leave-taking been considered for dynamic equivalents to the historic features of Christian liturgical gathering and sending? How long should gathering and sending take? Why? Who leads these events? Why? Are there matters from our local cultures that should be resisted in our practice of gathering and sending (e.g., greater honor accorded to people of wealth or status, too great a focus on charismatic individuals, too rigid or too relaxed a style, too individualistic or too faceless a manner in groups)? How do the needs and longings of the world and the reality of the local place, as these are before God, come to expression in these liturgical movements?

2. On hearing the word:
How does our congregation hear the word in Scripture and preaching? Is a lectionary used, connecting this assembly to the other churches ecumenically and/or locally? Is there always more than one reading? Does the sermon proclaim the crucified, risen and present Jesus Christ, on the basis of these readings? Is the place of the reading and preaching able to be recognized as a central and important place in the local cultural context? Is the book of the readings a book of dignity and significance? Does the congregational song, as well as the other arts of the assembly, bring the readings of the day to further expression? If there is a choir, does the choir act as the "rehearsed voices of the congregation," leading the congregation in its song around the word? What roles do psalmody, the traditional "alleluia" verses or sequence hymns, and the ecumenical creeds play in the service of the word? Does reading and preaching lead to intercessions? Are these really prayers for the world and for the unity of the church? Are the intercessions "sealed" with the kiss of peace? Is there one presider and many ministers — readers, singers and leaders of prayer — in this service of the word? Does the preacher have too great a role in this assembly? Too little? Is a strongly symbolic but richly accessible form of the local language and linguistic style used for reading and preaching? Have local cultural patterns been considered for dynamic equivalents to the noncentral historic features of the Christian liturgical word-service (e.g., the manner of reading and preaching, the place of the reading and

preaching, the form of the book, the character of the music, the roles of leadership, the vestments, the manner of intercessions, the kiss of peace)? Are there matters from our local cultures that should be resisted in our practice of the service of the word? Does the "word from ourselves" replace the word of God? Does our practice of the service of the word obscure the central matters of an assembly of the baptized, gathered around the judgment and mercy of God in Scripture and preaching, praying, and song?

3. On keeping the meal:

How does our congregation gather around the meal of Christ? Is this supper held every Sunday, as the principal service of our congregation? Does it include thanksgiving as well as eating and drinking? Does it include a collection for those in need? Is there a single presider and many ministers — singers, table servers and ministers of communion — in this service of the meal? Does the thanksgiving include the historic dialogue, praise to God for creation and redemption, the words of Christ at the supper, anamnesis, epiclesis, intercessions or commemorations, and a great Amen? Might appropriate local dynamic equivalents be considered for this historic flow of the prayer of thanksgiving? Does the thanksgiving involve response and participation by the whole assembly? Is it proclaimed with love and dignity, as a central event in the assembly? What food is used? Why? What vessels are used? Why? How do food and vessels relate to this local culture? How do they express the gift of Jesus Christ and the unity of his body? Are they, or do they need to be, countercultural or culture-transforming? Is the sharing of the food done with love and reverence, in a manner respectful of the gift of Christ and of the baptismal dignity of each communicant? What role do such historic matters as the presentation of the gifts, the setting of the table, the place of communion, and the procession of communicants or the singing of communion hymns play in our service of the meal? Have local cultural patterns been considered for dynamic equivalents to these noncentral historic features of the Christian liturgical meal? Are there matters from our cultures that should be resisted in our practice of the service of the table (e.g., conceptions of purity or of exclusive table fellowship)? Does our practice of the service of the meal obscure the central matters of thanksgiving and eating and drinking and remembering the need of the world? Does the entire service show forth Jesus Christ, crucified and risen, for the life of the world?

Something like these questions might be asked in all of our assemblies. These are — and will be — diverse assemblies, with diverse charisms, amid diverse cultures. But these assemblies — renewed again and again, receiving again and again the gifts that God gives in the gospel of Jesus Christ, finding again and again how God unites us through these gifts — can be reliable witnesses to God's love for the world and all its peoples. Our assemblies, then, can also be places where we encounter the fruit of the invincible beseeching of our Lord Jesus, as the Gospel of John puts it: "I ask not only on behalf of these, but also on behalf of those who will believe in me through their word, that they may all be one . . . so that the world may believe that you have sent me" (John 17:20-21; NRSV).

Susurrations Where Life Unites

Gláucia Vasconcelos Wilkey

Introduction

After affirming their common faith in the words of the creed, some 400 worshipers fell silent. Inspired by the susurration of the water flowing from the fountain, they remembered their own baptism. No one touched the water, lest there be any suggestion of "rebaptism"; but they let the water speak powerfully to them of their common incorporation into the one body of Christ.[1]

"Susurration": Ah, what a lovely word, close to the language of this writer's heart, Portuguese. In that language, "sussurro" (as a noun) is a sweet speech coming in whispers, the rustlings of leaves on a tree, but also gentle creeks and streams or fountains. In a world of dry loudness, discord, and divisions, words yet more sweet, and desired, and for those 400 worshipers named above, gathered in a meeting in Santiago de Compostela, the sounds of the very presence of the Spirit-come-in-baptism in the "water that speaks."

That welcome designation, "water that speaks," indicates a fortuitous grasp on baptism proposed in ancient texts, including in a witness from Ignatius of Antioch in the second century. The speaking water is named also by various contemporary theologians, including Gordon W. Lathrop, for example, in "Becoming a Christian: The Ecumenical Implications of Our

---

1. See Thomas F. Best, "A Faith and Order Saga: Towards *One Baptism: Towards Mutual Recognition*" (in this volume, pp. 302-19).

Common Baptism."[2] These waters speak of mercy and joy, of a particular kind of shout, as the psalmist sang long ago, "Happy are the people who know the festal shout" (Ps. 89:15).[3] For the church everywhere, they proclaim the presence and the gift of God, the three-in-one at the center of the Sunday meeting. But the sounds from these waters are not always gentle susurrations. They can also be bold and cajoling; they can and do remind and remake, admonish and press, for these waters first speak, of course, of death: "Do you not know that all of us who have been baptized into Christ Jesus were baptized into his death? Therefore, we have been buried with him by baptism into death." But this death is a harbinger of life newly envisioned, for "just as Christ was raised from the dead by the glory of the Father, so we too might walk in newness of life" (Rom. 6:3-4; NRSV).

In the Lord's Day meeting we call worship, the water is known and seen as the identity-giving word, indeed a speech that is as wide in its inclusiveness as it is enticing, and as borderless as it is demanding. Gordon Lathrop emphatically declares: "The baptized constitutes church. Period. All the baptized."[4] Powerful words — "the baptized" and "all" — for in them the *demands* of baptism become clear. No cultural or ecclesiological differences matter; no historical exclusions persist. So, in and from baptism and Jesus Christ's presence in word and sacrament, liturgical ministers and people will together make clear the meaning of these things: "With joy you will draw waters from the wells of salvation" (Isa. 12:3). And we are promised that wherever these waters go, "everything will be made fresh (Ezek. 47:1-12).

But these susurrations also speak of pain and decry disunity: "No one touched the water," says the narrative of the event at the gathering of the Fifth Faith and Order World Conference held in Santiago de Compostela in 1993, described in this volume by Thomas F. Best (see pages 302-19 above). On a first reading of Best's narrative, questions such as these might rush in: Why did no one touch the water? Was it that perhaps no one considered it

---

2. Gordon W. Lathrop, Thomas F. Best, and Dagmar Heller, eds., "Becoming a Christian: The Ecumenical Implications of Our Common Baptism," WCC Faith and Order Paper 184 (Geneva: WCC Publications, 1999), pp. 13ff.

3. This and all other biblical texts in this chapter are from the New Revised Standard Version of the Bible, Lutheran Study Bible (Minneapolis: Augsburg Fortress, 2009), © 1989 Division of Christian Education of the National Council of Churches of Christ in the U.S.A. (NRSV).

4. Gordon W. Lathrop, "Becoming a Christian: The Ecumenical Implications of Our Common Baptism," in *Holy Ground: A Liturgical Cosmology* (Minneapolis: Fortress, 2003), p. 118.

a "festal shout," but heard only common speech *about* Christian unity, perceived as unimportant and/or fraught with difficulties? Or is it that years of ecclesiological and cultural life in isolation set barriers beyond the reach of the most eager participant? Or could it be that respect for another's sense of baptism held back those who did hear the water speak, yet out of concern they refrained from the action, though this pained them? And where would we fit in the narrative, and why? In this story, though, there is a hopeful ending. Best tells us that the work of that gathering continued:

> Meanwhile, the liturgical experience around the fountain in Santiago de Compostela — truth be told, far more than the formal statements on baptism in the World Conference preparatory documents and reports[5] — energized a renewed Faith and Order commitment to work on baptism. Recognizing the fundamental significance of baptism for the churches' mutual recognition, an initial meeting was held in Faverges, France, in 1997 on the theme of "Becoming a Christian: The Ecumenical Implications of our Common Baptism." This stressed the importance of a common *ordo* of baptism, *explored issues of inculturation in relation to baptism,* and noted the ethical implications stemming from our common baptism into the one body of Christ.[6]

The water indeed spoke in Santiago de Compostela! And everyone heard its gift.

Baptismal Susurrations and the LWF Project

In 1994 the Lutheran World Federation (LWF) published the first of three volumes on worship and culture, direct results of a project that covered seven years (1992-1999) and involved theologians — Lutheran and others

---

5. See *On the Way to Fuller Koinonia,* "Discussion Paper, III.2, Sacramental Life," pp. 67, 283; Report of Section 3, Baptism," pp. 11-15, 247-48.
6. Thomas F. Best and Dagmar Heller, eds., "Becoming a Christian: The Ecumenical Implications of Our Common Baptism," Faith and Order Paper 184 (Geneva: WCC Publications, 1999). See the "Report of the Consultation," pp. 74-97 and, for the topics cited, esp. the chapters by Gordon Lathrop, "The Water that Speaks: The *Ordo* of Baptism and its Ecumenical Implications"; by Anscar J. Chupungco, "Criteria for the Inculturation of Baptism," pp. 54-64; and by Vigen Guroian, "On Baptism and the Spirit: The Ethical Significance of the Marks of the Church," pp. 65-73 (italics added).

— and churches from many countries. (See Norman A. Hjelm's introductory essay in this volume for full historical context of the project; see also Gordon W. Lathrop's essay for theological context.) In the preface to that first volume, Viggo Mortensen, then director of the LWF's Department for Theology and Studies, asked: "How are we to proclaim Christ in different cultures?" Then Mortensen suggested a response: "The message must first embrace us, and speak not only to our brains and senses but also our hearts. In order for this to happen it must be incarnated in the life of the people and their culture, just as it took root in one specific culture for the first time."[7] I concur with Mortensen: the message must first hold our own hearts and entice our very selves into a sense of humility before others' stories, songs, prayers, actions, and all of life in the midst of particular cultures. That is something we have known and heard in the past: "The word became flesh and lived among us" (John 1:14; NRSV). God in Christ still today takes body in all the world's cultures, and hence, "Let the same mind be in you that was in Christ Jesus . . . so that at the name of Jesus every knee should bend, in heaven, in earth, and under the earth, and every tongue confess that Jesus Christ is Lord, for the glory of God the Father" (Phil. 2).

Though they were aided by other participants in the project, including leaders from other church bodies, Lutheran pastor Gordon W. Lathrop and Roman Catholic priest Anscar Chupungco, OSB, were the two main theological pillars grounding, informing, and indeed sustaining the whole process of the Lutheran Study Series on Worship and Culture. S. Anita Stauffer facilitated the process as editor and contributed her own writings. For Stauffer and Chupungco, baptism is now fulfilled in their deaths. The work of their lives, which was united to Lathrop's before they died, could be seen not only in their gifts and their care for the church, but also in their mutual love and respect for each other, giving their contributions to this volume a great poignancy.

In the twenty years since 1994, Mortensen's question has beckoned multiple answers and birthed many more questions. The world's cultures are not so easily defined; the word "culture" itself calls for deeper inquiry into the multicultural and hybrid global village that we now inhabit as peoples and churches. One may side with definitions that are now historical, as enunciated, for example, by Clifford Geertz in 1973, who said that "culture denotes

7. Quoted in S. Anita Stauffer, ed., *Worship and Culture in Dialogue,* Reports of International Consultations in Cartigny, Switzerland (1993) and Hong Kong (1994) (Geneva: LWF, Department for Theology and Studies, 1994), p. 5.

an historically transmitted pattern of meanings embodied in symbols, a system of inherited conceptions expressed in symbolic forms by means of which men communicate, perpetuate, and develop their knowledge about and attitudes toward life."[8] Or one may agree with the interpretation of a group of scholars that opens one of Gordon Lathrop's essays in the first volume of the LWF series: "Culture is the symbolic-expressive dimension of social life." This includes aspects of human actions and words, stories, songs, food practices, and all things that are the basic practices of a community.[9] In this volume you have encountered many more definitions, each of them calling for reflection and critique, each of them opening and expanding horizons. "Hybridity" and "cultural multilayering," "postcolonialism" and "multiculturalism" — all these are bywords that, applied to liturgical concerns, challenge heretofore accepted understandings of inculturation and/or contextualization. In fact, those writers represented in this book question some of the assumptions and paradigms held in the original project's reports, even as they take to heart the meaning and scope of those assumptions. Worship is, after all, incarnational theology, the Word who is Christ, *this* day and in *this* place, guiding the church in the task of reconciling cultures and peoples.

"Inculturation" or "contextualization" are words we value in this conversation, but the Nairobi Statement also offers "cross-cultural," "transcultural" and "countercultural" as paradigms that might serve as lenses through which to engage cultural issues. But, we may ask, who decides, and on what bases, what is or is not faithfully contextual for the liturgical gathering anywhere, for example, or what is amenable to gospel culture, or which kinds of cross-cultural connections are appropriate and which are not? We may ask simpler questions, such as, How do we faithfully engage elements of our local culture without succumbing to demands or patterns that are countercultural to the gospel? A pastoral musician may contemplate songs from the global church and ask, How do we engage the gifts of other cultures in worship but steer clear of "liturgical tourism," or how do we make use of the gifts of other cultures solely as entertaining elements in worship, or as tokens of cultural recognition? And how can the fullness of the grace of God entice us to search for

8. Clifford Geertz, *The Interpretation of Cultures: Selected Essays* (New York: Basic Books, 1973), p. 89.

9. The group of scholars noted by Gordon Lathrop in note 1 in "Baptism In the New Testaments and Its Cultural Settings": Robert Wuthnow, James Davidson Hunter, Albert Bergesen, Edith Kurtzveil, and in Lathrop, *Cultural Analysis: The Work of Peter L. Berger, Mary Douglas, Michel Foucault, and Jürgen Habermas* (Boston: Routledge and Kegan Paul, 1984).

a "richer fare" of language for worship, beyond our practiced, localized, and familiar — but often parochial — texts that are limited and limiting?[10] And do the definitions of culture or cultural systems we embrace apply to churches? To denominations? What are the implications for our liturgical life then?

The LWF study series' case studies and reports are rich and offer much for theologians to ponder, but the work was fraught with difficulties. For example, interdisciplinary work between liturgical theologians and ethnomusicologists is not an easy task. Any attempt to deal with such significant issues must be approached with no small degree of humility. Theologians, musicians, liturgists, social-science scholars, and others involved in the LWF project had a sense of temporality embedded in that work. Chupungco, writing in the preface to *Shape a Circle Ever Wider,* says: "The topic of inculturation has many loose ends."[11] This is indeed true. For inculturation to happen, says Mark Francis later in the same volume — and in the same spirit revealed by Mortensen — one needs to develop and reveal a listening heart. Stauffer adds:

> Even before the seven-year LWF Study Series on Worship and Culture was proposed and approved, it was clear that such a study could never be the final word. The issues are too complex and controverted, and the cultures of the world are ever-changing and evolving. Furthermore, the work necessary in churches around the world cannot be done quickly, if it is to be deep and pastoral.[12]

Similarly, the texts that appear in this current volume are not, nor can they be, "the final word": much is left unsaid or unheard in the light of cultural and ecclesiological developments since the LWF study came to light. The transient nature of today's world cultures is vastly complex and calls for con-

10. Theologian Gail Ramshaw offers a deep well from which to draw insights into the matter of liturgical language and cultural context in her various publications, including *Treasures Old and New: Images in the Lectionary* (Minneapolis: Augsburg Fortress, 2002), and *Reviving Sacred Speech: The Meaning of Liturgical Language; Second Thoughts on "Christ and Sacred Speech"* (Akron: OSL Publications, 2000). This editor wishes to acknowledge Ramshaw's contributions to her own theological formation, an additional inducement in her desire to bring back to life and, in the process, reenvision the LWF Worship and Culture Study Series.

11. Mark R. Francis, CSV, *Shape a Circle Ever Wider* (Chicago: Liturgy Training Publications, 2000), p. viii. This is a thoughtful volume on the vision of the unity of the church and inculturation by this ecumenically sensitive Roman Catholic theologian.

12. Stauffer, "Worship: Ecumenical Core and Cultural Content," in S. Anita Stauffer, ed., *Christian Worship: Unity in Cultural Diversity* (Geneva: LWF, 1996), p. 19.

tinuing work. Yet, a cautionary note: whereas it is indispensable that we consider the temporal nature of our research and cultural systems, and work on the matter and pay attention to what social-science scholars tell us regarding cultures, we must also press and live the unchanging nature of Christian worship at its most fundamental level: where two or three are gathered in Christ's name, Christ himself is in the midst, in the assembly, in word, in water, in bread, and in wine.

With the people at the font in Santiago de Compostela, we say that no one culture, no one people, no one church will necessarily hear, experience, or interpret the waters' speech in the same way. However, we can hope that all will manifest a sense of wonder and humility, indeed grace, in face of the gifts in the other as we continue to ask, as in the past, "How is it that we hear, each in our own native language" — this coming anew of the Spirit in baptismal waters? Pentecostal fire comes out of the water, and this same Spirit, uniting all the baptized, speaks in and from the waters in various accents and colors, yet with the same grace's demand: "Make common identity clear, audible, visible; welcome diversity, celebrate others' gifts."

In his book *Cosmopolitanism: Ethics in a World of the Stranger,* Kwame Anthony Appiah challenges our use of familiar words, concepts, and questions that are commonly accepted definitions of culture while he decries our cultures' divisions for division sake, even as he offers venues for what the prophet Ezekiel's vision calls "the healing of the nations" (Ezek. 47:1-12). Two of the most challenging chapters in that volume, "Whose Culture Is It, Anyway?" and "Kindness to Strangers," can be heard or translated in the light of the concerns at the heart of this volume.

For example, think of the ecumenical vision and hear these words from Appiah:

> Each person you know about and can affect is someone to whom you have responsibilities: to say this is just to affirm the idea of morality. The challenge, then, is to take minds and hearts formed over the long millennia of living in local troops and equip them with ideas and institutions that will allow us to live together as the global tribe we have become.[13]

What might such an outlook suggest for each of our assemblies? Is it indeed reasonable to expect or hope that we, on the basis of our common

13. Kwame Anthony Appiah, *Cosmopolitanism: Ethics in a World of the Stranger* (New York: W. W. Norton, 2006), p. 12.

identity, do hold other churches and assemblies as part of our responsibility — at least in mutual care, affirmation, and admonition — equally gentle yet equally compelling? Can we then be led to see the both/and nature of "locality/globality"?

Appiah invites us to mutual responsibility, but some biblical texts point to the reasons for — and the scope of — that responsibility: "There are varieties of gifts, but the same Spirit; and there are varieties of services, but the same Lord. . . . To each is given the manifestation of the Spirit for the common good. . ." (1 Cor. 12:4-7). Diverse gifts given by God are, therefore, for the *common good*.[14] Don't these words actually invite us to more than Appiah's "common responsibility"? Could our local liturgies' prayers, songs, and actions reflect the notion of common good, both in and for the church everywhere, but also for the world beyond our places of worship? This is, of course, amply modeled in the familiar account of the life of the early church: "All who believed were together and had all things in common; they would sell their possessions and goods and distribute the proceeds to all, as any had need. . . . They broke bread at home and ate their food with glad and generous hearts . . ." (Acts 2:44-47). This way of being assumes that we are indeed mutually responsible for each other's lives, stories, and gifts — and for the common good of our churches and our world. Ecologists, anthropologists, and other social-science scholars go even further: for example, they speak of ecological destruction should we fail to live and work keeping the common good in mind.[15] What then? How do our liturgies live out the concerns of such knowledge? And what about the common good of peoples — and all created order — anywhere on the ground God called "holy"? What do our shared identities tells us in the watery speech but that baptism is not simply an event in time in the life of the Christian, but a lifelong process that, among other things, leads the baptized and assemblies into a growing realization of the interdependency of all things, including cultures and cultural systems, and all the waters of the earth? How do baptismal waters speak and lead to the care for the world's streams, lakes, rivers, and oceans? What images lead the baptized to see the connections among baptismal formation, the act of baptism, and the global water crisis?

In the middle of catastrophic events — floods and droughts, earthquakes

---

14. For more on the notion of "common good," see David Hollenbach, SJ, "The Common Good in a Divided Society," The Santa Clara Lectures 5, 1999.

15. Concerning these things, read Gordon Lathrop's *Holy Ground: A Liturgical Cosmology* (Minneapolis: Fortress, 2003).

and fires, things natural or those caused by relentless wars — can we go away from church on any given Sunday without having confessed our lack of attention and care for the very ground on which our church buildings and our lives are planted, or for the diminishing waters of the earth? Would a keener sense of interdependency aid our prayers and our actions? Do we raise such things to God's mercy in the Sunday liturgy, even as we acknowledge that in one way or another we very well may be accomplices to the misery surrounding us? If we invoke the gospel's message in all that we do in liturgy, would our concerns and pains and deep care for the holiness of the connections between us and all these things be made clear for the common good? "Yes," says United Methodist theologian Don E. Saliers:

> Among the requisites for participation in the form, content, and dynamism of Christian worship, two are central: a sense of wonderment and awe at the mystery of God's becoming flesh and an awareness of suffering and the interdependency of all things.... When the Christian assembly worships *without* awareness of human suffering and death, or without any sense of the injustice and pathos of the world, it is extremely difficult to "read" the texts and the patterns of God.[16]

If the words "culture" and "cultivate" are related, and they are, what are we "cultivating" in our Sunday prayers and actions? Is worship a culture itself? Some would argue that culture, in its basic understanding, includes not only recognition of national or territorial boundaries, race, and ethnicity, but also traditional gestures and visual symbols in any community, along with their stories and songs, expectations and ceremonies, foods and commitments — all things that fall into the category of "symbolic-expressive dimension of social life."

Consider this: "As many of you as have been baptized into Christ have clothed yourselves with Christ. There is no longer Jew or Greek, there is no longer slave or free, there is no longer male and female; for all of you are one in Christ Jesus" (Gal. 3:27-28). Jew/Greek, slave/free, male/female — "this or that." However, the "this or that" we see in some countries, and in some churches, displays such a localized, territorial, and parochial sense of nation and culture, religious or secular, that the idea of exceptionalism is now deeply embedded, for instance, in the United States' political — and increas-

---

16. Don E. Saliers, *Worship as Theology: A Foretaste of Glory Divine* (Nashville: Abingdon, 1994), p. 177.

ingly religious — discourse. In today's cultural ethos, when the realization of the deep meanings of symbols becomes more commonly shared across all boundaries, think of the incongruence of speaking of baptism as the source of a common identity, yet finding the presence of national flags in our houses of worship. Many of us have gone to great pains to set forth our liturgical environments so that they visibly display a particular yet common identity and story. In the face of troubled international times and in light of the growing multicultural and hybrid nature of our assemblies, what does the presence of a national flag — of any country — convey?

Turn, then, to the question of global musics and the commonly called "praise choruses" and "worship bands" now reaching every country in the globe. Consider the problematic nature of songs merely translated linguistically (English to Portuguese, for example), yet representing musical language in tones, rhythms, and harmonies that come from a powerfully rich marketing economy, the "contemporary songs" of the United States. Faithful contextualization or inculturation, something that has been long hoped for, is far removed from churches everywhere, as are any commitments to explore transcultural matters in worship and even less desire to inquire as to the countercultural nature of much in the world and church today, as Mark Bangert has shown in his thoughtful chapter above.

A recent volume on the history of my denominational body brings the questions raised in that text home. Bradley Longfield's *Presbyterians and American Culture: A History* is a fascinating report and reflection that covers the span of that branch of the church's life.[17] There was an undeniable allegiance and influence between church and political ideas and programs at the time of this nation's beginnings. Tomoko Masuzawa joins Longfield's voice, saying, "We often think of the mainstream culture of the United States as having been largely determined by particular strands of Protestant Christianity."[18] Jay Wilkey also reflects on that history in an essay on congregational song and its role in the life of the church and world, entitled "Music and the Making of the Nation."[19] The sung words in liturgy both express and shape our affections, our grasp of the meaning of "church," and set the patterns for our ecclesiological and political decisions, these writers suggest — individually and corporately.

17. Bradley J. Longfield, *Presbyterians and American Culture: A History* (Louisville: Westminster John Knox, 2013).

18. Tomoko Masuzawa, "Culture," in Mark C. Taylor, ed., *Critical Terms for Religious Studies* (Chicago: University of Chicago Press, 1998), p. 70.

19. Jay W. Wilkey, "Music and the Making of the Church," *Review and Expositor* 83, no. 1 (Winter 1976): 33-45.

Susurrations' Hope and Promise

As a student of liturgical theology and a woman of faith, I find much in our times that brings out in me a kind of despair concerning the worship of churches across this nation in general, and in the area where I live, central Texas, in particular. But not only here. Read and reflect on the reports of worship in many countries as noted in two recent volumes, *Christian Worship Worldwide: Expanding Horizons, Deepening Practices*, and *The Meaning of Christian Liturgy: Recent Developments in the Church of Sweden*.[20] The former volume includes ample quotes from the four statements in the LWF study series and narratives of case studies on worship in many countries. Reports on case studies are also, of course, at the heart of the original project that gave birth to the present volume. *The Meaning of Christian Liturgy* is a look into the worship life of the Church of Sweden, a text deeply rooted in the ecclesiological questions all liturgical practices raise. It is astonishing in what it reveals. In the words of a deacon in my part of the world, there might be a "low common denominator" in worship between what is taking place in liturgy and worship in Sweden and America's current liturgical practices, not only in Lutheran churches, but in all "mainline" churches. Sven-Erik Brodd says that worship in his country can be seen as "popular liturgy based on democracy as an ecclesiological category," or worship that seeks to mirror the history and the life of the national, political, and social culture in which it takes place. For example, Brodd proposes:

> At the end of the 1980s one idea, based on a survey by sociologists of religion, was to create liturgies in accordance with the needs of different generations and that there "might be more important factors to consider in construing the worship for the future than the more tradition-based historical reasons. . . ." It could perhaps be said that the most important ecclesiological change in recent years channeled through liturgy is what has been called the transition from church to well-being. These ideas have been greatly influenced by trends in the United States.[21]

20. Charles E. Farhadian, ed., *Christian Worship Worldwide: Expanding Horizons, Deepening Practices* (Grand Rapids: Eerdmans, 2007); see also Oloph Bexell, ed., *The Meaning of Christian Liturgy: Recent Developments in the Church of Sweden*, foreword by Gordon W. Lathrop (Grand Rapids: Eerdmans, 2012).

21. Sven-Erik Brodd, "Liturgy Crossing Frontiers: Interplay and Confrontation of Ecclesiological Patterns in Liturgical Change during the Twentieth Century," in Farhadian, ed., *Christian Worship Worldwide*, pp. 46, 48-49.

"Transition from church to well-being." This is as far as it can get from the understandings of liturgical life and its implications for ecclesiology and the world beyond the liturgy that are found in Lathrop, Stauffer, and Chupungco. This is also a source of continuing bafflement — and no small amount of pain — for many who find it difficult to sing with the psalmist of the gladness of the mere idea of going to the "house of the LORD" on the Lord's Day (Ps. 122).

But then, as hungry as I am for a continuing dominical life of word and sacrament that is faithful to a local parish's claimed liturgical ecclesiology and theology — yet faithfully ecumenical — I extend to you, the reader, an invitation: Look more closely at liturgical practices in your part of the world, as I do in what is a five-year-long look at culture and worship in the context of central Texas, and you may find reasons for hope. There are small susurrations being heard in some communities, and even some loud festal shouts. You might be surprised by hope and joy, particularly in the midst of the often confounding cultural links between church and state found in this part of the world. The three churches in this narrative are examples of liturgical life that go beyond what one would expect based on what we know of their ecclesiological/denominational claims. They seem to express in their practice and life, one way or another, the values and paradigms found in the heart of the LWF Study Series on Worship and Culture — the Cartigny, Nairobi, and Chicago statements. However, these narratives only focus on some basic facets of life as they gather as assemblies.

St. James Episcopal Church in Austin. Originally an African-American church, its Sunday assemblies today are clear demonstrations of what might happen when a congregation is committed to express, welcome, and forge — in worship and the life beyond worship — the wideness of God's mercies in diversity. As a rule, about 200-250 worshipers gather in one of two services, the second service entirely in Spanish. This is particularly meaningful in light of the troubled waters of the relationships between African Americans and Hispanics in the United States, about which the musical *West Side Story* spoke decades ago, but which persist today. That history is not lost; indeed, it is recognized in liturgy. There is always the sense that one is worshiping with people who bring as part of their story both the awful oppressions and horrors of African-American slavery, today's continuing racism, and the threatened way of life for so many Hispanics. A deeply lived theology of the cross pervades much that is said and done in prayers and songs. Lament is never too far away. Yet hope and joy in Christ's presence and the promise of victory of life over death is always strong and clear.

This is particularly seen on "festival" days. On the first Sunday in Advent, on Christmas Eve and Christmas Day, Epiphany, Easter, Pentecost, All Saints, and Christ the King festivals — then things are different. For those celebrations, about 400 or more cram the sanctuary for one shared liturgy. The worship aid is a full booklet with hymns, songs, and prayers in both English and Spanish. Organ and piano are now joined by a mariachi band in full regalia; spirituals and classic gems of hymnody from various parts of the world and from various cultures and stories are sung; prayers, liturgical texts, and the sermon are in both languages. The sanctuary itself merits consideration: the assembled take seats in groups that form a large semicircle facing the altar. The choir sits behind it, giving an impression of a full circle of the assembly. A liturgical mind was behind the design of these things. This church is where liturgical theologian William Seth Adams, who wrote specifically on liturgical spaces, served the congregation for quite some time. During the passing of the peace, the vibrancy and zest of diverse cultures mingle here in myriad tones. Abundant smiles speak of the wonder of God in granting humans such lovely diversity, color, and life. The list of special festivals is augmented by the addition of feasts and celebrations from African-American traditions and the Hispanic story of faith. This church seems to cultivate unity in diversity — inside and outside of the liturgy. There are no screens in the sanctuary. The assembly includes children and youth in large numbers. Unexpected graces abound.

First Baptist Church in Austin. This church is a study in surprise. It gathers in a very imposing sanctuary. The high and wide liturgical space holds a large cross, front and center, and a large submersion pool on one side, in the same axis with the pulpit and the communion table. On the first Sunday that my husband and I worshiped there, we were warmly greeted and then handed a worship aid that looked, surprisingly, as though its leaders used the Presbyterian *Book of Common Worship* to prepare the liturgy, in what looks very much like the ecumenical *ordo* that book proposes.[22] The liturgy of the word includes at least two texts, which are part of the common revised lectionary that so many of us embrace, again surprisingly in the context of worship life in this area's churches in the evangelical tradition. And there is the acclamation, "The word of the Lord," followed by the assembly's response, "Thanks be to God." Then we were very surprised to hear such a sermon as to confound not only this theologian but, as we later learned, others who routinely worship there — though they are not members of that

---

22. *Book of Common Worship* (Louisville: Westminster John Knox, 1993).

church. Many come because they are attracted precisely by the strength of the preaching and the striking blend of cultural worship traditions, which consistently call forth a gospel and a faith that, as my Jesuit brothers and Catholic sisters in Seattle would say, "do justice."

One is invited to hear denominational barriers — and surely expectations — crumbling in this setting as the Lord's Supper is celebrated. All are welcome. Here, via word and table, all hear the gospel interpreted and lived in ways that lead participants to understand the source of this church's passion for the work from the liturgy and in the world. This congregation is united in the strong opposition to the state's treatment of Hispanics and other immigrants in the area. In the local cultural ethos, in which nation is often the god, this is worthy of notice: this is an evangelical church where the sense of "evangelical" moves participants beyond a narrow-minded interpretation of that word. This is a church to which many flock in the certainty that word and table matters as they seek to reject the enticement of worship exclusively based on *theologia gloriae*. This church places any triumphalist nature of liturgy, common in this area, "down by the riverside"; instead, the congregation lives worship where *theologia cruci* is proclaimed and enacted. There are no screens in the sanctuary. The assembly includes children and youth in large numbers. Unexpected graces abound.

West Plano Presbyterian Church in Plano, Texas. This church is in a suburb of Dallas; about 200 worshipers gather normally. Though a predominantly white congregation, it is working slowly to attract its neighborhood, and it now counts among its members some who are recent immigrants from African nations. Congregational song, as in the two churches mentioned above, is rich both in traditional and contemporary "classic" hymnody, and in songs from the world's peoples, with a large array of instruments and styles. In this congregation, the prayers of the people, both thanksgivings and intercessions, flow in waves upon waves from the congregation, and so do prayers for the world's leaders and those nations in crisis of one kind or another. Prayers for ministers beyond the PCUSA are named. A large number of youth take on liturgical leadership as acolytes, lectors, and as those who bear the gifts of bread and wine to the table. Then this: during the offertory, baskets and baskets of food products are brought by worshipers to the foot of the communion table, as they come to receive bread and wine — and this dominically. These baskets include fresh produce grown in the church's own community garden. Immediately following the Eucharist, the baskets are taken to food banks for the homeless in the city.

Every Sunday these congregants, along with their pastor and other leaders, literally hear the susurrations as water is poured into the font at the outset of the confessional prayers and the declaration of pardon. The font is octagonal in design, resting on a wooden stand with a cross in its center, supporting a large clear acrylic bowl. It is placed on a special octagonal floor design in travertine tiles. The hope is that in the future there will be a larger space that will accommodate a full submersion pool, more in keeping with the church's deep commitment to baptismal formation, identity, and life. Most in the assembly touch the water, make the sign of the cross, and/or bow as they come to receive bread and wine in the liturgy of the table. These are people for whom the unity of the body of Christ is expressed every Sunday, week in and week out, often with texts that are part of the ecumenical language, a sign of their commitment to baptismal life's deep meanings. Cultural issues play themselves out in the light of word and sacrament. The historical and marvelous Rites of Initiation in the ministry of the catechumenate are fully celebrated in all their meaningful texts and actions.[23] There is coherence, then, in the fact that in this church the Triduum, or as Ramshaw reminds us, the "Three-Day Feast," is celebrated in its fullness every year, bringing to life the oft-declared reality that, as Sunday is to the week, so is the Three-in-One liturgy to the year.[24] This congregation seems to join the other churches, I am glad to note in this chapter, in their desire to cultivate diversity within fidelity to a way of being church that is all too rare these days: fidelity to its locality (ecclesiological and cultural) within fidelity to the globality of the gospel witnessed to in liturgy. There are no screens in the sanctuary. The assembly includes children and youth in large numbers. Unexpected graces abound.

This is simply the witness of one who has been a willing participant in a rather large number of churches' liturgical lives during these last years. This has been a journey that involved no small amount of pain, but also large doses of hope. It is my hope that these small segments of the life of the congregations described here offer the readers hope that all liturgies, in their places of celebration, are for the common good, for the sake of Jesus Christ, and for the world loved by God. They are witness to the fact that they and the authors here speaking well know both the festal shout and the susurrations of the font.

23. The church's pastor, Dr. David Batchelder, is well known in the Presbyterian Church (USA) as the foremost expert on these ancient rites of initiation, and he serves as consultant for other pastors and church leaders beyond the PCUSA on baptismal formation, theology, and practice.

24. Gail Ramshaw, *The Three-Day Feast: Maundy Thursday, Good Friday, Easter,* Worship Matters Series (Minneapolis: Augsburg Fortress, 2004).

Conclusion: Susurrations Where Life Unites[25]

The words around the baptismal font in the Chapel of St. Ignatius at Seattle University and on the logo of the School of Theology and Ministry of that institution are compelling. They imagine and offer a vision of a church beyond the cultural walls that divide Christians: exclusivism, parochialism, denominationalism, historical schisms, and liturgical life that far too often mirror the culture of spiritual individualism and entertainment rather than the countercultural grace — and risk — of common life envisioned in the gospel. Instead, based on Ephesians 4:4-6, the text on the rim of the font speaks of a common baptism and thus a common identity: "No barrier can divide where life unites: one faith, one fount, one Spirit, makes one people." These words, as found on the font at the Chapel of St. Ignatius, are part of a segment translated from an inscription in the baptistery of the Cathedral of Rome by the fifth-century St. John the Lateran and are foundational for the School of Theology and Ministry (STM). They provide lenses for the principles that served in the processes leading to the life of the institution's weekly ecumenical liturgical life, and for the Summer Institute for Liturgy and Worship (SILW), which this writer founded and directed for seven years. Other writers in this volume were part of the core faculty of that event — year in and year out. The Chapel of St. Ignatius is one of two chapels on campus.

The second chapel, the "Ecumenical Chapel," is a symbol of STM's commitment to its vision and mission. The space was renovated from the original sanctuary to serve the school's community and churches in partnership with STM during the second year of my work, with representatives from all churches in partnership with the institution. Attached to the back of this chapel there is also a multiple-faith space for quiet prayer and reflection that serves students from other faiths who desire to pray in their language, with spaces for ablutions and for vessels that are part of the story of faith for many (e.g., rugs for prayers).

The chapel itself is an enticing place: there is a large font at the entrance, round on the outside with water continually flowing to a cruciform pool in the inside, lined with shiny small tiles that reflect the metal cross suspended in the center of the space over the communion altar/table. Font, table, and

---

25. The segment that follows first appeared as a lecture presented at the 2006 Summer Institute for Liturgy and Worship, and in print in the *Journal of the Office of Theology and Worship of the PCUSA*, "Call to Worship."

pulpit are in a continuous axis, the assembly gathered around these things in semicircles facing the table in the center of the room. The font is the only immovable element in the space — and intentionally so: baptism is the base and framework from which all services took life in a community where students and faculty alike are part of a large array of churches and cultures. Liturgies of the hours, particularly morning and evening prayers, various services of word and/or services of word and sacrament began from the font — literally and metaphorically. To this day, as the community gathers in that space, a gentle susurration is always present. The waters still proclaim the common identity at the heart of the diverse offerings brought to liturgies in that space. The LWF study series' essays and stories were of profound significance for that work and ecumenical life, which were grounded in what that font's susurrations expressed. These are indeed waters that speak, as the *Chicago Statement on Worship and Culture* tells us:

> The foundational event in the life of any Christian community is the "one Baptism" (Eph. 4:5) which constitutes the Church to be a "royal priesthood," *proclaiming* the mighty acts of the life-giving God for all the world (1 Pet. 2:9). Baptism is the burial of Christians together with Christ in order that they may be raised with him to newness of life (Rom. 6:4) as signs of God's new creation. It is the "washing of water by the Word" (Eph. 5:26) that *proclaims* and gives the forgiveness of sins and, at the same time, identifies the Christian community with Jesus Christ, who identifies himself with outsiders and sinners and all the needy world.[26]

In a way, serving as editor of this volume continues to be, for this writer, the work of that worship life in Seattle's ecumenical story. I am keenly aware of the fact that the gifts of the presenters there — and writers here in this book — offer the vision of a shared story and shared faith beyond our localities, even as we continue to ask questions concerning culture and liturgical inculturation with open minds and hearts. As in Seattle, writers and readers from the Philippines to Australia alike, you have come with your gifts; from the Caribbean to Texas, you have brought your stories; from Philadelphia to Brazil, you have shared your songs. From diverse church communions you are seeking to bear with the rest of us the joys and the challenges that come with seeking to listen to the water that speaks, saying that we are one in

---

26. S. Anita Stauffer, ed., *Baptism, Rites of Passage, and Culture*, LWF Study Series, Department for Theology and Studies (Geneva: LWF, 1998), pp. 13-24.

Christ. We find in these waters that cultural or ecclesial diversities are to be received but also critiqued as gifts, ecclesiological and cultural difficulties notwithstanding, all to be held to the light of the gospel, which is Christ. For all of you who have been in this project — writers, friends, readers, sisters and brothers all — thanks be to God. As we sang in Seattle in blessing our speakers, "May you cling to wisdom, for she will protect you, and if you follow her, she will keep you safe."[27]

27. Text adapted from Proverbs 4. Adaptation and music, Steven C. Warner, Octavo, Copyright 1993 © World Library Publications.

Appendix: Participants in the Original LWF Project

Study Team on Worship and Culture: Lutheran World Federation (LWF) Department for Theology and Studies

PROFESSOR ADISS ARNOLD
Gurukul Lutheran Theological College, Madras, India

PROFESSOR MARK P. BANGERT
Lutheran School of Theology, Chicago, USA

PROFESSOR ØYSTEIN BJØRDAL
Norwegian Lutheran School of Theology, Oslo, Norway

REVEREND ERIC DYCK
Parish Pastor, Montreal, Canada

PROFESSOR MARCUS P. B. FELDE
Martin Luther Seminary, Lae, Papua New Guinea

RIGHT REVEREND JULIUS FILO
Evangelical Church of the Augsburg Confession in the Slovak Republic, Bratislava, Slovak Republic

RIGHT REVEREND WILLIAM GORSKI
Evangelical Lutheran Church in Chile, Santiago, Chile

PROFESSOR NELSON KIRST
Escola Superior de Teología, São Leopoldo, Brazil

OKR Hans Krech
United Lutheran Churches of Germany, Hannover, Germany

Professor Gordon W. Lathrop
Lutheran Theological Seminary, Philadelphia, USA

Professor Mark Luttio
Japan Lutheran Theological Seminary, Tokyo, Japan

Helena Tallius Myhrman
Architect, Bromma, Sweden

Reverend Nils-Henrik Nilsson
Church of Sweden, Commission on Congregational Life, Uppsala, Sweden

William Obaga
Musician, Nairobi, Kenya

Reverend C. Lisandro Orlov
Parish Pastor, Buenos Aires, Argentina

Professor Markus Roser
Ecole de Théologie de Baboua, Central African Republic

Reverend Louis Sibiya
Evangelical Lutheran Church in Southern Africa, Bonaero Park, Republic
of South Africa

Reverend Karen Ward
Evangelical Lutheran Church in America, Division for Congregational
Life, Chicago, USA

Professor Mabel Wu
Lutheran Theological Seminary, Hong Kong

Ecumenical Participants

Doctor Anscar J. Chupungco, OSB (Roman Catholic)
Paul VI Institute of Liturgy, Bukidnon, The Philippines

Reverend David Gilari (Anglican)
Diocese of Kirinyaga, Kutus, Kenya

Professor Karen Westerfield Tucker (Methodist)
Duke University Divinity School, Durham, NC, USA

LWF Staff

REVEREND S. ANITA STAUFFER
Study Secretary for Worship and Congregational Life, Department for
Theology and Studies

REGULA DOMINGUEZ
Secretary

Chicago Consultation Participants: LWF Worship and Culture Study Team (persons and positions at time of original publication, 1999)

PROFESSOR ADISS ARNOLD
Gurukul Lutheran Theological College, Madras, India

PROFESSOR MARK P. BANGERT
Lutheran School of Theology at Chicago, USA

PROFESSOR MUSAWENKOSI D. BIYELA
Lutheran Theological Seminary, Mapumulo, South Africa

PROFESSOR ØYSTEIN BJØRDAL
Liturgical Center, Trondheim, Norway

REVEREND ERIC DYCK
St. John's Lutheran Church, Montreal, Quebec, Canada

PROFESSOR NELSON KIRST
Escola Superior de Teología, São Leopoldo, RS, Brazil

OKR HANS KRECH
Lutherisches Kirchenamt, Hannover, Germany

PROFESSOR MARK LUTTIO
Japan Lutheran Theological Seminary, Tokyo, Japan

HELENA TALLIUS MYHRMAN
Architect, Bromma, Sweden

REVEREND NILS-HENRIK NILSSON
Church of Sweden Commission on Congregational Life, Uppsala, Sweden

REVEREND C. LISANDRO ORLOV
Buenos Aires, Argentina

REVEREND KAREN WARD
ELCA Division for Congregational Ministries, Chicago, IL, USA

PROFESSOR MABEL WU
Lutheran Theological Seminary, Shatin, N.T., Hong Kong, China

Ecumenical Participant

REVEREND THOMAS F. BEST
World Council of Churches (WCC), Commission on Faith and Order,
Geneva, Switzerland

Resource Persons

REVEREND ANSCAR J. CHUPUNGCO, OSB
Paul VI Institute of Liturgy, Bukidnon, The Philippines

PROFESSOR GORDON W. LATHROP
Lutheran Theological Seminary, Philadelphia, PA, USA

Consultants

REVEREND MARCUS FELDE
Versailles, IN, USA (former missionary to Papua New Guinea)

REGINA KUEHN
Oak Park, IL, USA (liturgical design consultant, St. Benedict the African
Church)

REVEREND PAUL R. NELSON
ELCA Director of Worship, Chicago, IL, USA

REVEREND MARKUS ROSER
LWD/DNK, Stuttgart, Germany (former missionary to the Central
African Republic)

LWF Staff

REVEREND S. ANITA STAUFFER
LWF Department for Theology and Studies, Geneva, Switzerland

ELCA Staff

RUTH ALLIN
ELCA Division for Congregational Ministries, Chicago, IL, U.S.A.

Listing in S. Anita Stauffer, ed., *Baptism, Rites of Passage, and Culture* (Geneva: LWF, 1998), pp. 275-78.

Listing in S. Anita Stauffer, *Christian Worship: Unity in Cultural Diversity,* vol. 2 (Geneva: LWF, 1998).

A Selected Bibliography on Worship, Culture, and the Unity of the Church

Abega, P. "Liturgical Adaptation." In *Christianity in Independent Africa*, edited by Edward Fasholé et al. Bloomington: Indiana University Press, 1978.

Abbott, Walter M., ed. *The Documents of Vatican II.* Translated by Joseph Gallagher. New York: America Press, 1966.

Adam, Júlio Cézar. "The Church Year in the Southern Hemisphere: A Case Study from Brazil." *Studia Liturgica,* 40 (2010).

———. Liturgia com os pés: estudo sobre a função social do culto cristão. São Leopoldo: EST/Sinodal, 2012.

Adler, Peter S. "Beyond Cultural Identity: Reflections on Cultural and Multicultural Man." In *Intercultural Communication: A Reader*, 2nd ed., edited by Larry Samovar and Richard Porter. Belmont, CA: Wadsworth Publishing, 1976.

Albuquerque, Amara C., ed. *Música brasileira na liturgia.* Petropolis: Vozes, 1969.

Amalorpavadass, D. S. "Theological Reflections on Inculturation." *Studia Liturgica,* Part 1, 20:1 (1990): 36-54; Part 2, 20:2 (1990): 116-36.

Anderson, Herbert, and Edward Foley. *Mighty Stories, Dangerous Rituals: Weaving Together the Human and the Divine.* San Francisco: Jossey-Bass, 1998.

Anderson, Herbert, and Robert Cotton Fite. *Becoming Married.* Louisville: Westminster John Knox, 1993.

Andrieu, M., ed. *Les Ordines Romani du haut moyen âge.* Vol. 2. Louvain, 1971.

Appiah, Kwame Anthony. *Cosmopolitanism: Ethics in a World of Strangers.* New York: Norton, 2006.

Aram, I. "The Incarnation of the Gospel in Cultures: A Missionary Event." *Ecumenical Review* 48, no. 1 (January 1996): 96-105.

Arazu, Raymond. "A Cultural Model for Christian Prayer." In *African Christian Spirituality*, edited by Aylward Shorter. Maryknoll, NY: Orbis Books, 1980.

Arbuckle, Gerard A. *Culture, Inculturation, and Theologians: A Postmodern Critique.* Collegeville, MN: Liturgical, 2010.

Avila, Rafael. *Apuntes sobre las implicaciones socio-políticas de la Eucaristía.* Bogota: Policrom Aries Gráficas, 1977. (English translation: *Worship and Politics.* Maryknoll, NY: Orbis Books, 1981.)

Baker, Jonny, Doug Gay, et al. *Alternative Worship.* London: SPCK, 2003.

Balbinot, Egídio. *Liturgia e política: a dimensão política da liturgia nas romarias da terra de Santa Catarina.* Chapecó: Grifos, 1998.

Bangert, Mark. "The Gospel about Gospel — The Power of the Ring." *Currents in Theology and Mission* 31, no. 4 (August 2004): 257-58.

Baptism, Eucharist and Ministry. Faith and Order Paper 111. Geneva: World Council of Churches, 1982-2007. (25th anniversary printing, with additional introduction, 2007.)

Baptism, Eucharist and Ministry 1982-1990: Report on the Process and Responses. Faith and Order Paper 149, Geneva: WCC Publications, 1990.

Barros, Marcelo. *Celebrar Deus da Vida: tradição litúrgica e inculturação.* São Paulo: Loyola, 1992.

Benson, Stanley. "The Conquering Sacrament: Baptism and Demon Possession among the Maasai of Tanzania." *Africa Theological Journal* 9, no. 2 (July 1980): 51-63.

Best, Thomas F., ed. *Baptism Today: Understanding, Practices, Ecumenical Implications.* A Pueblo Book. Collegeville, MN: Liturgical, 2008.

Best, Thomas F., and Dagmar Heller, eds. *Eucharistic Worship in Ecumenical Contexts: The Lima Liturgy and Beyond.* Geneva: WCC Publications, 1998.

————, eds. *Worship Today: Understanding, Practice, Ecumenical Implications.* Geneva, WCC Publications, 2004.

Bevans, Stephen B. *Models of Contextual Theology.* 2nd edition. Maryknoll, NY: Orbis Books, 2002.

Bexell, Oloph, ed. *The Meaning of Christian Liturgy: Recent Developments in the Church of Sweden.* Grand Rapids: Eerdmans, 2012.

Blount, Brian K., and Leonora Tubbs Tisdale, eds. *Making Room at the Table: An Invitation to Multicultural Worship.* Louisville: Westminster John Knox, 2001.

Bobb, Donald. "African Church Music." *Journey of Struggle, Journey in Hope: People and Their Pilgrimage in Central Africa,* edited by Jane Heaton. New York: Friendship Press, 1983.

Bobsin, Oneide. *Correntes religiosas e globalização.* São Leopoldo: CEBI/PPL/IEPG, 2002.

Bonhoeffer, Dietrich. *Letters and Papers from Prison.* Enlarged edition edited by Eberhard Bethge. New York: The Macmillan Company, 1971.

Boff, Leonardo. *Minima Sacramentalia: os sacramentos da vida e a vida dos sacramentos.* 18th ed. Petrópolis: Vozes, 1997.

Bos, Robert, and Geoff Thompson, eds. "Understanding the Church's Teaching on

Baptism (1988)." In *Theology for Pilgrims: Selected Theological Documents of the Uniting Church in Australia,* pp. 509-57. Sydney: Uniting Church Press, 2008.

Bowman, Wayne D. *Philosophical Perspectives on Music.* New York: Oxford University Press, 1998.

Bradshaw, Paul F., and Maxwell E. Johnson. *The Eucharistic Liturgies: Their Evolution and Interpretation.* A Pueblo Book. Collegeville, MN: Liturgical, 2012.

Bradshaw, Paul F., and John Melloh. *Foundations in Ritual Studies: A Reader for Students of Christian Worship.* Grand Rapids: Baker Academic, 2007.

———. *The Search for the Origins of Christian Worship: Sources and Methods for the Study of Early Liturgy.* 2nd ed. London: SPCK, 2002.

Brandão, Carlos Rodrigues, et al. *Inculturação e libertação:* semana de estudos teológicos CNBB/CIMI. 2nd ed. São Paulo: Paulinas, 1986.

Braukamper, Ulrich. "Aspects of Religious Syncretism in Southern Ethiopia." *Journal of Religion in Africa,* 21, no. 3 (August 1992): 194-207.

Brilioth, Yngve. *Eucharistic Faith and Practice: Evangelical and Catholic.* Translated by A. G. Hebert. London: SPCK, 1965.

Brown, Peter. "Christianity and Local Culture in Late Roman Africa." *Journal of Roman Studies* 58, nos. 1-2 (1968): 85-95.

Brunner, Paul. "Liturgical Adaption of Indigenous Music." *China Missionary Bulletin* 9 (December 1957): 668-69.

———. "The Liturgy of Baptism in the Missions." *China Missionary Bulletin* 11 (March 1959): 237-48.

Budde, Michael L. *The Borders of Baptism: Identity, Allegiances, and the Church.* Eugene, OR: Cascade, 2011.

Burns, Stephen. "Heaven or Las Vegas? Engaging Liturgical Theology." In *Mass Culture: The Interface of Eucharist and Mission,* edited by Pete Ward, pp. 95-112. Oxford: BRF, 2008.

———. *Worship and Ministry: Shaped Towards God.* Melbourne: Mosaic, 2012.

———, ed. *The Art of Tentmaking: Making Space for Worship.* Norwich, UK: Canterbury Press, 2012.

Burns, Stephen, and Anita Monro, eds. *Christian Worship in Australia: Inculturating the Liturgical Tradition.* Strathfield, NSW: St Paul's, 2009.

Buyst, Ione. *Símbolos na liturgia.* 4th ed. São Paulo: Paulinas, 2004.

———. Teologia e liturgia na perspectiva da América Latina. In: Favreto, C.; Rampon, Ivanir A. (Orgs), pp. 38-76. Passo Fundo: Berthier, 2008.

Candy, Susan. "Art and Asian Spirituality." In *Mission and Art,* edited by Masao Takenaka and Godwin R. Singh. Hong Kong: Christian Conference of Asia and Asian Christian Art Association, 1994.

Carroll, Kevin. "African Textiles for Church Linen and Vestments." In *Inculturation of Christianity in Africa,* pp. 241-48. Eldoret, Kenya: AMECEA Gaba Publications, 1990.

Cartford, Gerhard. "Public Prayer and Culture: An Ecumenical Journey." *Liturgy* 11, no. 3 (Winter 1994): 31-37.

Carson, D. A., *Christ and Culture Revisited*. Grand Rapids: Eerdmans, 2008.

Cenkner, William, ed. *The Multicultural Church: A New Landscape in U.S. Theologies*. New York: Paulist, 1996.

Chew, Hiang Chea John. "Church and the Inculturation of the Gospel." In *Theology and Cultures*, edited by Yeow Choo Lak. Vol. 2 of *Doing Theology with Asian Resources*. Singapore: Association for Theological Education in South East Asia, 1995.

Chupungco, Anscar J. *The Cultural Adaptation of the Liturgy*. New York: Paulist, 1982.

———. *Handbook For Liturgical Studies*. Vols. 1-5. Collegeville, MN: Liturgical, 1997.

———. *Liturgical Inculturation: Sacramentals, Religiosity and Catechesis*. Collegeville, MN: Liturgical, 1992.

———. "The Liturgical Year: The Gospel Encountering Culture." *Studia Liturgica* 40 (2010): 46-64.

———. *Liturgies of the Future: The Process and Methods of Inculturation*. Mahwah, NJ: Paulist Press, 1989.

———. *Shaping the Easter Feast*. Washington, DC: Pastoral Press, 1992.

———. *Towards a Filipino Liturgy*. Quezon City, Philippines, 1976.

———. *Tradition and Progress*. Washington, DC: Pastoral Press, 1994.

———. *What, Then, Is Liturgy? Musings and Memoirs*. A Pueblo Book. Collegeville, MN: Liturgical, 2010.

Collins, Mary. "Critical Ritual Studies: Examining an Intersection of Theology and Culture." In *Essays on Religion and Culture,* edited by John May. Chico, CA: Scholars Press, 1981.

Cone, James. *Speaking the Truth: Ecumenism, Liberation and Black Theology*. Maryknoll, NY: Orbis Books, 1986, 1999.

Congregatio pro Culto Divine, Citta del Vaticano. "Le Missal Romain pour les dioceses du Zaire." *Notitiae* 24 (1988): 454-72.

Cornehl, Peter. "Öffentlicher Gottesdienst zum Strukturwandel der Liturgie." In *Gottesdienst und Öffentlichkeit: zur Theorie und Didaktik neuer Kommunikation,* edited by Peter Cornehl and Hans-Eckehard Bahr. Hamburg: Furche Verlag, 1970.

Costen, Melva Wilson. *African American Worship*. Nashville: Abingdon, 1996.

———. "African Roots of Afro-American Baptismal Practices." *Journal of the Interdenominational Theological Center* 14, nos. 1-2 (1986-87): 23-42.

Crawford, Janet. "Becoming a Christian: The Ecumenical Implications of Our Common Baptism." Faith and Order Paper 184. Geneva: WCC Publications, 1999.

Crawford, Janet, and Thomas F. Best. "Praise the Lord with the Lyre . . . and the Gamelan? Towards Koinonia in Worship." *The Ecumenical Review* 46, no. 1 (January 1994): 78-96.

Crossan, John Dominic. *The Birth of Christianity*. San Francisco: HarperSanFrancisco, 1998.

Damatta, Roberto. *Carnavais, malandros e heróis: para uma sociologia do dilema brasileiro*. 6th edition. Rio de Janeiro: Rocco, 1997.

De Certeau, Michel. *The Capture of Speech and Other Political Writings*. Minneapolis: University of Minnesota Press, 1998.

De Clerck, P. "Le language liturgique: sa nécessité et ses traites spécifiques." *Questions liturgiques* 73, nos. 1-2 (1992).

Derrida, Jacques. "Des Tours de Babel." In *Acts of Religion*. New York: Routledge, 2002.

Di Sante, Carmine. *Jewish Prayer: The Origins of Christian Liturgy*. New York: Paulist Press, 1985.

Di Sante, C. "Cultura e Liturgia," *Nuovo Dizionario di Liturgia*. Rome, 1984.

Dix, Dom Gregory. *Jew and Greek: A Study in the Primitive Church*. Westminster, UK: Dacre Press, 1953.

———. *The Shape of the Liturgy*. London: A. C. Black, 1945.

Doemer, David I. "Comparative Analysis of Life after Death in Folk Shinto and Christianity." *Japanese Journal of Religious Studies* 4 (1977).

Donnella, Joseph A. *Like Other People's Children: The Danish West Indies Lutheran Mission; A Caribbean Prototype of Liturgical Inculturation*. Saarbrucken: Lap-Lambert Academic Publishing, 2010.

Donovan, Vincent J. *Christianity Rediscovered*. Maryknoll, NY: Orbis Books, 1983.

Echiegu, A. *Translating the Collects of the "Sollemnitates Domini" of the "Missale Romanum" of Paul VI in the Language of the African* (Münster, 1984).

Egbulem, Chris Nwaka. "An African Interpretation of Liturgical Inculturation: The Rite Zairois." In *A Promise of Presence*, edited by Michael Downey and Richard Fragomeni. Washington, DC: Pastoral Press, 1992.

Eliade, Mircea. *The Quest: History and Meaning in Religion*. Chicago: University of Chicago Press, 1969.

———. *Rites and Symbols of Initiation*. New York: Harper and Row, 1958.

———. *Sacred and Profane*. New York: Harcourt Brace Jovanovich, 1959.

"Epistle to Diognetus." Translated by Gordon W. Lathrop. Edited by Kirsopp Lake. In *The Apostolic Fathers*. Vol. 2. Cambridge, MA: Harvard University Press, 1959.

Farhadian, E. Charles, ed. *Christian Worship Worldwide: Expanding Horizons, Deepening Practices*. Grand Rapids: Eerdmans, 2007.

Farley, Edward. *Faith and Beauty: A Theological Aesthetic*. Burlington, VT: Ashgate, 2001.

Flannery, Austin, ed. *Vatican Council II: Constitutions, Decrees, Declarations*. English translation. New York: Costello, 1996.

Fisher, Eugene J., ed. *The Jewish Roots of Christian Liturgy*. New York: Paulist Press, 1990.

Fitzpatrick, Joseph P. *One Church, Many Cultures.* Kansas City: Sheed and Ward, 1987.

Fleming, Daniel Johnson. *Christian Symbols in a World Community.* New York: Friendship Press, 1940.

———. *Heritage of Beauty: Pictorial Studies of Modern Christian Architecture in Asia and Africa Illustrating the Influence of Indigenous Cultures.* New York: Friendship Press, 1937.

Foley, E. *Foundations of Christian Music: The Music of Pre-Constantinian Christianity.* Bramcote, Nottingham, UK: Grove Books, 1992.

———. *From Age to Age: How Christians Celebrate the Eucharist.* Chicago: Liturgy Training Publications, 1991.

Francis, Mark R. "Adaptation, Liturgical." In *The New Dictionary of Sacramental Worship,* edited by Peter Fink. Collegeville, MN: Liturgical, 1990.

———. *Liturgy in a Multicultural Community.* Collegeville, MN: Liturgical, 1991.

———. *Shape a Circle Ever Wider: Liturgical Inculturation in the United States.* Chicago: Liturgy Training Publications, 2000.

Francis, Mark R., and Keith Pecklers, eds. *Liturgy for the New Millenium: A Commentary on the Revised Sacramentary. Essays in Honor of Anscar J. Chupungco, OSB.* A Pueblo Book. Collegeville, MN: Liturgical, 2000.

Frith, Simon. *Performing Rites.* Cambridge, MA: Harvard University Press, 1996.

Gallagher, Michael Paul, SJ. *Clashing Symbols: An Introduction to Faith and Culture.* New York: Paulist Press, 2003.

Gardner, Howard. *Frames of Mind.* New York: Basic Books, 2011.

Garrigan, Siobhán. *The Real Peace Process: Worship, Politics and the End of Sectarianism.* London: Equinox, 2010.

Gay, Doug. *Remixing the Church: Towards an Emerging Ecclesiology.* London: SCM Press, 2011.

Gitari, David. *Anglican Liturgical Inculturation in Africa.* Alcuin/GROW Liturgical Study 28. Bramcote, Nottingham, UK: Grove Books, 1994.

Gittins, Anthony J. *Gifts and Strangers: Meeting the Challenge of Inculturation.* New York: Paulist Press, 1989.

Gordon, Edwin T. *Learning Sequences in Music.* Chicago: GIA Publications, 2012.

Gray-Reeves, Mary, and Michael Perham. *The Hospitality of God: Emerging Worship for a Missional Church.* London: SPCK, 2010.

Greive, Wolfgang, ed. *Communion, Community, Society: The Relevance of the Church.* Geneva: The Lutheran World Federation, 1998.

Greinacher, Norbert, and Norbert Mette, eds. *Christianity and Cultures (Concilium, 1994:2).* London: SCM Press, 1994. (French edition: *La Foi Chrétienne dans les Diverses Cultures* [*Concilium* 1994:251]; Paris: Beauchesne Eïditeur, 1994) (German edition: *Christlicher Glaube in unterschiedlichen Kulturen* [*Concilium* 30:1]; Mainz: Matthias-Grünewald-Verlag, 1994).

Griffiths, Bede. "Liturgy and the Missions." *China Missionary Bulletin* 12 (February 1960): 148-54.

Grimes, Ronald L. *Beginnings in Ritual Studies.* Lanham, MD: University Press of America, 1982.

Gy, Pierre-Marie. "The Inculturation of the Christian Liturgy in the West." *Studia Liturgica* 20, no. 1 (1990): 8-18.

Hahn, Ferdinand. *The Worship of the Early Church.* Philadelphia: Fortress, 1973.

Hao, Yap Kim. "Inter-Contextualization." *Asia Journal of Theology* 4, no. 1 (April 1990): 36-44.

Happel, Stephen. "Classicist Culture and the Nature of Worship." *Heythrop Journal* 31, no. 3 (July 1980): 288-302.

Harris, Mark. *Grave Matters: A Journey Through the Modern Funeral Industry to a Natural Way of Burial.* New York: Scribner, 2007.

Hastings, Adrian. "Western Christianity Confronts Other Cultures." *Studia Liturgica* 20, no. 1 (1990): 19-27.

Havea, Jione. "The Cons of Contextuality ... Kontextuality," In *Contextual Theology in the Twenty-first Century,* edited by Stephen B. Bevans and Katalina Tahaafe-Williams. Eugene, OR: Wipf and Stock, 2011.

Heller, Dagmar. *Baptized into Christ: A Guide to the Ecumenical Discussion on Baptism.* Geneva: WCC Publications, 2012.

Henderson, J. Frank. "Liturgical Inculturation among Native Peoples in Canada." *National Bulletin on Liturgy* 19, no. 105 (September-October 1986): 228-47.

Hess, M. Lisa. *Learning in a Musical Key: Insight for Theology in a Performative Mode.* Eugene, OR: Pickwick Publications, 2011.

Hesselgrave, David, and Edward Rommen. *Contextualization: Meanings, Methods, and Models.* Leicester, UK: Apollos, 1989.

Hiebert, Paul G. "Critical Contextualization." *International Bulletin of Missionary Research* 11, no. 3 (July 1987): 104-12.

Hillman, Eugene. *The Church as Mission.* New York: Herder and Herder, 1965.

Holeton, David R., ed. *Liturgical Inculturation in the Anglican Communion.* Bramcote, Nottingham, UK: Grove Books, 1990.

Hollenbach, David, S.J. *The Global Face of Public Faith: Politics, Human Rights, and Christian Ethics.* Washington, DC: Georgetown University Press, 2003.

Hollinger, David A. *After Cloven Tongues of Fire: Protestant Liberalism in Modern American History.* Princeton, NJ: Princeton University Press, 2013.

Hunsinger, George. *The Eucharist and Ecumenism: Let Us Keep the Feast.* Cambridge, UK: Cambridge University Press, 2008.

Irion, Paul E. *The Funeral: Vestige or Value?* Nashville: Parthenon Press, 1966.

Jagessar, Michael N. "Spinning Theology: Trickster, Texts and Theology." In *Postcolonial Black British Theology: New Textures and Theme,* edited by Michael N. Jagessar and Anthony G. Reddie, pp. 124-46. Peterborough, UK: Epworth Press, 2007.

Jagessar, Michael N., and Stephen Burns. *Christian Worship: Postcolonial Perspectives.* Sheffield, UK: Equinox, 2011.

Johnson, Clare V. "Inculturating the Easter Feast in Southeast Australia." *Worship* 78 (2004).

Johnson, Maxwell E., ed. *Sacraments and Liturgy.* Louisville: Westminster John Knox Press, 2012.

Jones, Paul H. "We Are How We Worship: Corporate Worship as a Matrix for Christian Identity Formation." *Worship* 69, no. 4 (July 1995): 346-60.

Jungmann, Josef A. *The Early Liturgy.* Notre Dame, IN: University of Notre Dame Press, 1959.

Kabasele, F. "Du canon roman au rite zaïrois." *Bulletin de théologie africaine* 4, no. 7 (janvier-juin, 1982): 213-28.

Kain, Anthony. "Jewish Roots of Christian Worship." In *The New Dictionary of Sacramental Worship.* Collegeville, MN: Liturgical, 1990.

———. " 'My Son's Bread': About Culture, Language and Liturgy." In *A Promise of Presence,* edited by Michael Downey and Richard Fragomeni. Washington, DC: Pastoral Press, 1992.

Kavanagh, Aidan. "Liturgical Inculturation: Looking to the Future." *Studia Liturgica* 20, no. 1 (1990): 95-106.

———. *The Shape of Baptism.* New York: Pueblo, 1978.

Keesing, F. *Cultural Anthropology: The Science of Custom.* New York: Rinehart, 1958.

Kelleher, Margaret. "Liturgy, Culture, and the Challenge of Catholicity." *Worship* 84, no. 2 (2010): 120.

Kinnamon, Michael. *The Vision of the Ecumenical Movement and How It Has Been Impoverished by Its Friends.* St. Louis: Chalice Press, 2003.

Kirst, Nelson, ed. *Culto e cultura em Vale da Pitanga.* São Leopoldo: IEPG, 1995.

Kolb, Robert, and Timothy J. Wengert, eds. The Augsburg Confession, Article XXIV (German Text) in *The Book of Concord: The Confessions of the Evangelical Lutheran Church,* Minneapolis: Fortress, 2000.

Koyama, Kosuke. "The Tradition and Indigenisation." *Asia Journal of Theology* 7, no. 1 (April 1993): 2-11.

LaCugna, Catherine Mowry. "The Baptismal Formula, Feminist Objections, and Trinitarian Theology." *Journal of Ecumenical Studies* 26, no. 2 (Spring, 1989): 235-50.

Lake, Kirsopp, ed. *The Apostolic Fathers.* Cambridge, MA: Harvard University Press, 1959.

Lange, Dirk G. "Confessions, Ecumenism, Ethnicity: A Lutheran Charism." In *Theological Practices that Matter: Theology in the Life of the Church.* Vol. 5. Minneapolis: LWF Lutheran University Press, 2009.

———. *Trauma Recalled: Liturgy, Disruption, and Theology.* Minneapolis: Fortress Press, 2009.

Lange, Dirk, and Dwight W. Vogel, eds. *Ordo: Bath, Word, Prayer, Time: A Primer in Liturgical Theology in Honor of Gordon W. Lathrop*. Akron, OH: OSL Publications, 2006.

Lathrop, Gordon W. "Berakah Response." *Proceedings of the North American Academy of Liturgy* (2007): 26-40.

———. *Holy Ground: A Liturgical Cosmology*. Minneapolis: Fortress, 2009.

———. *Holy People: A Liturgical Ecclesiology*. Minneapolis: Fortress, 1999.

———. *Holy Things: A Liturgical Theology*. Minneapolis: Fortress, 1993.

———. "*Ordo* and Coyote: Further Reflections on Order, Disorder, and Meaning in Christian Worship." *Worship* 80, no. 3 (2006): 194-213.

Leaver, Robin A. "Theological Dimensions of Mission Hymnody: The Counterpoint at Cult and Culture." *African Journal of Theology* 16, no. 3 (1987): 242-54.

Levitin, Daniel J. *This Is Your Brain on Music*. New York: Penguin Group, 2006.

Loh, I-to. "Toward Contextualization of Church Music in Asia." *Asia Journal of Theology* 4, no. 1 (April 1990): 293-315.

Lucarini, Dan. *Why I left the Contemporary Christian Music Movement*. Webster, NY: Evangelical Press USA, 2002.

Luther, Martin. *Liturgy and Hymns*. Vol. 53 of *Luther's Works*. American edition. Edited by Ulrich S. Leupold. Philadelphia: Fortress, 1965.

Lutheran World Federation. *Confessing Christ in Cultural Contexts*. 2 vols. Geneva: LWF Department of Studies, 1981, 1983.

———. *A Lutheran Agenda for Worship*. Geneva: LWF Department of Studies, 1979. (*O culto luterano*. Portuguese translation by Getulio Bertelli. São Leopoldo, 1982. *Temario luterano para el culto*. Spanish translation by Robert Hoeferkamp. Mexico City and Bogota, 1981.)

Mannion, M. Francis. "Culture, Liturgy and. . . ." In *The New Dictionary of Sacramental Worship*. Collegeville, MN: Liturgical, 1990.

———. "Liturgy and Culture." Four-part series. *Liturgy* 80 (April 1989, July 1989, October 1989) and *Liturgy* 90 (February-March 1990).

———. "Liturgy and the Present Crisis of Culture." *Worship* 62, no. 2 (March 1988): 98-123.

Maraschin, Jaci. *A beleza da santidade: ensaios de liturgia*. São Paulo: ASTE, 1996.

———. *Da leveza e de beleza: liturgia na pós-modernidade*. São Paulo: ASTE, 2010.

Martin, Gerhard Marcel. *Fest und Alltag: Bausteine zu einer Theorie des Festes*. Stuttgart/Berlin/Köln/Mainz: Kohlhammer, 1973.

Marty, Martin E. "From the Centripetal to the Centrifugal in Culture and Religion." *Theology Today* 51, no. 1 (April 1994): 5-16.

Martyr, Justin. *1 Apology*. Edited by L. Pautigny. Paris, 1904. Partial English translation: W. Jurgens. *The Faith of the Early Fathers*. Collegeville, MN: Liturgical, 1970.

Matta, Roberto da. *Carnavais, malandros e heróis: para um sociologia do dilema brasileiro*. 6th ed. Rio de Janeiro: Rocco, 1997.

———. *O que é o Brasil?* Rio de Janeiro: Rocco, 2004.

May, John R., ed., *The Bent World: Essays on Religion and Culture.* The Annual Publication of the College Theology Society. Chico, CA: Scholars Press, 1981.

Mazza, E. *The Eucharistic Prayers of the Roman Rite.* New York: Pueblo, 1986.

McFague, Sallie. *Metaphorical Theology.* Philadelphia: Fortress, 1982.

———. *Models of God: Theology for an Ecological, Nuclear Age.* Philadelphia: Fortress, 1987.

Menocal, Maria Rosa. *Ornament of the World.* Boston: Little, Brown, 2002.

Meyers, Ruth. "Liturgy and Society: Cultural Influences on Contemporary Liturgical Revision." In *Liturgy in Dialogue,* edited by Paul Bradshaw and Bryan Spinks. Collegeville, MN: Liturgical, 1995.

Miles, Margaret. *Images as Insight: Visual Understanding in Western Christianity and Secular Culture.* Boston: Beacon Press, 1985.

Miller, Vincent J. *Consuming Religion: Christian Faith and Practice in a Consumer Culture.* New York: Continuum, 2008.

Monro, Anita. *Resurrecting Erotic Transgression: Subjecting Ambiguity in Theology.* Gender, Theology, and Spirituality Series. London: Equinox, 2006.

———. "A View from the Antipodes. Juxtaposing Dingo and Baby: A Consideration of the Cycle of Light in the Australian Summer." *Studia Liturgica* 40 (2010): 94-101.

Need, Stephen W. *Human Language and Knowledge in the Light of Chalcedon.* New York: Peter Lang, 1996.

Nelson, Cary, and Lawrence Grossberg, eds., *Marxism and the Interpretation of Culture.* Basingstoke, UK: Macmillan, 1988, 271-313.

Nelstropp, Louise, and Martyn Percy, eds. *Evaluating Fresh Expressions: Explorations in the Emerging Church.* Norwich, UK: Canterbury Press, 2009.

Northcott, Michael. "BEM and the Struggle for the Liturgical Soul of the Emergent Church." In *BEM at 25: Critical Insights into a Continuing Legacy,* edited by Thomas F. Best and Tamara Grdzelidze, pp. 87-104. Faith and Order Paper 205. Geneva: WCC Publications, 2007.

Paxton, Frederick S. *Christianizing Death: The Creation of a Ritual Process in Early Medieval Europe.* Ithaca, NY: Cornell University Press, 1990.

Pelikan, Jaroslav. *Christianity and Classical Culture.* New Haven: Yale University Press, 1993.

———. *Jesus Through the Centuries: His Place in the History of Culture.* New Haven: Yale University Press, 1985.

Pereira, T. *Towards an Indian Christian Funeral Rite.* Bangalore, India, 1980.

Pietri, Charles. "Liturgy, Culture and Society: The Examples of Rome at the End of the Ancient World (Fourth-Fifth Centuries)." In *Liturgy: A Creative Tradition.* Vol. 162, no. 2 of *Concilium,* edited by Mary Collins and David Power. Edinburgh: T&T Clark, 1983.

Pilcher, Carmel. "Marking Liturgical Time in Australia: Pastoral Considerations." In

Christian Worship in Australia, edited by Stephen Burns and Anita Monro, pp. 47-58 (2007).

—————. "Ponsettia: Christmas or Pentecost — Celebrating Liturgy in the Great South Land that is Australia." *Worship* 81 (2007): 508-20.

Platten, Stephen, and Christopher Woods, eds. *Comfortable Words: Polity, Piety and the Book of Common Prayer.* London: SCM Press, 2012.

Power, David N. "Liturgy and Culture Revisited." *Worship* 69, no. 3 (May 1995): 225-43.

—————. *Unsearchable Riches: The Symbolic Nature of the Liturgy.* New York: Pueblo, 1984.

—————. *Worship: Culture and Theology.* Washington, DC: Pastoral Press, 1990.

Puglisi, James F., ed. *Liturgical Renewal as a Way to Christian Unity.* A Pueblo Book. Collegeville: Liturgical, 2005.

—————. "Unity in Diversity: Convergence in the Churches' Baptismal Practices." *Baptism Today: Understanding, Practice, Ecumenical Implications,* edited by Thomas F. Best, pp. 207-12. Collegeville, MN, and Geneva: Pueblo-Liturgical Press and WCC Publications, 1989.

Puthanangady, Paul. "Cultural Elements in Liturgical Prayer." In *Shaping English Liturgy,* edited by Peter Finn and James Schellman. Washington, DC: Pastoral Press, 1990.

Putnam, Robert, and David E. Campbell. *American Grace: How Religion Divides and Unites Us.* New York: Simon and Schuster, 2010.

Quivik, Melinda A. *A Christian Funeral: Witness to the Resurrection.* Minneapolis: Augsburg Fortress, 2005.

Radano, John A., ed. *Celebrating a Century of Ecumenism: Exploring the Achievements of International Dialogue.* Grand Rapids: Eerdmans, 2012.

Ramshaw, Gail. *Christian Worship: 100,000 Sundays of Symbols and Rituals.* Minneapolis: Fortress, 2009.

—————. *God Beyond Gender: Feminist Christian God-Language.* Minneapolis: Fortress, 1995.

—————. *Reviving Sacred Speech: The Meaning of Liturgical Language.* Akron: OSL Publications, 2000.

—————. *Treasures Old and New: Images in the Lectionary.* Minneapolis: Fortress, 2002.

Reif, Stefan C. *Judaism and Hebrew Prayer: New Perspectives on Jewish Liturgical History.* Oxford: Oxford University Press, 1993.

Richter, K. *The Meaning of the Sacramental Symbols.* Collegeville, MN: Liturgical, 1990.

Rivera-Pagán, Luis N., ed. "Called to be the One Church: An Invitation to the Churches to Renew Their Commitment to the Search for Unity and to Deepen their Dialogue." In *God in Your Grace,* pp. 255-61. WCC Assembly Text on Ecclesiology, Official Report of the Ninth Assembly of the WCC. Geneva: WCC Publications, 2007.

Roberts, Ainslie, and Charles P. Mountford. *The Dreamtime Book.* Adelaide, Australia: Rigby, 1973.

Roennfeldt, Robert. *Tiddalick: The Frog Who Caused a Flood.* Melbourne: Penguin, 1981.

Root, Michael, and Risto Saarinen, eds. *Baptism and the Unity of the Church.* Grand Rapids and Geneva: Eerdmans and WCC Publications, 1998.

Rose, Debra Bird. "Consciousness and Responsibility in an Australian Aboriginal Religion." *Traditional Aboriginal Society,* 2nd ed., edited by W. H. Edwards, pp. 239-51. Melbourne: Macmillan Education, 1998.

Russell, Letty. *Church in the Round: Feminist Interpretation of Church.* Louisville: Westminster John Knox, 1993.

———. *Just Hospitality: God's Welcome in a World of Difference.* Louisville: Westminster John Knox, 2009.

Rutherford, Richard, and Tony Barr. *The Death of a Christian: The Order of Christian Funerals.* Collegeville, MN: Liturgical, 1980.

Saliers, Don E. *Worship and Theology: Foretaste of Glory Divine.* Nashville: Abingdon, 1994.

Saliers, Don E., and Emily Saliers. "Liturgy in a Culture of Hype." *GIA Quarterly* (Fall 1995): 8-10

———. *A Song to Sing, a Life to Live: Reflections on Music as Spiritual Practice.* San Francisco: Jossey-Bass, 2005.

Schillebeeckx, E., OP. *Marriage: Human Reality and Saving Mystery.* New York: Sheed and Ward, 1965.

Schindler, Peter. *A Handbook on Inculturation.* New York: Paulist Press, 1990.

Schreiter, Robert J. *Constructing Local Theologies.* Maryknoll, NY: Orbis Books, 1986.

Schutz, Roger. "The Rule of Taizé." In *Parable of Community.* London: Mowbray, 1990.

Searle, Mark. "Culture." In *Liturgy: Active Participation in the Divine Life,* edited by James Moroney. Collegeville, MN: Liturgical, 1990.

Seasoltz, R. Kevin. "Cultural Pluralism and the Churches' Prayer." *Liturgy* 3, no. 2 (1983): 43-49.

Sedmak, Clemans. *Doing Local Theology: A Guide for Artisans of a New Humanity.* Maryknoll, NY: Orbis, 2004.

Senn, Frank C. "Ecumenical Covenants and Liturgical Inculturation." *Liturgy* 11, no. 3 (Winter 1994): 4-7.

———. "Invitational Evangelism: Hospitality and Inculturation." In *The Witness of the Worshiping Community,* edited by Frank C. Senn. New York: Paulist Press.

———. "Lutheran Liturgy in a Pluralistic and Ecumenical Age." *Dialog* 26, no. 4 (1987): 286-91.

———. *A Stewardship of the Mysteries.* Mahwah, NJ: Paulist, 1999.

————. *Toward a Theology of Inculturation.* London: Geoffrey Chapman, 1988.

Shorter, Aylward. *African Christian Theology: Adaptation or Incarnation?* New York: Macmillan, 1977.

Sigal, Phillip. "Early Christian and Rabbinic Liturgical Affinities: Exploring Liturgical Acculturation." *New Testament Studies* 30 (1984): 63-90.

Small, Christopher. *Musicking: The Meanings of Performing and Listening.* Hanover, NH: University Press of New England, 1998.

Spinks, Bryan. "Liturgy and Culture." In *Liturgy in Dialogue,* edited by Paul Bradshaw and Bryan Spinks. Collegeville, MN: Liturgical, 1995.

————. *Toward a Theology of Inculturation.* Maryknoll, NY: Orbis, 1994.

Stauffer, Anita, ed. *Baptism, Rites of Passage, and Culture.* Geneva: Lutheran World Federation, 1998.

————. *Christian Worship: Unity in Cultural Diversity.* Geneva: Lutheran World Federation, 1996.

————. *Worship and Culture in Dialogue.* Geneva: Lutheran World Federation, 1994.

Talley, Thomas J. *The Origins of the Liturgical Year.* New York: Pueblo, 1986.

Tanner, Norman P., S.J. "Chalcedon." In *Decrees of the Ecumenical Councils.* Vol. 1. *Nicaea I to Lateran V.* London: Sheed and Ward, 1990.

Taylor, Charles. *A Secular Age.* Cambridge, MA: Harvard University Press, 2007.

Taylor, Mark C., ed. *Critical Terms for Religious Studies.* Chicago: The University of Chicago Press, 1998.

Tentori, T. *Antropologia culturale.* Rome, 1980.

Thurian Max. "Baptism, Eucharist and Ministry." In *Dictionary of the Ecumenical Movement,* 2nd ed., editged by Nicholas Lossky, José Miguez Bonino, John Pobee, Tom F. Stransky, Geoffrey Wainwright, and Pauline Webb, 90-93. Geneva: WCC Publications, 2002.

Thurian, Max, ed. *Churches Respond to BEM: Official Responses to the Baptism, Eucharist and Ministry Text.* Vols. I-VI, Faith and Order Papers 129, 132, 135, 137, 143, 144. Geneva: WCC Publications, 1986-88.

Tillich, Paul. *Theology of Culture,* edited by Robert C. Kimball. New York: Oxford University Press, 1959.

Tovey, Phillip. *Inculturation of Christian Worship: Exploring the Eucharist.* Burlington, VT: Ashgate, 2004.

"Towards Koinonia in Worship." Report of a Consultation in Ditchingham, England, August 1994. Geneva: WCC Commission on Faith and Order, 1994.

Tracy, David. *Plurality and Ambiguity: Hermeneutics, Religion, Hope.* Chicago: The University of Chicago Press, 1987.

Triacca, A., and A. Pistoia, eds. *Liturgie et anthropologie. Conférence Saint-Serge. XXXVI Semaine d'études liturgiques.* Rome, 1990.

Tucker, Karen B. Westerfield. "Christian Rituals Surrounding Sickness." In *Life Cycles in Jewish and Christian Worship,* edited by Paul Bradshaw and Lawrence Hoffman. Notre Dame, IN: University of Notre Dame Press, 1996.

———. "Convergence and Divergence: Baptism Today." In *Baptism Today: Understanding, Practice, Ecumenical Implications,* edited by Thomas F. Best, pp. 213-24. Collegeville, MN, and Geneva: Pueblo-Liturgical Press and WCC Publications, 1989.

Turner, V. *The Ritual Process.* Chicago: Aldine, 1969.

Uzukwu, Elochukwu E. *Worship as Body Language: Introduction to Christian Worship; An African Orientation.* Collegeville, MN: Liturgical, 1997.

Villa-Vicencio, Charles. "Theology and Culture in South Africa: Beyond Multiculturalism." *Theology Today* 51, no. 1 (April 1994): 115-26.

Vischer, Lukas, ed. *Christian Worship in Reformed Churches Past and Present.* Grand Rapids: Eerdmans, 2003.

Von Bruck, Michael. "Religionswissenschaft und interkulturelle Theologie." *Evangelische Theologie* 3, no. 52: 245-61.

Vundla, Themba Jerome. "Traditional Initiation Rites among the Ngunis and Their Relationship to Christian Initiation." In *Growing in Newness of Life: Christian Initiation in Anglicanism Today,* edited by David R. Holeton. Toronto: Anglican Book Center, 1993.

Wainwright, Geoffrey. "Christian Worship and Western Culture." *Studia Liturgica* 12, no. 1 (1977): 20-33.

———. *Doxology.* London and New York: Oxford University Press, 1980.

———. *Embracing Purpose: Essays on God, the World, and the Church.* Epworth, 2007.

———. "The Eucharistic Dynamic of BEM." In *BEM at 25: Critical Insights into a Continuing Legacy,* edited by Thomas F. Best and Tamara Grdzelidze, pp. 45-86. Faith and Order Paper 205. Geneva: WCC Publications, 2007.

———. "The Localization of Worship." *Studia Liturgica* 8, no. 1 (1971): 26-41.

Wallin, Nils L. *Biomusicology.* Stuyvesant, NY: Pendragon Press, 1991.

Wallin, Nils L., Björn Merker, and Steven Brown, eds. *The Origins of Music.* Cambridge, MA: MIT Press, 2001.

Washington, James M., ed. Conversations with God: Two Centuries of Prayers by African-Americans. New York: Harper, 1995.

Werner, Eric. *The Sacred Bridge: The Interdependence of Liturgy and Music in the Synagogue and Church during the First Millenium.* New York: KTAV Publishing House, 1984.

———. *The Sacred Bridge: Liturgical Parallels in Synagogue and Early Church.* New York: Schocken Books, 1970.

Wessels, Anton. *Europe: Was It Ever Really Christian?* London: SCM Press, 1995.

Westerhoff, John H., III. "Celebrating and Living the Eucharist: A Cultural Analysis." In *The Eucharist.* Vol. 3 of *Alternative Futures for Worship,* edited by Bernard J. Lee. Collegeville, MN: Liturgical, 1987.

Westhelle, Vítor. "Creation Motifs in the Search for a Vital Space: A Latin American Perspective." In *Lift Every Voice: Constructing Christian Theologies from the Un-*

derside, edited by Susan B. Thistlethwaite and Mary P. Engel. New York: Orbis, 1998.

————, "Re(li)gion: The Lord of History and the Illusory Space." *Region and Religion: Land, Territory and Nation from a Theological Perspective,* edited by Viggo Mortensen. Geneva: LWF, 1994.

White, James E. *Christ Among the Dragons: Finding Our Way Through Cultural Challenges.* Downers Grove, IL: InterVarsity, 2010.

Wicker, B. *Culture and Liturgy.* London: Sheed and Ward, 1963.

Wills, Garry. *Font of Life: Ambrose, Augustine, and the Mystery of Baptism.* New York: Oxford University Press, 2012.

Witte, John Jr. *From Sacrament to Contract: Marriage, Religion, and Law in the Western Tradition.* Louisville: Westminster John Knox, 1997.

"World Council of Churches-Roman Catholic Church: Ecclesiological and Ecumenical Implications of a Common Baptism." *Joint Working Group between the Roman Catholic Church and the World Council of Churches.* Eighth Report, pp. 45-72 (1999-2005). Geneva: WCC Publications, 2005.

Young Lee, Jung. *Marginality: The Key to Multicultural Theology.* Minneapolis: Fortress, 1995.

Index

Adam, Julio Cézar, xvii; on worship
with a Brazilian face, 239-61
Adams, William Seth, 399
Ad Gentes Divinitus ("Decree on the
Church's Missionary Activity"),
59-61, 63
Ainslie, Peter, 222
Ambrose of Milan, 264
*American Grace: How Religion Divides
and Unites Us* (Putnam and Camp-
bell), 86, 94n
American Religious Identification
Survey (2001), 85-86n
"Amphibians," cultural, 12-13, 24
Anamnesis, 80, 83, 145, 229, 269;
cultural memory and memory of the
suffering, 255-58; and dynamic
equivalence, 270; and healing rites,
357
Al-Andalus, 12
Anderson, Scott, xv; on St. Andrew
Presbyterian Church (Renton,
Washington), 85, 90-92, 95-106
Anglican Communion (Church of
England), 36; and Cartigny consulta-
tion, 6, 35; *Common Worship*, 146,
150-51, 158; emerging church
constituency, 154-58; funeral rites,

360; *Mission-Shaped Church* (2004
report), 156; the *ordo*, 146-48, 149-51,
154-58
Anglican Province of Kenya, 207-8
Anglican Province of New Zealand,
208-9
Apostles' Creed, 77, 147, 216
Apostolic Tradition (AT), 79, 264-65,
352-53
Appiah, Kwame Anthony, 12, 21, 393-94
Architecture, church: Brazilian worship
places, 252-54; and the concern for
catholicity, 58; and contextualization,
210; Stauffer on, 38, 58, 65, 205, 207,
210
Armelagos, George, 184-85
Attali, Jacques, 122, 129
Augsburg Confession, 30, 40, 176-77,
179; Apology concerning the Mass,
40; Article 7 on the church and core
of Christian worship (word and
sacraments), 203-4; Article 24,
"Concerning the Mass," 169, 180; and
Cartigny Statement on significance of
worship for local churches, 55;
definition of the church as assembly
of believers, 54, 55; on the Holy
Communion, 184